UNIVERSITY LIBRARY

UNIVERSITY OF ILLINOIS AT URBANA-CHAMPAIGN

The person charging this material is responsible for its renewal or return to the library on or before the due date. The minimum fee for a lost item is **$125.00, $300.00** for bound journals.

Theft, mutilation, and underlining of books are reasons for disciplinary action and may result in dismissal from the University. *Please note: self-stick notes may result in torn pages and lift some inks.*

Renew via the Telephone Center at 217-333-8400, 846-262-1510 (toll-free) or circlib@uiuc.edu. Renew online by choosing the **My Account** option at: **http://www.library.uiuc.edu/catalog/**

UNIVERSITY H.S. LIBRARY

WITHDRAWN
University of
Illinois Library
at Urbana-Champaign

HOW THE
Gifted
Brain Learns

SECOND EDITION

Use what talent you possess:
the woods would be very silent
if no birds sang
except those that sang best.

—Henry Van Dyke

HOW THE Gifted Brain Learns

SECOND EDITION

David A. Sousa

UNIVERSITY H.S. LIBRARY

CORWIN
A SAGE Company

Copyright © 2009 by David A. Sousa

All rights reserved. When forms and sample documents are included, their use is authorized only by educators, local school sites, and/or noncommercial or nonprofit entities that have purchased the book. Except for that usage, no part of this book may be reproduced or utilized in any form or by any means, electronic or mechanical, including photocopying, recording, or by any information storage and retrieval system, without permission in writing from the publisher.

For information:

Corwin
A SAGE Company
2455 Teller Road
Thousand Oaks, California 91320
(800) 233-9936
Fax: (800) 417-2466
www.corwinpress.com

SAGE Ltd.
1 Oliver's Yard
55 City Road
London EC1Y 1SP
United Kingdom

SAGE India Pvt. Ltd.
B 1/I 1 Mohan Cooperative Industrial Area
Mathura Road, New Delhi 110 044
India

SAGE Asia-Pacific Pte. Ltd.
33 Pekin Street #02-01
Far East Square
Singapore 048763

Printed in the United States of America.

Library of Congress Cataloging-in-Publication Data

Sousa, David A.
How the gifted brain learns/David A. Sousa.—2nd ed.
    p. cm.
Includes bibliographical references and index.
ISBN 978-1-4129-7172-0 (cloth)
ISBN 978-1-4129-7173-7 (pbk.)
    1. Gifted children—Education—United States. 2. Gifted children—United States—Identification. 3. Brain—Localization of functions. I. Title.

LC3993.9.S68 2009
371.95—dc22   2009019964

This book is printed on acid-free paper.

09 10 11 12 13 10 9 8 7 6 5 4 3 2 1

Acquisitions Editor:	Carol Chambers Collins
Editorial Assistant:	Brett Ory
Developmental Editors:	Jessica Tyerman and Jennifer Beasley
Production Editor:	Cassandra Margaret Seibel
Typesetter:	C&M Digitals (P) Ltd.
Proofreader:	Theresa Kay
Cover Designer:	Tracy Miller
Graphic Designer:	Karine Hovsepian

Q.
371.95
So85h
2009
cop.2

Contents

About the Author

David A. Sousa, Ed.D., is an international consultant in educational neuroscience and author of seven best-selling books on how to translate brain research into educational practice. For more than 20 years he has presented at national conventions of educational organizations and has conducted workshops on brain research and science education in hundreds of school districts and at colleges and universities across the United States, Canada, Europe, Asia, Australia, and New Zealand.

Dr. Sousa has a bachelor of science degree in chemistry from Massachusetts State College at Bridgewater, a master of arts in teaching degree in science from Harvard University, and a doctorate from Rutgers University. He has taught high school science, served as a K–12 director of science, and was superintendent of the New Providence, New Jersey, public schools. He has been an adjunct professor of education at Seton Hall University and a visiting lecturer at Rutgers University. He is a past president of the National Staff Development Council.

Dr. Sousa has also edited science books and published articles in leading educational journals. He has received awards from professional associations and school districts for his commitment and contributions to research, staff development, and science education. He is a member of the Cognitive Neuroscience Society, and he has appeared on the NBC *Today* show and on National Public Radio to discuss his work with schools using brain research.

Acknowledgments

Corwin gratefully acknowledges the contributions of the following reviewers:

Mary Beth Cary, Teacher
Worth County Primary School
Sylvester, GA

Chris Godwin, Executive Director for General and Gifted Curriculum
Johnston County Schools
Smithfield, NC

J. Christine Gould, Ph.D., Associate Professor of Teacher Education
University of Wisconsin–Stevens Point

Steve Hutton, School Improvement Consultant
Villa Hills, KY

Debra K. Las, Science Teacher
Rochester Public Schools
Rochester, MN

Kathy Tritz-Rhodes, Principal
Marcus-Meriden-Cleghorn School
Marcus and Cleghorn, IA

Thea H. Williams-Black, Ph.D., Assistant Professor of Elementary Education
The University of Mississippi
University, MS

Leslie Owen Wilson, Ed.D., Professor of Teacher Education
University of Wisconsin–Stevens Point

Preface to the Second Edition

Welcome to the second edition! Since the publication of the first edition, there have been major developments in our understanding of how the human brain develops and functions. Brain imaging studies around the world number more than 1,500 a year, yielding additional insights into how we learn. Technologies, such as transcranial magnetic stimulation, have emerged to investigate cerebral processing. Meanwhile, researchers in genetics have found new links to the neurological processes involved in thinking. All of the chapters in this second edition have undergone major revision to include these developments and the findings of new studies. In addition, I have

- Combined Chapters 1 and 2 of the first edition to allow an earlier discussion of the characteristics of the gifted brain. The information on brain structures and memory systems that was in Chapter 1 has been distributed among other chapters to be closer to the text associated with it.
- Expanded and renamed the original chapter on "Musical Talent" to "Artistic Talent" so that it now includes music, dance, theater, and visual art.
- Moved the three chapters on specialized talents (language, mathematical, and artistic) so that they follow the chapters discussing broader characteristics of gifted brains.
- Added a new feature in most chapters called "From the Desk of a Teacher" to present specific examples of elementary and secondary classroom applications.
- Added more than 200 new references, including scientific studies for those who wish to read the original research.

Although the pace of neuroscientific research on the nature of giftedness is not as fast as some would like, it is, nonetheless, making progress in understanding the genetic and environmental triggers that result in extraordinarily high levels of academic achievement and talent. This revision delves into the research areas of greatest promise and highlights ways that the findings from that research can be used to develop instructional strategies that will help all students reach their full potential.

—David A. Sousa

Introduction

When the first edition of this book was published several years ago, our understanding of "giftedness" was largely based on theories and research in behavioral and cognitive psychology. Neuroscientists had barely begun to use their scanning technologies to look inside the working brain of gifted and talented people. But during the first decade of this twenty-first century, the field of neuroscience has just exploded, splintering into new disciplines, such as social cognitive neuroscience and behavioral neuroscience. Of particular interest to educators is the emergence of educational neuroscience, an area that promises to enrich pedagogy with new insights into how we can translate research in the neurosciences into educational practice.

This book is designed to examine the needs of gifted and talented students, to uncover what more we are learning about the gifted brain, and to suggest strategies and programs that can help our best and brightest students achieve their full potential. Classroom teachers, education specialists, school and district administrators, college instructors, and parents should all find items of interest in *How the Gifted Brain Learns*. Although many books have been written about the gifted, this book focuses primarily on insights to be gained about the gifted brain from the current explosion of research in neuroscience. It also reviews research information about the gifted learner for prospective and current teachers and administrators so that they may consider alternative instructional approaches.

WHAT DO WE MEAN BY GIFTED AND TALENTED?

Many terms are used to describe the student who demonstrates exceptional talent, and sometimes these terms themselves become a challenge to understand. *Gifted* is the most commonly used word, but it has hundreds of definitions, from legal to jargon. *Talented* usually describes an individual with a performance skill that has been refined through practice, such as music or dance. *Precocious* and *prodigy* are most commonly used to describe young children who display a high level of skill in a particular endeavor at a very early age.

In earlier times, *genius* was widely used, but it is now limited to the phenomenally gifted. *Superior* has recently come into vogue. Being a comparative term, it tempts one to ask superior to whom or to what, and to what degree. The vagueness of the term limits its usefulness in helping educators design an educational program for an individual student. *Exceptional* is an appropriate term when referring to a gifted child as being different from the regular school population, although it is also used to describe children with learning difficulties.

During the 1970s, the combined term *gifted and talented* came into common use. Although *gifted* and *talented* are often used interchangeably, Gagné (1985) differentiated between the two terms. For Gagné, *giftedness* is above-average aptitude (as measured by IQ tests) in creative and intellectual abilities, and *talent* is above-average performance in an area of human activity, such as music, mathematics, or literature.

1

In recent years, most researchers have moved away from defining *giftedness* solely in terms of IQ tests and have broadened its usage to include the characteristics of giftedness, such as creativity and motivation. Some definitions also consider the person's contributions to culture and society. People from diverse cultural and ethnic backgrounds may display their gifts and talents in ways that are recognized and valued by their own culture, but these individuals may not be recognized or valued by other cultures. Characteristics of gifted and talented children from across different ethnic groups have some common indicators (e.g., problem-solving ability, intense interest, and motivation) but each ethnicity has distinct and unique behavioral attributes. As a result, one of the greater concerns in the field of gifted education is the realization that gifted children from diverse cultural backgrounds, or who have some type of learning disability, will not be recognized as gifted in our schools.

The U.S. government added its own definition of giftedness in the No Child Left Behind Act of 2004. In Title IX, A, (22), gifted and talented students are defined as those "who give evidence of high achievement capability in areas such as intellectual, creative, artistic, or leadership capacity, or in specific academic fields, and who need services or activities not ordinarily provided by the school in order to fully develop those capabilities."

Given the various interpretations of the terminology used to describe students of high ability, I had to decide on a working definition that would be meaningful for all readers. For the purposes of this book, then, I use the term *gifted* to be an inclusive one in that it comprises high intellectual ability in academic areas as well as high levels of ability in areas of performance, such as music, theater, and dance. My simple definition is that a gifted person demonstrates (or has the potential for demonstrating) an exceptionally high level of performance in one or more areas of human endeavor. Not all readers may agree with this definition, and some may object that using it as an inclusive term de-emphasizes the importance of talent. That is certainly not my intent, which I think will become clear as one reads the book. However, to avoid any misinterpretation, and because the combined term is so widespread, many references to gifted and talented will be found in the text.

> For the purposes of this book, a gifted person is defined as one who demonstrates an exceptionally high level of performance in one or more areas of human endeavor.

Myths and Realities About Giftedness

Myths abound about the nature of giftedness, largely because public schools have not really had the resources to fully and accurately identify the gifted and to understand their needs. A prevailing notion for many years in public education has been that these students can take care of themselves and learn a great deal on their own. Consequently, schools have concentrated on providing a broad curriculum for mainstream students and then devoting a significant portion of remaining resources to students with learning difficulties. Little has been left over to identify or support the gifted, despite federal and state mandates to do so.

We are slowly gaining a greater understanding of the idiosyncracies of gifted children and the implications for parenting and teaching them. But to be successful at this, we must dispel the myths and look to credible research about the realities of being gifted and talented. The following list summarizes some myths and realities regarding gifted children (NAGC, 2009). Several of the topics are discussed in greater detail throughout the book.

Myth #1: Little is really known about how we learn. So how can we know about the gifted brain?	**Reality:** Research is providing a deeper understanding of how the human brain learns, including insights into the phenomenally gifted brain. See Chapter 1.
Myth #2: Academically gifted students have general intellectual power that makes them gifted in all areas.	**Reality:** Giftedness tends to be specific to a given domain of learning. Children can be gifted in one area and learning disabled in another. See Chapter 4.
Myth #3: *Gifted* refers just to academic ability, but *talented* refers to high ability in music and the arts.	**Reality:** There is no justification for this distinction. The domains of excellence are merely different, and in many cases the words can be used interchangeably. See Chapter 1.
Myth #4: Gifted students have lower self-esteem than nongifted students.	**Reality:** The majority of studies indicate that gifted students have a somewhat higher level of self-esteem than nongifted. However, they are at risk for isolation and loneliness, and they can become arrogant. See Chapters 1 and 4.
Myth #5: Giftedness in any domain requires a high IQ.	**Reality:** There is little evidence that giftedness in music or art requires an exceptional IQ. Moreover, IQ tests measure a narrow range of ability. See Chapters 1 and 7.
Myth #6: Acceleration options, such as grade skipping, early entrance, and early exit, tend to be harmful for gifted students.	**Reality:** Although it is important to consider the social and psychological adjustment of every student, there is little evidence that acceleration options are in any way detrimental. See Chapter 2.
Myth #7: Cooperative learning in heterogeneous groups provides academic benefits to gifted students and can be effectively substituted for specialized programs for academically talented students.	**Reality:** Recent studies show that gifted students receive greater academic benefit from being grouped with other gifted students. Cooperative learning can be a useful strategy, but it is not a replacement for specialized programs for academically talented students, such as new courses or acceleration options. See Chapter 2.
Myth #8: Giftedness is inborn, or giftedness is entirely the result of hard work.	**Reality:** True giftedness results from both genetic predispositions *and* hard work. See Chapter 1.

(Continued)

(Continued)

Myth #9: Creativity tests are effective means of identifying artistically gifted and talented students.	**Reality:** Creativity tests measure problem-solving and divergent thinking skills, but have not proved valid in predicting the success of students with high abilities in the visual arts. See Chapters 1, 7, and 8.
Myth #10: Pushy parents who drive their children to overachieve create gifted children.	**Reality:** Gifted children are usually pushing their parents, who are trying to accommodate and nurture them. However, some parents do try to live vicariously through their children and lose sight of the child's emotional well-being. See Chapters 2 and 3.
Myth #11: Early reading and writing skills should keep pace with each other.	**Reality:** Although this is a commonly held belief, there is no relationship between reading and writing skills in the development of young talented children. See Chapter 5.
Myth #12: All children are gifted, and there is no special group of children that needs enriched or accelerated education.	**Reality:** Although all children have strengths and weaknesses, some have extreme strengths in one or more areas. Extreme giftedness creates a special education need the same way that a learning disability does. See Chapters 2 and 4.
Myth #13: Highly gifted children go on to become eminent and creative adults.	**Reality:** Many gifted children, even prodigies, do not become eminent in adulthood, and many eminent adults were not prodigies. See Chapters 1, 4, 5, and 7.

Source: NAGC, 2009.

GIFTED AND TALENTED PROGRAMS IN TODAY'S SCHOOLS

Because some parents and educators believe that truly gifted children will remain gifted and fulfill their educational needs on their own, schools have historically done little to identify and encourage the gifted. As a result, potentially gifted students have gone through school without their gifts ever being recognized. This has been a long-standing problem as history will attest. Sir Isaac Newton was considered a poor student in grammar school. He left at age 14, was sent back at 19 because he read so much, and graduated at Cambridge without any distinction whatsoever. The poet Shelley was expelled from Oxford; James Whistler and Edgar Allen Poe were both expelled from West Point. Charles Darwin dropped out of medical school, and Edward Gibbon, the noted British historian, considered his education a waste of time.

Gregor Mendel, founder of the science of genetics, flunked his teacher's examination four times in a row and finally gave up trying. Thomas Edison's mother withdrew him from school after 3 months in the first grade because his teacher said he was "unable to perform." Winston Churchill ended up last in his class at the Harrow School. Albert Einstein found grammar school boring. It was his uncle, showing the boy tricks with numbers, who stimulated his interest in mathematics. For a long time and in many places, traditional academic programs have often been poorly suited to humans of extraordinary potential. One is left to wonder how many Edisons did not survive their educational experiences.

Our society has not given the same attention to the education of the gifted as it has given to other special groups. For example, we spend millions every year for the mentally handicapped. But, too often, children of superior intellect spend their time in a commonplace school, assimilating a curricular diet far below their potential. Thus, gifted children pose one of our greatest present-day problems, beginning in the home and ultimately becoming a concern of the school. Teachers at all grade levels have the responsibility to recognize and plan for the needs of the gifted.

Currently, the process of identifying gifted students and the programs designed to address their needs vary greatly by grade level and school district. Gifted students who are not identified and served by these programs are not likely to ever have their needs fully met while in school. The loss

> Our society has not given the same attention to the education of the gifted as it has given to other special groups.

of such potential is a serious blow to society as well as to the student and teacher. The student never feels fulfilled, loses self-esteem, and lacks direction. The teacher, meanwhile, is faced with student boredom, underachievement, and a litany of discipline problems that could have been avoided. One purpose of this book is to examine the current state of programs for the gifted and to suggest what we might do to make them better serve the gifts and talents of all students.

A Word About Elitism

Some parents, educators, and politicians object to any special programs for gifted children on the grounds of *elitism*. This word has acquired the negative connotations of snobbishness, selectivity, and unfair special attention at a time, critics say, when we should be emphasizing egalitarianism. Even some educators believe this notion of elitism has only been encouraged by federal efforts that emphasize increasing resources for less able students but do little to enhance programs for our most able students.

The reality is that gifted students are elite in the sense that they possess skills to a higher degree than most people in their class. The same is true for professional athletes, musical soloists, inventors, or physicians. Parents and schools must provide children with equal opportunity, not equal treatment. Treating all students as though they learned exactly the same way is folly. Therefore, schools have a responsibility to challenge gifted students to their fullest potential while, at the same time, challenging those who cry elitism to rethink the true meaning of the word and the real purpose of education.

ABOUT THIS BOOK

The serious problems of the twenty-first century (e.g., dealing with climate change, protecting the environment, and managing population growth) will require the concerted efforts of our best minds. Thus, more attention needs to be given to clarifying what constitutes a comprehensive and effective gifted program and what steps schools can take to ensure a broad and rich variety of educational experiences for our most gifted students.

Questions This Book Will Answer

This book will answer questions such as these:

- How different are the brains of gifted students from those of typical students?
- What kinds of strategies are particularly effective for students with specific gifts?

- What progress is brain research making in discovering the nature of intelligence and giftedness?
- Will brain research help us identify potentially gifted students sooner and more accurately?
- Are schools adequately challenging gifted students today? If not, what can we do about it?
- How can improving programs for the gifted and talented benefit other students?
- What can we do to identify and help gifted students who are underachievers?
- How can we identify students who are both gifted and learning disabled, and how can we help them?
- What insights are we gaining about students who are gifted in language, mathematics, and the arts?
- What progress are we making in identifying underrepresented minorities for gifted programs?

Chapter Contents

Chapter 1. What Is a Gifted Brain? This chapter looks at various conceptual schemes (e.g., psychological, socio-emotional) that attempt to define the nature of intelligence and giftedness. Of particular interest is the discussion over the long-standing debate about whether nature (i.e., genetic programming) or nurture (i.e., environment and upbringing) has greater impact on talent development. Several current models of giftedness are explained as well as a review of what current researchers suggest are the characteristics that gifted individuals are likely to display.

Chapter 2. Challenging the Gifted Brain. Here we examine specific suggestions for designing curricular and instructional strategies that are more likely to challenge the gifted brain. Because many teachers are faced with addressing the needs of gifted students within the context of the inclusive classroom, this chapter focuses on the concept of differentiated curriculum. Also discussed are acceleration, curriculum compacting, grouping formats, and other techniques that have been successful in developing the talents of gifted students.

Chapter 3. Underachieving Gifted Students. In this chapter, we investigate the various symptoms, causes, and types of underachievement in gifted students. A somewhat overlooked area of gifted education, this chapter presents ways of identifying these students and suggests strategies for reversing under-achievement. Particular attention is paid to the growing number of underachieving minority students and to ways for addressing their needs.

Chapter 4. The Twice-Exceptional Brain. Although the notion that a person can be both gifted and learning disabled may seem strange, this chapter examines the twice-exceptional student. The difficulties of identifying these students along with some of the more common combinations of giftedness and learning disabilities are discussed—for example, gifted children with attention-deficit hyperactivity disorder or autism.

Chapters 5, 6, and 7. Language, Mathematical, and Artistic Talent. These chapters deal with attempts to understand the nature of giftedness in three specific areas: language, mathematics, and the arts, respectively. As scientific evidence accumulated over the last few decades suggesting that the human brain is pre-wired for language, mathematics, and artistic capabilities, research resources were directed toward investigating the cerebral nature of these activities. Consequently, we include these areas because they currently have the largest base of research studies among all the school disciplines. Furthermore, there is little evidence at this time to indicate that the brain is specifically wired for science, economics, or history. According to current thinking, it is more likely that high ability in these areas results from high ability in one or more of the pre-wired areas (e.g., mathematics for science, and language for history) coupled with intense personal interest in, say, scientific phenomena or historical events.

Chapter 8. Putting It All Together. Finally, this chapter suggests some ways of identifying gifted children and setting up a learning environment where gifted students, along with their classmates, can excel in the inclusive classroom. The effectiveness of current programs to aid gifted students in elementary and secondary schools is also discussed.

Other Helpful Tools

Applications. At the end of each chapter is a section that offers suggestions on how to apply the research discussed in that chapter to educational practice. Although these applications can benefit all students, they often contain tips on how to challenge the gifted. Some of the applications contain specific classroom examples that have been used successfully by classroom teachers at the elementary and secondary levels.

Glossary. Many of the neuroscientific and psychological terms used in the text are described in a glossary.

References. Many of the citations in this extensive section are the original research reports published in peer-reviewed journals. These references will be particularly helpful for researchers and for those who would like more specific information on how the research studies were conducted.

Resources. This section offers some valuable Internet sites that will help teachers at all grade levels find many additional strategies for working with gifted students.

This book does *not* deal with exceptional performance in sports. How individuals become superb athletes is a separate and rich area of research. There are numerous books available that delve into this exciting field. Studies of athletic capabilities are beyond the scope of this book.

As we gain a greater understanding of the human brain, we may discover ways to identify gifted students more quickly and more accurately. This means that schools can begin to provide for student needs earlier and with greater effectiveness. Sometimes, these students are attempting to learn in environments that are designed to help but instead inadvertently frustrate their efforts. By looking for ways to differentiate the curriculum and by changing some of our instructional approaches, we may be able to move gifted students to exceptional levels of performance. My hope is that this book will encourage all school professionals and parents to learn more about how the brain learns so that they can work together for the benefit of all students.

CHAPTER 1
What Is a Gifted Brain?

Ask 50 people what is meant by giftedness and you will likely get 50 different definitions. And that becomes a major problem when deciding who is gifted. Nonetheless, some common elements will emerge from most of the descriptions. These might include describing a person's aptitude in a specific subject area or a talent in the visual or performing arts, or in sports. Also mentioned might be creativity, inventiveness, or just plain "intelligent in everything." Descriptions of giftedness also vary from one culture to another. For example, in a culture with no formal schooling, a skilled hunter might be the gifted one. Gifted abilities are also more likely to emerge when the individual's talents coincide with what is valued by the culture. Chess prodigies, for example, appear in cultures where such talent is valued and nurtured. So it can be said that giftedness is what others in a society perceive to be higher or lower on some culturally embedded scale.

> From one perspective, giftedness is what people in a society perceive to be higher or lower on some culturally embedded scale.

Even researchers in gifted education have a difficult time agreeing on what giftedness means. But they do agree on one thing: Giftedness derives from a well above average level of intelligence in one or more observable behaviors. So before we can understand what makes a person gifted, we have to take a closer look at what modern research has discovered about intelligence.

UNDERSTANDING INTELLIGENCE

Have We Found the Genes for Intelligence?

An obvious starting point in the search to understand intelligence is our genes. Impressive advances in methods for scanning our genetic makeup have inspired scientists to hunt for the specific gene or genes that can be linked to native intelligence. Imaging technologies that probe the workings of the brain are also valuable tools in this search because they may reveal the brain components that account for the differences in intelligence among individuals. The environment also plays an important role because some genes express their traits only when provoked by environmental influences.

Researchers often use studies of identical twins raised together and apart to explore whether certain traits are the result of genetics or the environment. Results of twin studies conducted over the past two decades have convinced some scientists that genes play a crucial role in intelligence but they do not act alone. So far, the hunt for specific genes related to intelligence has been disappointing. Comparing the DNA of highly intelligent people with each other and with the DNA of people with low and average intelligence can reveal patterns, called markers, which help identify neighboring genes. But tests have so far shown that these genes account for only a small variation in intelligence (Plomin & DeFries, 1998).

Gene Effects in Poor Children: Another factor is the discovery of expressive genes—those which express their traits when provoked by the environment. The same gene can have different effects in different environments. The environment seems to have a particularly powerful influence on genes related to intelligence in poor children. Eric Turkheimer and his colleagues at the University of Virginia analyzed the test scores of more than 300 sets of twins aged 7 years (Turkheimer, Haley, Waldron, D'Onofrio, & Gottesman, 2003). The study included a high portion of twins from racial minorities and impoverished families. Remarkably, the researchers found that the strength of the genes effect depended on the socioeconomic status of the family (as measured in part by family income and education level of the parents). About 60 percent of the variance in IQ could be accounted for by genes in the children from affluent families. But for children from impoverished families, genes accounted for almost none.

A similar study was conducted four years later. Here the researchers looked at how 839 sets of twins scored on the Merit Scholarship Qualifying Test in 1962, when most of them were 17 years old. Once again, genes played only a small role in the variance of scores among poor children, but played a far stronger role in the variance of scores among affluent children (Harden, Turkheimer, & Loehlin, 2007).

> The environment of poverty may exert powerful forces that suppress the genes associated with differences in intelligence from expressing themselves.

What is going on here? The researchers suggest that an impoverished environment includes powerful forces that shape intelligence from the womb through school and beyond, thereby suppressing the genes associated with differences in intelligence from expressing themselves. On the other hand, in children growing up in the relative stability of affluent families, gene-based differences are more likely to emerge (Zimmer, 2008). For example, if a child in an affluent home shows an interest in science, the parent is likely to get the child a book on science and a science kit. So reading about science and experimenting will make this child different from one in an impoverished home whose interest in science will likely go unnoticed or unfulfilled. The results from both of these studies ought to raise concerns over how much schools and communities are doing to address the plight of children in impoverished homes. Although there is some evidence that gene variations play a role in intelligence, their effect is small. The prevailing theory now is that there are many genes, each with a small effect, that together produce the full range of variation in intelligence. And their effects can be moderated by the environment. But finding those genes may take a long time. One thing seems certain: Genetic research demonstrates that intelligence levels can be inherited, but the idea that we are born with a few genes that set forever how intelligent a person is going to be is flawed (Zimmer, 2008). Furthermore, the debate over nature (genes) *versus* nurture (environment) is drawing to a close. Nature *and* nurture work together.

Is Brain Structure Related to Intelligence?

Another avenue of research has looked at changes in brain structure among individuals of different intelligence. Neuroscientists have long thought that intelligence is related to some aspects of brain structure. However, the way certain parts of the brain develop over time may be a much better predictor. Shaw and his colleagues (2006) have analyzed scans of developing brains. To control for individual variation, the researchers followed more than 300 children, ages 5 to 19, as they grew up over a period of 10 years. Most children were scanned two or more times, generally at two-year intervals. The scans were separated into three groups based on IQ test scores: superior (121–145), high (109–120), and average (83–108).

Shaw et al.'s (2006) attention was focused on the development of the cortex, a thin layer on the surface of the brain where most sophisticated information processing occurs. This part of the brain continues to grow and change in structure until about the age of 22 to 24 years. In all children, the cortex gets thicker as neurons grow and produce branches called *dendrites.* Then a pruning process begins to trim away underused dendrites and neurons. As a result, the cortex gets thinner and the brain becomes more efficient in the teen years.

The researchers discovered that the thickening and thinning processes varied among children with different levels of intelligence. Variations were particularly noticeable in the *prefrontal cortex.* This is the seat of abstract reasoning, planning, and decision-making, located just behind the forehead (Figure 1.1). The seven-year-olds in the superior group started out with a thinner cortex that thickened rapidly until age 11 or 12 before thinning. But in the same-age group of average intelligence, the cortex started out thicker but peaked by age 8, followed by gradual thinning. Those in the high intelligence group had a similar trajectory to the average group but with a thicker cortex (Figure 1.2). Although the cortex thinned out for all groups, the superior group showed the

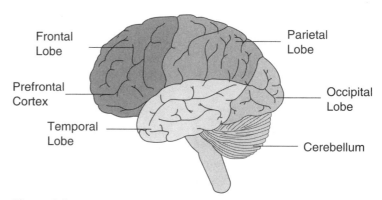

Figure 1.1 The major areas of the brain.

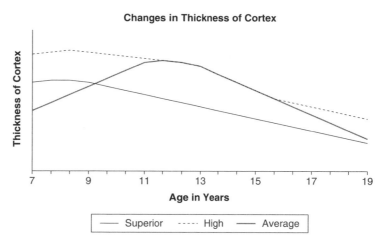

Figure 1.2 Changes in the thickness of the brain's cortex between the ages of 7 and 19 in individuals of superior, high, and average intelligence.

Source: Adapted from Shaw et al., 2006.

greatest rate of change. Children with average intelligence had a similar pattern but the changes were slower. In Shaw et al.'s (2006) words, "The most agile minds had the most agile cortex" (p. 678).

Implications: So what does it mean? The findings suggest that IQ is related—at least in part—to how the cortex matures. Perhaps the prolonged thickening process of the prefrontal cortex in children with superior IQ reflects an extended critical period for the development of high-level cognitive circuits. Thus, intelligence is not related so much to the size of the cortex, but to the dynamics of how it develops.

No one is sure what underlies the changes in cortical thickness. One theory is that the rapid thickening and thinning seen in the superior IQ group may indicate greater neural plasticity—the changes that occur in the brain as a result of experience. Having a high degree of neural plasticity may enable individuals to adapt better to the demands of their environment and may also be an indication of possessing a superior IQ (Garlick, 2002).

Richard Haier and his colleagues (2004) found a similar pattern in studies of adult brains. They gave IQ tests to 47 volunteers. The IQ scores, which ranged from 90 to 155, were then correlated with brain scans that look at volume of matter at different brain regions. People with high intelligence scores tended to have certain regions of the cortex that were larger than average (Haier, Jung, Yeo, Head, & Alkire, 2004). Furthermore, these

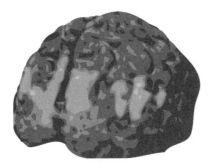

Figure 1.3 This front view of the brain shows the regions that some researchers believe are strongly associated with intelligence. They include the frontal and parietal lobes.

Source: Adapted from Haier et al., 2004.

regions were not limited to the frontal lobe where most scientists have long identified as the seat of intelligence. Rather, other brain regions located in the parietal lobe were also involved. Figure 1.3 shows a front view of the brain. The shaded areas represent those regions in the frontal and parietal lobes where larger mass correlated with higher intelligence. Shaw et al. (2006) suspect that some of the patterns will turn out to be the result of environmental influences, especially since neuron development is occurring at a rapid pace during the teenage and early adult years. But nature also plays a role. Studies show these brain regions to be the same size in identical twins, indicating that genes are also responsible for some of the differences in intelligence.

There are important implications here. If further research supports the theory that the environment is a principal factor affecting early cortical development, then we need to re-examine closely what schools do in the primary and intermediate grades. We must assess whether the learning environment is truly challenging and creative for all students. Of course, this should be the goal of all schools regardless, but the research implies that school experiences for this age group may have a significant impact on an individual's eventual level of intelligence. That bears repeating: What happens in classrooms may actually raise or lower a student's IQ—maybe even the teacher's!

> If further research finds the environment to be a principal factor affecting cortical development, then we need to re-examine primary and intermediate grade schooling.

Where in the Brain Is Intelligence Located?

One of the long-standing mysteries of science: Where in the brain lies intelligence? As mentioned earlier, scientists for a long time thought that the seat of intelligence lay in the frontal lobe (Figure 1.1). But in the study of adult brain structure mentioned earlier (Haier et al., 2004), the scans showed that intelligence was correlated with greater volumes of gray matter (cortex) in regions of the frontal and parietal lobes (Figure 1.3). These findings prompted Haier et al. to review other similar studies to determine whether there was any consistency among the areas correlated to intelligence.

The Parieto-Frontal Integration (P-FIT) Theory: After reviewing 37 imaging studies related to intelligence, including their own, Haier and Rex Jung of the University of New Mexico claimed to have identified a brain network related to intelligence (Jung & Haier, 2007). They found surprising consistency among the studies they reviewed even though the studies represented a variety of research approaches. It seems the brain areas related to intelligence are the same areas related to attention and memory as well as to more complex functions, such as language and sensory processing. This integration of cognitive functions suggests that intelligence levels might be based on how efficiently the frontal-parietal networks process information (Figure 1.3).

Information moves throughout the brain in the white matter located just below the cortex's gray matter. Think of the white matter as the wiring that connects distant areas of the brain to one another. Jung and Haier (2007) found that individuals with high intelligence tend to have tracts of white matter that are more organized than other individuals. High intelligence requires processing power and speed. The larger cortical areas provide it the processing power while the well-organized white matter gives it the speed. In this model individual differences in intelligence depend, in part, upon individual differences in specific areas of the brain and in the

> One theory suggests that high intelligence requires a lot of processing power and speed.

connections between them. Of course, one person may have higher processing power but lower speed, another the opposite, and others all the combinations in between. So you may have two people of equal intelligence, but their brains are arriving at that behavior in different ways. The model, dubbed the Parieto-Frontal Integration (P-FIT) Theory of Intelligence, provides a framework for future research.

THEORIES OF INTELLIGENCE AND GIFTEDNESS

Are you intelligent? Are you gifted? How do you know? Compared to whom? How could you tell if someone is more intelligent than you? And what about your students or your own children? How can you spot the highly intelligent or gifted ones? These sensitive questions have plagued researchers and educators for a long time. Yet to this day we still have no universally accepted definitions or measures of intelligence and giftedness. But many theories abound. What follows is a brief overview of why our understanding of giftedness went beyond IQ tests as well as some of the more predominant theories of what constitutes intelligent and gifted behavior.

Limited Value of IQ Tests

In the 1950s, researchers and psychologists described giftedness mainly in terms of intelligence: high IQ was the same as gifted. Creativity and motivation were soon added as other characteristics of gifted performers. Consequently, as the push in schools for special programs for gifted students got underway, IQ tests became the primary screening vehicle for program selection. But IQ tests had their own problems. They assessed analytical and verbal skills but failed to measure practical knowledge and creativity, components critical to problem solving and success in life. Some psychologists complained that because many IQ test items had a cultural and socioeconomic bias, students from minority or poor families were destined to get lower scores. It eventually became apparent that IQ tests were not a satisfactory measure of giftedness and that people could be gifted in different ways, such as in academic areas, sports, performing arts, or in business ventures. As early as 1951, researchers realized that IQ tests did not measure these capabilities (Lally & LaBrant, 1951).

Very few people are gifted in all areas. Paradoxically, some people can be gifted in some aspects of learning while displaying learning disorders in others (see Chapter 4). Clearly, relying on only one quantitative criterion (the IQ score) and maybe two qualitative criteria (creativity and motivation) was not adequate in the process of describing the collective and varied characteristics of gifted and talented people. More expansive theories of giftedness were needed.

Renzulli's Definition of Giftedness

In an effort to challenge the notion that *giftedness* meant demonstrating high performance in nearly all areas of intellectual and artistic pursuit, Joseph Renzulli (1978) proposed his own definition. He suggested that giftedness resulted from the interaction of the following three traits:

- *General abilities* (processing information, integrating experiences, and abstract thinking) or specific abilities (the capacity to acquire knowledge and to perform in an activity) that were above average
- *Commitment to task* (perseverance, hard work, endurance, perceptiveness, self-confidence, and a special fascination with a specific subject)
- *Creativity* (flexibility, fluency, originality of thought, sensitivity to stimulations, openness to experiences, and a willingness to take risks)

He named this the Three-Ring Conception of Giftedness (Figure 1.4). A few years later, he distinguished the following two types of gifted performance (Renzulli, 1986):

- *Schoolhouse giftedness,* which is characterized by the ease of acquiring knowledge and taking tests as demonstrated through high grades and high test scores. It is the type most often used for selecting students into special programs for the gifted.
- *Creative-productive giftedness,* which involves creating new products and ideas designed to have an impact on a specific audience or field.

Renzulli's position was that creative-productive giftedness was often overlooked in schools that relied primarily on traditional tests of aptitude, intelligence, and achievement. His work stimulated school districts to include more opportunities for creative expression in their programs for gifted students.

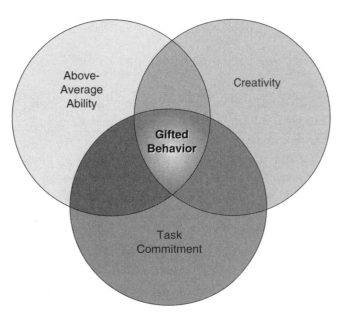

Figure 1.4   Renzulli's Three-Ring Conception of Giftedness. In this model, gifted behavior results from the interaction of above-average abilities, creativity, and task commitment.

Source: Renzulli, 1978.

Brain Research Support for Renzulli's Model: Most of the traits that comprise the Renzulli model are behaviors not easily associated with any specific brain region. The complex qualities included in general abilities, such as processing information, integrating experiences, and abstract thinking, all require input from the frontal lobe, parts of the emotional system (called the limbic area), and other regions as well. Commitment to task is often rooted in intrinsic motivation (the desire to do something because one enjoys doing it). Brain studies do confirm that motivated subjects rely heavily on elements in the limbic area to sustain interest and maintain attention. Creativity shows more promise. Recent imaging studies suggest that certain brain areas are highly activated when an individual is involved in creative work. Creativity is discussed in more detail in Chapter 2.

Gardner's Multiple Intelligences

During the 1980s, psychologists unleashed new and different models to describe intelligence. Harvard researcher Howard Gardner (1983) published a significant book suggesting that intelligence is not a unitary concept, that humans possess at least seven intelligences, and that an individual is predisposed to developing each of the intelligences to different levels of competence. The seven intelligences are *bodily-kinesthetic, logical/mathematical, musical/rhythmic, verbal/linguistic, visual/spatial, interpersonal,* and *intrapersonal.* (A few years later he added the *naturalist* intelligence, and most recently he proposed the *spiritualist* and *emotionalist* intelligences.) Figure 1.5 takes a closer look at eight of the intelligences and some of their relevant behaviors as described and revised by Gardner (1993). The diagram does not include the *spiritualist* and *emotionalist* because there has not been sufficient time to study and explore their characteristics and educational implications.

For Gardner, the intelligences represented ways of processing information and of thinking. He also suggested that the intelligences are the product of the interaction between genetic predisposition and the environment, a sort of nature-nurture combination that is not a question of either–or, but both–and. He selected an intelligence if it met the following eight criteria:

- Potential isolation by brain damage
- Existence of savants, prodigies, and other exceptional individuals
- An identifiable core operation or set of core operations
- A distinctive developmental history, along with a definable set of expert "end-state" performances
- An evolutionary history and evolutionary plausibility
- Support from experimental psychological tasks
- Support from psychometric findings
- Susceptibility to encoding in a symbol system

According to Gardner, the intelligences are not the same as thinking style, which tends to remain consistent and independent of the type of information being processed. Rather, individuals at any given time use those intelligences that will allow them to solve specific problems, generate new problems, or create products or services of value to their particular culture. As the information and tasks change, other intelligences are called into action. One of Gardner's legacies is the oft-quoted

> In Gardner's schema, giftedness can be defined as an individual being exceptionally competent in one or more of the intelligences.

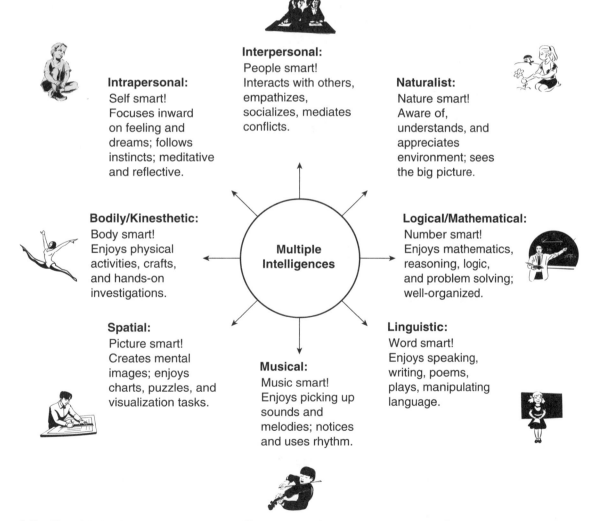

Figure 1.5 The eight intelligences describe the different types of competencies that we all possess in varying degrees and that we use in our daily lives.

Source: Adapted from Gardner, 1993.

aphorism, "Ask not how smart is the child, but how is the child smart?" Nevertheless, in this schema, *giftedness* can be defined as a individual being exceptionally competent in one or more of Gardner's intelligences.

In the 20-plus years since Howard Gardner proposed his theory of multiple intelligences, educators have been developing activities to apply his ideas to classroom practice.

Brain Research Support for Gardner's Model: You may be surprised to learn that there is little physical evidence from neuroscience to support Gardner's theory. About the best neuroscientists can say is that scanning studies show that different parts of the brain are used to perform certain tasks associated with Gardner's intelligences. For example, language processing is largely devoted to the left frontal lobe, while many visual-spatial operations are generally located in the right parietal lobe. Creating and processing music involves the temporal lobes, and running and dancing are controlled mainly by the motor cortex and cerebellum (Figure 1.1). Some theorists suggest that Gardner's model is simply a taxonomy of intellectual pursuits based on judgments that lack scientific support and ignore the notion and contribution of general intelligence (White & Breen, 1998).

Of course, there is plenty of anecdotal evidence to indicate different degrees and types of intelligences, as any veteran teacher will confirm. We encounter, for example, the star athlete (high bodily-kinesthetic) who can hardly write a complete sentence (low linguistic), or the mathematics whiz (high logical-mathematical) who rarely communicates with classmates (low interpersonal). Classroom observations and studies have shown that more students are likely to be motivated and succeed in classes where teachers use a variety of activities designed to appeal to students whose strengths lie in one or more of the intelligences described by Gardner (Shearer, 2004). However, it is important to remember that these intelligences describe the different types of competencies that we all possess in varying degrees and that we use in our daily lives.

Using Multiple Intelligences Theory With the Gifted

Multiple intelligences (MI) theory has been used in school systems all over the world to promote all sorts of curricular and instructional changes. Several curricular programs are almost exclusively based on MI. In his writings, Gardner (1983) has suggested that traditional measures for identifying gifted students rely too heavily on IQ tests that focus on linguistic and logical/mathematical skills. Consequently, schools are increasingly resorting to MI as an alternative means of identifying gifted students. However, the problem with this approach is deciding how to develop instruments that can measure each of the intelligences with reliability and validity.

> Educators need to be wary of the fad-like nature of some of the MI programs and recognize that, without further research support, they cannot depend on MI as a panacea for gifted education.

Although MI may be theoretically useful in identifying gifted and talented children, especially those from culturally diverse backgrounds, more empirical data are needed to help develop reliable measures for the identification process. Educators need to be wary of the fad-like nature of some of the MI programs and recognize that, without further research support, they cannot depend on MI as a panacea for gifted education.

Gardner himself has decried some of the misinterpretations and confusion surrounding his theory, including among educators of the gifted. He maintains that too many educators still hold that someone who is gifted scholastically will be very good at other things. It is this unitary notion of intelligence that his theory was designed to demolish, and yet after 20 years it still persists (Henshon, 2006).

Whether scientists will eventually discover the underlying neurological networks that comprise different intelligences remains to be seen. In the meantime, Gardner's theory can still be beneficial because it reminds teachers that students have different strengths and weaknesses, different interests, and that they learn in different ways. By using Gardner's ideas, teachers are likely to address the needs of a wider range of students, including the gifted.

Sternberg's Theories

The Triarchic Theory: Two years after Gardner's work appeared, Robert Sternberg (1985) at Yale proposed a theory that distinguishes three types of intelligence: analytical, creative, and practical. People with analytical intelligence (the analyzers) have abilities in analyzing, critiquing, and evaluating. Those who are creatively intelligent (the creators) are particularly good at discovering, inventing, and creating. By contrast, the practically intelligent (the practitioners) excel at applying, utilizing, and implementing. In this model, *intelligence* is defined by these three types of behavior, and *giftedness* results from the ability to perform the skills in one or more of these areas with exceptional accuracy and efficiency. According to Sternberg, various combinations of these three areas produce different patterns of giftedness (Figure 1.6). This concept was tested in several studies conducted by Sternberg and his colleagues.

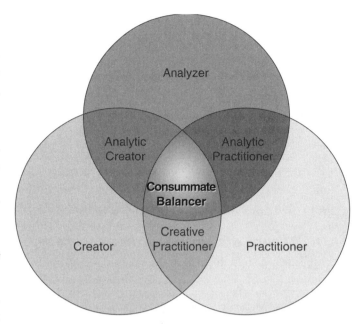

Figure 1.6 In Sternberg's model, the combination of the three types of intelligence produce different patterns of giftedness.

Source: Sternberg, 1985.

Students were assessed for their memory as well as their analytical, creative, and practical achievement. The results showed that those students who were taught in ways that best matched their achievement patterns outperformed those whose method of instruction was not a good fit for their pattern of abilities (Sternberg, Ferrari, Clinkenbeard, & Grigorenko, 1996; Sternberg et al., 2000).

The Pentagonal Implicit Theory of Giftedness: Ten years later, Sternberg and Zhang (1995) introduced another theory to describe giftedness. Their goal was to capture in one model most people's intuitions about what makes a person gifted (Figure 1.7). The result stated that a gifted person is one who meets the following five criteria:

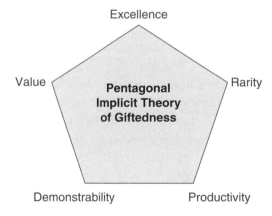

Figure 1.7 A model showing the five criteria comprising Sternberg and Zhang's Implicit Theory of Giftedness.

Source: Sternberg & Zhang, 1995.

- *Excellence.* The individual is superior in some dimension or set of dimensions relative to peers. The term "relative to peers" is important because that is the group against whom one is being judged. For example, a musical performance that would be extraordinary for a 10-year-old taking weekly music lessons, Sternberg notes, might be quite ordinary for another 10-year-old who has been trained at a conservatory since age 4.
- *Rarity.* The individual possesses a skill or attribute that is rare among peers. This criterion supplements the excellence criterion because a person may demonstrate high aptitude in a particular skill. But if that aptitude is not judged to be rare, then the person is not viewed as gifted. For instance, suppose we gave a difficult chemistry test to a group of high school seniors in an advanced chemistry class. Even if they all got perfect or near-perfect scores, we could not say they all were gifted.

- *Productivity.* The individual must produce something in the area of giftedness. It is not sufficient in this model to just get a high score on an intelligence test. The individual must be able to do something so that potential can be translated into productive work.
- *Demonstrability.* The skill or aptitude of giftedness must be demonstrable through one or more valid assessments.
- *Value.* The individual shows superior performance in a dimension that is valued by that person's society.

Sternberg and Zhang's theory helps provide a basis for understanding why we call some people gifted and others not. They caution, however, that although this theory can be helpful in identifying gifted individuals, it should be used in conjunction with other generally accepted assessment measures.

The Theory of Successful Intelligence: In 1997, Sternberg introduced his Theory of Successful Intelligence, which involves using one's intelligence to achieve the goals one sets for oneself in life, within a specific social and cultural context (Sternberg, 1997). Successfully intelligent people recognize their strengths and make the most of them while they recognize their weaknesses and find ways to correct or compensate for them. Both are important. Although students need to learn to correct aspects of their performance in which they are underperforming, they also must recognize that they probably will never be superb at all kinds of performance. It is intelligent to find ways around weaknesses, such as seeking help from others and giving it in return.

> Successful intelligence involves recognizing one's strengths and making the most of them while recognizing one's weaknesses and finding ways to correct them.

Sternberg explains that successfully intelligent people *adapt, shape,* and *select* their environment. For example, a teacher may adapt to the expectations of her principal by teaching in a way she believes the principal will support. Through shaping, individuals change the environment to fit them. In this example, the teacher may try to persuade the principal to support her new way of teaching even though it is different from what the principal has endorsed in the past. An alternative is selection, where individuals find a new environment. Here, the teacher may seek to transfer to another school if she is unable to convince the principal that her way of teaching is valid and will result in benefits for the students. In essence, successful intelligence is a direct extension of Sternberg's Triarchic Theory because these individuals accomplish their goals by finding a balance in their use of analytical, creative, and practical abilities (Sternberg, 1999).

Successful Intelligence in the Classroom. Teaching and assessment should provide a balanced use of the triarchic components of analytical, creative, and practical thinking. In this approach, teachers help students capitalize on their strengths and compensate for their weaknesses. Class work and assessments are largely centered around activities that require analysis, creativity, and application. This variety reaches more of the students' patterns of abilities so they are likely to be intrinsically motivated to succeed in their work. Sternberg suggests that teaching for successful intelligence improves student performance for the following reasons:

- It encourages *deeper* and more *elaborative* memory encoding than traditional teaching, so students learn and remember material in a way that enhances retrieval at test time.
- It encourages more *diverse* forms of encoding material, so there are more retrieval pathways to the material and a greater likelihood of recall.
- It enables students to capitalize on strengths and compensate for weaknesses.
- It is more motivating to both teachers and students.

Studies by Sternberg and others demonstrated that students taught and assessed with this approach, across many subject areas, performed better on assessments than students taught and assessed in conventional ways (Sternberg & Grigorenko, 2004). See specific suggestions on how teachers can use Successful Intelligence in their classrooms in the **Applications** section at the end of this chapter.

Brain Research Support for Sternberg's Theories: Sternberg's theories are also based on complex psychological traits, such as excellence and productivity, which most likely require contributions from many brain areas. To date, no brain studies have isolated the brain regions that appear to be specifically responsible for any of the traits in Sternberg's model. But that admission does not lessen the value of what Sternberg proposes. Although neuroscience has made some remarkable discoveries in recent years, it is still in its infancy. In the meantime, case studies and controlled research projects may still provide evidence that theoretical models, such as Sternberg's and others, when properly implemented, can result in improved student and teacher performance. In the meantime, Sternberg's triarchic model continues to influence decisions regarding instructional approaches that enhance giftedness.

Gagné's View of Giftedness and Talent

For many years in gifted education, the terms "gifted" and "talented" were often used interchangeably, and attempts to differentiate them were only moderately successful. Indeed, some researchers saw no real difference between the two. In the 1980s, Francoys Gagné (1985) of the University of Quebec at Montreal proposed a comprehensive model that made a distinction between the components of giftedness and the nature of talent (Figure 1.8).

Gagné (2003) differentiates between giftedness and talent, proposing that giftedness represents innate abilities in multiple domains, while talent is a skill in a single domain that has been systematically developed. The innate abilities fall into four aptitude domains: *intellectual, creative, socioaffective,* and *sensorimotor.* These aptitudes have a genetic basis and can be readily observed in the tasks that children perform in school.

Talents in this model emerge from a developmental process that transforms aptitudes into the skills that are characteristic of a particular field of human activity or performance. Figure 1.8 shows the many talent fields relevant to school-age youth. The model proposes that abilities and aptitudes are the raw constituents of talent. In other words, talent implies the presence of well above average natural abilities. One cannot be talented without having gifts. However, according to Gagné (2003), the reverse is not true. Some students with well above average natural abilities do not translate these gifts into talents, as evidenced by academic underachievement in intellectually gifted students. You may have encountered some of these students, although many go through school unidentified. We will have an in-depth discussion of them in Chapter 3.

> Some students with well above average natural abilities do not translate these gifts into talents, as evidenced by academic underachievement in intellectually gifted students.

Translating Aptitude to Talent: Gagné (2003) explains that the process of developing talent occurs when the child or adolescent engages in systematic *learning, training,* and *practicing.* The higher the level of talent sought, the more intensive these three activities will be. This process is helped or hindered by the action of two types of catalysts, *intrapersonal* and *environmental.* Intrapersonal catalysts include *motivation* and *volition,* which play an important role in initiating the process of talent development, guiding it, and sustaining it through obstacles, boredom, and occasional failure. *Temperament* and *adaptive strategies* also contribute significantly to support and stimulate, or slow down and even block, talent development.

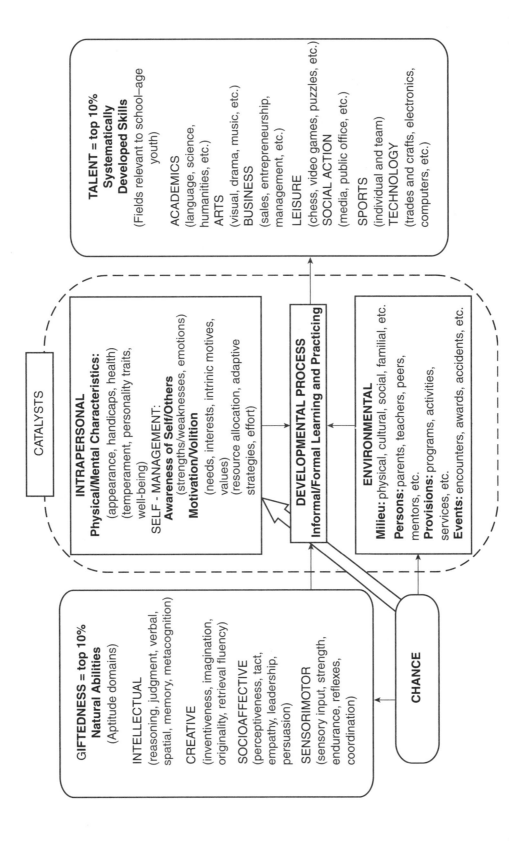

Figure 1.8 Gagné's differentiated model defines giftedness as innate abilities in multiple domains and talent as a systematically developed skill in a single domain.

Source: Adapted from Gagné, 2003.

20

Environmental catalysts exert their influence in various contexts. Many different *persons*, including parents, teachers, siblings, and peers, may exert positive or negative influences on the process of talent development. Gifted education programs within or outside the school belong to the category of *provisions* because they are a more systematic form of intervention to promote talent development. Finally, significant *events,* such as the death of a parent, winning an award, or suffering a major accident, can significantly influence the course of talent development.

Chance is a causal factor that affects the influence of other elements in the model, as for example, the chance of being born in a particular family, or the chance of the school in which the child is enrolled deciding to develop a program for gifted and talented students. Chance is also a major causal factor in determining genetic inheritance. According to Gagné, the power of chance should not be ignored or given too much weight when assessing one's potential talents (Gagné & Schader, 2006).

Practical Applications of Gagné's Model: Gagné believes that the model is most useful in differentiating giftedness from talent. He maintains that the persistent lack of differentiation has resulted in gifted and talented programs that focus mainly on the academically gifted and provide little or no support for highly talented students. He also suggests that, when properly interpreted, the model suggests the steps that schools and school districts should take to appropriately identify and serve gifted and talented students. See more about Gagné's specific suggestions in Chapter 8.

Brain Research Support for Gagné's Model: Studies in behavioral and cognitive psychology over the past few decades have shown that many of the components associated with Gagné's model contribute to student success in the gifted domains as well as in the various fields of talent (Bouchard & Shepard, 1994; Carroll, 1993; Fingelkurts & Fingelkurts, 2003; Mayer, Salovey, & Caruso, 2000), and are some of the studies that support components of the model. In neuroscience, however, a few studies using scanning technology have looked at how the brain responds when playing challenging games, getting motivated, solving logical and creative problems, and processing sensory input. But it will be a long while before studies in neuroscience can shed some light on how the many components of this model interact to reveal intellectual gifts and how they translate into talents.

Other Theoretical Models

The models we have just examined are among those that are cited most in the literature on gifted education. At least a dozen other models exist, many with common elements running through them. A full discussion of the other models goes beyond the scope of this book, but here is a brief explanation of two more recent models along with the Internet sites where readers can find additional information.

The Munich Model of Giftedness: This model was developed in Germany in the 1980s by Kurt Heller, Christopher Perleth, and Ernst Hany as part of the Munich longitudinal study of giftedness. It is based on the following four interdependent dimensions (Heller, 2004):

- **Talent factors (predictors of giftedness):** intellectual abilities, creative abilities, social competence, practical intelligence, artistic abilities, musicality, and psycho-motor skills
- **Non-cognitive personality characteristics (moderators of giftedness):** coping with stress, achievement motivation, learning and working strategies, test anxiety, and control expectations

- **Environmental conditions (moderators of giftedness):** family learning environment, family climate, quality of instruction, classroom climate, and critical life events
- **Performance areas (criteria for giftedness):** athletics and sports, art (music, painting), computer science, languages, mathematics, natural sciences, social relationships, and technology

A number of similar components can be found in the Munich and Gagné models. However, researchers with the Munich model have developed a series of instruments to measure the components of each of the four dimensions in students.

> For more information on the details of the Munich Model of Giftedness, visit the following Web site: www.pabst-publishers.de/psychology-science/3-2004/05.pdf.

The Actiotope Model of Giftedness: In this highly complex and dynamic model, developed by Albert Ziegler, gifts and talent are not personal attributes, but attributions made by scientists. These are based on our assumption that a person is in the position to carry out specific actions in the future. According to Ziegler, gifted behavior is displayed when a person has a wish to do something, the ability to do it, and the awareness that it can be done. Furthermore, the environment must consider this behavior as gifted. Giftedness is a characteristic that *changes* over time within an environmental context and is the result of various interactions between the individual and the environment (Ziegler, 2005).

CHARACTERISTICS OF GIFTEDNESS

Are the Gifted More Excitable?

Are gifted children more sensitive to touch and smell? Do they appear more impulsive? Are they more emotional? Do their imaginations run wild? For a long time, parents and teachers observed certain personality characteristics that were more noticeable in highly gifted children compared to their peers. The work of Polish psychiatrist and psychologist Kazimierz Dabrowski (1902–1980) provides a useful framework for understanding these characteristics. Dabrowski worked in Europe with genius and depravity during the pre–World War II years. After observing how highly gifted people reacted under stress, he developed the notion of *overexcitabilities*, as part of his larger Theory of Positive Disintegration. Dabrowski observed that innate abilities combined with overexcitability predicted an individual's potential for higher level development. Not all gifted people have overexcitabilities, he noted, but there are more gifted people with overexcitabilities than in the general population (Dabrowski, 1964).

> Overexcitabilities are innate characteristics that reveal a heightened response to stimuli. They are found more frequently in gifted individuals than in the general population.

Dabrowski's work was introduced to gifted education by his colleague Michael Piechowski in 1979 (Colangelo & Zaffran, 1979). The notion of overexcitabilities has gained popularity in recent years, especially among researchers who look at the social and emotional areas of giftedness. Some researchers also see overexcitabilities as a means for identifying gifted students that is different from the usual standardized tests.

Overexcitabilities: Overexcitabilities (OE) are innate characteristics that reveal a heightened ability to respond to stimuli due to increase sensitivity of the neurons. They are expressed through increased sensitivity, awareness, and intensity, and have an impact on an individual's quality of experiences. Dabrowski identified the five areas of intensity: *psychomotor, sensual, intellectual, imaginational,* and *emotional.* A person may possess one or more of these. Here is a brief description of each of the overexcitabilities (Lind, 2001).

- **Psychomotor overexcitability:** This is a heightened excitability of the neuromuscular system that results in movement for its own sake, surplus of energy demonstrated by rapid speech, enthusiasm, and intense physical activity. When tense, these individuals may talk compulsively, act impulsively, misbehave, display nervous habits (such as tics, nail-biting), show intense drive, and be highly competitive. Although they derive joy from their activity, others may find them overwhelming. At home and at school, these children seem to be constantly on the go and never still. As a result, they have the potential of being misdiagnosed as having attention-deficit hyperactivity disorder (ADHD).

- **Sensual overexcitability:** This is expressed as a heightened and more expansive experience of sensual pleasure or displeasure emanating from sight, smell, touch, taste, and hearing. These individuals have an early and increased appreciation of aesthetic pleasures such as music, language, and art. They may also feel overstimulated or uncomfortable with sensory input. When emotionally tense, some may overeat, go on shopping sprees, or seek the center of attention, while others may withdraw from stimulation. As children, they may find clothing tags, classroom noise, or cafeteria smells so distracting that schoolwork becomes secondary. These children may also become deeply absorbed in a particular piece of art or music to the exclusion of the outside world.

- **Intellectual overexcitability:** This is demonstrated by a need to seek understanding and truth, to gain knowledge, and to analyze and synthesize. These individuals have incredibly active minds, are intensely curious, avid readers, and keen observers. They are able to concentrate, engage in prolonged intellectual activities, and can be tenacious problem solvers. The enjoy elaborate planning, love thinking about thinking, and have excellent visual recall. They may focus on moral thinking, which often translates into strong concerns about moral and ethical issues, such as fairness on the playground, lack of respect for children, or even being concerned about the homeless, AIDS, or war. Sometimes, they appear impatient with others who cannot sustain their intellectual pace. They may be so excited about an idea that they interrupt the class at inappropriate times.

- **Imaginational overexcitability:** This reflects a heightened imagination with rich association of images and impressions, frequent use of metaphor, facility for invention and fantasy, and detailed visualization. These children often mix truth with fiction, and they escape boredom by creating their own private worlds with imaginary companions and dramatizations. They have difficulty paying attention in a classroom focused on teaching a rigid academic curriculum. In that case, they may write stories or draw instead of doing assigned work or participating in class discussions. A novel idea may send them off on an imaginative tangent and distract them from their classroom tasks.

- **Emotional overexcitability:** This is often the first OE to be noticed by parents. It is reflected in intense feelings, extremes of complex emotions, identification with others' feelings, and strong affective expression. It may also include physical responses, such as stomachaches, blushing, or concern with death and depression. These individuals have a remarkable capacity for compassionate and empathetic relationships and demonstrate strong emotional attachments to people, places, and things. They are acutely aware of their own feelings, of their own growth and change, and often carry on inner dialogs and practice self-judgment. Their concern for others, their focus on relationships, and the intensity of their feelings may interfere with everyday tasks like homework or household chores.

Research Studies on Overexcitabilities: A summary of the results of numerous studies conducted over the last two decades supported the application of OEs to gifted persons, especially in the imaginational, intellectual, and emotional OEs (Mendaglio & Tillier, 2006). A recent study of nearly 500 elementary and middle school students found that the OEs showed greater application to gifted students than their typical peers. The results also noted that (1) the power of the application was stronger among elementary students than among middle school students and (2) was stronger in all gifted females than gifted males in every OE except intellectual (Tieso, 2007). A study in Turkey of more than 700 students found the OE scores of highly intelligent, motivated, creative, and leader students in some OE areas were significantly greater than those of their typical peers. No gender differences are found in regard to OEs (Yakmaci-Guzel & Akarsu, 2006). As of this writing, there have been no studies using brain imaging technologies that looked specifically at the nature of Dabrowski's overexcitabilities.

Implications for Schools: Dabrowski's ideas and subsequent studies can help schools in at least the following two ways:

- Valid questionnaires based on the five OEs can be useful tools beyond traditional intelligence tests to identify gifted students. One such questionnaire was developed in 1999 and has shown consistent validity. The instrument is known as the Overexcitability Questionnaire-Two, or OEQ-II, and is available at www.gifteddevelopment.net (Falk, Lind, Miller, Piechowski, & Silverman, 1999).
- By describing the nature of the OEs, teachers and parents gain a better understanding of how to work with highly gifted students who display these OEs. Some strategies are suggested in the **Applications** section at the end of this chapter.

> For more information on the details of the Dabrowski and his work, visit the following Web site: www.positivedisintegration.com.

Thinking About Thinking

Some of the research on the characteristics of giftedness has focused on cognition and metacognition. In these studies, researchers observed how students identified as gifted thought through a given problem or situation (cognition), and how they reflected on their thinking throughout the problem-solving experience (metacognition).

Cognitive Strategies: Not surprisingly, the studies on cognitive strategies showed that gifted students acquired information and solved problems faster, better, or at earlier stages than other students, even in the primary grades (Cho & Ahn, 2003; Delcourt, Cornell, & Goldberg, 2007). Some studies showed that higher IQ individuals had more efficient memories, more information-processing strategies, larger and more elaborately organized knowledge bases, and a better ability to solve mathematical problems by employing their own symbolic encoding (Robinson & Clinkenbeard, 1998).

Sternberg has also investigated how different thinking styles in gifted students affect their academic performance (Grigorenko & Sternberg, 1997). The study found that there were no differences in thinking styles among groups of students at different ability levels, and that certain thinking styles contributed significantly to prediction of academic performance. For example, the style that involved analyzing, grading, or comparing things had the highest predictive value. Further, this contribution was independent of the type of instruction the students were given. One other finding of interest was that the gifted students performed best on assessment procedures that closely matched their thinking style. (This last finding corroborates the results of decades of earlier research on different types of student learning styles.) Other studies have found similar results (Rayneri, Gerber, & Wiley, 2006; Zhang & Sternberg, 2006).

Metacognitive Strategies: Research studies in metacognition (i.e., thinking about one's own thinking) have focused around three aspects:

- What do students know about thinking strategies?
- Can they use the strategies?
- Can they monitor their own cognitive processing?

Compared to other students, the studies showed that gifted students knew more about metacognitive strategies and could use them more easily in new contexts. The first edition of this book noted that several studies in the 1990s found that gifted students did not use a *greater variety* of metacognitive strategies than other students, nor did they monitor their strategies any more than the other students (Alexander, Carr, & Schwanenflugel, 1995). However, more recent studies have found that high performing elementary and secondary school students with strong metacognitive skills were aware of them and knew how to use them to successfully complete academic tasks (Coutinho, 2008; Steiner, 2006).

Neuroscientists—or more specifically, cognitive neuroscientists—also think about thinking. In recent years, they have explored what differences in the structure and functions of the gifted brain may allow it to achieve remarkable levels of performance. These researchers use many tools in their investigations. They include imaging technologies, such as PET scans and functional magnetic resonance imaging (fMRI), as well as electroencephalography (EEG) and magnetoencephalography (MEG). The techniques reveal similarities and differences in the function of high-performing brains compared with the brains of students showing no signs of the same kinds of giftedness. One area of particular interest is determining whether there is any difference in how information flows in gifted brains as compared to typical brains.

The Cerebral Hemispheres

Since the work of Roger Sperry in the 1960s, neuroscientists have accepted the notion that the two cerebral hemispheres are not mirror images of each other. That is, they differ structurally, biochemically, and functionally (Sousa, 2006). In most people, for example, the right frontal lobe protrudes over, and is wider than, the left frontal lobe. The left occipital lobe (at the back of the brain) protrudes over, and is wider than, the right occipital lobe. The neurotransmitter norepinephrine is more prevalent in the right hemisphere, while dopamine is more prevalent in the left hemisphere. Estrogen receptors are more prevalent in the right hemisphere than in the left hemisphere.

As for brain functions, more evidence is accumulating that the brain has a much greater degree of specialization than was previously thought. Even so, because of advancements in neuroimaging, the earlier idea that the brain is a set of modular units carrying out specific tasks has yielded to a new model, which holds that moving across the brain's surface results in a gradual transition from one cognitive function to another. Goldberg (2001) refers to this as the "gradiential" view of brain organization. This view does not discard the notion that particular areas of the brain perform specific functions. Rather, it uses recent evidence from neurological studies to suggest a pattern of organization whereby the boundaries between the specific areas are fluid, not fixed. The ability of certain areas of the brain to perform unique functions is known as *lateralization* or *specialization* (Sousa, 2006).

The left hemisphere monitors the areas for speech. It understands the literal interpretation of words, and recognizes words, letters, and numbers written as words. It is analytical, evaluates factual material in a rational way, and detects time and sequence. It also performs simple arithmetic computations. Arousing attention to deal with outside stimuli is another specialty of the left hemisphere. The right hemisphere gathers information more from images than from words, and looks for patterns. It interprets language through context—body language, emotional content, and tone of voice—rather than through literal meanings. It specializes in spatial perception; recognizes places, faces, and objects; and focuses on relational and mathematical operations, such as geometry and trigonometry (Gazzaniga, Ivry, & Mangun, 2002).

Specialization and Learning: The two hemispheres of the brain communicate with each other through a tight bundle of about 200 million nerve cells called the *corpus callosum*. Researchers have been particularly interested in how the specialized functions of each hemisphere affect new learning, and the degree to which they communicate with each other during that process. Early theories held that new learning occurs in the hemisphere mainly responsible for the functions associated with that learning. Thus, the left hemisphere would be largely involved in spoken language acquisition and sequential procedures, and the right side would support the learning of visual images and spatial relationships. These theories were based mainly on the results of tests done with patients who had damage to specific areas of the brain.

More recent research, however, lends credence to an alternative explanation. Goldberg (2001), for example, proposes that hemispheric specialization may center around the differences between novelty and routine. Closer examination of brain-damaged patients shows that those with severe right hemisphere problems experience difficulty in facing new learning situations, but can perform routine, practiced tasks (e.g., language) normally. Conversely, patients with severe left hemisphere damage can create new drawings and think abstractly, but have difficulty with routine operations.

Goldberg's notion gives us a different way of looking at how the brain learns (Figure 1.9). It suggests that upon encountering a novel situation for which the individual has no coping strategy, the right hemisphere is primarily involved and attempts to deal with the situation (Chong et al., 2008). With repeated exposure to similar situations, coping strategies eventually emerge and learning occurs because it results in a change of behavior. In time, and after sufficient repetition, the responses become routine and shift via the corpus callosum to the left hemisphere. The amount of time and the number of situational exposures needed to accomplish this right-to-left hemisphere transition vary widely from one person to the next. But it may be that one component of giftedness is the ability of that person's brain to make the transition in less time and with fewer exposures than average.

Studies using neuroimaging provide evidence to support Goldberg's theory. In one major study, researchers used PET scans to measure the changes in brain flow patterns when subjects were asked to learn various types of information. Changes in blood flow levels indicate the degree of neural activation. When the information was novel, regions in the right temporal lobe were highly activated. After the information had been presented several times to the subjects, activity in the right temporal lobe decreased dramatically (Figure 1.10). In both instances, however, the level of activation in the left temporal lobe remained constant (Martin, Wiggs, & Weisberg, 1997).

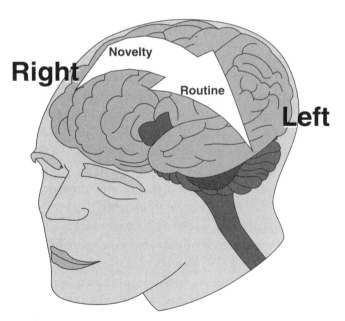

Figure 1.9 With repeated exposures, novel experiences become routine, and their main cortical processing areas shift from the right hemisphere to the left hemisphere.

Similar results were reported from other studies involving a variety of learning tasks, such as recognizing faces and symbols (Cycowisz & Friedman, 2007; Henson, Shallice, & Dolan, 2000; Speer & Curran, 2007), learning a complex motor skill (Shadmehr & Holcomb, 1997; Vogt et al., 2007), and learning and relearning different systems of rules (Berns, Cohen, & Mintun, 1997). The same shifts were detected no matter what type of information was presented to the subjects. In other words, says Goldberg, the association of the right hemisphere with novelty and the left hemisphere with routine appears to be independent of the nature of the information being learned.

The Prefrontal Cortex

Cognitive thought and related activities are located in the foremost part of the frontal lobes, called the *prefrontal cortex.* This area comprises about 29 percent of the total cortex and is interconnected to every distinct functional region (Figure 1.1). Often called the executive control area, the prefrontal cortex is embedded in a rich network of neural pathways so that it can coordinate and integrate the functions of all areas. Like the conductor of an orchestra, the prefrontal cortex blends individual inputs from various regions of the brain into a comprehensive and comprehendible whole. Its interpretations ultimately define personality, and its decision-making abilities determine how successfully an individual copes with each day.

To accomplish this task, the prefrontal cortex must converge the inputs from within an individual with those from the outside world. The brain's organization facilitates this process. As shown in Figure 1.11, sensory signals from the outside environment pass along the sensory nerves to the control center—called the *thalamus*—and are routed to other areas toward the back of the brain (reception). These inputs are then directed to specific sites in the parietal and temporal lobes, as well as in the limbic areas, for further analysis (integration). Finally, the frontal lobes combine this input with information from the individual's memory (interpretation) to determine what subsequent action, if any, should be taken (Bruguier, Preuschoff, Quartz, & Bossaerts, 2008).

The prefrontal cortex also seems to be strongly interested in task novelty. Several imaging studies show that when processing new information, cerebral blood flow levels in the frontal lobes reached their highest levels. But when the subject became familiar with the task, frontal lobe involvement—as measured by blood flow—dropped significantly (Goldberg, 2001; Habib, McIntosh, Wheeler, & Tulving, 2003). If a somewhat different task was introduced, frontal lobe activation picked up once again. We noted before that the right hemisphere was more

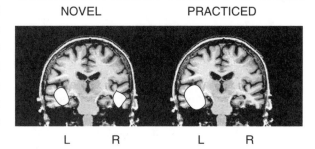

One component of giftedness may be the brain's ability to make the transition from novelty to routine in less time and with fewer exposures than average.

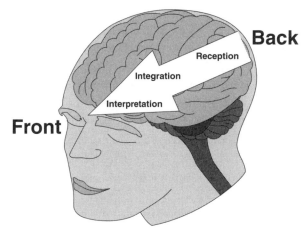

NOVEL   PRACTICED

L   R   L   R

Figure 1.10   In this representation of PET scans, the white areas show the changes in regional blood flow for novel and practiced tasks. The images reveal areas of high activation in the left and right temporal lobes for novel tasks, but only in the left temporal lobe for practiced tasks.

Source: Martin et al., 1997.

Figure 1.11   Stimuli from the outside world are received toward the rear of the brain, integrated in the center, and interpreted by the frontal lobes. Gifted individuals may be able to do this faster and with greater accuracy than typical individuals.

Gifted individuals may be able to carry out the reception, integration, and interpretation processes with greater speed and accuracy than typical individuals.

associated with novelty than the left. These findings infer that the frontal lobes are more closely aligned with the right hemisphere when dealing with novel learning situations. One can speculate, once again, that gifted individuals may be able to carry out the reception, integration, and interpretation processes with greater speed and accuracy than typical individuals.

Decision Making

The prefrontal cortex faces many decisions in the course of a day. Some involve simple concrete problems, such as the following:

"What is my doctor's telephone number?"

"How much money is left in my savings account?"

"When is my nephew's birthday?"

Each question is clear and the situations require searching for a single, indisputable answer. This process is called *veridical decision making*, or finding the single, true answer.

I may be faced with other questions as well:

"Am I sick enough to see the doctor or should I wait a few days?"

"Should I use some of my savings to buy stocks or bonds?"

"What gift should I get for my nephew's birthday?"

> Veridical decision making gets us through the day. Adaptive decision making gets us through life.

These questions are ambiguous and have no intrinsically unique answer. I will choose the answer for a variety of reasons. My decision to see the doctor might depend on whether my body temperature rises or falls. Buying stocks or bonds might depend on where I think the stock market may be headed in the next year. In any event, my brain is engaging in *adaptive decision making,* that is, I adapt the decision on the basis of context and my priorities at the moment. At another time and place, my decision might be different.

No one doubts that finely tuned veridical decision-making skills are valuable in certain technical occupations. But, life in general is fraught with ambiguities, and most critical decisions—personal and occupational—often require choosing from among equally valid options. Deciding among ambiguities is one of the most important functions of the prefrontal cortex. Studies show that (1) different parts of the brain are engaged, depending on the type of decision-making employed (Johnson et al., 2005); (2) individuals with damage to the prefrontal cortex have difficulty dealing with adaptive decision making, while damage to other parts of the brain does not seem to affect this process (Goldberg, 2001); and (3) drug addiction affects adaptive decision making much more than veridical decision making (Verdejo-García, Vilar-López, Pérez-García, Podell, & Goldberg, 2006).

To be successful, we need to be competent in both types of skills. Veridical decisions help us get through the day: What time do I need to be at work and when is my first appointment? How much gasoline is in the car? Who's picking up the kids after practice? Adaptive decisions, on the other hand, get us through life: Is this the person I should marry? Is this the right job for me? When should we start a family?

Neural Efficiency: When the frontal lobes gain more experience at making adaptive decisions and solving complex problems, the neuron pathways responsible for these processes should become more efficient and thus require less effort. Indeed, this concept—known as *neural efficiency*—has long been part of most theoretical models of the gifted brain. The idea is that gifted brains can perform tasks more quickly and accurately because they contain networks comprising neurons working together in vast arrays and with such efficiency that they require less cerebral energy than unorganized networks. One way to measure the level of brain activity is to monitor the pattern of waves produced by the brain's electrical activity.

Obtaining experimental evidence to support this idea requires using EEG technology to measure the activity of the brain while it was performing different functions. One study of chess players of various levels of intelligence and expertise showed that superior and brighter chess players performed better and with greater neural efficiency than less intelligent and lower expertise players (Grabner, Neubauer, & Stern, 2006).

EEG and fMRI Studies: When using the EEG to detect brain functioning, two wave patterns are of particular interest: alpha waves (8–13 cycles per second) and beta waves (14–60 cycles per second). Neurobiologists theorize that alpha activity is the result of neurons firing together (in synchrony) and resting together—an indication of neural pathway efficiency. Thus, alpha activity produces high voltage, rhythmic, and sinusoidal patterns. The higher the amplitude of the alpha wave (called *alpha power*), the more efficiently the neurons are firing, resulting in less mental effort.

Beta waves, on the other hand, result from the activity of neurons that are doing different things at different times (asynchrony), producing a low voltage, irregular pattern (Figure 1.12). Beatty (2001) offers the analogy of a marching band. When the band members are marching in synchrony, their footsteps are a loud beat with silence between the steps (alpha waves). But as the band members disperse after the march, one hears the constant sound of many steps at random intervals (beta waves).

Norbert Jausovec (2000) used EEG to study the differences in brain activity during problem solving in about 50 young adults who were separated into four groups based on their intelligence (average or high) and creativity (average or high). On the basis of their scores on various assessment measures, Jausovec placed them into the categories of intelligent, gifted, creative, and average (Figure 1.13). He then measured their alpha wave activity as they were solving closed problems (those requiring convergent and logical thinking) and creative problems (those requiring more adaptive decision making). His findings were threefold:

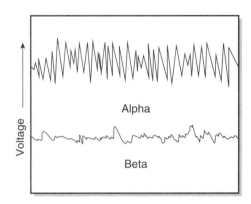

Figure 1.12 Typical activity patterns of alpha and beta brain wave activity.

- Alpha wave activity showed that high IQ individuals (gifted and intelligent) used less mental effort than the average IQ individuals (creative and average) when solving closed problems.
- Alpha wave activity showed that high creative individuals (creative and gifted) used less mental effort than average creative individuals (intelligent and average) when engaged in creative problem solving.
- Creative individuals showed more cooperation among brain areas than did gifted ones, who showed greater decoupling (disconnecting from each other) of brain areas when solving ill-defined problems.

These results first suggest that when individuals are solving problems in their area of strength, less mental effort is needed so the alpha power is high, an indication of neural efficiency. Second, the results appear to support the concept that creativity and intelligence are

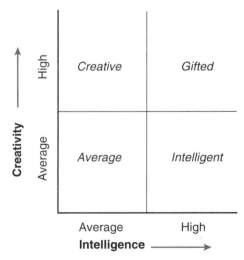

Figure 1.13 Jausovec's system for classifying subjects for the EEG study based on levels of creativity and intelligence.

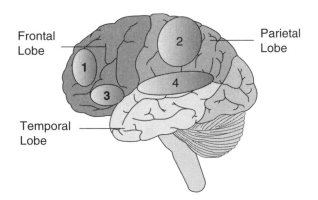

Frontal Lobe

Parietal Lobe

Temporal Lobe

Figure 1.14   Areas 1 and 2 show the brain regions with high alpha wave activity during the generation of creative ideas to solve a problem, as measured by EEG. Areas 3 and 4 show regions that are highly activated while performing a task, as measured by fMRI.

Source: Fink et al., 2009.

> Creativity and intelligence are different abilities that involve different areas of the brain while solving problems.

different abilities that involve different areas of the cortex while solving closed or creative problems. This finding enhances the position of those who urge that creativity be considered as a separate measure of giftedness.

Jausovec continued his EEG studies and found that individuals of average to low intelligence expend more neural energy—thus, have less neural efficiency—than high intelligence individuals when solving problems involving working memory (Jausovec & Jausovec, 2004).

Recently, researchers measured brain activity during creative thinking in two studies employing different technologies, EEG and fMRI. In both studies, participants worked on tasks that required generating creative ideas. The EEG was used to determine which brain regions produced synchronized alpha waves when the individual was generating creative ideas to solve a problem, essentially adaptive decision making. The fMRI was used to identify brain areas that were highly activated when the individual was completing a task, an activity more associated with veridical decision making.

The EEG study revealed that the generation of original ideas was associated with synchronized alpha wave pattern in the frontal lobe and with a widespread pattern over the parietal regions, as shown in areas 1 and 2 in Figure 1.14. When solving tasks, the fMRI study revealed strong activation in frontal regions of the left hemisphere, and task-specific effects in the parietotemporal brain areas, areas 3 and 4 (Fink et al., 2009). These results further strengthen the notion that the brain recruits different regions when confronted with veridical and adaptive decision making.

Implications for Schools: Far too frequently, what is taught in schools emphasizes veridical, rather than adaptive, decision making. Most course work—and the resulting tests—ask students to search for the unique answers to concrete and unambiguous questions. Some students adapt to this strategy quickly and excel at veridical decision making. As a result, their test scores are high, and they may even be considered gifted. However, when faced with ambiguous problems, they often vacillate and become indecisive. Seldom do schools offer students consistent opportunities to develop adaptive decision-making skills. Instead, these are acquired individually, through trial and error.

With such emphasis on veridical decision making in schools, one wonders what happens to students who favor adaptive decision making. Do they get bored easily and act out or become withdrawn? Do they get frustrated if teachers insist they find only the unique answer? Are there areas in the curriculum where they can excel with their adaptive skills? Is it possible that those students who prefer adaptive decision making will seem different from the rest of the class? Is it also possible that a high aptitude in adaptive decision making is a characteristic of the gifted brain?

Given the appropriate adjustments in curriculum, most students can be taught to improve their adaptive decision-making skills. This process involves helping students to make connections and to discover relationships

> Is it possible that a high aptitude in adaptive decision making is a characteristic of the gifted brain?

between the new learning and what they already know. One valuable strategy for accomplishing this is the frequent use of elaborative rehearsal. See the **Applications** section at the end of this chapter for suggestions on how to use elaborative rehearsal to enhance adaptive decision-making skills.

SOCIAL AND EMOTIONAL CHARACTERISTICS OF GIFTEDNESS

Social Characteristics

Despite stories that often circulate in schools about gifted students being loners, surveys indicate that preadolescent and adolescent gifted students were at least as popular as other students their age, and most gifted students felt good about themselves and their relationships with peers. However, highly gifted students had more difficulty with peer relationships and often developed coping strategies to deal with such circumstances. Several researchers have found that the most frequent coping strategies used by highly gifted students were hiding their giftedness, denying their giftedness, conforming to peer expectations, valuing peer acceptance, minimizing the importance of popularity, using humor, and helping others (Rudasill, Foust, & Callahan, 2007; Swiatek, 1995, 2001).

> Highly gifted adolescents use a variety of coping strategies when interacting with their peers, ranging from denying their giftedness to helping others.

The research studies revealed gender and age differences in selecting the coping strategies as shown in Table 1.1. Males tended to use humor to laugh off perceptions of their giftedness while females were more likely to use prosocial behavior in the form of helping others. Males were also more apt to minimize the importance of popularity while females preferred to deny their giftedness in order to fit into their preferred social circles. As for age differences, younger students tended to use conformity as a major coping strategy while older students were more apt to minimize popularity or deny and hide their giftedness. It should be noted that the gender and age differences found in these studies were not large, so caution should be used in interpreting the results. Nonetheless, one implication from these findings is that females seem to be using coping strategies to hide their aptitude rather than embracing it (Foust & Booker, 2007).

Some studies have also found a significant relationship between gifted students' self-concept and the coping strategies they chose. Those students who used positive strategies, such as helping others, also tended to have a higher self-concept. Conversely, gifted students who opted for more negative strategies, such as denying giftedness, had a lower self-concept. In other words, those students who have a more positive view of themselves select more positive coping strategies. This finding has implications for those who work with highly gifted students. There is research evidence that educators can change gifted students' views of

Table 1.1 Gender and Age Differences in Selecting Social Coping Strategies

	Males	**Females**
Gender	Using humor Minimizing the importance of popularity	Helping others Denying giftedness Valuing peer acceptance Conformity
	Younger	**Older**
Age	Conformity Minimizing the importance of popularity	Helping others Minimizing the importance of popularity Denying giftedness Hiding giftedness

Source: Foust & Booker, 2007.

themselves (Ziegler & Stoeger, 2004). This suggests that by improving gifted students' self-concepts, we may be able to help them select those coping strategies that enhance their academic achievement and contribute to a positive social adjustment.

Emotional Characteristics

Earlier in this chapter we discussed the notion of overexcitabilities in gifted children. One of these is emotional overexcitability, which is more evident in younger children. Apart from this characteristic, numerous studies in recent years on the emotional, personality, and motivational characteristics of gifted students have yielded similar results. In general, the studies showed that, when compared to average students, gifted students

- Were at least as well or somewhat better adjusted
- Possessed more personality traits considered to be favorable
- Displayed personality traits similar to older students
- Had lower levels of anxiety about school
- Scored higher on measures of self-concept
- Displayed higher levels of intrinsic motivation and autonomy, especially for reading, thinking, and solitude

Some gender and age differences have been noted. For example, gifted high school girls had significantly less self-confidence, more perfectionism, and more discouragement than younger gifted girls. Gifted high school boys, however, felt less discouragement than younger boys, and there were no age differences in self-confidence and perfectionism. High school girls scored higher on discouragement than high school boys (Cross, Cassady, Dixon, & Adams, 2008; Robinson and Clinkenbeard, 1998).

Although the studies present a useful profile, it is important to remember that some groups of gifted students will look quite different. For example, gifted students who are underachievers, and those whose talents are very far from the norm, are more likely to have difficulty fitting in socially and emotionally with their peers (see Chapter 7).

Asynchronous Development: One of the more puzzling observations with gifted children is how they can talk and act like an adult in one instance, and a few minutes later, throw a screaming fit because it is time to go to bed. This phenomenon may very well be due to *asynchronous development*. In typical children, intellectual, physical, and emotional development progresses at about the same rate. We can describe this development as synchronized. An average three-year-old has the intellectual and physical abilities as well as the emotional maturity of most other three-year-olds. However, in gifted children, the development of those areas is often not synchronized (or asynchronous) in that they do not progress at the same rate. For example, the developmental profile of three different gifted three-year-old children could look like this:

Child A	Child B	Child C
Intellectual ability: Age 6	Intellectual ability: Age 7	Intellectual ability: Age 6
Physical ability: Age 3	Physical ability: Age 3	Physical ability: Age 4
Emotional maturity: Age 2	Emotional maturity: Age 4	Emotional maturity: Age 3

Any other combination of the three developmental areas is possible, although intellectual ability is always advanced. The higher a child's IQ, the more asynchronous the development is likely to be. The advanced intellectual development of gifted children can lead teachers and parents to also expect more advanced behavior from these children. A six-year-old who can discuss global warming like a 10-year-old is often also expected to behave like a 10-year-old. When the child acts like a six-year-old instead, adults see that as immature behavior. Gifted children who are years ahead of their same-age peers are not always years ahead emotionally or socially. Advanced intellectual ability simply does not enable a gifted child to manage emotions any better than any other child.

As these children develop into adolescents, the asynchrony of the developmental areas may increase in some and diminish in others. An increase in asynchrony may produce difficulties, especially if emotional development lags while intellectual development leaps ahead. This imbalance could cause the adolescent to get anxious, frustrated, upset, overly sensitive, and self-critical (Alsop, 2003). These emotional needs should be addressed by parents, teachers, and counselors so that these gifted students can understand and deal with their developmental stages.

IMPACT OF PRAISE ON GIFTED STUDENTS

Gifted children should be commended for their good grades and high test scores. With restrained praise, gifted students are likely to attribute failure in a task to lack of effort rather than lack of ability (Assouline, Colangelo, Ihrig, & Forstadt, 2006). However, research seems to indicate that *excessively* complimenting children for their intelligence and academic performance may lead them to believe that good test scores and high grades are more important than learning and mastering something new (Mueller & Dweck, 1998). Six studies of 412 fifth-graders compared the goals and achievement behaviors of children praised for intelligence with those praised for effort and hard work under conditions of failure as well as success. Through their studies, the psychologists demonstrated that commending children for their intelligence after good performance might backfire by making them highly performance-oriented and thus extremely vulnerable to the effects of subsequent setbacks. In contrast, children who are commended for their effort concentrate on learning goals and strategies for achievement.

The researchers also observed that children who were commended for their ability when they were successful learned to believe that intelligence is a fixed trait that cannot be developed or improved. The children who were explicitly commended after their successes were the ones who blamed poor performances on their own lack of intelligence. They had a *fixed mind-set* about their abilities. However, when children praised for their hard work performed poorly, they blamed their lack of success on poor effort and demonstrated a clear determination to learn strategies that would enhance subsequent performances. They had a *growth mind-set.* Similar studies have demonstrated that children who are praised for their intelligence learn to value performance, while children praised for their effort and hard work value learning opportunities.

> Studies show that children who are praised for their intelligence learn to value performance, while children praised for their effort and hard work value opportunities to learn.

Virtually all of the findings were similar not only for boys and girls but also among children from several different ethnic groups in rural and urban communities.

One important study monitored 373 students for two years during their transition to junior high school (Blackwell, Trzesniewski, & Dweck, 2007). At the beginning of seventh grade, the students were asked whether they agreed or disagreed with a statement that said their intelligence is something very basic and cannot be really changed. Students with a growth mind-set believed that the more hard work you put into something, the better you became at it. Fixed mind-set students, however, were concerned about looking smart, and believed that hard work at something was a sign of low ability. These different mind-sets had an impact on academic performance. At the start of the seventh grade, the mathematics scores for both mind-set groups were similar. But as the work became more difficult, the growth mind-set students showed greater persistence and the gap in the mathematics grades over two years continued to widen, as shown in Table 1.2.

Table 1.2 Mathematics Grades of Growth and Fixed Mind-Sets				
	Fall 7th Grade	**Spring 7th Grade**	**Fall 8th Grade**	**Spring 8th Grade**
Growth mind-set	73.0	74.0	74.9	75.8
Fixed mind-set	71.1	71.0	70.8	70.7

Source: Blackwell et al. (2007).

These findings may also explain why bright young girls who do well in grade school often perform poorly in upper grades. In their desire to bolster young girls' confidence in their abilities, educators have praised them for their intelligence, which, these studies have shown, could have an undesired impact on their subsequent motivation and performance.

Labeling children as gifted or talented too soon may also have a negative impact on them. Such labeling may cause the children to become overly concerned with justifying that label and less concerned with meeting challenges that enhance their learning and mastery skills. They may begin to believe that academic setbacks indicate that they do not deserve to be labeled as gifted. Gifted and talented programs should emphasize how to meet challenges, apply effort, and search for new learning strategies. Furthermore, when students succeed, attention and approval should be directed at their effort and hard work rather than for the final product or their ability. In summary, researchers in this area stress that praise may undermine, enhance, or have no effect on children's intrinsic motivation. Praise is particularly motivating when it encourages solid performance, promotes autonomy, enhances competence without an over-reliance on "innate intelligence," and conveys standards and expectations that are attainable (Henderlong & Lepper, 2002).

APPLICATIONS

USING SUCCESSFUL INTELLIGENCE IN THE CLASSROOM

Teaching for successful intelligence is a method for helping students learn in a way that matches their patterns of ability. Based on Robert Sternberg's Triarchic Theory of Intelligence, the approach involves teaching in a way that balances learning for analytical, creative, and practical thinking. These methods help all students, including the gifted, reach their full potential. Here are some examples across the school curriculum suggested by Sternberg and Grigorenko (2004).

Teaching analytically: analyze, critique, judge, compare/contrast, evaluate, assess

- *Analyze* the development of the character of Fagan in *Oliver Twist.* (Literature)
- *Critique* the design of the experiment (just reviewed in class) showing that certain minerals improve plant growth while others do not. (Biology)
- *Judge* the artistic merits of Andy Warhol's op-art, discussing its strengths and weaknesses as fine art. (Art)
- *Compare and contrast* the American Revolution to the French Revolution, showing ways in which they were similar and different. (History)
- *Evaluate* the validity of the following solution to a mathematical problem, and discuss weaknesses in the solution, if there are any. (Mathematics)
- *Assess* the strategy used by the winning player in the tennis match you just watched, focusing on the techniques that were used to defeat the opponent. (Physical Education)

Teaching creatively: create, invent, discover, imagine if, suppose that, predict

- *Create* an alternative ending to *Romeo and Juliet* that shows a different way that things might have turned out for the main characters. (Literature)
- *Invent* a dialogue between an American tourist in Madrid and a Spanish police officer he encounters on the street from whom he is asking directions on how to get to the Prado museum. (Spanish)
- *Discover* the underlying principle that determines whether solutions will be acidic, basic, or neutral. (Chemistry)
- *Imagine if* the population of India continues to increase at its current rate over the next 15 years. What demands would that increase make on India's government? (Political Science)
- *Suppose that* you were to design a new musical instrument for a symphony orchestra. What would it look like and why? (Music)
- *Predict* changes that are likely to occur in the vocabulary and grammar of spoken French in the areas near the U.S.-Quebec Province border over the next 50 years as a result of continuous interaction between English and French speakers. (Languages/Linguistics)

Teach practically: apply, use, put into practice, implement, employ, render practical

- *Apply* the formula for computing compound interest to a problem that people are likely to face when planning for retirement. (Economics, Mathematics)

- *Use* your knowledge of Chinese to greet a new acquaintance in Beijing. (Chinese)
- *Put into practice* what you have learned about teamwork in basketball to make a classroom team project succeed. (Physical Education, Athletics)
- *Implement* a business plan you have written in a simulated business environment. (Business)
- *Employ* Ohm's Law to determine the voltage in this circuit. (Physics)
- *Render practical* the proposed design for a new building that is aesthetically inconsistent with the surrounding buildings, all of which are at least 100 years old. (Architecture)

It is not necessary to teach each curriculum topic in the three ways. Rather, the teacher alternates teaching styles so that the variety of student learning styles are addressed.

From a Teacher's Desk: *An Elementary Example*

Ways for Students to Demonstrate Various Intelligences:

Analytically

- Allow students self-assessment opportunities with expectations from a rubric or criteria chart to practice evaluation based on various modes of criteria. See next page for an example of a rubric.

Creatively

- Challenge students to predict the effects of an experiment, the solution in a story, or the consecutive trends of the economy. To add a component of creative thinking, prompt students to list many, varied outcomes and possibilities. Examples of specific prompts:

  "What many, varied, and unusual changes, or transformations, can you think of that might occur in the character throughout the story? Prove why some are purposeful and lead to another. Make a written list of your ideas."

  "What are other many, varied, and unusual examples of weather patterns that could follow this natural disaster? Make a written list of your ideas."

Practically

- Teach students to apply a learned skill or concept to a new content area or topic to enhance depth and promote transfer. For instance, after practicing how to change fractions to decimals, such as ¼ = 0.25, apply the skill to money for real-world application by relating the word form to the pictorial and decimal forms:

1/4 = one quarter of a dollar = $0.25 =

Name: _____	Topic: _____		Date: _____
Independent Study Project/Presentation Rubric			
	4 ☆ ☆ ☆ ☆	3 ☆ ☆ ☆	2 ☆ ☆	1 ☆
Knowledge	Conveys insightful information that helps others learn	Shares basic facts and information	Lacks clarity	Unfinished or does not include meaningful information
Accuracy	The information is cited from reliable sources	Some information is questionable or not clearly cited	No references are cited	There is evidence of plagiarism - copying others' words & ideas
Creativity	Display/ presentation demonstrates great unique thought and effort	Display/ presentation demonstrates some imaginative thought and effort	Display/ presentation demonstrates little thought and/or effort	Display/ presentation does not demonstrate any thought and/or effort
Communication	Terms and facts are defined, exemplified, and explained adequately so that audience understands	Some terms and facts are defined, exemplified, and explained so that audience understands	Few terms and facts are defined, exemplified, and explained	Little or no terms and facts are defined, exemplified, or explained
	My overall score: _____			

APPLICATIONS

SOME STRATEGIES FOR WORKING
WITH STUDENTS WHO EXHIBIT OVEREXCITABILITIES

It is often quite difficult and demanding to work and live with overexcitable individuals. Their behaviors may seem unexplainable, frequently incomprehensible, and often bizarre. Here are some strategies suggested by Lind (2001) that may help teachers and parents who work and live with students who demonstrate overexcitabilities. The first set are general strategies that are applicable regardless of which OEs are present.

General Strategies

- **Discuss the concept of overexcitability.** Share the descriptions of OEs with the family, class, or counseling group, as appropriate. Ask individuals if they see themselves with some of the characteristics. Point out that being overexcitable is understood and accepted.
- **Focus on the positives.** Discuss the positives of each OE when you first introduce the concept, and continue to point out these merits. Benefits include being energetic, enthusiastic, sensual, aesthetic, curious, loyal, tenacious, moral, metacognitive, creative, metaphorical, dramatic, poetic, compassionate, empathetic, and self-aware.
- **Cherish and celebrate diversity.** To some degree, the pursuit of educational and societal equity has diminished the celebration of diversity and individual differences. Highly gifted individuals, because of their uniqueness, may succumb to the public belief that they are not OK. When discussing OEs, it is essential that individuals realize that overexcitability is just one more description of who they are, such as being tall, or Asian, or left-handed. Since OEs are inborn traits, they cannot be unlearned. Therefore, we must accept our overexcitable selves, children, and friends. This acceptance provides validation and helps to free people from feelings of strangeness and isolation.
- **Use and teach clear verbal and nonverbal communication skills**. All people need to be listened to and responded to with respect. Overexcitable people need understanding and patience to a greater degree because they are experiencing the world with greater intensity and need to be able to share their intensity and feelings to thrive. Good communication skills are useful on several levels, from improving the chances of getting what you want, to nurturing and facilitating growth in others. The outcomes will include less stress, greater self-acceptance, greater understanding from and about others, and less daily friction at home, school, work, or anywhere else.

    When teaching communication skills, be sure to include verbal-listening, responding, questioning, telephoning, and problem solving. Nonverbal skills should include the use of time, interpersonal distance and touch, gestures and postures, facial expressions, tone of voice, and style of dress. Verbal and nonverbal strategies improve interpersonal communication and provide the skills individuals need to fit in when they wish to, to change the system if necessary, and to treat others with caring and respect.

- **Teach stress management as early as possible.** Everyone deals regularly with stress. But overexcitable individuals have increased stress reactions because of their increased sensitivity and reaction to external input. It is important to (1) learn to identify your stress symptoms: headache, backache, pencil tapping, pacing, etc.; (2) develop strategies for coping with stress: talk about your feelings, do relaxation exercises, change your diet, exercise, meditate, ask for help, develop organizational and time management skills; and (3) develop strategies to prevent stress: make time for fun, practice tolerance of your own and others' imperfections, and develop a group of people who will help, advise, and humor you.

- **Create a comforting environment whenever possible.** Intense people need to know how to make their environment more comfortable in order to create places for retreat or safety. For example, they need to find places where they can work or think without distraction, listen to music, look at a lovely picture, carry a comforting item, move while working, or wear clothing that does not scratch or cling. Learning to select one's environment to meet one's needs takes experimentation and cooperation from others, but the outcome will be a greater sense of well being and improved productivity.
- **Help to raise awareness of one's behaviors and their impact on others.** Overexcitable people are often insensitive and unaware of how their behaviors affect others. They may assume that everyone will just understand why they interrupt to share an important idea, or tune out when creating a short story in their head during dinner. It is important to teach children and adults to be responsible for their behaviors, to become more aware of how their behaviors affect others, and to understand that their needs are not more important than those of others. The key is to realize that you can show children and adults how they are perceived, you can teach them strategies to fit in, but they must choose to change.
- **Remember the joy.** When people discuss overexcitability, the examples and concerns are often mostly negative. Remember that being overexcitable also brings with it great joy, astonishment, beauty, compassion, and creativity. Perhaps the most important thing is to acknowledge and relish the uniqueness of an overexcitable child or adult.

Here are some strategies that are targeted to each overexcitability.

Psychomotor Strategies

- Allow enough time for physical or verbal activity, before, during, and after normal daily and school activities. These individuals love and need to be in motion. Build activity and movement into their daily routines.
- Ensure that the physical or verbal activities are acceptable and not distracting to those around them. This may take some planning, but the project should be fun and beneficial to all.
- Provide time for spontaneity and open-ended activities.

Sensual Strategies

- Whenever possible, create an environment that limits offensive stimuli (for example, loud noises, strong odors, or visual overload) and provides comfort.
- Provide appropriate opportunities for being noticed by giving unexpected attention, or facilitating creative and dramatic productions that have an audience. These individuals literally feel the recognition that comes from being the center of attention.
- Provide time for them to dwell in the delight of the sensual and to create a soothing environment.

Intellectual Strategies

- Show how to find the answers to questions. This respects and encourages the individual's desire to analyze, synthesize, and seek understanding.

- Provide or suggest ways for those interested in moral and ethical issues to act upon their concerns, such as collecting blankets for the homeless or writing to soldiers in Iraq. This enables them to feel that they can contribute, in even a small way, to solving community or worldwide problems.
- If individuals are critical or too outspoken to others, help them to see how their intent may be perceived as cruel or disrespectful. For example, saying "that is a dumb idea" may not be well received, even if the idea is truly dumb.

Imaginational Strategies

- Imaginational people may confuse reality and fiction because their memories and new ideas become blended in their mind. Help individuals to differentiate between their imagination and the real world by asking them to write down or draw the factual account before they embellish it.
- Help people use their imagination to function in the real world and promote learning and productivity. For example, instead of the conventional school organized notebook, ask the students to create their own system for organizing their work.

Emotional Strategies

- Accept all feelings, regardless of intensity. For people who are not highly emotional, this may seem particularly unusual. They may feel that those high in Emotional OE are just being melodramatic or seeking attention. But if we accept their emotional intensity as an innate trait and help them work through any problems that might result, we will facilitate their healthy growth and adjustment.
- Teach individuals to anticipate physical and emotional responses and to prepare for them. Emotionally intense people often are not aware when they are becoming so overwrought that they may lose control or may have physical responses to their emotions. Help them to identify the physical warning signs of their emotional stress such as a headache, sweaty palms, or stomachache. By knowing the warning signs and acting on them early, individuals will be better able to cope with emotional situations and not lose control.

From a Teacher's Desk: *An Elementary Example*

I had the challenging pleasure of two "twice exceptional" students in my class one year who evidenced several different kinds of overexcitability. Although they were both autistic and gifted, they were very different in their mannerisms. One student, Nathan, demonstrated sensual and imaginational overexcitability, while the other, Jamie, possessed psychomotor and intellectual overexcitability characteristics. Their varied intensities promised and delivered a year without a boring day!

In order to give the students an opportunity to evidence special abilities, one day I had the class play a PowerPoint *Jeopardy* game to review parts of speech. Jamie declared, "This is the best day ever!" Everyone wanted to be on his team because I set the scene with the facts that he regularly viewed the television show and had an excellent memory. He was quivering with enthusiasm at the prospect and desired to present the introductory part of the "show," which he recited verbatim. His team did end up earning the most points and more importantly, he had the chance to be a social leader and demonstrate his intellect at the same time.

Some students are simply dissonant with the routines and rules of standard school structure. As Nathan resisted compliancy and preferred to be in his imaginative world, drawing all day, I struggled to challenge him. Creative humor and exaggeration would get his attention and connect with him on a personal level, but wouldn't always produce results. Our "aha!" breakthrough moment was when I utilized independent study through technology. The Web site I found merged his interests and my expectations—he could research and explore his fascinations while also meeting standards. That day he changed from the stubborn underachiever who would hardly complete a sentence to a scholar that needed multiple pages to write down all of his ideas.

That year taught me some valuable ways to deal with overexcitability:

- Meet exaggeration with exaggeration
- Find humor in each intense situation
- Allow opportunity for intensities to be shown (get excited with and for them)
- Use specific phrases as the teacher and demonstrate for other students (e.g., "When you interrupt like that, it hurts my feelings because I feel disrespected and I lose my train of thought . . ." or "When you tap like that it distracts me and I can't concentrate" and "You see that child crying, with tears running down the face? That means they are sad and they need my help first-thing."
- Patience, patience, patience

Overexcited students can be exhausting one day and revitalizing another day. Basically, if you give them attention and patience, they will repay you with positive reinforcement and revelations.

APPLICATIONS

IMPROVING ADAPTIVE DECISION MAKING
THROUGH ELABORATIVE REHEARSAL

Rehearsal refers to the learner's reprocessing of new information in an attempt to determine sense and meaning. It occurs in two forms. Some information items have value only if they are remembered *exactly* as presented, such as the letters and sequence of the alphabet, spelling, poetry, telephone numbers, notes and lyrics of a song, and the multiplication tables. This is called *rote rehearsal*. Sense and meaning are established quickly, and the likelihood of long-term retention is high. Most of us can recall poems, songs, and telephone numbers that we learned many years ago.

More complex concepts require the learner to make connections and to form associations and other relationships in order to establish sense and meaning. Thus, the information will need to be reprocessed several times as new links are found. This is called *elaborative rehearsal*. The more senses that are used in this elaborative rehearsal, the more reliable the associations. Thus, when visual, auditory, and kinesthetic activities assist the learner during rehearsal, the probability of long-term storage rises dramatically. That is why it is important for students to talk about what they are learning *while* they are learning it, and to have visual models as well.

Elaborative rehearsal can also develop adaptive decision-making skills because students will have more opportunities to make new connections and to see relationships that would otherwise not be possible through rote rehearsal.

Rehearsal is teacher-initiated and teacher-directed. Much of what students practice in schools is rote rehearsal, which is essentially veridical decision making. Recognizing the value of elaborative rehearsal as a necessary ingredient for retention of learning, teachers should consider the following strategies when designing and presenting their lessons:

Elaborative Rehearsal Strategies

- *Paraphrasing.* Students orally restate ideas in their own words, which then become familiar cues for later storage. Using the auditory modality helps the learner attach sense, making retention more likely. For example:
    - After studying about the Declaration of Independence one could say: "This was a document that listed the many reasons why the American colonies should no longer recognize the British king as their ruler, and why they should become self-governing states."

- *Selecting and Note Taking.* Students review texts, illustrations, and lectures, deciding which portions are critical and important. They make these decisions on the basis of criteria from the teacher, authors, or other students. Students then paraphrase the idea and write it into their notes. Adding the kinesthetic exercise of writing furthers retention.

- *Predicting.* After studying a section of content, the students predict the material to follow or what questions the teacher might ask about that content. Prediction keeps students focused on the new content, adds interest, and helps them apply prior learnings to new situations, thus aiding retention. Some examples:
    - Having read to a certain point in a fable, predict its moral.
    - Predict how the earth's continued growth in population may affect the future.

○ Having read the first three acts of Shakespeare's *Romeo and Juliet,* predict a believable ending to the story based on what you already know.

- *Questioning.* After studying content, students generate questions about the content. To be effective, the questions should range from lower-level thinking of recall, comprehension, and application to higher-level thinking of analysis, synthesis, and evaluation. When designing questions of varying complexity, students engage in deeper cognitive processing, clarify concepts, predict meaning and associations, and examine options—all contributors to retention and to improving adaptive decision-making skills. Some examples:

  ○ What would be another way to solve this arithmetic problem?
  ○ What are some things I was wondering about when this was happening in the story?
  ○ How might the USA be different today if the Confederate states had won the Civil War?
  ○ What are the arguments for and against genetic engineering? Which side would you support and why?

- *Summarizing.* Students reflect on and summarize in their heads the important material or skills learned in the lesson. They can then share their summary with a partner or with the class. This is often the last and critical stage, in which students can attach sense and meaning to the new learning and thereby increase the likelihood that they will remember it. Here is a useful format to consider:

  ○ What did I learn today about . . .?
  ○ What did I already know that ties in to what I learned today?
  ○ How can what I learned today help me in the future?

CHAPTER 2

Challenging the Gifted Brain

Understanding the nature of the gifted brain is one thing; deciding how to help it learn is quite another. Here is a disturbing trend: A recent study showed a 5.0 percent high school dropout rate for gifted students compared to a 5.2 percent dropout rate for nongifted students (Phillips, 2008). Would some or all of these students have remained in school if we had advanced them to a grade or instructional level appropriate for their higher aptitude? Are we doing enough to ensure that our brightest students are getting the instructional

> A recent study showed a 5.0 percent high school dropout rate for gifted student compared with a 5.2 percent dropout rate for nongifted students!

opportunities they need to reach their full potential? Is the emphasis on leaving no child behind hampering our ability to move other children forward? These are not easy questions, but they will need to be addressed if schools are to meet their responsibility to serve *all* students.

Addressing the needs of gifted students can occur in different classroom settings, using a variety of curriculum resources and teaching strategies and having expectations of specific student products that demonstrate learning. As for classroom settings, elementary and middle school students identified as gifted might participate in a special pull-out class, and high school students can opt for advanced placement courses. But apart from these limited choices, most gifted students—except for those few with extraordinarily abilities—will get their learning opportunities in the normal school setting. Consequently, this chapter examines some considerations for selecting curriculum content, choosing teaching strategies, and deciding on the learning products of gifted students in the regular classroom.

DIFFERENTIATED CURRICULUM AND INSTRUCTION

Differentiated Curriculum

Although we have heard a lot in recent years about differentiating the curriculum, schools seem to be moving slowly. A 2003 study suggests that not much had changed in differentiation practices during the previous 10 years, despite considerable professional development time devoted to the topic (Westberg & Daoust, 2003). Because most gifted students—especially in elementary and middle school—will be taught primarily in the regular classroom, differentiating the learning experiences for these students may be the only way to meet their needs.

- Differentiating the curriculum means moving students beyond grade-level standards or connecting what is taught to their personal interests.

- Differentiating the processes means using the learning strategies that provide depth and complexity appropriate to the students' abilities.
- The products are differentiated in that they demonstrate student learning at an advanced level, going beyond paper-and-pencil tests and allowing students to develop their talents and curiosities and to present their findings to an appropriate audience.
- Differentiating the learning environment means allowing students to work more independently on their own projects, collaborate with other students, or pursue interests outside the regular classroom (Winebrenner, 2000).

Gifted students are expected to learn the same basic concepts, facts, issues, and skills as all other students. However, they make connections faster, work well with abstractions, and generally have the deep interests found in older individuals. Consequently, they need to work with the curriculum at higher instructional levels, at a faster pace, and using a variety of materials appropriate for their learning style and interests.

Federal regulations and those of most states require that school districts establish curriculum modifications to meet the needs of students identified as gifted. (Federal regulations on educational programs can be found on the Internet at http://www.ed.gov/legislation/FedRegister.) However, the standards movement will be of little value if it does not respond to the needs of all students, including the gifted. The standards need to be flexible so that gifted students can be assured access to a stimulating, rich, and thought-provoking curriculum. Furthermore, standardized tests should not be the primary means for measuring student achievement. A wide range of assessment tools, such as journals, learning logs, self-evaluation questionnaires, interviews, and portfolios, are likely to yield more accurate information about how much a student has learned. To assist districts in deciding what those modifications should be, the National Association for Gifted Children (NAGC) has published standards for preK through Grade 12 gifted programs in seven areas. Specifically, the standards (NAGC, 1998) suggest that

- Curriculum for the gifted learner should be differentiated and span Grades preK through 12.
- Regular classroom curricula must be adapted, modified, or replaced to meet the needs of the gifted.
- The pace of instruction must be flexible to allow for the accelerated learning of the gifted.
- Gifted students must be allowed to skip subjects and grades.
- Gifted learners must have opportunities that provide a variety of curriculum options, instructional approaches, and resources.

For more information on the details of the preK–Grade 12 standards, visit the NAGC Web site: www.nagc.org.

> The trick is to establish a flexible learning environment and differentiate the curriculum so that gifted students will be challenged rather than bored.

Exactly how to best address the different learning styles and needs of the gifted has been a question that schools have pondered for years. Some schools offer pull-out programs at the elementary and middle school levels, where gifted children can interact with their peers for a set time period. But for budgetary and philosophical reasons, schools in recent years have been moving away from pull-out programs and toward providing enrichment services to all students in the regular classroom environment. Some researchers in gifted education are alarmed at this trend, fearing that gifted students will not be appropriately challenged in this format. The trick is to establish a flexible learning environment and differentiate the curriculum content so that gifted students will be challenged rather than bored.

A differentiated curriculum is tailored to the needs of gifted learners. It offers learning experiences that are sufficiently different from the typical curriculum, delivered by a teacher trained in selecting appropriate instructional and assessment processes for gifted students. Curriculum designed for gifted students should focus on what is important for these students to know and be able to do at various stages of development. Van Tassel-Baska (2005) suggests that a differentiated curriculum for gifted learners is one that

- Links general curriculum principles to subject matter features and gifted-learner characteristics
- Identifies appropriate goals and outcomes
- Focuses on meaningful experiences that provide depth and complexity at a pace that honors the gifted learner's rate of advancement through the material
- Is standards-based and relevant to the thinking and doing of real-world professionals who practice writing, engage in mathematical problem-solving, or do science for a living
- Honors high-ability students' needs for advanced challenge, in-depth thinking and doing, and abstract conceptualization

Differentiated Instruction

Gifted learners prefer and benefit from instruction that includes

- A faster pace of learning
- Greater independence in study and thought
- Increased complexity and depth in subject content

Effective differentiation directly supports the learning needs of gifted students through activities that simulate real world problems, address multiple perspectives, and result in the development and sharing of a variety of authentic products. Differentiated instruction creates engaging and challenging activities that are student selected, interdisciplinary, open ended, inquiry based, and multi-faceted. Many of the strategies that are discussed later in this chapter and in the **Applications** section illustrate ways to differentiate instruction in mixed-ability classrooms.

A SUPPORTIVE LEARNING ENVIRONMENT

Teaching gifted students in an inclusive classroom requires a flexible and supportive learning climate that encompasses both the physical setting of the classroom and its climate. The teacher maintains a challenging environment by encouraging responsibility and autonomy, emphasizing student strengths, and addressing individual student needs.

Classroom Organization and Management

To organize the classroom for flexibility and openness, the teacher provides space for students to work independently and in small groups. Students may move around the room freely as long as they remain on task. They may also go to the computer lab, library, or other in-school location, if appropriate. In this setting, the teacher's role changes from presenting the curriculum to selecting and creating learning opportunities, guiding students, and assessing their progress. Students are given choices and allowed to schedule their activities, at least for part of the classroom time. Of course, students are still responsible for completing specific activities or periodically demonstrating what they have learned. However, they can choose how and when they will work.

Social and Emotional Climate

A positive learning environment includes the elements of safety and acceptance. Teachers create this atmosphere by modeling care and respect for all members of the classroom, emphasizing every student's strengths. All students need to recognize and appreciate their own strengths and those of others. Acceptance is a particularly important component of classroom climate because gifted learners are prone to being perfectionists and thus place great emphasis on completing a task quickly and getting the right answer. Their unusual abilities may make them outsiders among their classmates, or they may be accustomed to having a higher status than others in the classroom.

Gifted students sometimes feel insecure when presented with problem-solving activities or open-ended inquiry. They want to know the procedures that will ensure that they do it the right way. Here the teacher needs to remind these students that mistakes are an important part of the learning process and that there may be several "right" ways to solve a problem.

Not all gifted students like to display or explain their work. Some see this as redundant or as slowing them down. Assure students that explaining how they got an answer is as important as being correct. Using a scoring guide or rubric may help these students recognize the value of the steps used to work through a problem.

CURRICULUM CONTENT INITIATIVES FOR GIFTED LEARNERS

Gifted students need to work at higher instructional levels and at a faster pace than nongifted students. Several initiatives have emerged to enhance content within the context of the self-contained classroom as well as within the middle and high school curricular formats. Numerous studies in recent years have investigated the impact of these initiatives on student performance, the extent of which is assessed by a statistical measure known as *effect size*.

A Note About Research and Effect Sizes

One way to measure the impact of an educational strategy on student achievement is with a statistical measure known as *effect size* (ES). It is determined by dividing the standard deviation of the control group into the difference between the mean scores of the treatment and control groups.

$$\text{Effect Size} = \frac{(\text{Mean of Treatment Group}) - (\text{Mean of Control Group})}{\text{Standard Deviation of Control Group}}$$

An effect size of 0.25 or greater is considered educationally significant. In classroom terms, an effect size of 1.00 is approximately equal to one school year. Thus, if a study found an effect size of 0.33, it would mean that the treatment group outperformed the control group by 1/3 of a school year, or about 3 grade-equivalent school months of additional achievement.

In the following sections, references are made to effect size results if they are available. For more information on effect size, see Cortina and Nouri, 1999.

Acceleration

Acceleration assumes that different students of the same age are at different levels of learning. This requires a diagnosis of the learning level and the introduction of curriculum at a level slightly above it. Essentially, acceleration recognizes that different students will learn different material at different rates in different subject areas and at different stages of their development. However, schools have found great difficulty in achieving the flexibility required to meet these varying student needs. No one pretends that this is easy, and several components need to be considered.

Early Entrance and Exit: One component should allow for early entrance and early exit of students who complete the curricular requirements at any grade level. Getting into high school early eliminates the slower moving middle school years. Despite the cry over standards, they do provide a clear way to determine mastery of curriculum, thus allowing students to move ahead.

Content-Based Acceleration: Another component involves content-based acceleration in all subject areas while the student remains in grade. Although schools are now more open to acceleration in mathematics, other areas of acceleration languish. Gifted learners with verbal, scientific, and artistic abilities need access to accelerated programs in these subjects as well. Some educators and parents express concern that gifted children should not accelerate more than six months to a year for fear they will get too far out of step with the curriculum or socially with their peers. Yet, there is little reliable research to support either of these fears.

Telescoping: Courses often overlap material and skills from one grade level to the next. Because gifted students learn and remember material faster, telescoping reduces the amount of time a student takes to cover the curriculum. An example is when a student completes Grades 7 and 8 mathematics in one year, thus allowing the student to move on to more challenging work.

Grade-Level Advancement: Acceleration can involve advancing students who have learned all areas of a grade's curriculum, to the next grade. This step is particularly warranted for students who demonstrate more than 2 years' advancement in all school subjects. Once again, the concerns raised about the potential mismatch of social and emotional growth between these students and their new peers seems unfounded, especially when compared with how grade acceleration can counter the boredom and disenchantment of our most able learners. Given its powerful effect sizes (see box that follows), grade advancement should be far more common than it is.

Yet many practitioners continue to have concerns about this practice and use it infrequently (Stanley & Baines, 2002). However, when it does occur, skipping a grade is not always accompanied by adaptations to the curriculum to meet the needs of the advancing student. Because grade skipping is applied to an individual student, a curriculum plan needs to be designed to ensure that appropriate curriculum experiences will occur for that student in the new placement.

Advanced Study Programs: In high school, acceleration has traditionally meant enrollment in the College Board's Advanced Placement (AP) Program or the International Baccalaureate (IB) program. About 14,000 high schools offer AP programs, and about 500 offer IB. Both programs allow students to engage in college-level work and get the reward of college placement or credit for work done during their high school years. However, concerns about the integrity of these programs have led to changes in both programs' curriculum and exams. A recent report from the Thomas B. Fordham Institute gave high marks to the revised programs and cited high academic standards and goals as well as exams that are aligned to the standards, testing students on the content of their courses and considerably more (Byrd, 2007).

Students in these courses also seem to be pleased with them, although they recognize limitations. In interviews with 200 students in 23 U.S. high schools, students believed that AP and IB courses provided a greater level of academic challenge and more favorable learning environments than other existing high school courses. However, the students also felt that the curriculum and instruction within AP and IB courses were not a good fit for all learners, particularly those from traditionally underserved populations (Hertberg-David & Callahan, 2008).

Dual Enrollment: Acceleration can also mean dual enrollment at local community and four-year colleges, where students can sample the college environment and gain the opportunities needed for early academic and socialization processes to occur. In some areas, high school students can receive college credit for successfully completing the course.

Acceleration Through Technology (Distance Learning): Advances in telecommunications now permit university online courses to reach distant rural areas. Some of these distance learning courses (e.g., the Stanford Education Program for Gifted Youth) are tailored for younger students, and others offer the equivalent of freshman-level college courses. Online communications also offer independent study with university faculty and opportunities to work on research projects.

Acceleration and Effect Sizes

After conducting an exhaustive search of research literature on gifted education through 2007, Rogers (2007) performed an analysis of acceleration formats and found the following effect sizes (ES):

- Early Entrance and Exit: ES = 0.49
- Content-Based Acceleration: ES = 0.59
- Telescoping: ES = 0.45
- Grade-Level Advancement: ES = 0.56 (Academic effect); 0.31 (Socialization effect)
- Advanced Study Courses: ES = 0.29
- Dual Enrollment: ES = 0.32
- Distance Learning: ES = 0.33

Curriculum Compacting

Compacting is one of the most common curriculum modifications for academically gifted students. This strategy reduces the amount of time the student spends on the regular curriculum. It allows students to demonstrate what they know, to do assignments in those areas where work is needed, and then to move on to other curricular areas. The strategy makes appropriate adjustments for students in any curriculum area and at any grade level. Essentially, the process involves defining key concepts and skills of a specific curriculum unit, determining and documenting which students have already mastered most or all of the learning objectives, and providing replacement strategies for material already mastered that result in a more challenging and productive use of the student's time (Reis, Burns, & Renzulli, 1992a).

Occasionally, there will be specific areas in which the student is still developing competence. In this instance, the teacher can ask the student to rejoin the class at strategic points during the unit. The student may also need to join the class for discussions and inquiry or for problem-solving activities.

Teachers can compact basic skills as well as course content. Compacting basic skills involves determining which ones the students have mastered and eliminating the repetition or practice of those skills. For example, beginning algebra students who demonstrate mastery of some algebraic functions have little need for drill and practice in those areas and should move on to more complex course content.

Compacting is also useful for those gifted students who have not mastered the course material at the regular classroom pace but can do so at an accelerated pace. They usually have some understanding of the content but may require only minimal instructional time to reach mastery.

Some elementary teachers are reluctant to use curriculum compacting for fear that doing so could cause declines in students' scores on achievement tests. However, a recent study looked at the achievement scores of a national sample of 336 high-ability students

> A teacher's fear that curriculum compacting will cause decreases in students' achievement scores is not supported by research studies.

from second- through sixth-grade heterogeneous classrooms in urban, suburban, and rural settings. The teachers selected one to two students who demonstrated superior knowledge of the material prior to instruction and eliminated 40 to 50 percent of the curriculum across content areas for those students. The results of the Iowa Test of Basic Skills indicated that the achievement scores of the students whose curriculum was compacted did not differ significantly from the scores of similar students whose curriculum was not compacted (Reis, Westberg, Kulikowich, & Purcell, 1998).

In a study of language arts curriculum for advanced learners in Grades 4 through 6, teachers replaced the regular readings with selections that were advanced for the grade levels in which they were introduced. The readings emphasized abstract concepts in literary analysis, such as mood, tone, theme, and motivation. Outcome measures showed that the learners who received the advanced material outperformed students in the comparison groups in three areas: on a reading assignment that focused on literary analysis, on a persuasive writing assignment, and on an objective measure of grammatical understanding (VanTassel-Baska, Johnson, Hughes, & Boyce, 1996). See the **Applications** section at the end of this chapter for procedures for compacting the curriculum.

Curriculum Compacting and Effect Sizes

Different effect sizes were found in the research literature on curriculum compacting, depending on the type of replacement activity provided.

ES = 0.83 for the replacement of math and science curriculum with advanced math and science at the student's true learning level and at an accelerated pace.

ES = 0.26 for the replacement of social studies and reading curriculum with enrichment activities in those areas (Rogers, 2007).

When regular readings in Grades 4 through 6 were replaced with advanced-level readings for gifted students, ES = 0.99 is for writing; ES = 1.57 is for grammatical understanding (VanTassel-Baska et al., 1996).

Grouping

Grouping can be an effective component in educating all students. But this technique is particularly effective with gifted students because it is an ideal medium for differentiation. Furthermore, several studies have found that gifted students benefit most from like-ability grouping because they are able to access more advanced knowledge and skills and to pursue their learning tasks in greater depth (Kulik, 2003). Grouping formats run the gamut from within-class ability groupings to independent grouping options, such as internships and mentor programs. See the **Applications** section at the end of this chapter for strategies for flexible grouping.

Within-Class Ability Grouping: This format can occur at all grade levels. In elementary schools, many classes are now heterogeneous and inclusive—settings where little challenge or differentiation is provided for

Gifted students benefit most from like-ability grouping because they can get more deeply involved in the learning task.

the gifted learner. In secondary schools, instruction in even the honors, Advanced Placement, or International Baccalaureate programs are set for the norm. Thus, high ability students may find the instructional pace too slow and miss out on opportunities for more in-depth and challenging work. Within-class groups can be formed around term papers, for example, allowing advanced students more latitude for their work. Groups for differentiated reading assignments can have the same effect.

Pull-Out Grouping: This program is particularly popular at the elementary level and is one of the primary ways to deliver differentiated curriculum. Students identified as gifted from different classes meet as one group on a regular basis. In this setting, effective acceleration practices can be used for individual students because the content level of the class, by its very nature, needs to be more advanced.

Full-Time Ability Grouping: This format usually starts in upper elementary grades. Students are in the same group for most of the day and tend to remain in that group throughout their school year. This arrangement allows students to pursue a more advanced series of courses through middle and high school. The recent trend toward heterogenous classes has diminished full-time ability grouping, especially in middle school where it all started. Where it still occurs, it usually provides for special grouping in mathematics and language arts, but not in science and social studies. To be truly successful, full-time grouping should apply across all subject areas, where the school size allows.

Cluster Grouping: Cluster grouping is different from full-time ability grouping in that the group is composed of only three to six students, usually the top five percent of ability in the class. This format allows the gifted children to learn together while avoiding permanent grouping arrangements with students of other ability levels. If the cluster group is kept to a manageable size, teachers report a general improvement in achievement for the whole class. This is probably because teachers who learn how to provide opportunities for gifted students also modify those opportunities for the rest of the class, raising achievement for all. Cluster groups can also be

---

Grouping Formats and Effect Sizes

There are only a few reliable studies on pull-out groups, so the effect size numbers may be inflated.

- ES = 0.34 for within-class ability grouping
- ES = 0.65 for pull-outs that are a direct extension of the regular school curriculum
- ES = 0.44 for pull-outs that focus on thinking skills
- ES = 0.32 for pull-outs that focus on creative skills

For full-time ability grouping:

- ES = 0.49 for the yearly effect of all academic areas for elementary gifted students (Grades K–6)
- ES = 0.33 for secondary students (Grades 7–12)
- ES = 0.62 for cluster grouping of gifted students

Mentor programs can advance gifted students in many ways:

- ES = 0.47 for the socialization effect
- ES = 0.42 for the self-esteem effect
- ES = 0.57 for the academic effect (Rogers, 2007).

formed in secondary schools in any heterogeneous classroom, especially in smaller schools, where there may not be enough students to form an advanced section in a particular subject (Winebrenner & Devlin, 2001).

Independent Work Grouping: This format offers students options for more personalized opportunities for intellectual growth. It can occur by one or two students working on a well-designed independent project, interning in a professional setting (e.g., a hospice or senior care center), or associating with an adult mentor who has expertise in an area of the student's interest. Such options require close collaboration between school and community leaders.

INSTRUCTIONAL PROCESSES FOR GIFTED LEARNERS

Processes refers to the instructional strategies that engage students during the learning episode that will help them find sense and meaning. This is more likely to happen if the instructional techniques help students see purpose to the new learning and have opportunities to probe for understanding and relevancy. Such process skills might involve higher-level thinking, creative thinking, problem solving, and independent or group research.

Higher-Level Thinking and Bloom's Revised Taxonomy

Trying to classify levels of human thought is no easy feat. But that has not kept psychologists from trying. One model, published more than 50 years ago by Benjamin Bloom (1956), has passed the test of time and remains useful as a starting point for understanding the complexity of human thought. I have discussed the value of Bloom's Taxonomy at great length in a previous publication (Sousa, 2006) so my purpose here is just to present a short version to set the stage for discussing thought processes further.

Bloom's original taxonomy contained six levels that many readers can no doubt recite from memory. Moving from the least to the most complex, they are *knowledge, comprehension, application, analysis, synthesis,* and *evaluation.* From 1995 through 2000, a group of educators worked to revise the original taxonomy based on more recent understandings about learning. The group published the results of their work in 2001 and the basic revision is shown in Figure 2.1 (Anderson et al., 2001).

Revising the taxonomy provided the opportunity to rename three categories and interchange two of them, as well as change the names of all levels to the verb form to fit the way they are used in learning objectives. The original *Knowledge* level was renamed *Remember* because it more accurately describes the recall process occurring at this level. Also, knowledge can be acquired at *all* levels. *Comprehension* was renamed *Understand* because that is the term most commonly used when teachers discuss this level. *Application, Analysis,* and *Evaluation* were changed to the verbs *Apply, Analyze,* and *Evaluate.*

Synthesis changed places with *Evaluation* and was renamed *Create.* This exchange was made because the researchers felt that recent studies in cognitive neuroscience suggest that generating, planning, and producing an original product demands more complex thinking than making judgments based on accepted criteria. Although there are still six separate levels, the hierarchy of complexity is not as rigid, and it recognizes that an individual may move easily among the levels during extended processing.

Levels of Bloom's Taxonomy
Revised Version (2001)

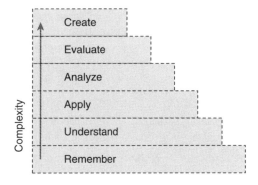

Figure 2.1 The revised taxonomy changes the labels to verb form, renames three levels, and interchanges the top two levels. The dotted line suggests and more open and fluid model, recognizing that an individual may move among the levels during extended processing.

Convergent and Divergent Thinking: The first three levels of Bloom's revised taxonomy describe what can be called *convergent* thinking whereby the learner recalls and focuses what is known and comprehended to solve a problem through application. While using the upper three levels, the learner often gains new insights and makes discoveries that were not part of the original information. This describes a *divergent* thinking process.

Here are brief definitions of each level:

- **Remember:** The mere recall of rote learning, from specific facts, to a memorized definition or complete theory. This is the lowest level of learning and there is no presumption that the learner *understands* what has been recalled.
- **Understand:** This level describes the ability to make sense out of the material, goes beyond recall, and represents the lowest level of comprehension. Here the material becomes available for future use to solve problems and to make decisions.
- **Apply:** This level refers to the ability to use learned material in new situations with a minimum of direction. It includes the application of such things as rules, concepts, methods, and theories to solve problems. The learner uses convergent thinking to select, transfer, and apply data to complete a new task. Practice is essential at this level.
- **Analyze:** This is the ability to break material into its component parts so that its structure may be more thoroughly understood. It includes identifying parts, examining the relationships of the parts to each other and to the whole, and recognizing the organizational principles involved. The learner must be able to organize and reorganize information into categories. The brain's frontal lobes are working hard at this level. This stage is more complex because the learner is aware of the thought process in use (metacognition) and understands both the content and structure of the material.
- **Evaluate:** This level describes the ability to judge the value of material on the basis of specific criteria and standards. The learner examines criteria from several categories and selects those that are the most relevant to the situation. Activities at this level almost always have multiple and equally acceptable solutions. This is a high level of cognitive thought because it contains elements of many other levels, plus conscious judgments based on definite criteria. At this level, learners tend to consolidate their thinking and become more receptive to other points of view.
- **Create:** This refers to the ability to put parts together to form a plan that is new to the learner. It may involve the production of a unique communication (essay or speech), a plan of operations (research proposal), or a scheme for classifying information (a taxonomy). This level stresses creativity, with major emphasis on forming *new* patterns or structures. This is the level where learners use divergent thinking to get an *Aha!* experience. Although most often associated with the arts, this process can occur in all areas of the curriculum.

The Important Difference Between Complexity and Difficulty: Complexity and difficulty describe completely different mental operations, but are often used synonymously (Figure 2.2). This error, resulting in the two factors being treated as one, limits the use of the taxonomy to enhance the thinking of all students. By recognizing how these concepts are different, the teacher can gain valuable insight into the connection between the taxonomy and student ability. *Complexity* describes the *thought process* that the brain uses to deal with information. In Bloom's Taxonomy, it can be described by any of the six words representing the six levels. The question, "What is the capital of Florida?" is at the remember level, but the question, "Can you tell me in your own words what is meant by a state capital?" is at the understand level. The second question is more *complex* than the first because it is at a higher level in Bloom's Taxonomy.

Difficulty, on the other hand, refers to the *amount of effort* that the learner must expend *within* a level of complexity to accomplish a learning objective. It is possible for a learning activity to become increasingly difficult without becoming more complex. For example, the question, "Can you name the states of the Union?" is at the remember level of complexity because it involves simple recall for most students. The question, "Can you name the states of the Union and their capitals?" is also at the remember level but is more difficult than the prior question because it involves more effort to recall more information. Similarly, the question, "Can you name the states and their capitals in order of their admission to the Union?" is still at the remember level, but it is considerably more *difficult* than the first two. It requires gathering more information and then sequencing it by chronological order.

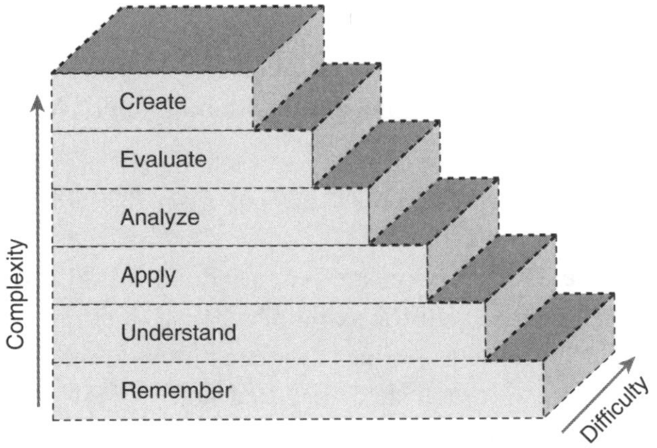

These are examples of how a student can exert great effort to achieve a learning

Levels of Bloom's Taxonomy
Revised Version (2001)

Figure 2.2 Complexity and difficulty are different. Complexity establishes the level of thought; difficulty determines the amount of effort within each level.

task while processing at the lowest level of thinking. When seeking to challenge students, classroom teachers may unwittingly increase difficulty rather than complexity as the challenge mode. This may be because they do not recognize the difference between these concepts or that they believe that difficulty is the method for achieving higher-order thinking. Moreover, for all sorts of reasons, including the overcrowded curriculum and the continued educational emphasis on fact acquisition, more class time is spent with instruction at the lower levels of the taxonomy. Obviously, all students benefit when teachers include activities that engage students at the upper levels of analyze, evaluate, and create. Gifted students, particularly, can pass through the first three levels quickly and schools do these students a great disservice if they fail to provide opportunities for higher-level thinking. See the **Applications** section at the end of this chapter for examples of activities that increase difficulty and complexity.

Creative Thinking

Is creativity the result of innate abilities or of a learned set of behaviors? Psychologists and others have debated this question for decades, more often siding with the view that creativity is a gift from nature or the result of genetic heritage. Now studies in cognitive neuroscience seem to be indicating that creativity is more likely the result of a series of cognitive processes that can be developed in most individuals. Surely, genetic heritage still has some influence. But the notion that some degree of creativity can be *taught* is exciting, and strategies to accomplish this will make valuable additions to a teacher's repertoire.

> When seeking to challenge students, classroom teachers may unwittingly increase difficulty rather than complexity as the challenge mode.

In Bloom's model, "create" is the level most closely associated with creativity, but there certainly are other ways to define creative thinking, usually in terms of the learning behaviors creativity evokes. Four behaviors often associated with creativity are

Fluency: This describes the ability to generate new ideas. This skill is required for students to explain what they know, to think of ways to solve a problem, to develop ideas for writing or speaking, and to draw diagrams or models. A question like, "In what ways can we do this?" evokes fluency.

Flexibility: This behavior requires generating a broad range of ideas, such as "How many different ways can we do this?"

Originality: This behavior refers to unusual or unique responses to a situation. Original responses usually occur at the end of an idea-seeking activity and after the more obvious ideas have been rendered. A question to provoke originality might be, "What is the most unusual way to accomplish this?"

Elaboration: Here, other ideas and details are added to the reasoning. "What else can we do here?" and "Can you tell me more?" are questions that elicit elaboration.

These four behaviors are skills, and like all skills they can be learned and refined. An average-IQ student who has learned well the skills of creative thinking might be more creative than a high-IQ individual who has not. Neuroscience brings us interesting revelations. A recent study measuring blood flow looked at which brain areas were activated in gifted and typical individuals when completing creativity tests measuring fluency, originality, and flexibility (Chávez-Eakle et al., 2007). The study's results showed that when processing originality the brain recruited some different brain areas than it did when processing fluency and flexibility. Here was further evidence that specific neural networks are associated with different components of the creative process.

The researchers also found higher activation in gifted individuals in certain brain regions than in typical individuals while they were taking the tests. This result came as no surprise, but it does raise the chicken-and-egg question. Were these individuals already genetically endowed with high IQ that led to increased activity in those brain areas, or did environmental experiences that challenged and thus developed those brain areas lead to a higher IQ? The question is important to answer because it may mean that appropriately trained teachers could be successful in developing creative thinking in *all* their students.

> Creative thinking can be developed in the classroom regardless of an individual's innate abilities.

Another study of high-IQ and average middle school students may have shed more light on the answer to this chicken-and-egg question (Russo, 2004). The study assessed the students' creative thinking abilities on fluency, flexibility, originality, and elaboration. They were given pretests, followed by one 90-minute session per week for six months to improve their problem-solving skills in each of the four areas. The posttests revealed that the average students actually scored higher than high-IQ students in some areas, especially in the area of elaboration. An important implication is that creative thinking can be developed in the classroom regardless of the individual's innate abilities.

Creativity as Decision Making: If being creative is more a learned pattern of behavior than genetic heritage, the question arises as to what behaviors or skills are likely to develop creativity. Sternberg (2000) suggests that students can develop their creativity by learning the attitudes they will need to be successful in their work. Thus, they develop what Sternberg calls "creative giftedness" as a decision-making skill. He describes ten decisions that students can make to be more creative:

1. **Redefine Problems.** Creative people take a problem and force themselves to see it differently from the way most other people see it. For example, Manet and Monet challenged artistic representations, Beethoven redefined classical music, and Einstein totally altered our views of the universe.

2. **Analyze One's Ideas.** Creative people analyze the value of their ideas, recognizing that not all of them are worthy of pursuit and that they will make mistakes. This self-skepticism prevents them from believing that they have all the answers and encourages them to admit when they are wrong.

3. **Sell One's Ideas.** Because creative ideas usually challenge existing methods, they will not be easily accepted and thus need to be sold to the public.

4. **Knowledge Is a Double-Edged Sword.** Knowledge can help people decide what new areas need to be explored, or it can entrench people so that they lose sight of other perspectives.

5. **Surmount Obstacles.** Creative people inevitably confront obstacles and must have the determination to surmount them.

6. **Take Sensible Risks.** Creative people must be willing to take reasonable risks, recognizing that they will sometimes fail and sometimes succeed.

7. **Willingness to Grow.** Creative people avoid getting stuck with one idea forever. Rather, they look for new ways to expand the idea or add new ones.

8. **Believe in Yourself.** Creative people maintain their belief in themselves even when their ideas are poorly received and when other sources of intellectual and emotional support are gone.

9. **Tolerance of Ambiguity.** Creative people often face ambiguity when trying creative things. A high tolerance for ambiguity is important if the creative venture is to succeed.

10. **Find What You Love to Do and Do It.** Creative people are at their best when they are doing what they love to do.

Sternberg proposes that anyone can make the decision to be creative. Because the ten decisions are not fixed abilities, teachers can encourage students to decide in favor of creativity and to reward those students who do. See the **Applications** section at the end of this chapter for suggestions on how to teach for creativity.

Problem-Based Learning

Problem-based learning places students in the position of trying to solve a multifaceted problem of significant complexity. The problem resembles a real-life situation in that the students lack some of the information they need to solve the problem or are not clear on the steps they will need to take. The students critically analyze the problem from different points of view, look for alternative solutions, select a solution, and develop a plan of action for its implementation.

Students usually work in groups and are responsible for retrieving the additional information and resources they will need. In addition, students decide which group members will focus on the various parts of the problem and on how to present their findings to demonstrate what they have learned. Their presentations can be in the form of portfolios, videotapes, exhibits, or written reports. The teacher's role in problem-based learning is to act as a metacognitive coach by asking questions, helping students plan their work, guiding them toward the questions they need to pursue, and assessing their progress. In this format, the teacher is more of a guide than a provider of information.

The open-ended nature of problem-based learning allows for considerable differentiation of curriculum and instruction. The process calls upon the varied strengths of the learners, involves a multitude of in-school and out-of-school resources, and provides opportunities for students to pursue their interests. Several studies have shown that problem-based learning, while time-consuming, leads to long-term retention of the content as well as mastery of problem-solving and collaboration skills (Hmelo-Silver, 2004). See the **Applications** section at the end of this chapter for guidelines for problem-based learning activities.

The Triarchic Approach

In Chapter 1 we discussed the Triarchic Theory of Intelligence (Sternberg, 1985). To apply the theory in the classroom, present instruction so that at different times it engages the students in analytical, creative, and practical thinking while solving problems. The problem-solving cycle involves five steps: identifying the problem, acquiring the resources for solving the problem, devising a strategy for solving the problem, and monitoring and evaluating the problem solving (see Figure 2.3). Properly implemented, the cycle promotes the three different types of thinking. For example, evaluating the problem-solving approach might involve analytical thinking. Creative thinking would help to formulate the strategy, and practical thinking would be helpful in determining and acquiring the resources for solving the problem at hand.

In the triarchic approach, teachers plan their lessons not only for memory but also for analytical, creative, and practical processing. Analytical thinking occurs and then teachers ask students to judge, compare and contrast, evaluate, and critique. Creative thinking activities would have students suppose, invent, imagine, explore, and discover. Practical thinking is involved when students implement, use, apply, and contextualize. Classroom applications of the theory have shown positive results in terms of student achievement (Sternberg et al., 1996; Sternberg et al., 2000). See the **Applications** section at the end of this chapter for suggestions on how to use the triarchic model in the classroom.

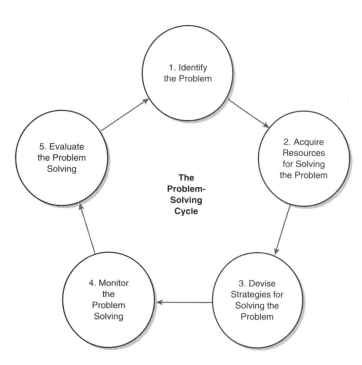

Figure 2.3   The five steps in the problem-solving cycle.

Independent Study

Independent study can be a useful strategy for differentiating curriculum. However, students generally need help in learning how to become independent workers. But with proper teachers' guidance, students can learn to pursue interests on their own by setting learning goals, establishing criteria for judging their work, assessing their progress, and presenting their work products to an audience. The goal of this program is to help the student move from being teacher-directed to being self-directed.

These ventures are more likely to be successful if the student has a clear focus on what material and skills are to be learned. The selected independent learning activities should help develop creative and critical thinking skills as well as time management strategies and research skills. Maintaining a learning log and a portfolio of results also is an important component of a successful independent study program. Note that assessment results of the effect size of independent study are inconclusive. This lack of impact could result if the measurement of achievement did not have any items that directly corresponded to what was learned in a highly individual study project. Another explanation is that the gifted learners may not have possessed the skills to meaningfully engage in independent study (Rogers, 2007). See the **Applications** section at the end of this chapter for suggestions on how to guide students for independent study.

Tiered Assignments

Tiered assignments provide for differentiation by allowing students at different ability levels to work on the same content. Students are grouped for instruction based on their prior background knowledge in a given subject area. They seek out the answers to different questions and are assigned different activities based on their ability. One approach is to teach Bloom's Taxonomy and to ask them to design questions and activities at the different levels of complexity. The teacher then works with the students to decide which questions they will pursue and to set the criteria for evaluating their results.

Before starting on tiering, identify the core elements—those components that *all* students should master. The teacher then devises separate versions of the activities so that the low-, middle-, and high-ability students are adequately challenged. The advantage of this approach is that, with a little advance planning, the teacher can keep students of differing ability levels engaged and working toward the same learning objective through differentiated tasks.

Tiered learning activities work. In one study, students were either in a control secondary science classroom or a classroom in which instruction was tiered. The tiered instruction was designed to match high, middle, or low levels of background knowledge on astronomy and Newtonian physics. Seven control classes received middle-level non-tiered instruction while seven other classes received three levels of tiered instruction. Test scores of low background knowledge learners who received tiered instruction were significantly higher than the scores of low background learners who did not receive tiered instruction, and indication that tiered instruction may be especially beneficial for lower level learners. The researchers also found that professional support for teachers was critical to the success of tiered instruction (Richards & Omdal, 2007). See the **Applications** section at the end of this chapter for steps for developing tiered activities.

Cautions About Discovery-Based Teaching

When differentiating instruction for gifted students, teachers often select open-ended, discovery type, problem-based, and independent study activities. Although it appears that many high-ability students can work on their own to solve problems and learn new content, there are some cautions that need to be mentioned here for this strategy to be successful. The cautions center around what we know about the limits and contributions of human memory during learning. Let us briefly examine the basic components of memory to understand why caution is necessary when using open-ended, discovery-centered approaches, even with gifted students.

Memory Systems: Neuroscientists generally agree that there are three basic types of temporal memory: *immediate memory* and *working memory* for temporary interactions and *long-term memory* for permanent storage (Figure 2.4).

Immediate Memory. Immediate memory is the ability to hold on to items, from a few seconds up to about a minute, to accomplish a particular task. Repeating a short list of items or remembering a telephone number just

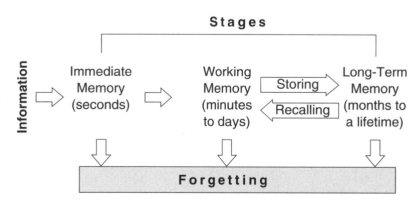

Figure 2.4 This diagram shows the three basic stages of memory. Conscious processing occurs in working memory, which has a limited capacity.

long enough to dial it are examples of using immediate memory. The task is often completed subconsciously and the memory of it quickly fades.

Working Memory. Working memory is the ability to hold items long enough to consciously process and reflect on them and to carry out related activities during that processing, which can take from minutes to days. Studies of working memory indicate that it has a limited capacity of about six to seven verbal items for most people, but may be as low as four (Cowan, 2001). This capacity is likely to be greater for highly talented individuals and less for those with learning problems.

Working memory capacity seems to be closely related to the amount of attention one gives to situations requiring problem solving. Individuals with higher working memory capacity give more controlled attention to problem solving tasks and are less likely to be diverted by other distractions (Cowan et al., 2006). Working memory also shows a strong connection to general intelligence, probably because working memory's connections within the frontal lobes keep the new representations active for further processing (Engle, Laughlin, Tuholski, & Conway, 1999; Jarrold & Towse, 2006; Tuholski, Engle, & Baylis, 2001).

Long-Term Memory. Long-term memory is the ability to store information in a permanent form for months, years, and even a lifetime. Storing occurs when specialized brain structures encode information into one or more long-term memory areas. The encoding process takes time and usually occurs during deep sleep, resulting in permanent physical changes to neurons and an increase in the efficiency of transmission in the neural areas associated with the memory. Note that forgetting can occur in all stages of memory.

Memory Systems Affect New Learning: During learning, memory systems are actively involved in at least two major ways. First, we noted earlier that working memory has a limited capacity. Even though that capacity may be greater for high-ability students, it is still limited. Second, past learning always affects new learning. When learning something new, long-term memory loads into working memory those stored items it perceives as related to the new information. These items interact with the new learning to interpret the information and provide meaning. This is part of the powerful principle of learning called transfer (Sousa, 2006).

Any problem-solving activity requires the learner to not only deal with new information but also to recall stored items and concepts that can help with a solution. Researchers refer to this process as the *cognitive load.* Without guidance, working memory will continue to search long-term memory for information relevant to the problem. Because high-ability students tend to have a larger store of knowledge than typical students, working memory can be overwhelmed by the transfer process. During that time, working memory is unavailable to process the new information and learn. It is possible to search for considerable periods of time without any changes to long-term memory.

What the Research Says: Although it may seem that open-ended learning involving unguided or minimally guided instruction would be more effective than guided instruction, especially for high-ability students, research findings do not support this approach. Mayer (2004) reviewed numerous studies during the previous three decades and found that guided instruction clearly emerged as more effective, regardless of the students' ability. More recent studies confirm these findings (Moreno, 2004), and although some high-ability students fared well with the minimally guided instruction, their performance did not exceed those of the students who had guided instruction (Klahr & Nigam, 2004). Researchers in this area suggest several ways to ease the burden of cognitive overload on working memory. See the **Applications** section at the end of this chapter for techniques on providing guidance to students who are using open-ended learning formats.

THE PRODUCTS OF GIFTED LEARNERS

Products are the vehicles through which students demonstrate what they have learned as a result of their engagement with a particular body of knowledge and skills. The products referred to in this context are culminating activities that result from a considerable amount of student time and involvement with the learning unit; they are not the worksheets or quizzes that are part of daily routine. To be effective, the culminating products need to be able to do the following (Tomlinson, 1995):

- Offer students opportunities to extend their knowledge, stretch their abilities, and pursue authentic and challenging learning experiences.
- Evolve from advanced materials, original research, or primary documents.
- Transform information so that students are not merely repeating information but creating a new idea or product.
- Be similar to those created by professionals in that the products address real-world problems and are intended for real audiences, for example, are published in student literary magazines, displayed in public places (banks, malls, and shop windows), or prepared as oral history tapes for a library.
- Be assessed by experts associated with the field of endeavor, such as researchers, college professors, or other professionals.

Student products can be centered around tiered assignments, independent studies, the Triarchic and Multiple Intelligences models, and any complex investigations that result in the learning of a body of knowledge and skills. They can include the following:

☞ Written reports	☞ 3-D sculptures
☞ Oral reports	☞ Storyboard displays
☞ Plays, skits, or pantomimes	☞ Audiotapes
☞ Songs	☞ Poems
☞ Charts and graphs	☞ Oral history tapes
☞ Photo essays	☞ Charcoal sketches
☞ Demonstrations	☞ Watercolors
☞ Videotapes	☞ Puppet shows

See the **Applications** section at the end of this chapter for the components of effective culminating products.

GIFTED VISUAL-SPATIAL LEARNERS

Linda Silverman (1989a) was among the first researchers to identify visual-spatial learners as a result of working with children with many types of giftedness. She identified two groups of gifted visual-spatial learners. The first group scores extremely high on IQ tests because they have high ability in tasks requiring visual-spatial processing as well as those tasks requiring sequential thinking processes. The second group consists of students who are brighter than their IQ scores would indicate but do not score well because they have weaknesses in sequential processing skills. Although these students may have difficulty achieving their potential in school, they may not have a learning disability, but perhaps a teaching-style disability. That is, traditional teaching methods tend to favor strong sequential learners. Concepts are usually presented step-by-step, practiced with drill and repetition, reviewed, and then tested under timed conditions. Consequently, gifted visual-spatial learners may have greater difficulty in traditional classrooms and their talents may not be fully recognized.

There is no single test to determine visual-spatial giftedness. Identification is best accomplished by looking for a collection of behaviors that often indicate visual-spatial preference. For example, IQ tests generally show higher scores on nonverbal tasks compared with verbal tasks. Essentially, this type of learner enjoys constructing toys and rarely follows directions. These students are reflective and need time to think.

Table 2.1 Characteristics of Visual-Spatial Learners
• Rely on vision and visualization • Preoccupied with space at the expense of time • Intuitive grasp of complex systems • Prefer synthesis approach • Simultaneous processing of concepts • Active use of imagery • Prefer visual directions • Poorly organized • Prefer puzzles, jigsaws, computer games • Get difficult concepts, struggle with easy ones

Consequently, they may appear off task when they are really probing some inner meaning or mentally creating a new conceptual scheme. As children, they often pull toys apart, trying to determine how they work. Organizational skills are not their strong point and they have difficulty keeping to schedules and being on time. Table 2.1 lists some of the characteristics of visual-spatial learners (Silverman, 1989b), who thrive on complex ideas, abstract concepts, holistic methods, multidisciplinary studies, inductive learning strategies, and any other activities requiring synthesis of thought.

Once visual-spatial learners create a mental image of a concept, it creates a permanent change in the students' understanding and awareness. Repetition is unnecessary and may cause difficulty because it emphasizes their weaknesses instead of their strengths. These students are ideally suited for the kinds of activities and learning experiences associated with programs for the gifted. However, to reach their full potential, visual-spatial learners must be placed in a learning environment that is a good match between their learning style and the way they are taught. As adults, they often have careers in computer technology, science, mathematics, engineering, aeronautics, and the fine arts.

As for neuroscience, nearly all studies to date on visual-spatial aptitude have dealt with individuals with psychological or physical disabilities. There was one recent EEG study that measured brain activity of gifted and typical students performing tasks requiring visual-spatial processing. Students in the gifted group showed much more brain activity during the processing, especially in the right hemisphere, generally accepted as the area for visual interpretation (Jin, Kim, Park, & Lee, 2007). See the **Applications** section at the end of this chapter for strategies for working with gifted visual-spatial learners.

AVOIDING THE PITFALL OF ACADEMICS VERSUS THE ARTS

Much of the research in areas related to programs for the gifted and talented focuses on the education of students with high ability in academic areas. Little research exists that suggests how to develop curriculum, teach, or assess students who are artistically gifted, probably because educators—and the communities they serve—generally place much greater emphasis on the academic areas than the arts. Furthermore, researchers and educators traditionally have used the terms *gifted* and *talented* to describe different things. *Gifted* often referred to high ability in one or more academic areas; *talented* usually meant superior abilities in the visual or performing arts. Researchers in the past often claimed that there was little direct evidence that students who were talented in the arts also exhibited high abilities in academic areas. To this day, it is not unusual to find school districts that have separate programs for the academically and artistically gifted.

Researchers today, who have worked with both types of high-ability students, argue that academically gifted students are often equally gifted in the arts, and vice versa. In a study of teenage students at a summer institute for the arts, all the participants were superior students in academic areas as well (Clark & Zimmerman, 1998). Perhaps we need to adopt a broader view of giftedness that includes all areas of both academic and artistic talents for all students who participate in gifted education programs. The theories of Renzulli, Sternberg, and Gardner discussed in Chapter 1 define a wide range of abilities that contribute to a more inclusive description of what constitutes programs for gifted students. This multidimensional approach allows for the inclusion of students with abilities in a wide range of school subjects and from all racial, ethnic, and socioeconomic groups.

Fortunately, the growing recognition that students may have multiple abilities, such as mathematics and music, has prompted school districts to use multiple criteria to identify students for special programs. Given the enormous economic and technological threats facing our society, we need to expand our efforts to identify and support all the gifts of our children, for it is their knowledge and skills that will ultimately determine the nature and quality of our lives in the future. See the **Applications** section at the end of this chapter for suggestions on how to integrate academic and arts-related activities for gifted students.

APPLICATIONS

ASSESSING THE LEARNING ENVIRONMENT

The following list of questions is designed to help teachers assess the effectiveness of the learning environment for gifted students in their classroom:

- Have you helped students become more aware of their learning styles?

- Have you asked students what helps them learn effectively?

- Do you model the process of talking about *how* we learn, rather than just *what* is learned?

- Have you established an environment in which wrong answers are a productive opportunity for learning?

- Do you actively encourage creative thinking by asking open-ended questions to which there are no single right answers?

- Do you encourage students to question themselves, each other, and other adults in the classroom?

- Are students involved in self-assessment?

- Do you encourage students through challenging and interactive displays?

- Have you developed a resource collection including Web sites and in-school and out-of-school resource centers, and how do you know if the resources are being well used?

APPLICATIONS

PROCEDURES FOR COMPACTING CURRICULUM

Compacting curriculum means determining what students already know about a particular unit of instruction, deciding what they still need to learn, and replacing it with more interesting and challenging material that they would like to learn. There are eight basic steps to the process (Reis, Burns, & Renzulli, 1992a):

Define and Assess Key Concepts and Skills	1. The first step is to identify and define the key concepts and skills for the unit to be taught. Teachers' manuals, district curriculum guides, scope-and-sequence charts, and even some textbooks list the goals and key learning objectives for each curriculum unit. 2. Examine these key objectives to decide which represent the acquisition of new learning and which review and practice material is already presented in earlier grades or courses. Comparing the scope-and-sequence charts or tables of contents of basic textbooks will often reveal new versus repeated material.
Identify and Assess Student Candidates for Compacting	3. Identify the students who have the potential for mastering the new material at a faster than normal pace. Use completed assignments, scores on previous tests, classroom participation, and standardized achievement tests as some of the measures for identifying potential candidates for compacting. 4. Develop appropriate techniques for assessing specific learning objectives. Any unit pretests can be helpful here. The analysis of the pretest results will help determine proficiency and identify instructional areas that may need additional practice. 5. Streamline the instruction and practice activities for students who demonstrate mastery of the learning objectives. 6. Provide individualized or small-group instruction for students who have not yet mastered all the objectives, but who are able to do so more quickly than their classmates.
Provide Acceleration and Enrichment Options and Keep Records	7. Offer more challenging learning alternatives based on student interests and strengths. Deciding which replacement activities to use is guided by space, time, and the availability of resource persons and materials. Resource persons can be other classroom teachers, media specialists, content area or gifted education specialists, and outside mentors. The materials can include self-directed learning activities, instructional materials that focus on developing particular thinking skills, and a variety of experiences designed to promote research and investigative skills. 8. Use a simple three-column form (see below) for maintaining a record of the compacting process and of the instructional alternatives provided. In the first column, list the objectives of a particular unit of study and data on the students' proficiency in those objectives. Use the second column specifically to detail the pretest measures and their results. In column three, record information about the acceleration and enrichment options that were used.

Guidelines. Curriculum compacting takes time and energy at first, but usually saves time once teachers and students are familiar with the process. For educators who are hesitant to try curriculum compacting, here are a few guidelines that are likely to increase your chances of success (Reis, Burns, & Renzulli, 1992b):

- Start with one or two responsible students who have a positive attitude and who are more likely to welcome the change and be successful with the replacement activities.
- Talk with these students and discuss the content with which they feel comfortable. Select the appropriate activities, but be sure to give them some options.
- Try a variety of methods to determine how much they already know about the material. Sometimes a brief conversation with the students is just as reliable as a formal pretest.
- Compact the topic rather than the time. Because the alternative activities are usually more interesting, students may take more time to complete them than you estimated.
- Define proficiency in learning the material or skills based on conversations with school staff, administrators, and parents.
- Do not hesitate to request help from other school personnel or from community volunteers to accomplish the replacement activities.

Teachers who use curriculum compacting on a regular basis report increased interest and enthusiasm among their students and thus often expand the compacting program from just one or two students to a broader segment of the class. The process can be used at any grade level and in any subject area and is not aligned with any specific curricular reform. It is adaptable and flexible to meet the needs of almost any classroom. More information on this strategy is available from the National Research Center on the Gifted and Talented (see the **Resources** section).

From a Teacher's Desk: *A Secondary Example*

Many secondary level teachers find Curriculum Compacting a difficult strategy to try at first. Yet it is a valuable strategy for a wide variety of students. Compacting means reducing the amount of time a student spends on what is being offered in the regular curriculum and moving the student to areas where they really need to spend their time. For teachers just getting started with this strategy, the use of contracts or agendas may make the transition easier. Teachers applying the compacting strategy must first pre-assess students to find out which concepts or skills the students already have mastered. After the pre-assessment, a teacher may create an agenda that guides the students' next steps in the curriculum. Here is an sample agenda created for an Algebra I class unit on probability. The "imperatives" represent the material that is most essential for that student, whereas the "negotiables" and "options" represent the accelerated material that a teacher is using to engage and challenge the student.

Algebra I Agenda

Imperatives (You must do these):

1. Complete the "meteorology simulation" on pages 88–89 of your textbook.

2. Create a list of 10 pairs of events. Five pairs should contain events that are dependent and five pairs should contain events that are independent. Explain each classification.

3. Complete the "frequency table" assignment on pages 506–507 of your textbook.

4. Examine the attached list of functions and determine which functions represent probability distributions.

Negotiables (You must do at least one of these):

1. Design a game spinner that has this probability distribution: P(red) = 0.1; P(green) = 0. 2; P(blue) = 0.3; P(yellow) = 0.4.

2. Suppose a dart lands on a dartboard made up of four concentric circles. For the center of the board (the "bull's eye"), r =1.5; the remaining rings have widths of 1.5. Use your understanding of area and probability to determine the probability of (1) hitting a "bull's eye" and (2) landing in the outermost ring.

3. Work with a partner to analyze the game of "Primarily Odd." See your teacher for game cubes and further instructions.

Options (You may do one or more of these):

1. Work with a partner to analyze the game of "Primarily Odd." See your teacher for game cubes and further instructions.

2. Figure the probability of "Murphy's Law" and make a case for whether or not it should indeed be a "law."

APPLICATIONS

STRATEGIES FOR FLEXIBLE GROUPING

Grouping is common in the elementary school classroom. Creating small groups of gifted students to work together provides a productive learning situation. Here are some guidelines to consider when organizing these groups (Smutny, 2000).

Create Ground Rules

Certain ground rules need to be established to ensure that all participants have an opportunity to participate and share ideas. Discuss these ground rules with the class. The rules should be grade- and age-appropriate, but most need to include the following:

- If you cannot agree on what to do, move on to another idea
- Listen to others in your group and respond to their comments
- Take turns sharing ideas
- Help each other
- Make your best effort
- If you don't understand something, talk it out with your group
- Seek the teacher's help when needed

Provide Variety

Organize a variety of groups based on the learning objective. Groups can be formed around student interests, motivation, and the complexity level of the assignment.

Offer Choices

When appropriate, allow students to choose their group members as well as their topic. Of course, teacher discretion may be necessary to allow for variety of groupings over time or to ensure that certain students do not always dominate a group.

Assess Students Individually

Although some reward can be given to the group upon completion of their work, it is important to assess each student individually. Assessment measures can include checklists, portfolios, mastery tests, drawings, written compositions, and oral responses.

Compact the Curriculum

Compress the essentials so that students can move beyond what they have already mastered. Assess their level of mastery and then allow students to choose activities of particular interest to them. Another option is to design an activity related to the current lesson that challenges their abilities. Some teachers find that signing a learning contract with a student can be effective. The contract stipulates the chosen activities or projects, the conditions for their completion, and the expected outcomes. See the Application on compacting curriculum in this chapter.

Incorporate Creative Thinking

Using creative thinking activities benefits all students. The "what if" questions are always interesting to pursue and they challenge students to come up with alternative explanations. Teachers can then suggest other resources to help students with their new explorations. Brainstorming and other metacognitive strategies can stimulate discussions and add to the depth of understanding that students have about a particular subject or theme.

Using Flexible Grouping in the Classroom

Forming and Maintaining Groups

Flexible grouping requires frequent evaluation by the teacher in order to move a student who is progressing in one group to another group based on assessment evidence. A mistake that is often made is forming groups of students at the beginning of the year without pre-assessments and then maintaining those same groups throughout the school year. The two different types of ability grouping, heterogeneously and homogenously, should vary. There are several additional ways grouping can be flexible:

- Group names can vary by color, region, number, animal, etc. to establish ambiguity about the groups' strengths and weaknesses. As students progress, be sure to change their level or name individually or as an entire group.
- The number of students in each group can vary as needed. Perhaps during earth science, students will collaborate in teams of four but in reading for language arts, six students will work together. While it is preferable for many content areas to have students divided equally into groups, sometimes it is impossible to do so if you are grouping by homogenous ability.
- Ideally and realistically, students should work with different peers in each content area (e.g., language arts, mathematics, science, social studies, etc.). Often students that are linguistically gifted do not have the same strengths in all areas of mathematics, so the groups should be adjusted accordingly. The opportunity to work with and appreciate the different abilities of all peers, at one time or another, is valuable for establishing camaraderie and recognizing various talents.
- Within each content area, there are various topics and concepts that require different kinds of thinking. For example, the strands of science (physical, earth, life) and mathematics (number sense, algebraic functions, mathematical reasoning, etc.) as well as language arts (reading fluency, reading comprehension, writing conventions, etc.) are all topical areas wherein some students have already mastered concepts while others are struggling. As the topic or focus changes, groups should as well.

Using Independent Study

Strategic Methodology

A well-structured independent study can start with teacher guidelines that encourage the student to take on the responsibility with autonomy. Similar to the problem-solving cycle (see Figure 2.4), steps of independent study can become a cyclical process.

- First, the learner must **define the topic or area of study**. The more narrow the focus, the more in-depth and meaningful the research will be. Teachers can aid students in narrowing the subject (e.g., animals → sheep → cloning sheep → the ethical issues and implications of cloning sheep).
- Second, the student should **formulate a set of study questions** to initiate and guide their learning throughout the investigation. Ideally, the questions should vary in complexity and type. They can start

with factual questions (*who, what, when, where*) but should graduate to analytical and evaluative questions to answer the conundrums of *why* and *how* such occurs. Teachers can assist with prompting question stems (*What if. . .?* or *Is there another way. . .?*) and rewording questions to be more profound. Of course, the learner should also continue asking questions throughout the study, which will lead to both unanswered questions as well as potential independent studies for the future.

- Third, the learner will **gather information and data** about the chosen subject area. The research materials should answer questions posed in step 2, while also adding to a general wealth of information they will accumulate as they essentially become an "expert" in the topic. Teachers and parents can provide varied resources for the student (primary and secondary) to encourage cross-referencing and application of research skills.

- Fourth, the student will **organize and summarize information**. Research skills, teacher-taught or self-learned, are essential for this step. Graphic organizers and note-taking basics can guide students that need a structure established for them. Others can develop their own systems to code and interpret information, depending on the subject area.

- Fifth, the student must choose a way to **present the information**. With all the options that the media and technology offer today, this step has unlimited possibilities. Presentations may include anything from a basic report or display board to an annotated PowerPoint presentation or informative brochure. The presentation can be written and/or verbal.

- Finally, the learners should reflect on their research experience and **evaluate progress**. Assessment from the teacher is separate from this step. The self-evaluation is purely for students to measure their success according to their own goals and expectations. They can measure their progress on a rubric or similar assessment tool, or simply answer questions such as, *What did I learn? What would I do the same or differently next time? What step required the most effort?*

APPLICATIONS

TWO GUIDED INSTRUCTION TECHNIQUES FOR OPEN-ENDED LEARNING ACTIVITIES

When assigning open-ended learning activities, such as those involving problem-based, inquiry, discovery, experiential, and constructivist approaches, more students are likely to be successful with teacher guidance strategies that reduce the cognitive load. The guidance should be tailored to the expertise level of the student, and should focus on how to cognitively manipulate new information so that it is eventually stored in long-term memory. Here are a few suggestions that the research has shown to be effective (Kirschner, Sweller, & Clark, 2006).

- **Worked Examples.** This is a print, audio, or video sample that shows how to solve a problem or perform an task. Worked examples are commonly found in mathematics and geometry textbooks, but are also used in other fields. The clues from the worked example help guide the student to perform a more limited and targeted search of long-term memory, thus lowering the cognitive load. Students who are new to the area being investigated should get a more complete step-by-step example than those who have more knowledge of the subject. Highly-skilled students may not need worked examples at all, and may get turned off by them, a phenomenon known as the *expertise reversal effect* (Kalyuga, Ayres, Chandler, & Sweller, 2003).
- **Process Worksheets.** Process worksheets provide a description of the steps the learner should go through when solving the problem as well as hints that may help to successfully complete each step. Students can consult the process worksheet while they are working on their learning tasks and they may use it to note intermediate results as they work through the problem-solving process. For example, a student could use the problem-solving cycle shown in Figure 2.3 and fill in the information in each circle while moving through the five steps for a specific problem.

APPLICATIONS

BLOOM'S REVISED TAXONOMY: INCREASING COMPLEXITY

Examples become more complex from bottom to top, and more difficult from left to right.

	BLOOM'S LEVEL	INCREASING DIFFICULTY →	
↑ INCREASING COMPLEXITY	CREATE	Rewrite the story from the point of view of the dog.	Rewrite the story from the points of view of the dog *and of the cat.*
	EVALUATE	Compare the two main characters in the story. Which would you rather have as a friend and why?	Compare the *four* main characters in the story. Which would you rather have as a friend and why?
	ANALYZE	What were the similarities and differences between this story and the one we read about the Civil War hero?	What were the similarities and differences between this story, the one we read about the Civil War hero, *and the one about the Great Depression*?
	APPLY	Think of another situation that could have caused the main character to behave that way.	Think of at least *three* other situations that could have caused the main character to behave that way.
	UNDERSTAND	Write a paragraph that describes the childhood of any one of the main characters.	Write a paragraph that describes the childhood of each of the *four* main characters.
	REMEMBER	Name the major characters in this story.	Name the major characters and the *four locations* in this story.

APPLICATIONS

DIFFERENTIATING CONTENT

Content refers to what the student needs to know, understand, and be able to do as a result of a particular unit of study. It should be highly relevant to students, coherent, transferable through instructional techniques, and authentic. Content includes any means by which students acquire information and skills. The teacher promotes differentiation through the use of the following (Tomlinson, 1999):

- ✓ Multiple textbooks
- ✓ Field trips
- ✓ Supplementary readings
- ✓ Videos
- ✓ Guest speakers
- ✓ Demonstrations
- ✓ Lectures
- ✓ Computer programs
- ✓ Internet

- ✓ Learning contracts
- ✓ Mentors
- ✓ Media centers
- ✓ Experiments
- ✓ Interest centers
- ✓ Audio tapes
- ✓ Internships
- ✓ Group investigations

APPLICATIONS

TEACHING FOR CREATIVITY

Sternberg (2000) proposes that creativity results from a set of 10 decision-making skills that can be learned. He further suggests that teachers can encourage students to be creatively gifted by doing the following:

Decision	Teacher Activity
1. Redefine Problem	• Goal: To help students see an aspect of the world in a different way from which it is usually seen. • Example: Select or have students provide a well-known phenomenon, such as seasonal differences in the northern and souther hemispheres. "Summer vacation" in the USA has to be redefined for students living in Australia.
2. Analyze One's Ideas	• Goal: To help students critique strengths and weaknesses of their ideas. • Example: Have students analyze the phenomenon they presented above. What were its strengths and weaknesses? How can they improve the idea?
3. Sell One's Ideas	• Goal: To teach students the importance of selling their ideas to others. • Example: Have students present an oral or written report in which they explain, defend, and promote an idea in which they truly believe. Remind them to defend their idea against possible criticism.
4. Knowledge Is a Double-Edged Sword	• Goal: To help students realize that theories apply only to a limited range of behavior. • Example: Lead students to study a major idea (e.g., any person born in the United States can become president). What kind of information would we need to determine if this really applies to all children? What other factors could limit this statement's validity?
5. Surmount Obstacles	• Goal: To help students realize that new ideas are not immediately accepted. • Example: Ask students to reflect on ideas they may have encountered (e.g., Darwin's Theory of Evolution, the Wright brothers' concept of flight, or the "big bang" theory of the formation of the universe) or on one of their own ideas that others had difficulty accepting. What strategies would help these ideas gain acceptance? Can we relate them to ideas people already accept?
6. Take Sensible Risks	• Goal: To help students realize that creativity involves some degree of risk. • Example: Have students write a brief essay critiquing an interpretation you (the teacher) gave in class. They must support their belief and their criticism must be constructive. Assure the students that you welcome alternative interpretations. Evaluate their essay and offer ways for them to improve their critique. Here they realize they can take a sensible risk and be rewarded.
7. Willingness to Grow	• Goal: To encourage students to grow by challenging their own beliefs. • Example: Ask students to select a belief they have about human behavior, such as why people fall in love, why they get angry, how they chose their friends, or whether capital punishment is effective (or ineffective). Have them commit to this belief in writing and then compose an essay that persuasively supports an opposite point of view. Afterwards, ask if writing this essay helped them to better understand people who disagree with them.

Decision	Teacher Activity
8. Believe in Yourself	• Goal: To show students that if they believe they can do something, they often can. • Example: Ask students to select a task they think would be very difficult to do (e.g., learning to play an instrument, losing weight, or achieving an athletic goal), and then ask them to develop a plan for accomplishing that task. In some cases, students may be encouraged to follow through on their plan and report on their progress periodically.
9. Tolerance of Ambiguity	• Goal: To help students recognize and appreciate that ambiguity is inherent in much thinking in the academic disciplines. • Example: Ask students to read a piece that seems to present a theory, analysis, or explanation persuasively. The ask them to read a critique of what they have read and to let you know if the original analysis is still convincing. Why or why not? The reading and critique can be on any set of opposing ideas, such as communism versus capitalism, the North's and South's views of the Civil War, or capital punishment versus life without parole. Students should realize that attaining understanding can be a slow process and that one must tolerate ambiguity for a long time in order to better understand the world.
10. Find What You Love to Do and Do It	• Goal: To show students how any field of endeavor can accommodate a wide variety of outside interests. • Example: Ask students to reflect on an interest they have that is outside a field of study and to relate orally or in writing this interest to the field being studied. These investigations might relate music or art to a scientific field, or compare science fiction to real science, or delve into the psychological makeup of a literary character. The point is to show that they can pursue a diversity of interests while still following a specific area of study.

APPLICATIONS

CREATIVE THINKING THROUGH QUESTIONING

Open-ended questions are effective for encouraging creative thinking because they rarely have one answer and they stimulate further inquiry. They ask for clarification, probe for assumptions, search for reasons and evidence, and look for implications and consequences. Here are a few examples of these types of questions:

- What would you have done? Why do think this is the best choice?

- Could this ever really happen? What might happen next?

- What do you think might happen if . . . ? What do you think caused this?

- Is what you are saying now consistent with what you said before?

- How is it different from . . . ? Can you give an example?

- Where do we go next? Where could we go for help on this?

- What do you mean by that expression?

- Can we trust the source of this material?

- In what other ways could this be done? How can you test this theory?

- What might be the consequences of behaving like that?

- Do you agree with this author/speaker? Why or why not?

- How could you modify this? How would changing the sequence affect the outcome?

The Question Spinner. Here is a tool to promote creative questioning. Make a copy of this page. Cut out the arrow. Insert a paper fastener through the white dot on the arrow and through the center of the inner circle. A student spins the arrow and answers the indicated question.

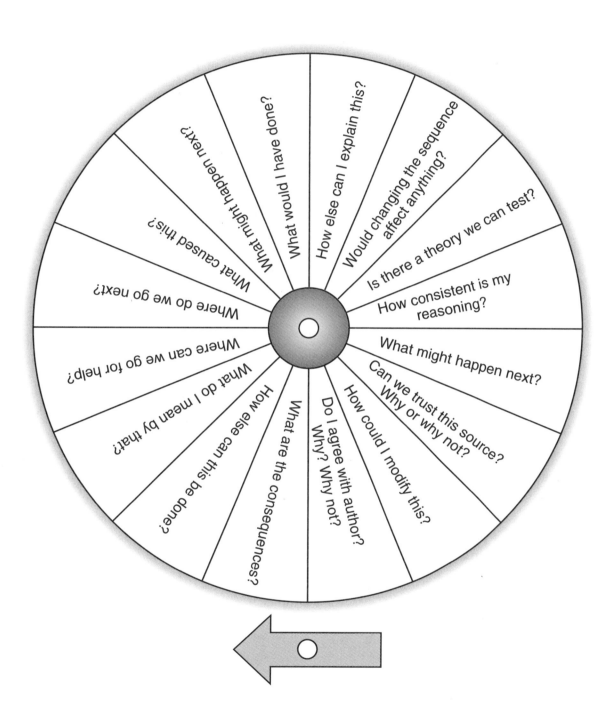

APPLICATIONS

GUIDELINES FOR PROBLEM-BASED LEARNING ACTIVITIES

Problem-based learning activities are usually labor-intensive and time consuming. Before embarking on these activities, consider working with other teachers to plan the problem that the students will undertake. Here are some guidelines to consider (Burruss, 1999):

- Identify some complex issues or problem situations. Selecting a local issue, such as environmental preservation or city planning, adds relevancy to the process. The following are examples of local issues:
  - Should a city park be sold for commercial development to increase dwindling property tax revenues?
  - What can be done to prevent or lessen the runoff of fertilizers into the community's water table?
  - What are the advantages and disadvantages of building a strip mall next to the middle school?
  - Should smoking be banned from all indoor public areas?
  - Should our city councilors be subject to term limits?
- Examples of regional and national issues can be found in books, newspapers, magazines, and television news and documentary programs. Here are a few examples:
  - Should members of Congress be subject to term limits?
  - What are the pros and cons of electing the US president by popular vote?
  - Should Americans give up some liberties in the fight against terrorism?
- State the problem in a way that is interesting for students and that puts the situation in an intriguing context. The statement should suggest avenues they can pursue but should not provide all the information and resources they need.
  - What are the implications of starting high school an hour later? Think about such things as the effects on our sports schedules and school buses. How could any potential problems be resolved?
  - Should we adopt an evening curfew for teenagers?
- Because your program may have time restrictions, be sure to align the problems with the curriculum and standards. Think about the curriculum areas involved and the skills the students will use as they pursue the problem and generate solutions. Some topics cut across several curriculum areas.
  - What can be done to stem the continuing rise of AIDS in Africa?
- Carefully select the best time to discuss and present the problem in class, and make sure to allow sufficient time for students to complete their work.
- To ensure a productive start and reduce off-task time, give the students a partial list of materials and resources they may need at the onset of their work. Insist on periodic progress reports to ensure a timely conclusion to the project.
- If the project falters, revise the problems as needed to resume progress.

APPLICATIONS

USING THE TRIARCHIC MODEL IN THE CLASSROOM

Practical applications of Sternberg's Triarchic model in the classroom require that the teacher incorporate activities that provoke analytical, creative, and practical thinking whenever students are involved in complex problem solving (Sternberg, 1985; Sternberg et al., 2000). This approach to differentiated instruction helps all students, but is particularly beneficial for gifted students who can use their strengths for in-depth study.

General Guidelines

- Use *analytical activities* at times that encourage students to compare and contrast, analyze, evaluate, judge, and critique.

- Use *creative activities* at times that encourage students to discover, imagine, explore, invent, and create.

- Use *practical activities* at times that encourage students to use, contextualize, apply, and put into practice.

- Allow all students occasionally to capitalize on their strengths.

- More often, enable students to correct or compensate for their weaknesses.

- Use assessments that match the analytical, creative, and practical activities you are using, as well as testing for memory skills.

- Value the diversity of learning styles in all students.

Examples

Activity	Science	Language Arts	Social Studies
Analytical	• Draw the major parts of an animal cell, and explain what the parts do.	• Identify simile, analogy, and metaphor, and explain their function.	• Describe the steps necessary for a bill to become law in the state legislature.
Creative	• Write a story (or play) using characters representing the parts of an animal cell, and describe a potential conflict.	• Using unusual materials, act out simile, analogy, and metaphor in mime, and see if other students can guess them.	• Become a state senator, and use your position to help us think about the merits and problems of laws to restrict campaign financing.
Practical	• Find a system in the world around you that mimics the activities and relationships in an animal cell, and explain it	• Demonstrate how someone would use similes, analogies, or metaphors in their work or life.	• Underage drinking is a problem here at school. Devise legislation that would address this problem.

APPLICATIONS

GUIDING STUDENTS FOR INDEPENDENT STUDY

Independent study is another useful strategy for differentiating curriculum and instruction, especially in the self-contained, mixed-ability classroom. However, even gifted students often need guidance in pursuing learning objectives independently. Here are some considerations.

- Prepare options in advance for the students to select as part of the curriculum unit's work. These options should include a variety of ability levels, involve different skills, and address different learning styles.

- Encourage students to select the option they feel is most relevant to their topic. The teacher may need to help with this decision by discussing with the students how the options match their needs, strengths, and desires.

- Guide students toward appropriate resources that they can seek out independently.

- Ensure students that they can also develop other options for the curriculum unit, but that they should discuss them with the teacher before embarking on any work with the options.

- Suggest to students that they can occasionally work in small groups if necessary to accomplish their learning objectives.

- Encourage students to seek out other environments, such as another classroom, the media center, or computer lab, that will help them with their task.

APPLICATIONS

STEPS FOR DEVELOPING TIERED ACTIVITIES

In a classroom with students of mixed abilities, tiered activities offer choices for accomplishing a learning objective at different levels of complexity. The following guidelines are useful for planning tiered activities (Tomlinson, 1999).

- Decide which concepts, themes, and skills *all* students will be expected to learn in the instructional unit. These selections are the core fundamentals for developing an understanding of the curricular material.

- Use simple assessments to determine the range of readiness of the students who will be studying this unit. Other measures and previous experience will also allow you to determine the students' interests, talents, and learning styles as they pertain to the learning objectives.

- Select a past activity, or create a new one, that focuses students to use an important skill to understand an important idea. This activity should be interesting, relevant, and able to engage students in higher-level thought, such as at the upper levels of Bloom's Revised Taxonomy.

- Next, chart the complexity of the activity along some linear scale (Tomlinson suggests a ladder) that runs from low to high complexity. Think about the students who will be using the activity you developed in the previous step and place it on that scale. Its placement will help you determine what other versions of the activity need to be developed. For example, will the lesson challenge only the average ability students? If so, you will need to develop versions for the low- and high-ability learners.

- Devise the versions of the activity needed along the scale at the different degrees of complexity. These versions can be created by varying the material the students will use (from basic to very challenging) by developing a range of applications of the learning (from those that are close to the student to those that are very remote), and by allowing different products that students can use to demonstrate achievement.

- Finally, match each version of the activity to the appropriate students based on their learning profile and the requirements of the learning task. The goal is to closely match the degree of complexity to the students' readiness, but to also add a measure of challenge.

From a Teacher's Desk: *A Middle and Secondary Example*

Unit Objective: To understand the issues involved in global warming (Grades 5+)

Introduction: To determine prior knowledge, the teacher asks the question, "What do you already know about global warming?" The students record their answers. The teacher then asks, "If we were scientists, what criteria should we use to judge the validity of the information about global warming that is coming from so many different sources?" The students discuss the judgment criteria and they are posted for future reference. Students are then asked to develop a concept map representing what they already know about the issue.

(Continued)

Preliminary Assessment: Using these two pre-assessment techniques, the teacher determines that there are three distinct levels of readiness to accomplish the learning task. All students will use the posted criteria to judge the information they will gather and use for the activity.

Tiers:

Tier I: Students will use reading material that discusses the required information about global warming. They will conduct a survey of science teachers and students to determine their awareness of the issue, what they believe about it, and why they hold that belief. Students will apply the validity criteria to the information gathered and present their findings.

Tier II: Students will use grade-level reading material to gather secondary information and develop and conduct a survey of a least two scientists currently investigating the issue. Students will apply the validity criteria to the information gathered and present their findings.

Tier III: Students will compare their knowledge of global warming with at least one other environmental issue, such as fertilizer chemicals in the drinking water, and note the similarities and differences in the evidence that is presented by each side of the issue. Each issue being addressed must meet the established validity criteria. Students will then present their findings.

Culminating Activity: Students present their findings on global warming and explain how this issue is an example of conflicting views being used as a catalyst for change. After all presentations are completed, the teacher asks, "What can we generally say now about global warming? Based on our current knowledge, what predictions can we make about this issue? What value, if any, do the validity criteria have in drawing defensible conclusions?"

From a Teacher's Desk: *A Secondary Example*

Unit Objective: Predicting Weather Patterns (Grades 8+)

Introduction: Mr. Humphrey often uses tiered assignments in his eighth-grade science class. Although much of the information he teaches is new for his students, he knows that many of his students are at different readiness levels in terms of reading and interpreting information. In his upcoming unit on predicting weather patterns, he would like for all of his students to understand that energy transfer between the sun and the Earth and its atmosphere drives weather and climate on Earth.

Preliminary Assessment: After administering a preliminary assessment, he found that some of the students were more comfortable with the concepts being taught during his weather unit, whereas many of his students were unfamiliar with the concepts in this unit. For one of his first assignments, Mr. Humphrey thought it would be helpful for students to access materials that would challenge not only the students who were struggling, but students who were more familiar with the topic as well.

Tiers: For his tiered task, he designed two tasks for his students:

Tier I: This group had the most difficulty with comprehending this topic. They were asked to write a public service announcement for citizens of their town about an upcoming weather system that was typical of their area of the country. This group had access to reading materials and graphic organizers that would assist them in preparing this public service announcement.

Tier II: This group was more comfortable with the concepts behind predicting weather patterns. They were asked to conduct a survey of peer awareness and understanding about weather patterns in their state. Mr. Humphrey challenged them by having them use a professionally constructed survey to serve as a model for designing, conducting, analyzing, and reporting their own survey. Although the teacher limited the number of questions they could ask and the number of students they could poll, they had access to reading materials from the American Meteorological Society that informed their questions and final report to the class.

No matter which group the students were in, their final product was designed to report about weather patterns found near them, and how energy transfer between the sun and the Earth and its atmosphere drives their weather.

APPLICATIONS

COMPONENTS OF EFFECTIVE CULMINATING PRODUCTS

A culminating product created by students at the end of a major unit of inquiry is an excellent opportunity to assess how much the students have learned. Teachers can use differentiation in their classes when they allow students to select from a broad variety of possible culminating projects. This venture is more apt to be successful if the teacher does the following (Tomlinson, 1999):

- Makes clear to students what they should transfer, demonstrate, explain, or apply to show what they have learned and what they can do as a result of their inquiry.

- Allows students to choose from among a variety of product possibilities, such as videos, photo essays, charts and graphs, and written reports.

- Presents specific expectations about what
  (1) type of information, concepts, and resources constitute high-quality content;
  (2) steps should be used in developing the product, such as planning, editing, effective use of time, and originality; and
  (3) details describe the nature of the product itself, such as size, durability, format, construction, accuracy, and the anticipated audience.

- Supports student efforts by providing in-class workshops on how to use research materials, for brainstorming ideas, for discussing timelines, and for peer reviewing, critiquing, and editing.

- Provides for variations in student learning styles, interests, and learning readiness.

APPLICATIONS

STRATEGIES FOR WORKING WITH GIFTED VISUAL-SPATIAL LEARNERS

Gifted visual-spatial learners do best with a holistic approach to learning. They prefer complex systems, abstract concepts, and inductive reasoning and problem solving. Recognizing the strengths and weaknesses of these learners, and making a few simple academic modifications, can help these students become successful and innovative leaders. Here are some strategies that have been found to be effective with visual-spatial learners (Silverman, 1989b).

- Use visual aids, such as overhead projectors, computers, diagrams, graphic organizers, and other visual imagery.

- Give them the larger scheme at the beginning of each unit and explain the major objectives so that the students understand the instructional goal.

- In spelling, use a visualization approach: Show the word, have students close their eyes and visualize it, have them spell it backward (this is visualization), then spell it forward, and then write it once.

- Find out what they have already mastered about the unit's topics before teaching them.

- Use manipulative materials for hands-on experiences.

- Avoid rote memorization. Use more conceptual and inductive approaches.

- Help students discover their own methods of problem solving. When they succeed, give them a harder problem to see if their system works.

- Emphasize concepts over details. Encourage new insights, creativity, and imagination.

- Avoid drill and repetition. Instead, have them try the hardest tasks in the unit with at least 80 percent accuracy. If they accomplish this, then the students may not have to complete the rest of the assignment.

- Group gifted visual-spatial learners together for instruction. Give the group handouts if they have difficulty with dictation.

- Allow them to accelerate in school.

- Give them abstract, complex material at a faster pace.

- Use real-life scenarios and service-oriented projects whenever possible.

- Allow students to construct, draw, or create other visual representations of concepts.

- Have students discuss the moral, ethical, and global implications of their learning.

- For foreign language learning, total immersion is much more effective than being in the typical classroom setting for these students.

- At the end of each class or school day, ask the students to take a few deep breaths, close their eyes, and visualize what happened during the class (or day) and what they will need to do for homework.

APPLICATIONS

INTEGRATING ACADEMIC AND ARTS-RELATED ACTIVITIES FOR ALL GIFTED STUDENTS

Many academically talented students are also capable of being high performers in artistic endeavors. Because the artistic areas are often ignored in gifted programs, educators should incorporate the visual and performing arts into comprehensive gifted and talented programs. Here are some recommendations for accomplishing this task (Clark & Zimmerman, 1998).

- The arts should be included as an integral part of all comprehensive gifted and talented programs. This type of program will more likely accommodate the varying needs of the wide variety of abilities represented in a comprehensive program that includes academically and artistically gifted students.

- Just as scientifically talented students need access to modern, well-equipped laboratories, artistically gifted students should have access to facilities that resemble the studios, stages, and other workplaces of artists who are trying to solve problems in the arts. The goals of programs designed to educate artistically gifted students should be carefully integrated with those for students who are academically gifted so that all students benefit from comprehensive and enriching experiences.

- Traditionally, schools often encourage academically gifted students to take advanced classes in academic subjects within the school but suggest that they pursue artistic endeavors outside the school. Teachers, administrators, and parents need to be educated about the importance of including the arts as an integral part of the gifted education program, and to encourage all students to pursue the arts within the school setting.

- Educators who teach academically and artistically talented students should collaborate in planning programs that provide equity and excellence, that reinforce shared goals, and that emphasize common strengths for the benefit of their students and the entire school community. Such collaboration would inevitably benefit all students who participate in programs that develop talent.

- More work needs to be done on developing resources and teaching strategies that incorporate the arts into the comprehensive programs for gifted students. If these resources are available, teachers are more likely to include them as a regular part of their repertoire. Furthermore, these strategies need to be appropriate to the learning styles and cultural backgrounds of individual students.

- Developing integrated programs should not be solely the responsibility of teachers. Local, community, and state resources should be gathered to support these efforts and to establish liaisons with out-of-school entities (e.g., organizations, government agencies, and businesses) that can contribute to the success of the comprehensive program.

CHAPTER 3

Underachieving Gifted Students

The phrase "underachieving gifted students" may sound like an oxymoron. By definition, gifted students are those of above average intelligence who consistently display high levels of performance. Underachievement implies failure to perform. How can these two phrases be used together to describe one individual? But gifted underachievers do exist, and most likely in larger numbers than we believe. Underachievement can result when a gifted student acquires—for whatever reasons—some complex behaviors that erode academic performance. Whether it occurs quickly or slowly, underachievement prevents gifted students from reaching their potential. Consequently, it is an issue that must be addressed and remedied as much as any other obstacle to learning.

WHAT IS UNDERACHIEVEMENT?

Defining underachievement is not easy, especially among gifted students. Part of the problem lies in the definition of giftedness. Each school district has its own definition, although most rely on the use of an intelligence or achievement test score and teacher recommendations. These measures are not always reliable because few mentally gifted students truly excel in all subjects and on all academic tasks. Another problem is the definition of *underachievement*. Rimm (1997) defines underachievement as a discrepancy between a student's performance in school and some index of that student's ability. A student's actual performance is measured by class grades and teacher evaluations, while the student's ability or expected performance is measured by intellectual ability assessments and standardized achievement test scores. To be considered an gifted underachiever, the discrepancy between expected and actual academic performance must not be the result of a diagnosed learning disability. Gifted students who also have a learning disability are considered as *twice-exceptional* students, and they are fully discussed in Chapter 4.

SOME CAUSES OF UNDERACHIEVEMENT

A combination of factors, both in the home and at school, can cause underachievement. Of all the possible causes, the following seem prevalent (McCoach & Siegle, 2003).

- **Academic Self-Concept.** Students who are confident about their skills are more apt to engage in different types of activities. Self-perceptions influence the types of activities students select, how much they challenge themselves at those activities, and the persistence they display once they get involved in these activities. Academic self-concept involves both internal and external comparisons.

Students compare their own performance with that of their classmates (an external comparison), as well as with their own performance in other areas they pursue (an internal comparison).

As much as one-third of achievement can be accounted for by academic self-concept alone. Self-concept can become a self-fulfilling prophesy. If students see themselves as failures, they eventually place self-imposed limits on what is possible. Good grades are dismissed as accidents or luck, but poor grades serve to reinforce a negative self-concept. Students with this attitude often give up trying because they assume that failure is inevitable. The results are low self-concept and limited incentive to change.

- **Attitudes Toward School.** Not surprisingly, research studies have found that students' attitudes toward school have an impact on their achievement. The more positive the attitude, the higher the achievement, especially for girls. Underachievers exhibit more negative attitudes toward school than average and high achievers do.

- **Attitudes Toward Teachers and Classes.** Many underachievers have difficulty with authority figures, including teachers and school personnel. As a result, their attitudes toward their teachers and classes may have a negative impact on their academic achievement. Prevailing instructional methods may not be compatible with the learning style of highly gifted students. The level of instruction may be below these students' capabilities, and classroom rules and restrictions may discourage their full participation. Classrooms that are over-competitive or under-competitive may also lead to achievement problems.

- **Motivation and Self-Regulation.** Self-regulation refers to the self-generated thoughts, feelings, and actions that students regularly use to attain their goals. Self-regulation is a significant predictor of academic achievement, and the use of internalized self-regulatory strategies helps students achieve in school. However, students also must be motivated to use these strategies as well as regulate their effort. Underachievers may lack motivation, self-regulation skills, or both.

- **Goal Valuation.** How students value their achievement is a critical component of their academic motivation and self-regulation. Whenever students value the goals of school, they are more likely to engage in academics, expend more effort on their schoolwork, and do better academically. Students may withdraw from participating in school if they sense a conflict in the values of the school and the culture from which they come. For example, some students may underachieve because they do not want to be perceived as bookworms or nerds by their peers.

Adjusting to Giftedness

Some gifted students, especially adolescents between the ages of 11 and 15, may underachieve because they have serious problems adjusting to their giftedness. Perfectionism, unrealistic appraisal of their gifts, rejection from peers, competitiveness, and confusion over mixed messages about their talents can all erode their achievement in school.

Obstacles to Adjustment: Researchers cite the following as some of the obstacles that can interfere with an adolescent's adjustment to giftedness (Buescher & Higham, 1990; Peters, Grager-Loidl, & Supplee, 2000).

- **Ownership of Talents.** It is not unusual for some talented adolescents to deny their talent, often because of peer pressure to conform and the adolescent's sense of being predictable. These individuals lack self-esteem and have doubts about the objectivity of their parents or teachers in identifying their gifts.

- **Giving of Themselves.** Because they have received gifts in abundance, talented adolescents sometimes feel that they must give of themselves in abundance and that their abilities belong to their teachers, parents, and society.
- **Dissonance.** Gifted adolescents have learned to set high standards, to expect to do more, and to be more than their abilities might allow. In this drive toward perfection, these students experience real dissonance between how well they expect to accomplish something and how well it is actually done. This dissonance can be far greater than teachers or parents may realize.
- **Taking Risks.** Gifted adolescents are less likely to take the risks they took at an earlier age because they are more aware of the repercussions of their activities. Thus, they tend to be more cautious in weighing the advantages and disadvantages of possible choices, and in examining alternatives. They may even reject all risk taking, such as enrolling in advanced courses, competitions, or public presentations.
- **Competing Expectations.** The expectations of others (parents, teachers, peers, siblings, and friends) may compete with the gifted adolescent's own plans and goals. In effect, the adolescent's own expectations must face the onrush of the demands and desires of others. The greater the talent, the greater the expectations of others and outside interference. Trying to meet these expectations can drain energy and dampen the desire to succeed.
- **Impatience.** Gifted students can be just as impatient as other adolescents when looking for quick solutions to difficult questions or trying to develop social relationships. This impulsiveness makes them intolerant of ambiguity and unresolved situations. They can get angry if their hasty solutions fail, especially if other less capable students gloat over these failures. A string of such failures may prompt these students to withdraw.
- **Premature Identity.** For gifted adolescents, the weight of competing expectations, a low tolerance for ambiguity, and the pressure of multiple options all contribute to very early attempts to achieve an adult-like identity, even while in their early to middle teens. In an attempt to complete this identity, they may reach out for career choices that are inappropriate for their true age and that may interfere with the normal processes of identity resolution and acceptance.

Developing a Sense of Identity: Many gifted students continue to struggle with their giftedness because they have a difficult time developing a sense of identity. Teachers and counselors who are trained in recognizing this struggle can provide needed support for these students. To date, very few models are available to assist in the identity development and counseling of gifted people. Andrew Mahoney (2008), who counsels individuals struggling with their giftedness, has developed and uses a matrix called The Gifted Identity Formation Model. This model includes identity and its formation as crucial variables in the counseling process, and it uses identity as the baseline for intervention. The model aids with assessment and helps counselors devise interventions that explore and strengthen the identity formation of gifted people. The model is based on the following four constructs:

- **Validation.** This is an acknowledgment that one's giftedness exists as corroborated by others or by oneself. Giftedness can be validated through identification by an academic gifted program, acknowledgment of one's giftedness by a significant other, or by coming to one's own realization through exceptional accomplishments.
- **Affirmation.** This construct requires acknowledgment of giftedness from many supportive individuals or processes. It is the continual reinforcement of the nuances of an individual's giftedness from learning, experiences, environment, parents, teachers, and enrichment. It is the ongoing, interactive process between self as gifted and the world. The process reinforces in the self the notion that "I am gifted."

- **Affiliation.** This construct represents an association with others of similar intensities, passions, desires, and abilities. It means being received in fellowship or integrated into a group or society without loss of identity (or the self). Affiliation provides a reason for existing by offering a pathway toward connecting the self with another community. Gifted affiliation provides a forum in which individuals are appreciated and accepted for their uniqueness.

- **Affinity.** The fourth construct is an attraction toward that which nourishes and resembles a mating of souls, spirit, and philosophy. Affinity connects the self to the world and the mystery of life. Often affinity needs are set aside when the identity process is not complete. Unmet affinity creates anguish, making life more tenuous. Individuals feel that if they cannot fulfill their calling, then they will never have a sense of fulfillment and relief from their anxiety.

In Mahoney's model, these four constructs represent important building blocks in development of the self. Put into a matrix (Figure 3.1), they will interact with 12 systems to help shape and influence identity formation in the gifted: Self, Family, Family of Origin, Culture, Vocational, Environmental, Educational, Social, Psychological, Political, Organic-Physiological, and Developmental. These interactions, according to Mahoney, represent both the internal and external forces that affect the formation of a gifted person's identity.

The model is a guide for understanding the complexity and nuances of gifted students. It provides a counseling framework that helps gifted individuals become aware of the effect their giftedness has on their own identity formation, so that they can better understand themselves as gifted people. Mahoney stresses that the model is not meant to be used as a criteria scale for mental health or to compare the development of different individuals. Rather, it has three primary counseling purposes: serving as an assessment tool, assisting in the development of counseling interventions, and acting as a guide in the counseling process.

Systems Affecting the Identity Formation of the Gifted

Systems ↓ Constructs →	Validation	Affirmation	Affiliation	Affinity
Self				
Family				
Family of Origin				
Cultural				
Vocational				
Environmental				
Educational				
Social				
Psychological				
Political				
Organic-Physiological				
Developmental				

Figure 3.1 This matrix is the basis for the Gifted Identity Formation Model, describing the interaction between four constructs and 12 systems involved in the formation of one's identity.

Source: Mahoney, 2008. Reprinted with permission.

Furthermore, it allows for giftedness to be placed in a positive context of human development rather than be mischaracterized as abnormal or pathological.

The four constructs in this model get support from current research in the field of social cognitive neuroscience. This is a new science that attempts to understand the complex and dynamic relationship between the brain and social interaction (Ochsner, 2007). Using brain imaging technology, researchers have found that neural systems that process social stimuli, such as forming relationships or comparing oneself to others, are different from those that process non-social stimuli. Studies to date confirm that social development is a critically important part of human development. This importance is signaled in the brain by the activity of specific regions that help individuals understand themselves as social beings, infer the intent of others, and decide the appropriate behavioral response for different social situations (Sousa, 2009).

> For more information on the Gifted Identity Formation Model, visit the following Web site: www.counselingthegifted.com.

IDENTIFYING GIFTED UNDERACHIEVERS

The problem of unidentified gifted underachievers has become more evident in recent years. Typical changes in school systems include the following:

- Use of more sophisticated and varied measures of intelligence and achievement
- A jump in the number of teacher referrals for special education services because of behavioral and learning problems
- Increase in efforts to recognize and develop the potential abilities of culturally different and minority children
- More reports by parents of out-of-school behaviors that demonstrate advanced interests and skills

General Characteristics

Some of the most common characteristics and patterns of underachievement in gifted—as well as other—students are shown in Figure 3.2 (Reis & McCoach, 2000). Because gifted underachievers continue to fail in some areas, they tend to exhibit three general behavior patterns: *aggressive, withdrawn,* or *passively compliant.* Aggressive behavior is characterized by stubbornly refusing to comply with requests, disrupting others, rejecting drill activities, alienating peers, and lack of self-direction in decision making. In contrast, withdrawn behavior patterns include lack of communication, working alone, little attempt to justify behavior, and little participation in classroom activities. Those who are passively compliant will conform and acquiesce to classroom expectations, but without revealing their high ability. Behaviors in all three groups reflect a belief in their inability to influence outcomes in school, a low or unrealistic self-concept, and negative attitudes toward school in general. They also tend to be easily distracted, supersensitive, and socially isolated (Grobman, 2006).

Characteristics of Gifted Underachievers

(Not all characteristics may be present in the same person.)

- High IQ score
- Lack of effort
- A skill deficit in at least one subject area
- Frequently unfinished work
- Inattentiveness to current task
- Low self-esteem
- Poor work and study habits
- Intense interest in one area
- Seeming inability to concentrate
- Failure to respond to usual motivating techniques

Figure 3.2

Source: Reis & McCoach, 2000.

Five Types of Gifted Underachievers

1. Low grades, high test scores

2. Low test scores, high grades

3. Low performance in all subjects

4. Low performance in certain subjects

5. Unnoticed

Figure 3.3

Studies classify underachieving gifted students into five types (Figure 3.3). The first type has low grades in general but high test scores (often on both criterion- and norm-referenced tests). In contrast, the second type displays low test scores but high course grades. The third type performs consistently below the level of capability in all subjects, and the fourth type underachieves only in certain subjects. Students whose underachievement goes unnoticed while in school comprise the fifth type. The existence of this type is most disconcerting because it means that these students will go through school seldom experiencing the educational opportunities that could have challenged them to reach their true potential.

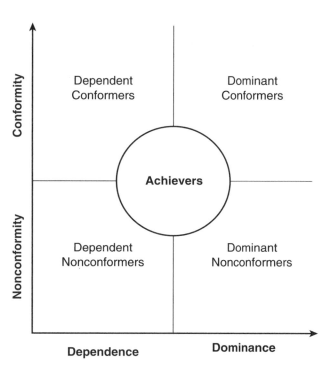

Figure 3.4 The quadrants represent different types of underachievers.

Source: Adapted from Rimm, 2008.

Dependence and Dominance

Underachieving gifted students often protect themselves by developing defense mechanisms. These temporary adaptations use dependency and domination patterns. Sylvia Rimm (2008) is a pediatric psychologist who suggests that underachievers can adopt patterns of behavior that fall on one spectrum that describes their dependence or dominance and another spectrum that represents their degree of conformity. The interaction of these elements results in a chart of quadrants (see Figure 3.4).

According to Rimm, dependent children (left side of figure) have learned how to manipulate adults and get so much help from adults that they lose self-confidence. Because they do less, parents and teachers expect less. As a result, they can become overly sensitive, anxious, and even depressed. These children often go unnoticed.

In contrast, the dominant children (right side of figure) select only those activities they feel they can master. They manipulate adults by trapping them into arguments that can be about almost anything. Rimm maintains that if these children lose arguments, they develop enmity toward adults and use that as an excuse not to do their work or take on responsibilities. When the adults respond negatively to the manipulation, these dominant children complain that the adults do not like or understand them.

The upper and lower portions of the figure (conformity to nonconformity) represent the degree of severity of these children's problems. Those in the upper quadrants have minor problems and are likely to outgrow them. If they do not, however, then they may slip into the lower quadrants and their problems become more severe. Most dependent children will change to dominant by adolescence, although some retain a dependent-dominant mix, varying their response according to the situation. Rimm believes that teachers and parents are often frustrated by these underachievers and inadvertently reinforce the undesirable patterns. Although children should be encouraged to be independent and creative, they should not be over-empowered so that adult guidance becomes impossible. Underachievement can be reversed, and in Rimm's model, that means adopting strategies that move the underachievers into the central circle of achievers—those children who are not dependent on defense mechanisms but who have confidence, an internal locus of control, and who are resilient.

Spatially Gifted Students

Some individuals have unusually high spatial ability. This involves the visual manipulation of objects as well as complex visual materials, and the ability to comprehend the relationships between fluid, changing patterns. While individuals with strong verbal skills can express themselves easily with words, those with strong spatial skills are adept at using images to express their thoughts and solve problems.

Using imaging technologies, neuroscientists have found that verbal and spatial processing require distinct and separate networks that are part of the brain's working memory. You may recall that working memory involves the temporary manipulation and storage of information. Figure 3.5 shows the model used to represent this system (Baddeley, 2003). The *central executive* regulates two subsystems: the

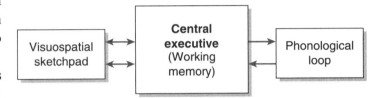

Figure 3.5 A model of working memory, showing the central executive controlling two sub systems: the phonological loop that encodes acoustical information, and the visuospatial sketchpad responsible for encoding visual information. The double arrows between the visuospatial sketchpad and the central executive represent a strong association.

Source: Baddeley, 2003.

phonological loop that manages verbal material, and the *visuospatial sketchpad* responsible for processing visual and spatial material. One surprising finding from these studies is that the strength of association between the visuospatial sketchpad and the central executive indicates that the assessment of spatial tasks may be more closely related to general intelligence than to tests of verbal skills (Brunyé & Taylor, 2008; Miyaki et al., 2001).

Because language skills remain the most frequently used measure of academic giftedness, students who are strong in visual-spatial skills but weak in verbal skills are often perceived as underachievers. Consequently, if they are poor in language skills, their teachers are more likely to focus on remediation and overlook any hint of giftedness. One major study at the University of Illinois in Urbana-Champaign found that, compared with other gifted students, students gifted in spatial ability were performing below their capabilities. Furthermore, this group had interests that were less compatible with traditional course work and received less

> Studies suggest that the assessment of spatial tasks may be more closely related to general intelligence than to tests of verbal skills.

college guidance from school counselors. The students were also less motivated by their educational experience and generally aspired to, and achieved, lower levels of academic and occupational success (Gohm, Humphreys, & Yao, 1998).

Spatial ability is closely linked to visual thinking, but it is not a single entity. It involves the coordination of several brain regions, primarily in the right hemisphere. There is no one set of characteristics that describes all individuals with high spatial ability, as there is considerable variation from one person to another. Table 3.1 shows some of the possible strengths and weaknesses that studies show are common among spatially gifted individuals (Mann, 2005).

A 20-year longitudinal study revealed that many students with high spatial ability were not being identified by the current practices schools use to determine giftedness. These students scored high on tests of spatial ability but did not meet the verbal or mathematics minimum scores for participation in gifted programs or talent searches. The researchers were concerned when they found that if school districts selected the top three percent of students based solely on their verbal and mathematical abilities, it would result in an

Table 3.1   Possible Strengths and Weaknesses in Spatially Gifted Individuals

Strengths	Weaknesses
The individual: • Can manipulate visual images • Displays a vivid imagination • Often uses reflective thinking • Seems preoccupied with many ideas • Shows an excellent memory for detailed information • Displays creative talent • Often speaks with metaphors and uses them effectively • Deals easily with complex and higher-level content • Comprehends relationships between systems • Displays competency with mathematical concepts	**The individual:** • Is slow at processing verbal communication • Has difficulty putting stories into written form • Often daydreams • Displays weak social skills • Does not deal well with rote memorization • Often struggles in traditional academic settings • Rarely uses concise descriptions in language • Has problems with easy or basic content • Does not grasp isolated details • Displays poor mathematical computation skills

Source: Adapted from Mann, 2005.

unfortunate loss of more than *half* of the students in the top one percent of spatial ability (Shea, Lubinski, & Benbow, 2001). Clearly, assessing verbal and quantitative abilities alone were insufficient for identifying intellectually gifted students. See the **Applications** section at the end of this chapter for teaching strategies that are effective with spatially gifted students.

Despite the increased awareness of underachievement in gifted students, educators should work harder to ensure that these students are identified as early as possible for several reasons. The most obvious one is the potential loss of their contributions to society. The second—and less obvious reason—is the underachiever's vulnerability to significant social and mental health problems. It is not uncommon for the gifted underachiever to become a major behavioral problem at school and at home. This misbehavior results from the conflict between the individual's personal psychological needs and the lack of appropriate learning opportunities in the school. Additionally, having a better chance at reversing the patterns of underachievement is another reason for early identification of these students.

UNDERACHIEVEMENT AMONG GIFTED MINORITY STUDENTS

Although most states have written policies that call for recognizing all gifted students, including underrepresented minorities, ths issue of underrepresentation persists. The most recent data available from the U.S. Department of Education (Figure 3.6) show the minority enrollment in gifted programs nationwide in 2004. The percentage of Black and Hispanic students remains less than half that of White students (USDE, 2007). American Indian/Alaska Native enrollment is about three-fourths, while Asian student enrollment is one-and-a-half times that of the White enrollment.

As efforts continue to identify more minority gifted students, attention must also be focused on underachievement among the minority student population, especially culturally and linguistically

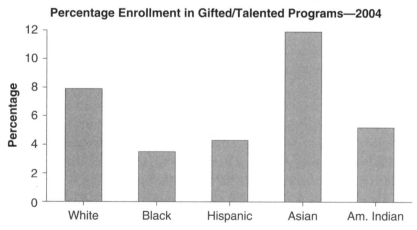

Percentage Enrollment in Gifted/Talented Programs—2004

Figure 3.6   Percentage enrollment in K–12 gifted and talented programs in 2004 by race/ethnicity.

Source: USDE, 2007.

different students. Estimates of the number of gifted minority who underachieve vary, and no reliable data are available to date.

Why Minority Students Underachieve

Several factors must be explored to understand why minority students underachieve. These factors fall into three major categories: sociopsychological, family-related, and school-related (Ford et al., 2002).

- **Sociopsychological Factors.** Low academic self-concept and poor self-esteem are major contributors to underachievement. Racial identity must also be explored as a possible contributor. For example, How do students feel about their racial and ethnic heritage? Do they have a strong positive racial identity? If not, they may be especially vulnerable to negative comments by peers, such as "acting White" or "selling out," which contributes to low effort and low achievement. Especially for adolescents, taking advanced classes, working hard to get good grades, and working with a teacher on a special project are examples of achievement behaviors that may be in conflict with cultural expectations. Many of these students must choose between their need for achievement and the need for peer affiliation. Too often, the need for affiliation wins (Ford, Grantham, & Whiting, 2008; Niehart, 2006).

> Minority students need to choose between their need for achievement and the need for peer affiliation. Too often, the need for affiliation wins.

Minority students can attribute their outcomes to external factors, such as discrimination, and may thus put forth less effort than students who attribute outcomes to internal factors, such as ability and effort. Those minority students who substitute their belief in the power of work with their beliefs in glass ceilings and social injustices are not likely to reach their potential in school.

- **Family-Related Factors.** Numerous studies of gifted programs have found that family variables can influence the success of gifted students in school. The few studies that have examined the family influence on underachieving Black students found that the parents
  - expressed feelings of helplessness and hopelessness,
  - were less involved and assertive in their children's education,
  - set unclear and unrealistic expectations for their children, and
  - were less confident of their parenting skills.
- **School-Related Factors.** Factors in schools can influence the achievement of gifted minority students. Underachieving Black students often report
  - less positive student-teacher relations,
  - too little time to understand the material,
  - less supportive classroom climate, and
  - being disinterested and unmotivated in school.

Teacher expectations play a big role in student achievement. Teachers who lack objectivity or training in gifted education and multicultural education may have different views of giftedness and underachievement, and thus are less likely to refer minority students for gifted education programs. Some teachers may have lower expectations for minority and low-income students than for other students. Consequently, minority students may not be identified as either gifted or underachieving. Eventually, these students underachieve due to frustration, disinterest, and lack of challenge (Miller, 2005).

A few research studies have identified key attributes of minority students' learning styles. For example, Black students tend to be field-dependent, concrete, and visual learners, but schools often emphasize abstract and verbal approaches. This mismatch between learning and teaching styles can result in confusion, frustration, and underachievement (Hale, 2001).

The Deficit Orientation: Some researchers believe that the low referral rate and underachievement of minority students in gifted programs is due to a pervasive deficit orientation that prevails in our schools. They contend that deficit thinking can cause educators to misinterpret the cultural characteristics of minority groups. For example, some minority students have strong psychomotor preferences and need to be actively involved and mobile during learning. Teachers may misinterpret this behavior and view these students as hyperactive, inattentive, and immature. Also, in some cultures, children express themselves easily with emotions and are "feeling" oriented. With these traits, the student may be perceived as too emotional and immature, and may even be considered weak in cognitive skills (Ford et al., 2002).

As teachers become more aware of cultural differences, the likelihood increases that more high ability minority students will gain entrance to gifted programs. The next step is to ensure that the program is sufficiently differentiated so that these students can be appropriately challenged and successful. Furthermore, we need to make every effort to reverse patterns of underachievement in all students.

Identifying Gifted Minority Students: More school districts are becoming aware of the need to revise policies regarding their identification of gifted and talented students in order to address the problem of underrepresented minorities. Callahan (2005) offered the following nine solutions for identifying these students:

Solution 1: Expand Conceptions of Intelligence and Giftedness. The first step is to expand our notions of aptitude and intelligence, such as those offered by Howard Gardner and Robert Sternberg (see Chapter 1). Of equal importance is the ability to see giftedness as something other than pure precocious behavior or genius that must exhibit itself across all realms of performance for the student to be considered gifted. Giftedness does not mean that a student exhibit outstanding abilities in all areas. Students may be gifted or talented in just one area of performance.

Solution 2: Provide Exemplars of Gifted Performance and Use the Identification Process to Enhance Understanding. Teachers can be advocates in the nomination, screening, and identification of gifted students from underserved populations. Thus, it is important they be provided with examples of how various talents may manifest themselves in performance outside of the usual indicators in reading and writing. Districts should provide examples of students from target populations in classroom settings exhibiting the behaviors associated with all aspects of talent, including nontraditional examples of verbal ability. These examples may be in writing or presented as video clips. Teachers should also be involved in the descriptions of what giftedness may look like in multiple cultural groups. Participation gives the teachers ownership of their new conception, expands their understanding, and creates additional advocates who will disseminate information about the existence of talent in underserved populations.

> Districts should establish in the primary grades a program of talent development based on student interest, with highly relevant and motivating tasks, and with the use of high-level and sophisticated thinking skills.

Solution 3: Develop a Program for Talent Development. Districts should establish in the primary grades a program of talent development based on student interest, with highly relevant and motivating tasks, and with the use of high-level and sophisticated thinking skills. The activities in this program should be built around the real world and relevant to the lives of the children.

Solution 4: Identify Early and Often. The research literature shows that the gaps on readiness to learn and achievement in the early grades of ethnic minority groups compared to White populations increase dramatically over time (Donovan & Cross, 2002). By acting quickly in the early years to identify signs of exceptional performance and nurture that performance, we may stand a far greater chance of enhancing achievement and the development of talent. We should develop strategies for ongoing, persistent talent searches and be continually alert for indicators of talent.

Solution 5: Use Valid and Reliable Tools. Assessment tools to assess the talents of any student must present evidence of reliability and validity. On reliability: Would the rating scale yield about the same score if completed by two teachers who knew the child equally well? Would the same teacher rate the child about the same on two different days? On validity: Do scores on this instrument really reflect the definition of giftedness we are using? Do scores on the instrument predict that the child will be successful in the proposed differentiated curriculum?

Solutions 6: Use Authentic Assessments. Assessment tools should emphasize genuine performance tasks that are part of the student's world. These types of tools have greater validity for students who are threatened or turned off by paper-and-pencil intelligence, aptitude, or achievement tests that often contain items not related to their everyday existence. For example, authentic tools could assess creative problem-solving ability by including problems that might be encountered in school, such as truancy, and home, such as a crisis while caring for younger siblings. By using authentic assessments and collecting data over time, educators can observe the ways students respond to open-ended, real-life, challenging, and complex tasks.

Solution 7: Gather Data Over Time and Use Portfolios. Teachers in the talent-development process should be watching how students respond to the high-level challenge that require creativity, critical thinking and analysis, and in-depth inquiry. By documenting this development in a portfolio that includes commonly assigned tasks and student-selected tasks, they provide information that is validly indicative of the student's potential to continue excelling at such tasks.

Solution 8: Eliminate Policies or Practices That Limit the Number Served in the Gifted Program. One of the most inhibiting factors in expanding services to minority students is the belief that there is a magic number of gifted and talented students who can be served by the gifted program. The number of gifted students is not fixed in any community. However, the competition for slots naturally sets up an artificial conflict between those who are traditionally identified and those who might emerge through alternative procedures. When a continuum of services model is implemented, all gifted students can be served.

Solution 9: Rewrite Procedures for Nomination, Screening, and Identifying to Reflect an Inclusive, Expanded Definition of Giftedness. Policies for the process of identifying and placing gifted students should allow for multiple avenues and paths into and through the identification process.

In a study of 25 programs designed to identify culturally, linguistically, and ethnically diverse gifted and talent students, Briggs and her colleagues found that five categories contributed to the success of these programs (Briggs, Reis, & Sullivan, 2008). The categories were the following:

Category 1: Modified Identification Procedures. The procedures had three categories of identification strategies: (a) use of alternative pathways for program identification; (b) early identification, usually at the primary grade level; and (c) inclusion of information about broader perspectives of student performance. Alternative pathways to identification included the use of different assessment tools and elimination of formal identification procedures, combined with the use of special consideration. In cases of special consideration, students who did not necessarily meet typical standards for inclusion but who showed potential for advanced-level work were provided with gifted services to nurture their talents. Early identification was followed by student preparation for later program participation. Student preparation focused on advanced and enriched learning experiences for students who did not have access to these experiences at home, in regular classrooms, or in their communities. Student performance assessments included observations of students during enriched lessons to watch for signs of gifted behaviors, student work portfolios indicating students' strengths and talents, and probationary placement in gifted services to provide opportunities for students to demonstrate their abilities.

Category 2: Front-Loading. Front-loading is the process of preparing students for advanced content and creative and critical thinking prior to the formal identification process or before advanced-level courses are offered. Front-loading bridges the gap in the readiness of some students, nurtures their abilities, and prepares them for success in advanced content programs.

Category 3: Curriculum Changes. Curriculum strategies used by gifted programs in this study included three subcategories: (a) implementation of a continuum of services, (b) adoption of a specific curriculum framework, and (c) an emphasis on directly addressing the needs of the diverse students. A continuum

> Front-loading is the process of preparing students for advanced content and creative and critical thinking prior to the formal identification process.

of services included individualized instruction, use of advanced content, training in research skills, and development of creative and critical thinking skills. The programs also emphasized differentiation, questioning strategies, project- and interest-based activities, hands-on experiences, problem solving, and enrichment opportunities. Three different specific curricular frameworks were used in these programs. First, curricular frameworks were used to guide instruction, including areas such as dual language/bilingual methods, field-specific knowledge and skills, and service learning. Second, some programs implemented specific national curriculum models, such as the Schoolwide Enrichment Model (Renzulli & Reis, 1985). Third, two programs created a specific framework for their individual needs.

The curricular practices specifically adopted to meet the unique needs of these students included mentor opportunities whereby research professors from culturally diverse backgrounds were invited to make research presentations to students. Other practices gave students early access to enriched experiences, and to important learning opportunities prior to identification for the gifted program. Some programs provided dual language classroom opportunities in which bilingual students could learn in both English and their first language. In other programs, opportunities for integrating cultural traditions into the learning process occurred.

Category 4: Parent-Home Connection. Strategies used to increase communication and interaction included involving parents as volunteers, consistently disseminating program information, and making family and culture connections. In the majority of the programs, parents volunteered for field trips and fund-raising activities, often serving as chaperones or supplying food or services. To ensure dissemination of information to parents, programs held parent meetings and support groups, issued newsletters and program brochures, held parent-teacher conferences, and maintained Web sites. In programs reporting family and culture connections, educators used translators for meetings and print materials, gave student homework that required family participation, and fostered collective decision making between students and parents concerning course selections.

Category 5: Program Evaluation. Program evaluation included stakeholder satisfaction, student achievement reports, increased enrollment of these students in gifted programs, and retention of students in gifted services. Information on program satisfaction was gathered through parent, student, and teacher surveys. The majority of program coordinators reported unsuccessful attempts to measure gains in student achievement because the district test data did not disaggregate the performance of gifted students on statewide assessments. Lacking access to this information, student improvement was reported from classroom observations. Qualitative findings included students becoming better at problem solving, more able to implement higher order thinking skills, and developing facility with more challenging content.

Documentation of increased representation of students in gifted programs was found by comparing the number of students currently served to previous numbers or compared to other schools in the district. As to retention of students in the gifted programs, students who left the program were reported to have continued to receive gifted services in other academic sites that included middle school placement, college enrollment, and identification for within-school gifted programs.

Gifted English Learners (EL): Between 1979 and 2006, the number of school-age children (ages 5 to 17) who spoke a language other than English at home increased from 3.8 to 10.8 million, or from 9 to 20 percent of the student population in this age range. During the more recent period of 2000 to 2006, it increased from 18 to 20 percent (USDC, 2007). Despite this growing population, the underrepresentation of English learners (EL) in gifted and talented programs remains an issue of concern and has been cited in research reports for years. Because of the inherent language barrier, EL students have fewer opportunities compared to their native English-speaking peers to be noticed by teachers for those behaviors that would qualify them as being gifted and talented (Aguirre, 2003). Gifted aptitudes and talent potential in EL students are often embedded in EL students' cultural, linguistic, and ethnic backgrounds. Identification procedures for EL students, therefore, should concentrate on a broader idea of giftedness and include nontraditional measures that consider different cultures.

Two major barriers appear to affect the assessment of EL as gifted and talented. First, teachers of gifted and talented students often do not communicate with teachers of other special populations, such as special education and EL students. This lack of communication reduces the opportunity to see EL students in multiple educational settings. Second, despite some progress in this area, there continues to be a lack of explicit policies regarding the identification of gifted and talented students from underrepresented groups. Other barriers include tracking and low expectations for EL students, negative reactions from some teachers toward non-English speaking students, and failure to communicate with parents who often do not speak or read English (Harris, Rapp, Martínez, & Plucker, 2007).

> Gifted aptitudes and talent potential in English learners are often embedded in their cultural, linguistic, and ethnic backgrounds.

Identifying Gifted EL Students: As the population of EL students continues to grow, educators have to examine their practices for identifying and selecting EL student for gifted and talented programs. The following three-step process suggested by Coleman (2003) and adapted by Harris et al. (2007) can be used for the identification of gifted EL students. The reader will note some similarities to the suggestions made earlier by Callahan (2005).

Step 1. General Screening or Student Search. This phase establishes a school- or district-wide screening system that involves all students, including the EL population. Screening methods can rely on data that are available for all students, such as standardized scores on state or district assessments, and other cognitive and academic assessments given as part of the screening process. Assessments should be administered in the student's native language as well as in English. Districts should use multiple criteria to gain a complete picture of the EL student's giftedness and potential. These assessment procedures should gather information from multiple sources, such as families, teachers, students, and others with significant knowledge of the students. They should also collect information in different ways, such as through observations, performances, products, portfolios, interviews, as well as in different contexts, such as in-school and out-of-school settings.

Caution is advised when using nonverbal tests. It seems logical to assume that nonverbal tests would be useful to assess the abilities of EL students who have difficulty with spoken and written English. But this may not necessarily be the case. One recent study of nearly 1,200 elementary school children compared the validity of three nonverbal tests to identify academically gifted EL students. Approximately 40 percent of the participants were ELs. All were administered the Raven Standard Progressive Matrices (Raven), the Naglieri Nonverbal Ability Test (NNAT), and Form 6 of the Cognitive Abilities Test (CogAT). Results showed that the EL children in this study scored 8 to 10 points lower than non-EL children on the three nonverbal tests. Furthermore, there appeared to be errors in the national norms. When using national norms,

UNIVERSITY H.S. LIBRARY

both the Raven and NNAT substantially overestimated the number of high-scoring children. None of the nonverbal tests predicted achievement for EL students very well (Lohman, Korb, & Lakin, 2008).

School districts should provide information about the district's gifted program and identification practices to parents in their native language. This information should include both the characteristics to look for in their child that might indicate giftedness, and the procedures for notifying the district's gifted coordinator if such traits are observed. Screening should be dynamic and ongoing throughout the school year so that migrant and immigrant EL students who arrive at different times in the school year have an opportunity to participate in the assessment and identification process.

Step 2. Review of Students for Eligibility. In this phase, the data for the EL students who demonstrated potential based on the screening process should be reviewed by a team of school personnel that includes gifted and talented and EL teachers. Parents and general education teachers should also be active members of the team. After reviewing teach student's data, a team decision is made to either collect additional data about the student, or to immediately place the student in the program for gifted and talented children. Adaptations to the curriculum may be necessary, particularly with regard to the student's native language.

Step 3. Match Students to Services. EL students who have demonstrated high potential are now offered appropriate educational services. These may include an alternate placement, such as a class for gifted and talented students, or enriched services, such as an after-school class. The curricular services should be individualized to the EL student's unique strengths. To increase the representation of EL students in gifted and talented programs, the district may identify a certain number of slots for EL students. Periodically, the appropriateness of the services should be monitored and reviewed to make sure it is still a good fit for the student.

Although it is important to develop appropriate identification procedures for EL students, teachers, school administrators, and their policies must also promote and emphasize these procedures. Successful identification of gifted and talented EL students requires proactive work and visionary leadership.

REVERSING PATTERNS OF UNDERACHIEVEMENT

Approaches to reversing patterns of underachievement are successful if they are based on the view that the poor performance has been shaped by forces within the school that can be changed. These forces include the social messages communicated by the teacher and peers that invite or discourage the student to participate, and the degree to which the curriculum and instructional strategies are compatible with the learning style of the underachiever. Thus, successful interventions will create positive forces that shape achievement behavior. These interventions must address three critical questions.

1. What does it mean to be gifted and what are the associated problems?

2. What are constructive ways of coping with the inevitable conflict that arises by the significant gap between performance level and cognitive ability?

3. How can a student develop a healthier, more realistic self-concept?

Despite the frustration of working with students who are performing below their potential, strategies do exist that are effective in reversing underachievement. The following three types of strategies are worth considering.

- **Supportive Strategies.** These strategies focus on allowing students to feel that they are part of a group where problems and concerns can be discussed, and where curriculum activities can be chosen based on student needs and interests. Students may also be allowed to omit assignments for which they have already shown competency.

- **Intrinsic Strategies.** By accepting the notion that students' desires to achieve academically are closely linked to their self-concepts as learners, teachers use this type of strategy to encourage attempts, not just successes. Teachers also invite students to provide input on classroom rules and responsibilities. Students may also be allowed to evaluate their own work before submitting it to the teacher.
- **Remedial Strategies.** Underachievement is more likely to be reversed when teachers recognize that students make mistakes, and students can have individual strengths and weaknesses in addition to their intellectual, social, and emotional needs. Remedial strategies, therefore, are designed to allow students to excel in their areas of strength and interest. At the same time, teachers provide opportunities in the specific areas of each student's learning deficiencies. The classroom climate is one in which mistakes are considered part of the learning process for teacher and student alike.

See the **Applications** section at the end of this chapter for suggested classroom strategies in these three categories.

Reversing Underachievement in Minority Students

Efforts need to be made to reverse or prevent underachievement in gifted minority students. These interventions should (Ford et al., 2008)

- Use valid and reliable measures for determining underachievement in minority populations;
- Improve students' skills in organization, studying, time management, and taking tests;
- Build self-esteem, social and academic self-concept, and racial identity;
- Involve family members as partners in the educational process; and
- Provide appropriate school staff with training in gifted and multicultural education, which includes strategies for improving classroom climate and teacher expectations.

Bernal (2002) maintains that an effective way to improve achievement in gifted culturally and linguistically different (CLD) students is to change the nature of traditional gifted programs so that more of these students will qualify. He proposes the following remedies to address this problem of underrepresentation:

- **Evaluation:** Districts that have already had success in admitting and retaining CLD students need to evaluate their programs and share their data. The evaluation should focus on questions, such as
  - Who are the students that the program currently admits?
  - What are the students like who succeeded in the program, and who failed?
  - What modifications have been made to the gifted program to accommodate these students, and what have been the outcomes?
- **Multicultural Curriculum:** For CLD students to be successful in a gifted program, the curriculum must be multicultural. Districts need to train teachers in multicultural methodologies. This training should show teachers how to
  - Use examples from different cultures to make learning more interesting to a wider group of students;
  - Demonstrate how new knowledge is influenced by ethnicity, history, and individual perspectives;
  - Use cooperative learning groups to promote positive interaction among students of diverse backgrounds; and
  - Establish a classroom climate that makes CLD students feel wanted.
- **Recruitment:** Schools need to recruit authentic representatives of their respective minority groups into the gifted program's teaching staff. These individuals model some of the intellectual content and values of their cultural traditions for the benefit of all gifted students.

We noted earlier that researchers have suggested using a variety of assessment approaches to enhance the identification of gifted minority students. Some approaches to the identification of gifted minority students use a variety of information sources including rating scales, checklists, referrals, and peer nominations. Peer nomination forms are valuable because students can often identify their bright peers, and they may be less biased toward cultural differences than their teachers (Brown et al., 2005).

Peer nomination instruments are often criticized for their lack of reliability and validity. However, a study involving 670 students in Grades 4 through 6 did show that a peer nomination form designed to identify gifted Hispanic students had sufficient reliability and validity to warrant its use (Cunningham, Callahan, Plucker, Roberson, & Rapkin, 1998). The researchers recommended that the instrument be used with other minority groups, e.g., African Americans, Native Americans, and Asian Americans. A copy of the form used in this study can be found in **Applications** section at the end of this chapter.

There is no simple answer to the problem of underachievement among gifted students. Some gifted students are high achievers in a highly-structured environment, but are underachievers if they have low self-esteem and cannot focus on a selected number of activities, establish priorities, and set long-term goals. Teachers and parents must remember that achievement and resilience can be taught. By doing so, they build the competencies and confidence that students will need as they grow and mature.

APPLICATIONS

STRATEGIES FOR HELPING SPATIALLY GIFTED STUDENTS

Spatially gifted students do not easily adapt to the sequential structure generally found in many classrooms. The following lists suggest the teaching strategies that are likely to be more effective and less effective with students who have strong spatial ability (Mann, 2005).

Effective Strategies

- Focus on concept development
- Time for reflection
- Opportunities for discovery
- Reading instruction that emphasizes sight words
- Activities that use manipulatives
- Interdisciplinary units
- Open-ended problem solving

Less Effective Strategies

- Focus on rote memorization
- Emphasis on rapid recall
- Mostly lecture and oral directions
- Reading instruction emphasizing phonics
- Lots of drill and repetition
- Step-by-step learning
- Note-taking and outlining

From a Teacher's Desk: *A Secondary Example*

Often strategies can be combined to provide differentiation for students with different learning styles. One effective combination is using manipulatives to let children have opportunities for discovery. Math and science are excellent content areas in which to use these strategies. For example, as students work with magnets, they will discover the properties as well as the rules of attraction and repulsion. Also, allowing students to use base-10 blocks for regrouping will assist in a conceptual understanding of place value.

Rhythm can be used across all disciplines to motivate and make connections between text or information and music. Using clapping or snapping to count syllables for spelling words is an easy way to teach students to learn the strategies themselves. Historical songs about wars, revolutions, movements, etc. can tell stories with words and movement. Any syncopation that can be added to a concept will encode information meaningfully into memory and trigger retrieval for all students.

APPLICATIONS

PROGRAMMING COMPONENTS FOR REVERSING UNDERACHIEVEMENT IN GIFTED STUDENTS

Programs designed specifically to reverse underachievement in gifted students can occur in the regular classroom, in resource rooms, or through the development of a plan that involves a mentor in the school or community. Achor and Tarr (1996) suggest that the program should contain at least the following five elements.

Teacher	The teacher's perception of the student's problem is critical to the program's success. Consequently, the teachers must accept the fact that the student is gifted, does not want to underachieve or fail, needs to develop constructive coping skills, and has low self-esteem. To be successful, the teacher should be skilled in guidance techniques, have an accurate understanding of the nature of giftedness, and possess a positive attitude toward the challenge of working with this type of student.
Curriculum	Program success is more likely if the curriculum is challenging, relevant, and rewarding to the student. The curriculum should have a balance between basic skill development and more advanced exploration of the arts and sciences. Critical elements also include the development of personal interests and career possibilities. There should be plenty of opportunities for challenge and success.
Instruction	Instructional techniques should include minimal memorization and drill/practice activities and maximal opportunities for inquiry, creative production, and scientific inquiry. Nurturing the student's self-discipline is important, as well as encouraging self-directed learning activities. The instructional climate should foster anticipation, excitement, low pressure, and personal satisfaction.
Peer Group	The peer group should include at least a few other gifted students, possibly underachievers, who can become good friends. The group must be accepting of individual differences and diversity. Their interactions can help develop needed social skills.
Special Services	Appropriate special services should be provided for gifted underachievers who are also handicapped, for those requiring remedial instruction, and for group counseling. These students sometimes require family counseling as well as supplemental medical and psychological services.

APPLICATIONS

STRATEGIES FOR UNDERACHIEVING GIFTED STUDENTS

The following types of strategies are effective in preventing and reversing underachievement behavior in gifted students. They can be used by both teachers and parents (Delisle & Berger, 1990).

- **Supportive Strategies**
  - Do not assume that advanced intellectual ability also means advanced social and emotional skills.
  - Provide an atmosphere that is non-authoritarian, flexible, mutually respectful, and questioning.
  - Establish reasonable rules and guidelines for behavior.
  - Give consistently positive feedback.
  - Provide strong support and encouragement.
  - Help them to accept their limitations as well as those of others, and to help others as a means of developing tolerance, understanding, empathy, and acceptance of human limitations.
  - Be a sounding board and listen to their questions without comment.
  - When it is time for solving problems, suggest possible solutions and encourage students to come up with their own solutions and strategies for choosing the best one.
  - Show enthusiasm for students' interests, observations, goals, and activities.
  - Avoid solving problems that the student is capable of managing.
  - Avoid establishing unrealistic expectations.
  - Provide a wide variety of opportunities for the students to experience success and to gain confidence in themselves.
  - Reserve time to have fun and to share daily activities.

- **Intrinsic Strategies**
  - Recognize that intellectual growth and development is a requirement for these children, and not merely an interest or a temporary phase that they are going through.
  - Avoid giving assignments that are too easy or too difficult.
  - Because learning style can affect achievement, ensure that these students are in programs that are sufficiently flexible and that have teachers who can address various learning style strengths and weaknesses. For example, gifted children are often strong in visual-spatial ability and weak in sequencing skills. They may also not do well in spelling, foreign languages, and mathematics, especially if they are taught in the traditional way.
  - Look for opportunities that allow students to explore topics in-depth, to participate in hands-on learning, and to develop adult expert-mentor relationships.
  - Encourage students to pursue their interests, recognizing, however, that some students will spend hours on a project and fail to submit required work. They need to be reminded that others may not be sympathetic to tardy or incomplete work.
  - Early career guidance can help these students set short- and long-term goals, complete required assignments, and plan for college.
  - Be aware of the fine line between encouragement and pressure. Encouragement emphasizes the process, steps, and effort used to achieve a goal; appraisal and evaluation are left to the student (intrinsic rewards). In contrast, pressure to perform focuses on outcomes and grades for which the student receives praise (extrinsic reward). Underachieving gifted students often reject praise as artificial and not authentic.

- **Remedial Strategies**
  - ○ Be cautious about statements that may discourage the student, such as "Why did you get a C? You know you are gifted." Statements like these are rarely effective.
  - ○ Avoid putting these students in situations where they are either winner or losers, and avoid comparing them to others. Rather, show them how to function in competition and how to deal with losing.
  - ○ Special tutoring may help concerned students who are experiencing short-term academic difficulties. The tutor should be carefully selected to match the interests and learning style of the student.
  - ○ Long-term underachievers rarely benefit from special tutoring or from study skills and time management courses. Other interventions that more directly address the causes of the underachievement need to be explored.

From a Teacher's Desk: *A Middle School Example*

Team Work. At Morris Middle School, gifted teachers and counselors work together to provide support for their students. They realized that by pooling their resources, they could work with academically and socially diverse gifted students who often felt like they were "different" from their classmates. For example, the school counselor and gifted teachers cooperatively teach stress management lessons that provide their students with strategies to overcome stressful situations such as high-stakes test sessions.

The counselor also works with the gifted teachers to implement a comment box in the classroom. This box provides students with an opportunity to anonymously ask questions or even ask for help without drawing attention in class. One gifted teacher saw that his students were often competitive in class, and some students who seemed frustrated by that did not want to risk raising their hand and possibly getting the wrong answer. By providing the comment box, more of his students felt comfortable getting help that way.

Finally, the counselor and teachers provided special monthly family homework nights in which they invited students and family members to come to the school library and work on homework together. They found that parents not only felt more connected to the school, but became more aware of what their child was learning in school and how to better support him/her at home. Morris Middle School has found that by working together as a team, counselors and teachers can provide more opportunities for students to feel success in school.

Motivating Underachievers Through the Anchor Activity. Underachievement can stem from many factors, such as self-concept and attitudes toward school or teachers. For these students, school can seem like a long list of imperatives without much room for divergence. One strategy that has potential for success is the Anchor Activity. Anchor Activity is a term used by Tomlinson (2003) to describe any activity that students may do when they have finished with work in class. Teachers often use Anchor Activities to extend what the class is learning. For students who struggle with motivation, the Anchor Activity can provide an opportunity to tap into student interest and give students choice in learning. The following is an example of some anchor activities that were given to a seventh-grade English class during their study of *The Giver* by Lois Lowry.

During the novel study of *The Giver* by Lois Lowry, students who finished their classroom work early or were given time during the unit could work on anchor activities. Although many activities were offered, students could choose the ones they were most interested in. All students were expected to complete at least two by the end of the novel study. Students were also given the opportunity to work with a partner or small group on their anchor activities provided there were students available during their work time.

Sample Anchor Activity Cards

Where does the word "Utopia" come from? What is its opposite?

When we discuss the term "Utopia" in relation to *The Giver*, are we using it in a way that is consistent with its original meaning?

What is the professional title of a person who studies the origins of words?

What is the professional title of a person who researches the way languages change over time?

What might someone who studies language usage conclude about the way Jonas' people use words such as "release"?

Jonas' community represents an attempt to create a Utopian society. Different groups have attempted to establish alternative, closed societies to distance them selves from the mainstream culture. Some have been more successful than others. Research one of these societies. Give some brief information about the values, practices, history and success or failure of the society. Based on your research, what factors might have led to its success or failure? (provide examples)

Jonas becomes upset when he learns that a game his friends play actually simulates the painful events of war. Over time, the sometimes-tragic origins of children's games are forgotten. Research the origins of a common children's game. (provide examples)

Through *The Giver,* Lois Lowry suggests that one person's actions can change the course of a whole society. Research the life of someone from history who changed the course of the society he or she lived in. Based on your research, which characteristics of the individual or the society do you think enabled the person to become so influential?

Members of Jonas' community have been genetically engineered so that they can't distinguish color. Research the way the eye perceives color.

APPLICATIONS

ADDITIONAL STRATEGIES FOR UNDERACHIEVING MINORITY STUDENTS

In addition to the strategies suggested in the previous pages, here are some other considerations for enhancing achievement in minority students (Ford et al., 2002).

- **Supportive**
  Provide opportunities for these students to discuss their concerns with teachers and counselors who are trained in gifted and multicultural education. Classroom activities should focus more on cooperation than competition, and these students should get genuine positive reinforcement and praise when appropriate. Use activities that include multicultural components, mentors, and role models (such as teachers) from different ethnic and racial groups. Find substantive ways to involve family members and suggest ways that they can encourage the student at home.

- **Intrinsic**
  Allow students to have choices in selecting projects and in areas of interest. Vary teaching style to accommodate different learning styles. Use biographies of minority role models when appropriate. Include curriculum components that are multicultural, relevant, and personally meaningful to students.

- **Remedial**
  Implement academic counseling as soon as needed. Include tutoring and the teaching of study, time-management, organizational, and test-taking skills. Individual learning contracts and learning journals are also helpful.

APPLICATIONS

USING PEER NOMINATION FORMS
TO IDENTIFY GIFTED MINORITY STUDENTS

Students tend to enjoy the process of completing surveys, especially when it involves them. At the same time, they take the process seriously, as evidenced by their many questions to make sure they are accomplishing the task correctly. As with any assessment instrument, specific wording is imperative so that students interpret the question or task uniformly. For elementary students, two-part questions might only return a one-sided answer. For example, the prompt for a student who "learns quickly but doesn't speak up in class very often" could return results mostly for a student who is quiet, not necessarily a student who learns quickly.

While everyone in the class might turn up on the surveys somewhere (even sometimes self-nominated), there will be certain students who stand out in each category as well as in several categories overall. Those individuals who peers identify as having multiple strengths should be recommended for gifted identification if they have not already been. Students that are said to excel in certain areas, such as dance, music, or art, might need a special referral matching their talent (depending on the district guidelines) and should also be recommended.

Cunningham et al. (1998) used the following peer nomination form in a major study to help identify gifted Hispanic students in Grades 4 through 6. Because of the instrument's high reliability and validity in their study, the researchers recommend that the instrument also be used with other minority groups, e.g., African Americans, Native Americans, and Asian Americans.

The 10 questions address intellectual abilities (questions 1, 2, 3, 9, and 10) and creative and artistic abilities (questions 4, 5, 6, 7, and 8). The directions on the form ask students to consider all of the peers in their classes, and the instructions ensure the confidentiality of their responses. The form gathers different information from that provided by standardized tests and should be just one part of a multiple assessment process.

The researchers suggest that the items on the form be used independently or in appropriate clusters to nominate students. Therefore, rather than using an overall cut-off score, students should be considered for selection on the basis of the proportion of nominations (i.e., the number of nominations divided by the class size) in the area of giftedness—intellectual abilities or creative and artistic abilities.

Peer Referral Form

Teacher's Name _____

I am going to ask you to think of your classmates in a different way than you usually do. Read the questions below and try to think of which child in your class best fits each question. Think of the boys and girls, quiet kids and noisy kids, best friends and those with whom you don't usually play. You may only put down one name for each question. You may leave a space blank. You can use the same name for more than one question. You may not use your teacher's name or names of other adults. Please use first and last names. You do not have to put your name down on this form, so you can be completely honest.

1. What boy OR girl learns quickly, but doesn't speak up in class very often?

2. What girl OR boy will get interested in a project and spend extra time and take pride in his or her work?

3. What boy OR girl is smart in school, but doesn't show off about it?

4. What girl OR boy is really good at making up dances?

5. What boy OR girl is really good at making up games?

6. What girl OR boy is really good at making up music?

7. What boy OR girl is really good at making up stories?

8. What girl OR boy is really good at making up pictures?

9. What boy OR girl would you ask first if you needed any kind of help at school?

10. What girl OR boy would you ask to come to your house to help you work on a project? (Pretend that there would be someone to drive that person to your house.)

Note: Adapted from Peer Referral as a Process for Locating Hispanic Students Who May Be Gifted (unpublished doctoral dissertation, University of Arizona), by A. J. Udall, 1987.

Source: Cunningham, Callahan, Plucker, Roberson, & Rapkin, 1998. Reprinted with permission.

CHAPTER 4

The Twice-Exceptional Brain

The notion that a gifted child can have learning disabilities seems bizarre. As a result, many children who are gifted in some ways and deficient in others go undetected and unserved by our schools. Only in recent years have educators begun to recognize that high abilities and learning problems can coexist in the same person. But even with this recognition, many school districts still do not have procedures in place to screen, identify, and serve the needs of children with dual exceptionalities. Districts that do identify these students provide services for either their giftedness or learning disability, but generally not both (Newman, 2004). What makes dual exceptionalities even possible is that the individual's strengths and weaknesses lie in different areas. Early observations of these students led to the term paradoxical learners, due to the many discrepancies in their school performance. Today, they are more commonly referred to as the twice-exceptional student.

IDENTIFYING TWICE-EXCEPTIONAL STUDENTS

Gifted children who display learning problems can be placed into three distinct groups (Baum & Owen, 2004):

1. *Identified gifted, but also learning disabled.* The first group includes students identified as gifted but who exhibit learning difficulties in school. They often have poor spelling and handwriting and may appear disorganized or sloppy in their work. Through low motivation, laziness, or low self-esteem, they perform poorly and are often labeled as underachievers. Teachers expect them to achieve because they are labeled as gifted. As a result, their learning disabilities remain unrecognized until they lag behind their peers.

2. *No identification.* The second—and perhaps largest—group represents those students whose abilities and disabilities mask each other. They often function at grade level, are considered average students, and do not seem to have problems or any special needs. A majority of these students are unassertive, doing what is expected of them but not volunteering information about their abilities or interests. Although they may be seem to be performing well, they are in fact functioning well below their potential. In later high school years, as course work becomes more difficult, learning difficulties may become apparent, but their true potential will not be realized. Because neither exceptionality is identified, students in this group will not receive the educational programs necessary to meet their needs.

3. *Identified learning disabled, but also gifted.* The third group includes students who have already been diagnosed with learning disabilities but whose high abilities have never been recognized. This may

be a larger group than one might believe at first. They are often placed in a learning-disabilities classroom where their difficulties suppress their intellectual performance. Little attention is given to their interests and strengths. Over time, they may become disruptive and find ways to use their creative abilities to avoid tasks. If their high ability remains unrecognized, then it never becomes part of their educational program, and these students never benefit from services to the gifted.

Students in all three groups are at risk for social and emotional problems when either their potential or learning disabilities go unrecognized. The problem is further compounded by the identification process because the activities used to select students for either learning disability or gifted services tend to be mutually exclusive. Consequently, these students often fail to meet the criteria for either type of service.

The Difficulties of Identification

No actual data exists to date on how many gifted students have learning disabilities, although some estimates suggest that between 120,000 and 150,000 attend American schools (Davis & Rimm, 2003). The number of possible combinations of intellectual giftedness and learning disabilities is so great that any attempt to devise a single set of reliable measures is probably futile. For example, gifted students with language or speech impairments cannot respond to tests requiring verbal answers. Students with hearing problems may neither be able to respond to oral directions nor possess the vocabulary necessary to express complex thoughts. Vision problems could prevent some students from understanding written vocabulary words. Learning disabilities could prevent some students from expressing themselves through speech or in writing. Moreover, dual exceptionality students often use their gifts to hide their disabilities, further complicating the identification process.

Nonetheless, researchers agree that a battery of measurements should be developed to assess these students. Assessment should include an achievement battery, an intelligence test, indicators of cognitive processing, and behavioral observations. Teachers should be given lists of characteristics, such as the "Characteristics of Gifted Children with Learning Disabilities" at the end of this chapter, to increase their awareness of behaviors displayed by students who are gifted and have a learning disability. Parent interviews, self-concept scales, and talent checklists are just some of the tools that can be used to assess whether a child is gifted. The goal is early identification and intervention for gifted students with learning disabilities so that their needs and talents are recognized and appropriately addressed by the school staff.

Cline and Hegeman (2001) propose that the identification of gifted students with disabilities is particularly difficult for the following reasons:

- **Focus on Assessing the Disability.** Assessment of the disability should include looking for particular strengths, such as superior mental or artistic ability, and creativity. Besides medical information, test administrators should look at participation in extracurricular activities and performance in music, visual arts, drama, or dance.
- **Stereotypic Expectations.** The long-held perception that gifted students are motivated and mature while learning disabled children are unmotivated and sluggish needs to be overcome if we are to successfully identify this population.
- **Developmental Delays.** Delays in a student's cognitive development may result in disabilities that mask talents. Students with visual impairments, for example, will have difficulty with any abstract thinking that requires visual representation, but may have high capabilities in other areas of language expression.
- **Deficits in Experiences.** Students in families with limited resources may not have had many opportunities for a variety of learning experiences (e.g., travel), thus inhibiting the expression of their unique abilities.

- **Narrow Views of Giftedness.** Too many educators still hold a narrow view of giftedness as intellectual potential in mathematics and language. However, the works of Howard Gardner, Robert Sternberg (see Chapter 1), and others have provided broader conceptions of intelligence that may help in the identification of gifted students with learning disabilities.
- **Disability-Specific Concerns.** Because a specific disability may affect a student's performance in certain parts of the testing process, test administrators may need to make adaptations or accommodations to the testing procedures. These alterations should be appropriate to the specific disability and could include omitting certain questions or extending the time for taking the test.

The Potential for Misdiagnosis

As psychologists and educators become more aware of the behaviors that suggest learning disabilities, concerns are now being raised that gifted students may be misdiagnosed as having psychological disorders as a result of the very behaviors that make them gifted. For example, many gifted students are intense in their work, engage in power struggles with adults, and are extremely sensitive to emotional situations. They are often impatient with themselves and others, displaying an intense idealism and concern for moral and social issues, which can create depression and anxiety. Further, gifted students are often bored in the regular classroom and their peer relations can be difficult. These problems, which can be associated with the characteristic strengths of gifted students, can be mislabeled and ultimately lead to misdiagnosis.

> Gifted students may be misdiagnosed as having psychological disorders as a result of the very behaviors that make them gifted.

Psychologist James Webb has long been interested in the misdiagnosis of gifted students. Table 4.1 lists a few of the possible problems that he suggests may be linked to the typical strengths of gifted children (Webb et al., 2005). Webb contends that inexperienced health professionals are misreading the problems and mistakenly diagnosing some gifted children with attention-deficit hyperactivity disorder (ADHD), oppositional defiant disorder, bipolar disorder, and obsessive-compulsive disorder. No doubt, giftedness can coexist in students who have psychological disorders, but Webb believes that number is far smaller than currently diagnosed.

Similarly, some gifted students are being misdiagnosed with learning disabilities. This can happen when health professionals misinterpret any of the following as a sign of learning dysfunction (Rizza & Morrison, 2003; Webb et al., 2005; Winner, 2000):

- Large differences between the verbal IQ and performance IQ on the Wechsler intelligence tests
- Large differences between the individual subscales on the intelligence and achievement sections of the Wechsler Intelligence Scale for Children
- Poor handwriting
- Poor sleep habits
- Parental reports that the child is strong-willed, impertinent, weird, argumentative, and intense

Misdiagnosing Giftedness as Attention-Deficit Hyperactivity Disorder (ADHD)

In looking at Table 4.1, it is apparent that many of the possible problem behaviors linked to gifted students can readily be associated with the characteristics of attention-deficit hyperactivity disorder (ADHD). In Chapter 1 we discussed Dabrowski's notion of "ovexcitabilities" which could possibly be misinterpreted by some as a sign of hyperactivity. Specifically, the gifted characteristics of high motor activity, sensitivity, intensity, and impatience can easily be mistaken for ADHD. Surely, some gifted children suffer from ADHD, but many do not. So how do health and education professionals determine whether a

Table 4.1	Possible Problems Linked to the Typical Strengths of Gifted Children
Strengths	**Possible Problems**
Quickly acquires and retains information.	Looks bored; gets impatient with slowness of others.
Enjoys intellectual activities and can conceptualize and synthesize abstract concepts.	May question teachers' procedures; resists practice and drill; omits details.
Seeks to organize things and people.	May be seen as rude or domineering.
Is self-critical and evaluates other critically.	Intolerant toward others; may become depressed.
Enjoys inventing new ways of doing things.	May reject what is already known; seen by others as different.
Strong desire to be accepted by others; has empathy for others.	Expects others to have similar values; sensitive to peer criticism; may feel alienated.
Has diverse interests and abilities.	Frustrated over lack of time; may appear disorganized.
Strong sense of humor.	Often sees the absurdities of situation; humor may not be understood by others; becomes class clown to get attention.
Displays intense efforts, high energy, eagerness, and alertness.	Eagerness may disrupt others; frustrated with inactivity; may be seen as hyperactive.

child's behavior is merely the expression of giftedness or the sign of a gifted child with ADHD? Answering this question requires considering the settings and situations in which the child displays the problem behavior, as well as other potential explanations.

- **Consider the Setting and the Situation.** Gifted children do not exhibit the problem behaviors in all settings. For example, they may appear ADHD-like in one class, but not in another; or they may have problems on the ball field, but not at their music lessons. By contrast, children with ADHD exhibit their problem behaviors in all settings, although the intensity of their display may vary from one situation to another.

   Gifted children may be perceived as being off-task when their behavior might be related to boredom, mismatched learning style, lack of challenge in the curriculum, or other environmental factors. Providing more challenge will usually get them back to work. ADHD children have a difficult time focusing on their work no matter how interesting it may be.

   Hyperactivity is a common characteristic of gifted and ADHD children. However, for the gifted, their activity is highly focused and usually results in productive work or achievement of a specific goal. For ADHD children, their hyperactivity is found across all different types of situations and is often unfocused and unproductive.

- **Consider Other Sources.** Clinical studies report that a small percentage of gifted students suffer from borderline hypoglycemia (low blood sugar) and from various kinds of allergies (Webb et al., 2005). Physical reactions in these conditions, coupled with the sensitivity and intensity characteristics of gifted children, can result in behavior that mimics ADHD. Once again, the intensity of their display will vary with diet, time of day, and other environmental factors.

Some highly gifted boys exhibit levels of behavior problems similar to boys who have learning disabilities.

Some empirical evidence exists that assesses the possibility of misdiagnosis between giftedness and ADHD (Harnett, Nelson, & Rinn, 2004). Case studies add their findings to the mix as well. For example, one study found that highly gifted boys exhibit levels of behavior problems similar to boys who have learning disabilities (Shaywitz et al., 2001). Surely, some gifted children have true learning disabilities, and their dual exceptionality should be addressed. However, health care professionals need to become more familiar with aspects of giftedness so that they are less likely to conclude that certain inherent characteristics of gifted children are signs of pathology.

Guidance and Counseling Interventions

Twice-exceptional college students often report that they received little guidance in elementary and high school to help them reconcile their academic talents with their learning difficulties. Some still believe they are dumb because of negative comments made to them during their years in school. Other heard that they were lazy and if they worked harder, their learning problems would diminish or disappear. No school counselors were available to help these students (Reis & Colbert, 2004).

School counselors can provide guidance and counseling services that benefit gifted students with learning disabilities. These services can often help students develop positive social relationships, raise their self-esteem, and improve their overall behavior. Furthermore, counselors can advocate on behalf of these students by raising awareness of their unique needs. By assisting in the identification process, using individual and group counseling, consulting with parents, and sharing academic strategies, counselors become important collaborators and facilitators in ensuring the academic success of gifted students with learning disabilities (McEachern & Bornot, 2001).

GIFTEDNESS AND ATTENTION-DEFICIT HYPERACTIVITY DISORDER

Some gifted children do have attention-deficit hyperactivity disorder (ADHD). Unfortunately, this dual exceptionality often means that such children are not recognized as having either exceptionality. Therefore, their needs for an appropriate education often go unmet (Zentall, Moon, Hall, & Grskovic, 2001).

What Is ADHD?

Attention-deficit hyperactivity disorder (ADHD) is a syndrome that interferes with an individual's ability to focus (inattention), regulate activity level (hyperactivity), and inhibit behavior (impulsivity). It is one of the most common learning disorders in children and adolescents. It affects and estimated five percent of youths ages 9 to 17. About 3 times more boys than girls are diagnosed. ADHD usually becomes evident in preschool or early elementary years, frequently persisting into adolescence and adulthood. Many adults outgrow the hyperactivity part of ADHD.

Although most children have some symptoms of hyperactivity, impulsivity, and inattention, there are those in whom these behaviors persist and become the rule rather than the exception. These individuals need to be assessed by health care professionals with input from parents and teachers. The diagnosis results from a thorough review of a physical examination, a variety of psychological tests, and the observable behaviors in the child's everyday settings. A diagnosis of ADHD requires that six or more of the symptoms for inattention or for hyperactivity-impulsivity be present for at least six months, appear before the child is seven years old, and be evident across at least two of the child's environments, such as at home, in school, on the playground, etc. ADHD has been classified into three subtypes: predominantly inattentive, predominantly hyperactive-impulsive, and the combined type (APA, 2000).

What Causes ADHD?

The exact causes of ADHD are unknown. Scientific evidence indicates that this is a neurologically based medical problem and researchers are coming closer to understanding the causes. The biological basis of the disorder appears to lie in differences in brain structure and function as well as the presence of certain genetic abnormalities (Sousa, 2007).

The Attention Loop: Because one of the main characteristics of ADHD (as well as attention deficit disorder, ADD) is the inability to control attention, recent research has focused on how the brain attends to

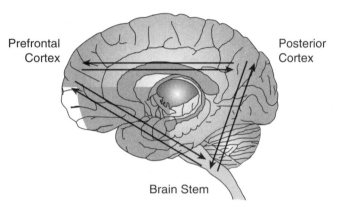

incoming and internal stimuli. Attention seems to be the result of a loop-like process that involves the brain stem, the posterior (rear) cortex, and the prefrontal cortex (Figure 4.1). The brain stem collects the incoming data and sends it to the posterior cortex, which integrates the data. Interpreting the data is the job of the prefrontal cortex, and its interpretation can modify what the brain stem transmits, thus completing the loop. Any breakdown in this loop will interfere with attention, and the degree of breakdown will affect the nature of the attention deficit, some with and others without hyperactivity (Goldberg, 2001).

Figure 4.1 The attention loop involves the brainstem, the prefrontal cortex, and the posterior cortex.

Because gifted children have a higher functioning prefrontal cortex than their average peers, breakdowns in the attention loop are more likely to occur in the posterior cortex (sensory integration and emotional input) and in the brain stem. This may explain why gifted children with ADHD are more prone to have social and emotional problems rather than cognitive ones.

Characteristics of Gifted Children With ADHD

Assuming proper diagnosis, gifted children with ADHD do differ from average children with ADHD in the following ways (Lovecky, 2004).

- **Testing.** Gifted children with ADHD show great variability on tests of achievement and intelligence. Their performance is scattered and they miss many easy items while answering the difficult items correctly. Because of their excellent memory, they tend to score high on the subtests involving mathematics. They also tend to score high in abstract reasoning ability.
- **Study Skills.** These children often learn more rapidly and exhibit more mature metacognitive strategies (e.g., using of mnemonics; grouping by category, patterns, or spatial characteristics; and recalling by association) than their age peers. However, they sometimes forget to use the strategies or may not use them efficiently. They tend to have more problems with study skills, such as note taking, organizing ideas, and outlining.
- **Developmental Issues.** Gifted children with ADHD show greater differences in their degree of social and emotional development than their average peers. They may behave less maturely than their peers in some situations and more maturely in others. They form friendships with those who will share their complex interests with the same intensity. However, they often misread social cues and show poor understanding of group dynamics and goals. They tend to be more emotional and show greater sensitivity than their age peers.
- **Interests.** Compared to their age peers, these children usually have more specialized interests and seek out activities that have greater complexity. Their interests are generally intense and last for years.

Gifted children with ADHD differ from other gifted children in that they

- Show greater degrees of differences in development across cognitive, social, and emotional areas and in their ability to act maturely.
- Have less ability to think sequentially and to use working memory adequately.
- Experience greater difficulty solving problems that use part-to-whole relationships because they have trouble selecting the main points among data.
- Tend to complete less work, hurry through it, take too long to complete simple things, and often change topics on projects.
- Find it difficult to work in groups, even with groups of gifted children.
- Do not feel a high degree of satisfaction or intrinsic reward for completing a project.

GIFTEDNESS AND AUTISM

To understand this twice-exceptional population, let us first examine the nature of autism and then look at some unique characteristics of individuals who are both gifted and autistic.

What Is Autism Spectrum Disorder?

In autism spectrum disorder (or autism), neurological problems develop that make it difficult for a person to communicate and form relationships with others. It is a spectrum disorder that runs the gamut from mild to severe. In 2007, the Centers for Disease Control and Prevention issued a report that looked at thousands of eight-year-olds and found that the prevalence of autism has risen to 1 in 150 American children, and almost 1 in 94 boys (CDC, 2007).

The symptoms of autism usually appear before the age of three. Children with autism do not interact well with others and may avoid eye contact. They may resist attention and affection, and they rarely seem upset when a parent leaves or show pleasure when the parent returns. Understanding the cues of others—such as a smile, wink, or grimace—is difficult for them as well. Some children with autism also tend to be physically aggressive at times, particularly when they are in a strange or overwhelming environment. At times they will break things, attack others, or harm themselves.

There is no general agreement on the causes of autism, and given that this is a spectrum disorder, it is likely that there are multiple causes. Researchers have found that autism may be associated with genetic defects (autistic characteristics tend to run in families), with structural abnormalities in the frontal lobes and brain stem, or with low concentrations of serotonin and melatonin. There has been an enormous increase in the number of children diagnosed with autism in the last 10 years. At first, researchers thought the increase was due to two factors: the broadening of the diagnostic criteria for autism and the greatly increased diagnosis of autism at younger ages. Both these factors could make it seem like there are more autism cases than there were before. However, a recent California study concluded that these two factors accounted for less than half of the increase. Clearly, some other factors are involved. This study suggests that scientific research should focus on fetal and early childhood exposure to environmental factors, such as pesticides, viruses, and harmful chemicals in household products (Hertz-Picciotto & Delwiche, 2009).

Types of Autism: Autism spectrum disorder includes the following five types:

- **Classical or Kanner-Type.** Sometimes called early infantile autism, this type is characterized by the early onset of symptoms, lack of eye contact, late speech, repetitive behaviors, and in some cases, possible mental retardation.

- **Asperger Syndrome.** A pervasive developmental disorder on the autism spectrum characterized by social deficits, relatively normal cognitive and language development, and the presence of an intense, idiosyncratic interest in a single object or topic to the exclusion of all others.
- **Pervasive Developmental Disorder (PDD).** Also known as atypical autism, this is a catchall category for children who do not meet the defining criteria before the age of 3. Sometimes this classification is used when the condition appears less severe or inconsistent with the general criteria. It is usually more closely aligned with classical autism than with Asperger syndrome.
- **Rett's Disorder.** A rare disorder that almost exclusively affects females. Rett's children begin to develop normally. Then they begin to lose their communication and social skills. Beginning at the age of 1 to 4 years, repetitive hand movements replace purposeful use of the hands, and they have difficulty controlling their feet.
- **Childhood Disintegrative Disorder.** These children develop normally for at least two years, and then lose some or most of their communication and social skills. Loss of vocabulary is more dramatic than in classical autism.

For the purposes of this book, we will focus on classical (Kanner-type) autism and Asperger syndrome because these are the two types that are most likely to coexist with giftedness.

Impact of Giftedness on Individuals With Classic (Kanner-Type) Autism

Giftedness also runs on a spectrum from mildly gifted to genius. It is sometimes difficult to separate a high functioning individual with mild autism from someone who is gifted because they can both share many similar traits. For example, both the gifted and autistic tend to focus intently on objects, behaviors, and activities. They display similar negative behaviors, such as stubbornness, indifference to socialization and dress, discourteousness, and resistance to teacher authority. Both groups are powerful visual thinkers and have keen senses. Individuals who are both gifted and autistic are difficult to identify because their strengths and weaknesses can mask each other. Nonetheless, they have to manage and adjust to their environment. Having these dual exceptionalities can result in the following positive and negative impacts (Cash, 1999).

> It can be difficult to separate a high functioning individual with mild autism from someone who is gifted because they can both share many similar traits.

- **Positive Impacts.** The key to the success of gifted/autistic individuals often starts in school where they can learn compensatory strategies to manipulate their autistic weaknesses and tendencies. Through behavior modification programs and by using metacognitive strategies, they can gain acceptance and credibility, and be more easily accepted by society.
- **Negative Impacts.** Gifted/autistic individuals frequently move from one environment that praises their strengths to another that misunderstands and fears their unusual and perplexing characteristics. In school, gifted/autistic students may be placed in classes where their seemingly contradictory behaviors and non-traditional social interactions often confuse uninformed teachers and peers. As a result, the gifted/autistic students may be criticized and suffer social rejection. Although some of these dual-exceptional students are insensitive to the lack of connectedness (a typical autistic characteristic), others are frustrated by the ostracism.

Too often, gifted/autistic individuals do not receive intellectual opportunities and are frequently placed in classes with mentally-challenged students. The school focuses on addressing only their weaknesses and remediation becomes the sole educational goal. Consequently, these students can suffer from depression, low self-esteem, and lack of

Too often, gifted/autistic individuals do not receive intellectual opportunities and are frequently placed in classes with mentally-challenged students.

motivation. On the other hand, more educators are becoming aware that some autistic children may also be gifted, and are exploring interventions, such as early identification and screening, the use of diagnostic instruments, coordinated teacher and parent training, parent support networks, behavior modification programs, and learning theory reform. If prompt identification and appropriate interventions begin in school, there is a greater likelihood that gifted/autistic individuals can develop into important and contributing adults (Cash, 1999).

Asperger Syndrome

Identified in 1944 by Austrian physician Hans Asperger, this syndrome is a developmental disorder with many of the same symptoms of autism. Asperger syndrome (AS) may occur in as many as 36 out of 10,000 children, or about 1 in 280. The number of occurrences is changing as AS becomes better known and as the number of professionals diagnosing it increases. AS has often been referred to as High-Functioning Autism (HFA) because people with the disorder generally display higher mental performance than those with typical autism. But there are some differences. Compared to high-functioning autism, it is believed that in AS

- The onset is generally later (Autism is not usually diagnosed until around the age of 3, whereas AS usually is not diagnosed until the child is 6 or 7 years of age.)
- The outcome is usually more positive
- Social and communication deficits are less severe
- Targeted interests are more prominent
- Clumsiness is seen more frequently
- Neurological disorders are less common
- Visual processing speeds are faster
- Language skills are significantly better

Because of these differences and the results of recent studies, researchers are still debating whether AS and HFA are just different variations along a continuous spectrum (Ring, Woodbury-Smith, Watson, Wheelwright, & Baron-Cohen, 2008) or are, in fact, separate disorders (Spek, Scholte, & van Berckelaer-Onnes, 2008; Tsatsanis, 2005).

Because of the results of recent studies, researchers are debating whether Asperger syndrome and High-Functioning Autism are variations along a continuous spectrum or are separate disorders.

Like classical autism, AS is a lifelong condition. The first symptoms of the condition usually appear after the age of 18 months and are characterized by poor motor coordination and late mobility. As the child develops, other symptoms become evident, such as routinized obsessive-compulsive behaviors, poor motor coordination with clumsy gait, strong attachments to places, poor eye contact, difficulty in relating to people, lack of empathy for others, and depression. Speech is often repetitive and pedantic, with monotone intonation and the absence of first person pronouns.

That individuals with AS have problems with social interaction can be a particularly burdensome characteristic because it carries into adulthood, causing social isolation and frustration. Children with AS are often unable to understand the social customs associated with dating or to pick up on nonverbal social cues, such as eye contact, voice intonation, or gesturing. As a result, individuals with AS often devise a set of rules to cope with social interactions. The rules are generally inflexible and serve only to further isolate these individuals rather than help them succeed in social situations. Several programs have been devised to help students with AS enhance their social skills.

Genetic Components: There is substantial evidence that both classical autism and AS have genetic components. First, both conditions have a significantly high male to female ratio. These gender differences are far too great to be explained entirely by differences in socialization. They more likely reflect developmental differences between the two sexes regulated by genetic information. Second, there is an increased incidence of AS profiles among relatives of children with AS. Third, there is an increased incidence of other developmental disorders among the siblings of children with AS.

One early study investigated the genetic connection through a series of cognitive performance tasks to test whether the parents of children diagnosed with AS displayed similar cognitive traits (Baron-Cohen & Hammer, 1997). Mothers and fathers of children with AS performed better than the control subjects on those tasks associated with AS strengths, but worse on the tasks associated as weakness in AS profiles. This finding lent support to the notion that parents of children with AS carry mild forms of the disorder. Another finding was that male parents performed lower on all tasks than female parents, suggesting that the genetic factors that contribute to AS are more closely linked to males. However, it is likely that AS results from many contributing factors, including genetic ones.

More recent studies have centered on trying to identify specific gene variants that may be associated with traits common to autism and AS. It appears that different sets of genes are responsible for the social, communication, and behavioral impairments. In separate studies, researchers have found genetic linkages to restricted and repetitive behavior (Shao et al., 2003) and to language delay and social interaction (Depienne et al., 2007). The search continues.

Brain Imaging: Only a handful of studies have used brain imaging techniques to examine differences in cerebral functions of children with AS compared to children without AS. Using fMRI, one study found some differences in frontal lobe activity of children with and without AS during a task involving social judgment (Oktem, Diren, Karaagaoglu, & Anlar, 2001). A comparison MRI study of 21 adults with AS and 24 matched controls found significant reductions in gray matter (the surface cortex) volume in frontal lobes and cerebellum. There was also an increase in white matter in the limbic area of the left hemisphere. A third finding was that the controls exhibited age-related changes in the volume of the cerebral hemispheres and in gray matter but the AS group did not. A follow-up study extended this study substantially and demonstrated a consistent pattern of findings across age, severity of autism, race, and ethnicity (McAlonan et al., 2002). Only further research will tell us whether these findings can help in the diagnosis and prevention of autism and its related spectrum disorders.

General Characteristics of AS: More studies on AS have been undertaken in recent years as researchers try to further understand this exceptionality. Surveys of these studies found that children and adolescents with AS tended to have the following characteristics (Barnhill, 2001; Henderson, 2001; Lee & Park, 2007):

- An IQ range similar to the general public
- High oral language skills; low written language skills

- Fluent verbalization but poor problem-solving skills
- Knowledge of simple vocabulary but difficulty with inferences and abstract language
- Pronounced emotional difficulties recognized by others but not by themselves
- An approach to new learning that resembles a learned helplessness
- Low sensory thresholds causing a sensory overload that may be overwhelming
- Low ability to plan use of time or estimate time passage
- Difficulty with social/emotional cues
- Difficulty acknowledging that a perspective different from their own can exist

Direct and specific skill strategies can be used to help individuals with AS cope with the challenges posed by these characteristics, especially in school and social situations.

Identification of Gifted Students With AS: Until recently, AS was generally diagnosed much later than classic autism, most likely because individuals with AS had relatively normal early development. As practitioners become more familiar with AS, earlier diagnosis means earlier intervention and appropriate services. Early diagnosis becomes even more important for gifted individuals with AS so that programs can be devised to address their gifts as well as their disabilities. Finding the measure to accurately identify gifted students with AS has not been easy. However, Henderson (2001) reports that the behavioral patterns, motor skills, gifted and talented characteristics, and leadership can be measured reliably by various instruments.

> When given educational support and appropriate opportunities, many students with Asperger syndrome are academically successful and attend college.

To parents and teachers, AS appears a serious disability, especially because it inhibits social interaction. Yet, individuals with AS develop deep interests in narrow topics and can often succeed in areas where attention to detail is critical and social discourse minimal. When given educational support and appropriate opportunities, many students with AS are academically successful and attend college. Many persons with AS are drawn to science, inventions, mathematics, and computers and can have successful careers in these areas.

Misdiagnosis of AS: Just as the characteristics of giftedness can be misread as signs of psychological disorders and learning disabilities, so can they lead to a misdiagnosis of Asperger syndrome. Intense fascination with a specific subject, an uneven profile of abilities, original problem-solving methods, and exceptional concentration are not only components of AS, but of giftedness as well. Someone not familiar with the asynchronous development of gifted children that we discussed in Chapter 1 could mistake these characteristics as signs of AS.

Although there can be similarities between a gifted child and a child with AS, there are some very clear differences. For example, the *Diagnostic and Statistical Manual for Mental Disorders* (APA, 2000) cites a qualitative impairment in social interaction as one of the two main characteristics of AS. A highly gifted child's atypical social interactions or unusual modes of commenting could be misinterpreted as being characteristics of AS. However, a lack of social or emotional reciprocity is characteristic of AS while gifted children most often show a tremendous concern for

> Someone not familiar with the asynchronous development of gifted children could mistake their characteristics as signs of Asperger syndrome.

others. The gifted children may not always know how to express it appropriately, but the concern is there.

The manual's second major diagnostic component of AS describes an encompassing preoccupation with one or more interests that is abnormal either in intensity or focus. The special interest may come and go, but it will dominate the child's free time and conversation. When engaged in their special interest, children with AS display an uneven profile of abilities with remarkable long-term memory, exceptional concentration, and original methods of problem solving. At the same time, they may show motor clumsiness and a lack of motivation and attention for activities that would engage peers of their age.

All of these characteristics may be seen in gifted children and can easily be mistaken as AS by someone not familiar with the special needs of gifted youth. The unusual behaviors of many gifted children do strike those who are not familiar with gifted characteristics as a qualitative impairment in social interactions. However, these interactions are of a different nature and likely have different causes.

HYPERLEXIA

Although there is not a precise definition of hyperlexia, the term is applied to children who exhibit precocious reading skills but have significant problems with learning and language as well as impaired social skills. Children with hyperlexia often exhibit behaviors associated with other developmental disorders. As a result, they may also be diagnosed with autism, pervasive development disorder, attention deficit disorder, or Asperger syndrome. Others receive no diagnosis and are considered just precocious readers. Researchers are still not in agreement as to whether hyperlexia is a form of autism or a separate and distinct language disorder.

> Researchers still do not agree whether hyperlexia is a form of autism or a separate and distinct language disorder.

PET scans detect significant differences in activity in the brain of a child with hyperlexia compared to that of a typical reader of the same age. Figure 4.2 shows how the brain of a child with hyperlexia recruits more areas during reading than the brain of peer who does not have the disorder (Restak, 2001). Another study using fMRI technology found similar patterns (Turkeltaub et al., 2004).

 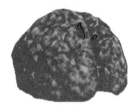

Figure 4.2 These PET scans show how the brain of a young reader with hyperlexia (left) is much more active (red areas) during reading than that of an age-matched reader without hyperlexia.

Source: Adapted from Restak, 2001.

Identification of Hyperlexia

The frequency of hyperlexia appears to be about the same in girls as in boys (Grigorenko et al., 2002). Children are suspected of having hyperlexia if they exhibit the following three characteristics (Kupperman, Bligh, & Barouski, 2002):

- **Precocious Reading Ability.** By the age of 18 to 24 months, parents are amazed by the child's ability to name letters and numbers. This skill was not taught to the child by parents. By 3 years of age, these children see printed words and read them, sometimes before they have really learned to talk. They are fascinated by the printed word.
- **Peculiar Language Learning Disorders.** Of those children who talk (there are also nonverbal hyperlexics), nearly all display echolalic speech (repeating what others have said) and good auditory memory for songs learned by rote, the alphabet, and numbers. They also show impairment in the ability to initiate or sustain a conversation, despite adequate speech.
- **Problems in Social Development.** The behaviors that may be observed include the following: noncompliance, extreme need for sameness, difficulty with transitions, difficulty in socializing with peers, and impaired ability to make peer friendships.

Types of Hyperlexia

Because behavioral symptoms subside in many children as their language comprehension and expression improve, identification of true hyperlexia is difficult. The studies on hyperlexia seem to indicate that there are three types (Kupperman et al., 2002):

- **Just Precocious.** These are children who have very precocious reading skills and who are normal in all other aspects of development. They do not display any long-lasting autistic behaviors. Rather, these are normal children who just enjoy reading and whose brains are considerably more active when reading (see Figure 4.2).
- **Precocious Reading/Autistic-Like Behaviors.** These children display exceptional reading skills coupled with autistic-like behaviors, such as echolalia (the involuntary parrotlike repetition of a word or phrase just spoken by another person), and impaired social skills. But these children are not autistic and may represent the group where a specific diagnosis of hyperlexia is most appropriate. The long-term outlook for this group is good.
- **Savant Behavior.** These children have such extraordinary reading skills that they display savant skills, associated with autism or some other developmental disorder. In this case, the hyperlexia is but one symptom of a more serious spectrum disorder.

Dealing With Hyperlexia

Because of the various types of hyperlexia, a comprehensive assessment by a knowledgeable team is essential for proper diagnosis. For instance, it is important to differentiate these children from those whose language disorders may be related to a hearing loss, autism mental retardation, or emotional disturbance. Although children with hyperlexia are like other children with language learning disorders, they are more fortunate in that they have the reading skill to use as a supportive resource.

> Many children with hyperlexia lose their autistic-like characteristics by second or third grade.

Nonetheless, hyperlexia is puzzling because it raises questions about the relationship between reading and language. A child may display exceptional reading ability while also presenting a collection of linguistic, behavioral, and social deficits.

Many children with hyperlexia show remarkable improvement from the time they are first diagnosed at the age of 2 or 3 until they enter second grade. At first, their behavior looks autistic (i.e., they are echolalic and not able to understand much language). However, as their language comprehension and expressive language improve, these children emerge out of their autism. By the time they reach first or second grade, they lose most of their autistic characteristics but may still remain aloof from other children. At this point, they can be taught social skills. Emphasis should be placed on intensive speech and language therapy because the success of these children depends on the development of their comprehension and use of language (Kupperman et al., 2002).

APPLICATIONS

CHARACTERISTICS OF
GIFTED CHILDREN WITH DISABILITIES

Although recognizing giftedness in children with disabilities is no easy task, some characteristics do emerge that can help educators (and parents) in this process. Tables 4.2 and 4.3 on the following pages are adapted from the work of Colleen Willard-Holt (1999) who surveyed the research literature and collected characteristics of children with dual exceptionalities. Her work remains the most comprehensive survey to date.

Table 4.2 shows the characteristics of gifted students who also have physical, hearing, and vision impairments. Table 4.3 describes the characteristics of gifted students who also have learning disabilities and attention problems. It is important to note that some students are misdiagnosed with attention-deficit hyperactivity disorder (ADHD) when in fact they are gifted and are reacting to an inappropriate learning environment.

One way to distinguish between the two is to examine the persistence and pervasiveness of the problem behavior. Gifted children are more likely to act out in specific situations where they are not challenged. Students who display problem behavior in all situations may have ADHD. It is also possible for a child to be both gifted and have ADHD.

Table 4.2   Characteristics of Gifted Students With Physical, Hearing, and Vision Impairments

Gifted With Physical Disabilities	Gifted With Hearing Impairments	Gifted With Vision Impairments
❑ Development of compensatory skills ❑ Creative in finding alternative ways of communicating and accomplishing tasks ❑ Impressive store of knowledge ❑ Good sense of humor ❑ Superior memory ❑ Insightful ❑ Ability to set and strive for long-term goals ❑ Advanced academic skills ❑ Good problem-solving skills ❑ Persistence and patience ❑ Greater maturity than age mates ❑ High motivation to achieve ❑ Self-criticism and perfectionism ❑ Possible difficulty with abstractions ❑ Possible limited achievement due to pace of work	❑ Development of speech and reading skills without instruction ❑ Early reading ability ❑ Function in regular school setting ❑ High reasoning ability ❑ Rapid grasp of ideas ❑ Excellent memory ❑ Nontraditional ways of getting information ❑ Self-starter ❑ Intuitive ❑ Ingenuity in problem solving ❑ Delays in concept attainment ❑ Symbolic language abilities ❑ Wide range of interests ❑ Good sense of humor ❑ Enjoys manipulating the environment	❑ Fast rate of learning ❑ Excellent memory ❑ Superior verbal communication skills and vocabulary ❑ Advanced problem-solving skills ❑ Motivation to know ❑ Excellent ability to concentrate ❑ Creative production of thought that progresses more slowly than sighted students ❑ Slower rate of cognitive development than sighted students

Source: Adapted from Willard-Holt, 1999.

Table 4.3 Characteristics of Gifted Students With Learning Disabilities and Attention Problems

Gifted With Learning Disabilities	Gifted Who Are Bored	Gifted With ADHD
❑ High abstract reasoning ❑ Advanced vocabulary ❑ Good mathematical skills ❑ Sophisticated sense of humor ❑ Keen visual memory and spatial skills ❑ Insightful ❑ Creative ❑ Imaginative ❑ Good problem-solving skills ❑ High performance in science, music, arts ❑ Difficulty with memorization, computation, phonics, spelling ❑ Grasp of metaphors and satire ❑ Understanding of complex systems and models ❑ Often fails to complete assignments ❑ Difficulties with sequential tasks	❑ Poor attention and daydreaming ❑ Low tolerance with tasks that seem irrelevant ❑ Question school customs, rules, and traditions ❑ High activity level ❑ May need less sleep ❑ Begin many projects but take few to completion ❑ Lose or forget homework ❑ Disorganized ❑ Judgment lags behind intellectual growth ❑ Intensity may lead to power struggle with authorities ❑ May appear careless ❑ Difficulty restraining desire to talk ❑ High sensitivity to criticism ❑ Do not exhibit problem behavior in all settings	❑ Poor sustained attention ❑ Shift from one uncompleted activity to another ❑ Diminished persistence on tasks not having immediate consequences ❑ Impulsive ❑ Poor delay of gratification ❑ More active and more restless than other children ❑ Often talk excessively ❑ Poor adherence to requests to regulate behavior in social settings ❑ Inattentive to details ❑ Often interrupt or intrude on others ❑ Highly sensitive to criticism ❑ Often lose things required for tasks at school or at home ❑ Problem behaviors exist in *all* settings, but are more severe in some ❑ High variability in task performance and in time used to accomplish tasks

Source: Adapted from Willard-Holt, 1999.

APPLICATIONS

SOME TEACHING STRATEGIES FOR GIFTED/LEARNING DISABLED STUDENTS

Several successful teaching strategies and practices have been suggested in the literature. These should be considered in addition to providing supplemental gifted services for students who are both gifted and learning disabled (Baum & Owen, 2004; Dix & Schafer,1996; Rivera, Murdock, & Sexton,1995; Winebrenner, 2003).

Instruction

- **Staff Development.** Ongoing staff development is necessary to ensure that educators have the information they need to screen, identify, and successfully teach gifted/learning disabled students.
- **Basic Skills.** Teachers should continue with their instruction in basic skills because these students often have learning problems in these areas.
- **Technology.** Incorporate modern technology into lessons whenever possible. Equipment such as cameras, calculators, computers, and audio and video recorders can help students reach their potential and produce quality work. It also teaches students a useful life skill.
- **Student Strengths and Weaknesses.** Students already know their weaknesses; help them find, appreciate, and use their strengths. Offer options that allow students to use their strengths and preferred ways of learning.
- **Classroom Materials and Assessment.** When possible, students need to select from a variety of classroom materials to show mastery of the learning in a manner that matches their strengths. A variety of assessment tools, such as performance measures and portfolios, should also be available. Consider allowing students to take tests in separate, supervised environments so they can either read the test aloud to themselves or have someone else read it to them. Some students have difficulty concentrating on tests and a quiet place allows a student to focus. Furthermore, listening to a voice read the questions aloud helps the student better understand the questions.
- **Compensation Strategies.** Teachers should neither focus on students' weaknesses nor ignore them. Students need to be taught compensation strategies to address their weaknesses. For example, they can learn calculator skills to do mathematics computation or learn to use a computer and a spell checker to compensate for poor spelling.
- **Instructional Approaches.** For most of these students, it is better to teach the concepts first and details second. Make sure students see the big picture before they try to learn its pieces. Other strategies could include having students watch a video before and after studying a novel or other unit of work, hear a story read aloud before reading it individually, and work from graphic organizers that fit on one page so that students can see the entire unit content. Emphasize higher-order abstract thinking, creativity, and a problem-solving approach. Promote active inquiry, discussion, and experimentation.
- **Teaching Strategy and Learning Disability.** Whenever possible, match the teaching strategy to address the learning disability. For example, if a student has auditory processing difficulties, avoid a quick-response format as these students will need more time to respond to verbal inquiries.

- **Number of Instructions.** Remember that working memory has a limited capacity, so limit the number of instructions given at any one time.
- **Using Boards.** Because many of these students need visual tools to help them remember directions or steps in a procedure, use a board to write down important information.
- **Modeling.** Allow students to observe others who are successfully performing a task before they try it themselves. Develop models that demonstrate different ways of thinking and communicating.
- **Visual and Tactile-Kinesthetic Activities.** Many students with learning difficulties are global learners who prefer visual and tactile-kinesthetic formats. Some students with learning problems may have sensory challenges. Classroom strategies that include visual and hands-on activities take advantage of these students' learning strengths. Use musical chants, raps, rhymes, or rhythms for students who respond to those methods. For many students, singing or chanting the content makes mastery much easier to achieve. Build movement into learning tasks. Ask students to stand or jump to indicate their responses to questions. Use team games where students can walk to different areas of the room to indicate a response. Such opportunities meet students' needs to learn from the concrete to the abstract.
- **Self-Concept.** Find opportunities to assist in strengthening the students' self-concept. Help students set realistic short-term goals and to take credit for reaching those goals, even if they represent only a part of the entire task. This approach is highly effective in helping discouraged learners become positively motivated to put more effort into their work because it makes larger assignments seem more manageable.
- **Time.** Provide for individual pacing in areas of the students' strengths and disabilities.

Classroom Dynamics

- **Proximity and Quiet.** Place students with attention problems near the teacher, and provide for them a quiet space with a minimum of distractions. Another option is to offer these students choices of different work areas. They can choose the place to do their work as long as they follow three simple rules: (1) Do not bother anyone while you are working, including the teacher, (2) Do not call attention to yourself or the fact you are doing something different from other students, and (3) Do the work you are supposed to do. Students who follow these expectations can choose where they will work. Those who do not will have their work area chosen by the teacher, one day at a time.
- **Eye Contact.** These students often have short attention spans and are easily distracted. Before giving individual instructions, make eye contact with the student to ensure that attention is focused on you.
- **Expectations.** Expect students to participate in all activities and strive for normal peer interactions whenever possible. Facilitate acceptance and demand respect for all members of the class. Treat a student with a disability the same way you would treat a student without that disability.
- **Differences.** Model ways to celebrate individual differences. Take time at the beginning of the school year to help all your students appreciate, respect, and support individual differences in everything from observable physical differences to apparent differences in learning abilities. At appropriate times throughout the year, discuss the implications of talents and disabilities with the class.
- **Help With Getting Organized.** Give specific instruction in organizational techniques. Consider providing color-coded notebooks by subject areas and two sets of texts, one that can be kept at home. Teach students to organize their lockers, desks, and supplies. Help students learn to use an assignment notebook or personal desk assistant to keep track of assignments and long-term projects.

From a Teacher's Desk: *A Secondary Example*

Mr. Darron teaches the technology class "Engineering Design and Development" at Monument High School. During the semester, students work individually to construct a solution to an open-ended engineering problem. This year Mr. Darron has several students who are having difficulties completing work. They have the background knowledge and desire to complete their individual work, but they seem to lack the attention needed to follow through. To help students who were having problems staying on task, he created some tools to aid in student success. The three tools he chose to use were (a) timelines, (b) self-assessments, and (c) progress reports.

Timelines. Some of his students benefited from shorter timelines with frequent check-in times. These students needed due dates that were closer together in order for them to feel like they could be successful. Students had broken down the steps they needed to complete the work and Mr. Darron provided check-in dates individualized to each student's needs.

Self-assessments. Mr. Darron included self-assessments during each stage of the students' work process. He found that these self-assessments helped his students connect their progress in class with their work habits, and also helped them understand which strategies were working better for them so they could adjust for the next due date. An example of what this is:

How Is My Progress?

Tasks	Evaluation
Today I worked on: 1) _____ . _____ Completed? Y N 2) _____ . _____ Completed? Y N	Check ONLY if you did this to the best of your ability _____ I completed my goals. _____ I used my time wisely.
Prediction Next week, I plan to focus on: 1) _____ 2) _____	**Needs** Questions I have after today: Materials/resources I want to use next week:

Progress Reports. Finally, Mr. Darron included progress reports within the structure of the semester. All students presented regular progress reports to the class. These progress reports as well as their final written report helped prepare them for the final defense of their solutions to a panel of outside reviewers at the end of the semester. Students were motivated by each other's progress and helped students discuss potential dilemmas in their project solutions. The final defense also engaged the students in real work of an engineer, which led to students finding the tasks relevant and worth completing.

Teachers who have integrated technology into their classes offer the following suggestions:

- All instruction should be contoured according to students' strengths and weaknesses, especially when addressing twice exceptional students. Their needs and abilities are more extreme than most students. Technology is an excellent tool to use as a motivator as well as an instructor for meeting their needs.
- For the student that works quickly and autonomously, allow them to use the computer to type their work, whether in class or at a computer lab, with a partner or alone.
- For students who best interpret information using auditory senses, let them listen to eBooks (electronic books, often free) online or books on tape and compact discs (CD).
- For students who learn visually, allow them to draw on the board and/or project an image using an overhead or document camera.
- For students with verbal/linguistic strengths, encourage and allow them to share mnemonics using instruments and even record them with handheld devices to playback for others.

Often these students' strengths can be harnessed as models for other students, and it is they, in fact, who become the teachers. They will bestow the greatest gifts of all—creative, revolutionary ways to consider and comprehend ideas and information.

APPLICATIONS

STRATEGIES FOR GIFTED YOUTH WITH SPATIAL STRENGTHS

Gifted youth with spatial strengths and verbal deficiencies need to have their strengths recognized and nurtured by working with complex material that requires creativity and higher order thinking skills. Teaching strategies that are not generally successful in teaching gifted students with spatial strengths and verbal deficiencies include rote memorization, forced oral reading, text-based instruction, and use of teacher-directed activities. The following four specific strategies can be successful for use with all students. Studies indicate that they are especially helpful for learners with spatial strengths and verbal weaknesses (Mann, 2006).

- **Offer Students Choices.** Students should have choices for how they obtain information and the methods in which they communicate their findings. Student products should be assessed based on the content they contain rather than the venue in which they were developed.

- **Explore Student Interests.** Knowledge of individual student's interests, strengths, and weaknesses help the teacher provide meaningful choices and opportunities for students to be successful. Classroom instruction should focus on student strengths rather than dwell on weaknesses. In an environment where remediation is the principal goal, students are constantly focused on what is perceived as "wrong" with them rather than areas in which they can be successful. While core knowledge and skills are important, information can be more effectively acquired in an environment that looks to student strengths.

- **Provide Opportunities for Authentic and Experiential Learning.** Students need to find value in the tasks in which they are asked to perform. Authentic and experiential activities allow student to encounter a variety of skills and the information they need to acquire to be successful.

- **Emphasize Conceptual Understandings With a Whole-to-Part Approach.** Students with spatial strengths tend to process information holistically, so they benefit from instruction that provides them with the big picture. Once they have a vision of the conceptual framework, they can assess how individual concepts fit into that picture. By focusing on conceptual understandings rather than recall of specific facts, these students will build their own scheme of interconnected ideas and make connections to concepts in a wide variety of disciplines.

APPLICATIONS

SOME COUNSELING STRATEGIES FOR
GIFTED STUDENTS WITH LEARNING DISABILITIES

School counselors can play an important role in helping gifted students with learning disabilities adjust and succeed in school. Counselors can contribute in the following ways (McEachern & Bornot, 2001; Reis & Colbert, 2004):

- **Consulting With Parents.** Parents seek answers as to why their child can exhibit intellectual abilities while having difficulty in school performance. Counselors can do the following:
  - Provide parents with information on the diagnosis and suggest strategies that support the education of their child when at home.
  - Reduce tension between parents, teachers, and students and suggest appropriate emotional responses.
  - Set up support groups among parents so they can share similar concerns, discuss strategies for change, and gain confidence in parenting.

- **Sharing Academic Strategies With Teachers.** Counselors can work with teachers to design curriculum and instruction activities that are more likely to keep gifted students with learning disabilities engaged and successful. Here are some ways that counselors can help:
  - Urge that the curriculum focus on exploratory, discovery, and investigative learning, including provisions for the various learning styles of these students. Activities that involve art, photography, drama, and other self-directed and unconventional methods should be encouraged.
  - Include technology in the curriculum, such as using computers for word processing, to improve language and writing skills, and for individualized instruction and introducing calculators and tape recorders (audio and video) as instructional tools.
  - Advise teachers to develop student strengths as well as to remedy student weaknesses. Overemphasis on student weaknesses will lower their self-esteem and confidence. Advise teachers, too, on the importance of providing emotional encouragement and assurance that tell students they can be successful.
  - Use film, videos, books, and guest speakers to expose these students to local and nationally known role models of gifted individuals with learning disabilities who have been successful.
  - Collaborate with teachers of the gifted to discuss ways of supporting the social and psychological needs of these students. These teachers may also agree to conduct small-group counseling sessions and behavior modification interventions in the classroom, so that students do not have to be taken out of class for such activities.
  - Increase teachers' understanding of students who are gifted and have learning disabilities by facilitating and coordinating workshops that offer guest speakers who can give expert information and resources. Counselors can prepare special materials that will help teachers identify these students for referral as well as select and incorporate learning strategies that are likely to be successful.

- **Individual and Group Counseling With Students.** Gifted students with learning disabilities often have difficulty facing the fact that they have some areas of high performance and others in which they are less capable than their peers. Teachers sometimes tell these students that they are bright but lazy and that they are not living up to their potential. The pressure to excel and meet others' expectations often puts these students at greater risk for stress, self-blame, depression, and suicide. Counselor interventions, individual or group, can include the following:

○ Helping these students understand that inadequacy in one area or skill does not mean inadequacy in all areas. Offer ideas on ways to use their strengths to build up their weaknesses.

○ Discouraging negative thinking by helping students rephrase the negativism into positive expressions. Suggest both stress-reduction strategies and healthy coping behaviors.

○ Using art therapy as a creative and symbolic way for relieving the pressure these students feel and for discussing problems and setting goals.

○ Conducting sessions on the use of problem-solving strategies to identify and address areas of strengths and weakness. Also helpful are sessions to teach about constructive peer interactions, goal-setting, and positive study habits, such as note taking, summarizing, and preparing for tests.

• **Advocacy.** Counselors can become effective advocates for these students by

○ Discussing with other school personnel the problems and general needs of these students.

○ Monitoring the progress of these students through their school experiences, assuring that their courses are consistent with their career goals, and encouraging that they are participating in appropriate extracurricular activities.

○ Using peers as tutors in the academic areas for which the gifted students with learning disabilities need assistance.

○ Assuring, as members of the child study team, that these students receive appropriate services, including referrals to outside agencies, if necessary.

Working as a team, school counselors are in a unique position to serve as facilitators, teachers, and advocates for the under-served population of gifted students with learning disabilities.

From a Teacher's Desk: *A Middle School Example*

Middle schools teachers often collaborate with each other during team meetings. This is a great opportunity to discuss students who may need special assistance in classes. These meetings provide fertile ground for collaboration between special resource teachers as well, such as the learning disabilities teacher and the gifted teacher. In one middle school, this has been in place for over five years now with much success.

As part of the Response to Intervention (RTI) model, Pleasant Valley Middle School has been using their "Team Time" to bring together the gifted and resource teachers for planning. They have found that there are many instances in which a student may have needs in terms of gifted issues as well as learning disability issues. These twice-exceptional students benefit from all teachers working together on their behalf.

During one particular session, teachers were coming up with ideas to help a student who was identified gifted, but struggling when he was in the Language Arts block. The gifted teacher had many ideas of how to challenge him when he was in the mathematics and social studies blocks, but when the conversation turned to the latest novel study, the teacher was unsure of some of the latest strategies for struggling readers. The resource teacher was there to help. She suggested that the teacher begin front-loading vocabulary, which means giving the student the vocabulary for the upcoming chapter at least a day or two ahead of time. She also suggested using a graphic organizer for taking notes on the chapter content in order to better prepare for quizzes. The gifted teacher said that she would incorporate some of the graphic organizers into other subjects as well in order for the student to begin to adjust to the note taking strategy.

Due to the collaboration between the general education teachers, gifted teacher, and resource teacher, the staff left the meeting that day with some strategies to help the student reach his goals, not only in the subjects where he was finding much success, but in other subjects as well.

APPLICATIONS

WORKING WITH GIFTED CHILDREN WITH ADHD

Interventions for gifted children with ADHD have to be somewhat different from those recommended for average children with ADHD. Here are some items to consider when developing the Individualized Education Plan (IEP) for these children (Lovecky, 2004):

- **Acceleration.** These children may need acceleration while being taught the metacognitive skills to support the higher level of thinking required for more challenging work. This suggests a differentiated program rather than just being placed in an advanced class.
- **Enhance Strengths, Build on Weaknesses.** Gifted children with ADHD need academic programs that will allow them to enhance their strengths while building on their weaker areas. For example, they may need to be taught organizational and study skills in the context of their high-level work—learnings that their gifted peers without ADHD usually acquire without difficulty. Their program should also provide mentors in their areas of strength to maintain the stimulation and complexity needed to enhance their cognitive development.
- **Team Approach.** Without a comprehensive educational plan that includes addressing their cognitive, social, and emotional needs, these children will not enhance their ability to focus and sustain attention. Further, they may develop ineffective work habits and achieve less. If they lose their interest in learning, emotional and behavioral problems may emerge that can further affect their achievement. A team of specialists with expertise in both giftedness and ADHD is an effective approach for meeting the unique needs of these children.
- **Accommodations.** Consider the following accommodations for students who are gifted and who have ADHD:

Physical Accommodations:

- ○ Preferential seating near the teacher, between well-focused students, and away from distractions
- ○ Quiet areas for study, written work, and hands-on activities
- ○ Post all schedules and classroom rules on board
- ○ Organize workspace

Instructional Accommodations:

- ○ Keep oral directions clear and simple
- ○ Ask the student to repeat back directions when possible
- ○ Make eye contact
- ○ Provide directions in written form
- ○ Divide long-term assignments into manageable tasks
- ○ Allow student to use tape recorder or computer
- ○ Provide extra homework reminders

Behavioral Accommodations:

- ○ Give tasks that can be completed
- ○ Provide positive verbal or written feedback
- ○ Develop private signals with the student as behavior reminders
- ○ Offer reward systems and incentives
- ○ Be consistent with rewards and consequences

- ○ Provide student with responsibilities
- ○ Assign jobs that can be performed well
- ○ Create tangible goals with a reasonable timetable
- ○ Use appropriate school staff for support
- ○ Communicate regularly with parents through letters, meetings, and phone calls

Testing Accommodations:

- ○ Provide a distraction-free area
- ○ Allow extended time

APPLICATIONS

MANAGING STUDENTS WITH ASPERGER SYNDROME

Although students with Asperger syndrome (AS) can be managed in the regular classroom, they often need educational support services. Occasionally, the resource room or tutoring can be helpful by providing individualized instruction and review. However, some students with high-functioning AS are able to adapt and function in school with educators who are understanding, knowledgeable, and flexible. Here are some suggestions for managing students with AS in an instructional setting (Bauer, 2008; Moreno & O'Neal, 2008).

- Keep classroom routines as consistent, predictable, and structured as possible because students with AS do not like surprises.
- Prepare students in advance for any changes or transitions, such as an assembly, substitute teachers, vacation days, and holiday breaks.
- Apply rules carefully. Rules should be clearly expressed and written down. However, they should be applied with some flexibility. That is, instructions do not need to be exactly the same for students with AS as for the rest of the class. This approach also models tolerance for student peers.
- Use visuals (e.g., charts, schedules, lists, and pictures) and emphasize the visual cues that can be used for retention. Although many students with AS have strong visual preferences as part of their learning-style profile, they also have poor visual memory.
- Take full advantage of the student's special area of interest when teaching. Allowing the student access to special interest areas can also be used as a reward for completing other tasks or for displaying appropriate behavior.
- Protect the student from bullying. One approach is to educate peers about learning differences so that the class becomes a supportive social as well as educational environment.
- If your class involves pairing off or choosing partners, either draw numbers or use some other arbitrary means of pairing. Consider asking an especially kind student to agree to choose the student with AS as a partner before the pairing takes place. Students with AS are most often the individuals left with no partner. This is unfortunate since these students could benefit most from having a partner.
- Look for ways to take advantage of the special interest areas of students with AS, such as using them occasionally to help other students. This technique can help the student with AS gain acceptance from peers, who begin to recognize the value of the AS students' capabilities.
- Help students with AS gain proficiency in frontal lobe executive functions by teaching strategies to improve their organizational skills and study habits. Strategies could include having the students put a picture of a pencil on the cover of their notebook or maintaining a list of assignments to be completed at home. Always praise the students when they remember something that was previously forgotten.
- Avoid escalating power struggles. Displays of authority may cause these students to become rigid and stubborn, and their behavior can rapidly get out of control. If that occurs, it is often better to back away and let the situation cool down. Avoid asking vague questions such as, "Why did you do that?" Instead, say, "I did not like it when you slammed your book down when I said it was time for gym. Next time put the book down gently and tell me you are angry. Were you showing me that you did not want to go to gym, or that you did not want to stop reading?" Preventative measures, such as negotiating and offering choices at the outset, may avoid the confrontation entirely.
- Do not take misbehavior personally. Students with AS are typically not manipulative, scheming people who are trying to make your life difficult. Misbehavior is often the result of efforts to survive experiences that may be confusing, disorienting, or frightening. People with AS are, by virtue of their disability, egocentric. Most have extreme difficulty reading the reactions of others.

- Keep the teaching on a concrete level because students with AS have difficulty understanding abstract language forms, such as metaphors, idioms, figurative speech, and sarcasm. When possible, try to recast abstract concepts into simpler and more concrete components.
- Interrupt when students with AS use repetitive verbal arguments or repetitive verbal questions. Continually responding or arguing back seldom stops this behavior. The subject of the argument or question is not always the subject that has upset them. More often they are communicating a feeling of loss of control or uncertainty about someone or something in the environment. Request that they write down the question or argumentative statement, and write down your reply. This has a calming effect and stops the repetitive activity. If that does not work, write down the repetitive question or argument and ask them to write down a logical reply. This distracts from the escalating verbal aspect of the situation and may give the students with AS a more socially acceptable way of expressing frustration or anxiety.
- Assume nothing when assessing skills. For example, a student with AS may be a "whiz" in Algebra, but not able to make simple change at a cash register. Others may have an incredible memory about books they have read, speeches they have heard, or sports statistics, but still may not be able to remember to bring a pencil to class. Uneven skills development is a hallmark of AS.
- Ensure that other members of the school staff who come in contact with students with AS are properly trained in management approaches and are aware of their needs.
- Work closely with the student's parents because they are usually familiar with the management and instructional strategies that have worked in the past. Do not rely on students with AS to relay important messages to their parents about school events, assignments, school rules, etc., unless you try it on an experimental basis with follow-up or unless you are already certain that the students have mastered this skill. Even sending home notes for their parents may not work. The students may not remember to deliver the note or may lose it before reaching home. Phone calls to parents work best. Frequent and accurate communication between the teacher and parent (or primary care-giver) is very important and more likely to result in parents and educators working toward similar and productive solutions.

From a Teacher's Desk: *An Elementary Example*

Children with AS are as exciting as they are exhausting. They often make uninhibited statements that are difficult not to take to heart. They might say things as worse as, "You're the worst teacher in the whole world!" and as wonderful as, "This is the greatest day ever!" The contrast in their expressions and emotions is an analogous parallel for the roller coaster you can join them on, or get sick watching. Sometimes they are looking for attention (positive or negative), or for validation.

The old saying, "Turn that frown upside down" is a good model for changing negative expressions and actions to the positive. It is essential to model appropriate interactions with these students so that classmates can understand and replicate moral behaviors. Here are some statements students with AS might say (sometimes repeatedly until a response is given) and what some classroom teachers have done to change the mood:

Student:	"Why do we have to do this?" (challenging)
Teacher:	(Allow other students to give input) "Who can answer that question?"
Teacher:	(Use logic, reasoning, and/or humor) "Well, my understanding is we do this to learn. If you're learning and you know it, clap your hands!" (CLAP-CLAP–like the primary song) "Okay, if you're ready and you know it and you really want to show it; if you're ready and you know it, stomp your feet!" (STOMP-STOMP). Repeat until all are participating and ready to move on.
Student:	"I don't like this assignment." (manipulating)

Teacher:	(Be patient, gracious) "Thank you for your honesty. What about the assignment do you like?" (If no response, offer an idea) "I like the feeling of accomplishment when I complete a task. Do you feel the same way?"
Teacher:	(Don't fall for the trap. Respond with an unexpected phrase or question.) "What assignments do you like?" (Let them give a few examples.) "Great. When you finish this assignment, you can choose to do one of those tasks."
Student:	"I was bad. I shouldn't have done that. I need to be punished." (self-negativity)
Teacher:	"I am impressed with your self-monitoring. We all make mistakes. How can you overcome this one?" (Let them think for a moment and possibly offer responses.)
Teacher:	"I know when I make a mistake, I make up for it with a 'take two.' I find a balance by making a right for my wrong. What right thing can you do right now?"

Usually such statements are reactions to adverse, unexpected changes in environment or plans that upset the child, which is why they should be taken seriously but not personally.

APPLICATIONS

ENHANCING THE SOCIAL INTERACTION SKILLS OF STUDENTS WITH ASPERGER SYNDROME

Students with Asperger syndrome (AS) usually have difficulty engaging in the social interactions expected for their age. This often leads to social isolation and frustration. Marjorie Bock (2001) has developed a social behavioral learning strategy for students with AS to guide their social interactions. The strategy is composed of four components and is called SODA, an acronym for Stop, Observe, Deliberate, and Act. Each component contains three to five questions or statements that can be individualized to meet the specific needs and age level of students.

STOP

This component helps the student understand the social setting, determine the sequence of events that will occur, and select a low-traffic area to complete the rest of the tasks. The typical questions are the following:

> *What is the room arrangement?*
>
> *What is the activity schedule or routine?*
>
> *Where should I go to observe?*

OBSERVE

The second component helps students note social cues by observing what the people are doing. If they can hear what people are saying, they should listen for similarities across conversations, note the length of a typical conversation, as well as what the people do when the conversation ends. The typical questions are the following:

> *What are the people doing?*
>
> *What are the people saying?*
>
> *What is the length of a typical conversation?*
>
> *What do the people do after they have visited?*

DELIBERATE

The third component helps the students decide what they would like to do and say as well as look for cues to let them know if the people would like to visit longer or end the visit. The typical questions are the following:

> *What would I like to do?*
>
> *What would I like to say?*
>
> *How will I know when others would like to visit longer or would like to end this conversation?*

A C T

The last component helps students interact with others. They select the person with whom they would like to converse and present a greeting. They then listen to the speaker and decide what they would like to learn more about. They share some of their own related experiences and then look for cues to decide if the person wants to continue talking or end the visit. The typical statements are the following:

> *Approach person(s) with whom I like to visit.*
>
> *Say, "Hello, how are you?"*
>
> *Listen to person(s) and ask related questions.*
>
> *Look for cues that this person would like to end or continue the visit.*

This is the basic SODA format. Other questions can be added to each component as needed. Bock suggests that teaching SODA should involve at least one session to present and explain the model, and at least three sessions to demonstrate each component. Students then practice the strategy in class for three sessions, followed by at least three out-of-class situations. The goal here is to get students with AS to replace their inflexible and ineffective social interaction rules with SODA so that they can recognize and attend to social cues, selecting the appropriate response to various social situations.

APPLICATIONS

HELPING STUDENTS WITH HYPERLEXIA

Educators are just beginning to recognize that children who enter school diagnosed with hyperlexia need some special attention. Early intervention seems to be the best remedy for improving their comprehension and use of language as well as their social skills. The American Hyperlexia Association recommends the following considerations in designing school programs for children with hyperlexia (Kupperman et al., 2002).

Placement	Although children with hyperlexia can spell, decode, and write at much higher levels than their peers, their language comprehension and socialization may preclude them from regular school programs. However, their verbal language skills are the reverse of normal development, and special education teachers need to be adequately trained for this unusual developmental situation.
Educational Goals	Instruction should aim to • Facilitate accommodation to school structure and group learning • Develop language comprehension and expression • Improve social interaction with peers • Develop alternative learning strategies • Address behavioral issues
Classroom Conditions	Classrooms (regular or special) that include students with hyperlexia should • Be small so that these students are not overwhelmed with too much peer input • Contain a strong language development component that includes expressive, receptive, and written and oral language activities • Have a structured but not rigid class routine. These children do best when they can anticipate what is happening next and when they get help for schedule changes. • Use a variety of behavioral interventions. Too rigid a behavioral modification system may be frustrating, and these children may not accept behavioral rewards. • Use visual and manipulative materials • Provide opportunities for social interactions with an appropriate peer group • Include opportunities for mainstreaming in areas such as arts, music, athletics, recess, and lunch • Offer the services of speech/language pathologists
Types of Classrooms	KINDERGARTEN Regular Kindergarten: Some children with hyperlexia adjust easily to regular kindergarten with supportive services, such as an aide. Adjustment is easier if these students are given both written and verbal instructions, and given individual as well as group directions. Large class size is often a problem. Developmental Kindergarten: Although the smaller class size and more individualized program can be helpful, other children in the class may have difficulties in areas that are strengths for the child with hyperlexia (e.g., working on letter recognition or shapes). There also may be too much emphasis on the development of pre-reading skills. PRIMARY GRADES Regular Education: This format can work for children with hyperlexia who have had early intervention on language and behavioral skills. The regular education teacher and the class need to be prepared for the child with hyperlexia. Support services and parent involvement may be necessary.

Communication Disorders Classroom: Because of their strong emphasis on language intervention and academic orientation, these classes are usually appropriate for children with hyperlexia. Mainstreaming into regular education is possible, and generally there is enough variety in the peer group to include children with hyperlexia with age-appropriate social skills.

Learning Disabilities Classes: Some children with hyperlexia succeed in these classes where the academic work is highly individualized. However, because children with hyperlexia are quite different from the typical learning-disabled child who has trouble reading, the focus should be on language and socialization issues.

Behavior Disorders and Emotionally Handicapped Classes: These classes are generally inappropriate for children with hyperlexia because their behavioral issues are related to their language disorder. As language skills improve, so does the behavior.

CHAPTER 5

Language Talent

One of the most extraordinary features of the human brain is its ability to acquire spoken language quickly and accurately. We are born with an innate capacity to distinguish the distinct sounds (phonemes) of all the languages on this planet. Eventually, we are able to associate those sounds with arbitrary written symbols (graphemes) to express our thoughts and emotions to others. Ever since Paul Broca discovered evidence in 1861 that the left hemisphere of the brain was specialized for language, researchers have attempted to understand the way in which typical human beings acquire and process their native language.

SOURCES OF LANGUAGE ABILITY

In most people, the left hemisphere is home to the major components of the language processing system (Figure 5.1). Broca's area is a region of the left frontal lobe that is believed to be responsible for processing vocabulary, syntax, and grammar. Recent imaging studies indicate that regions toward the rear of the brain are also involved during the processing of syntax (Tyler & Marslen-Wilson, 2008). Wernicke's area is part of the left temporal lobe and is thought to process the sense and meaning of language. However, the emotional content of language is governed by areas in the right hemisphere.

This strong predisposition for language processing regions to be in the left hemisphere (called *lateralization*) begins at a very early age. Brain imaging studies of infants as young as 4 months of age confirm that the brain possesses neural networks that specialize in responding to the auditory components of language. Using EEG recordings, researchers measured the brain activity of 16 four-month-old infants as they listened to language syllables and acoustic tones. After

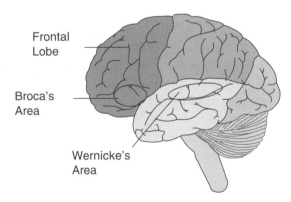

Figure 5.1 In most people, the language system is in the brain's left hemisphere and is comprised of Broca's area and Wernicke's area.

numerous trials, the data showed that syllables and tones were processed primarily in different areas of the left hemisphere, although there was also some right hemisphere activity. For language input, various features, such as the voice and the phonetic category of a syllable, were encoded by separate neural networks into sensory memory (Dehaene-Lambertz, 2000).

In a later study, imaging researchers exposed infants aged 6 to 9 months to both visual and linguistic stimuli and then to visual stimuli alone. They discovered that the infant brain was able to clearly distinguish between the two types of stimuli and process them in separate regional networks (Bortfeld, Wruck, & Boas,

2007). These remarkable findings suggest that, even at this early age, the brain is already organized into functional networks that can distinguish between language fragments and other acoustical or visual input.

The predisposition of the brain to the sounds of language explains why most young children respond to and acquire spoken language quickly. How long the brain retains this responsiveness to the sounds of language is still open to question. However, there does seem to be general agreement among researchers that the window of opportunity for rapidly acquiring language within the language-specific areas of the brain begins to taper off for most people around 10 to 12 years of age. Obviously, one can still acquire a new language long after that age, but it takes more effort because the new language will be spatially separated in the brain from the native language areas.

This spatial separation represents a decrease in the effect of language lateralization, and no one knows exactly why it occurs. However, a recent study may offer a possible clue. Researchers used fMRI scans to examine the effect of age on language lateralization in 170 healthy right-handed children and adults ages 5 to 67. Their findings indicated that language lateralization to the dominant hemisphere (usually the left) increases between the ages of 5 and 20 years, plateaus between 20 and 25 years, and slowly decreases between 25 and 70 years (Szaflarski, Holland, Schmithorst, & Byars, 2006). It seems that as we get older, other brain regions are recruited for processing, and perhaps acquiring, language.

Structure of Language

Languages consist of distinct units of sound called *phonemes*. Each language has its own unique set of phonemes. Linguists cannot agree on the total number of phonemes that comprise all the world's languages, but the range is from 150 to 400. These phonemes consist of all the speech sounds that can be made by the human voice apparatus. Around the age of 6 months or so, infants start babbling, an early sign of language acquisition. Their babbling consists of all those phonemes, even ones they have never heard. Within a few months, however, neural pathways to the phonemes that the brain hears most frequently get strengthened, while those that are rarely or never heard grow weak. Pruning of the weak pathways soon begins, and by about one year of age, the neural networks focus primarily on the sounds of the language being spoken regularly in the infant's environment (Gazzaniga et al., 2002).

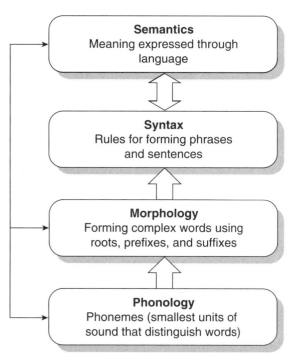

Figure 5.2   The levels of hierarchy in language and in language acquisition. Although the process usually flows from the bottom to the top, recycling from the top to lower levels occurs during complex processing, as indicated by the arrows to the left.

Syntax and Semantics

With more exposure, the brain begins to recognize the hierarchy of language. Phonemes, the basic sounds, can be combined into morphemes, which are the smallest units of language that have meaning. Morphemes can then be combined into words, and words can be put together according to the rules of syntax to form phrases and sentences that have meaning. Toddlers show evidence of their progression through these levels when simple statements, such as "Candy," evolve to more complex ones, "Give me candy." They also begin to recognize that shifting the words in sentences can change their meaning. Figure 5.2 illustrates the hierarchy. When an individual is learning language, the process usually flows from bottom to the top. However, as language skill increases and language processing becomes more complex, recycling from upper to lower levels also occurs.

The brain's ability to recognize different meanings in sentence structure is possible because Broca's and Wernicke's areas establish linked networks that can understand the difference between "The dog chased the cat" and "The cat chased the dog." A significant fMRI study found that Broca's and Wernicke's areas work together to determine whether changes in syntax or semantics result in changes in meaning. For example, "The policeman arrested the thief" and "The thief was arrested by the policeman" have different syntax but the same meaning. The fMRI showed that Broca's area was highly activated when subjects were processing these two sentences. Wernicke's area, on the other hand, was more activated when processing sentences that were semantically—but not syntactically—different, such as "The car is in the garage" and "The automobile is in the garage" (Dapretto & Bookheimer, 1999).

How is it that Wernicke's area can so quickly and accurately decide that two semantically different sentences have the same meaning? The answer may lie in two other recently discovered characteristics of Wernicke's area. One is that the neurons in Wernicke's area are spaced about 20 percent further apart and are cabled together with longer interconnecting fibers than the corresponding area in the right hemisphere of the brain (Galuske, Schlote, Bratzke, & Singer, 2000). The implication is that the practice of language during early human development results in longer and more intricately connected neurons in the Wernicke region.

The second recent discovery regarding Wernicke's area is its ability to recognize predictable events. An MRI study found that Wernicke's area was activated when subjects were shown differently colored symbols in various patterns, whether the individuals were aware of the pattern sequence or not (Bischoff-Grethe, Proper, Mao, Daniels, & Berns, 2000). This predictability-determining role for Wernicke's area suggests that our ability to make sense of language is rooted in our ability to recognize

> The ability to understand language may be rooted in the brain's ability to recognize predictability.

syntax. The researchers noted that language itself is very predicable because it is constrained by the rules of grammar and syntax.

Subsequent studies have reaffirmed how Broca's and Wernicke's areas work together to help the brain understand differences in word form, semantics, and syntax. The studies have also noted that these areas get support from other brain regions during this process when required. Certain regions of the left temporal lobe located to the right of Wernicke's area (see Figure 5.1) were more active during semantic processing, while regions to the left of Wernicke's area were more active during syntactic processing (Heim, Eickhoff, & Amunts, 2008; Humphries, Binder, Medler, & Liebenthal, 2006; Tyler, Marslen-Wilson, & Stamatakis, 2005).

Genes, Language, and the Environment

The production of phonemes by infants is the result of genetically determined neural programs; however, language exposure is environmental. These two components interact to produce an individual's language system and, assuming no pathologies, sufficient competence to communicate clearly with others. Scientists, of course, are interested in the exact nature of that interaction in an effort to determine how genes can be modified by the environment, and vice versa. These gene-environment relationships are called *genotype-environment correlations* (GECs). Research on GECs helps to explain the degree to which a child's genetic destiny can be modified by environmental experiences. Three types of GECs have been described: evocative, active, and passive (Scarr & McCartney, 1983).

Evocative GEC occurs when young students who are talented in language are identified by their teachers and provided with special opportunities to enhance their gifts. In other words, they evoke reactions from other individuals on the basis of their genetic predispositions. Consequently, these students will receive more verbal input and be better stimulated than students without such talents. Over time, the talented group's environment and genetics mutually influence each other, favoring the development of greater language ability.

Active GEC occurs when students talented in language arts seek out environments that are rich in language experiences. For example, they may want to associate with like-talented peers or take part in poetry or essay contests. Once again, this type of GEC can enhance language skills due to the different groups that the students place themselves into over time.

Passive GEC occurs when students talented in language arts inherit both the genes from their similarly talented parents *and* the environment that promotes the development of language ability. Hence, the children passively receive a family environment that is closely correlated to their genetic predispositions.

Evocative and active GECs can occur inside or outside the family and become increasingly important as the child moves outside the family and becomes involved in other environments. Passive GEC, on the other hand, occurs only within the biological family and tends to decrease in importance as the child matures. Consequently, children who are passive GEC candidates are the most appropriate group to study when trying to determine how much various environmental factors moderate genetic traits.

To that end, a major longitudinal study of passive GEC looked at language development in children from about 400 families over a 12-year period (Gilger, Ho, Whipple, & Spitz, 2001). In order to isolate the genetic propensities from the environmental influences on linguistic development, the children were selected from an almost even split of adoptive and nonadoptive families. Language-related assessment measures were administered to the subjects during the second, fourth, seventh, tenth, and twelfth years.

Evidence emerged from this study that genetic predispositions *can* dampen the influence of four environmental variables: the provision of toys and games in the home, the degree of maternal involvement in the child's language development, the number of people living in the home, and the degree of intellectual/cultural orientation in the home. Using statistical analysis, the researchers estimated the genetic contribution to these variables to range from 11 to 100 percent. A similar recent study of 380 seven-year-old twins also found that over half of the variance in these children's language skills was accounted for by genetic effects. Furthermore, these was little evidence of significant environmental influence (DeThorne et al., 2008).

Keep in mind that passive GECs decrease in importance as the child ages because the family becomes less significant than peers and other adults in the child's environment. Two major implications arise from these studies: (1) It is important to avoid drawing conclusions from family data about the impact of the environment on language-based skills of children, and (2) children possessed of genetic predisposition for high language ability, but raised in family environments that do not evoke the ability, can still realize their potential when they encounter teachers who recognize and nurture these talents.

> Environmental variables in the home may not be reliable predictors of a child's language ability.

Gender Differences: For many years research investigations using anecdotal data and case studies suggested that females generally possess a greater facility for language acquisition and processing than males. This observation has been further supported by evolutionary geneticists who propose that this advantage resulted from the role our female ancestors played in prehistoric societies. While the males were off hunting for food, females took care of the children and had to keep them in the cave to protect them from dangerous predators lurking outside. They told stories to maintain the children's interest, and taught them the tribe's language and culture. Thus, the female's family and tribal obligations helped her develop better language processing skills than her male counterpart. Single females with good language skills were more likely to find a mate than those with poor language skills, and pass their genes on to their offspring.

Now, in the last decade or so, neuroscience has contributed its findings. The first discovery came with PET scans in the mid-1990s. They revealed that female brains generally use more brain regions to process language than

Studies confirm that females generally have an advantage in language processing over males.

males. Female processing used not only Broca's and Wernicke's areas in the left hemisphere, but regions in the right hemisphere as well. Male processing used fewer regions, primarily in the left hemisphere (Shaywitz, Shaywitz, & Gore, 1995). The second discovery was that the bundle of nerves that allows communication between the two hemispheres, called the *corpus callosum,* was proportionately larger and thicker in females than in males. Assuming that function follows form, this would suggest that the female language advantage results from the combination of dual-hemisphere processing and more efficient between-hemisphere communications. Subsequent studies continue to support this notion (Schmithorst & Holland, 2007; Wilke, Holland, & Krägeloh-Mann, 2007).

Learning to Read

Speech will develop in the human brain without any specific instruction. Reading, on the other hand, is an acquired skill. To read correctly, the brain must learn to connect abstract symbols (the alphabet) to those sound bits (phonemes) it already knows. In English, the brain must first learn and remember the alphabet, and then connect those 26 letters to the 44-plus sounds of spoken English that the child has been using successfully for years. Thus, reading involves a recognition that speech can be broken into small sounds and that these segmented sounds can be represented by symbols in print.

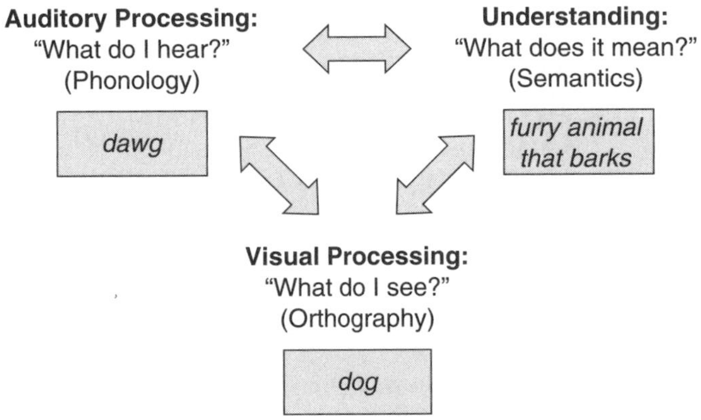

The brain's ability to recognize that written symbols can represent sounds is known as the alphabetic principle. Unfortunately, the human brain is not born with the insight to make these sound-to-

Auditory Processing: "What do I hear?" (Phonology) — *dawg*

Understanding: "What does it mean?" (Semantics) — *furry animal that barks*

Visual Processing: "What do I see?" (Orthography) — *dog*

Figure 5.3 Successful reading requires the coordination of three systems: visual processing to see the word, auditory processing to hear it, and semantic processing to understand it.

symbol connections, nor does it develop naturally without instruction. Children of literate homes may encounter this instruction before coming to school. If these children possess any type of genetic predispositions for high language ability, they are likely to learn quickly the complex process of reading earlier than other children of the same age.

Successful reading involves the coordination of three neural networks: visual processing (orthography), sound recognition (phonology), and word interpretation (semantics). In reading the word *dog*, for example, the visual processing system puts the symbols together. The decoding process alerts the auditory processing system that recognizes the alphabetic symbols to represent the sound "dawg." Other brain regions, including the frontal lobe, search long-term memory sites for meaning. If all systems work correctly, a mental image emerges of a furry animal that barks (Figure 5.3).

Learning to read also requires good memory systems. Working (temporary) memory has to keep words available long enough so that letter sounds found at the beginning of the word can be connected to those found at the end of the word. Eventually, the learner has to be able to remember the meaning of the word if future reading is to be successful. Because so many words in English have different meanings in different contexts, the learner must also remember every word in the sentence in order for the brain to select the correct meaning and put everything together.

Some brains acquire the skills associated with reading, such as phonemic awareness and the alphabetic principle, very quickly, and reading becomes an easy task. Most neuroscientists who study how the brain reads agree that genetic predispositions likely enhance processing within various neural networks that contribute to reading. In rare cases, the predisposition is so strong that it produces a condition known as *hyperlexia*, where the child becomes a voracious reader at the expense of developing spoken language and communication skills. We discussed hyperlexia in Chapter 4.

IDENTIFYING STUDENTS GIFTED IN LANGUAGE ARTS

Students who are gifted in the language arts of reading, writing, and communication skills will demonstrate competencies in some or all of the following areas:

- **Awareness of language.** These students understand the nature of language and show special interest in language features, such as rhyme, accent, and intonation in spoken language, and the use of grammar in written texts. They often have an interest in other languages and demonstrate an awareness of the relationship between the sounds and words of other languages.
- **Communication skills.** These students can easily gain the attention of an audience by exploiting the humorous or dramatic components of a situation in imaginative ways. They tend to write and talk with a creative flair that is exceptional for their age, often using metaphors and poetry. They can also express ideas elegantly and succinctly, in ways that reflect the knowledge and interests of specific audiences. They will guide a group to achieve its shared goals, while being sensitive to the participation of others.
- **Reasoning and arguing.** These students can use reasoned arguments at an abstract and hypothetical level in both spoken and written language. They can justify their opinions convincingly, and they know how to use questioning strategies to challenge the points of view of others.

Van Tassel-Baska (2002) recommends that any assessment model designed to identify students who may be gifted in language arts should

- Use multiple and varied types of measures, such as portfolios of students' work, product evaluation, and observational checklists of student behaviors.
- Incorporate long-term and short-term measures. A combination of frequent quizzes and less frequent tests is a more desirable approach to student assessment of learning than only one or the other. The use of short-term products combined with one long-term project is more revealing of what has been learned than only short-term projects or only one long-term one. This combination allows the teacher to determine how students have progressed incrementally.
- Incorporate multiple approaches to assessing learning. A good combination might be to use pre-post, time-series, and product assessments. Because gifted learner outcomes are geared to higher levels than typical student outcomes, teachers should not rely on one approach to measure the desired outcomes. Moreover, gifted curriculum outcomes are frequently incompatible with the use of a single assessment.
- Be developed early, preferably at the time of designing learner outcomes. For each learner outcome in a language arts curriculum for the gifted, a corresponding assessment should be identified. It is much easier to do this while the overall planning process is evolving, rather than after the instructional features have been put in place. Moreover, the assessment approach should also influence choices made in the instructional design.

See the **Applications** section at the end of this chapter for a rating scale and a rubric that can help teachers (and parents) determine whether a student has language talent.

DEVELOPING LANGUAGE ABILITY

Students talented in language arts will develop their abilities when they are challenged by experiences involving sophisticated language. Too often in the regular classroom, the reading materials and language activities are not sufficiently challenging for gifted students, who then become bored when their learning needs are not being adequately met. For these students to grow, they should be given language problems that are not easily solved, that are open-ended, and that force them to think, study, reread, and reformulate. Thus, a curriculum designed for these students should build upon the characteristics of the intellectually gifted. It should carefully identify which components and strategies will be used at each grade level in order to eliminate the content redundancy that plagues too many curriculum guides.

As explained earlier, teachers can have a great impact on evoking language-related talents in students. The teachers in this program should be highly intelligent, emotionally secure, comfortable interacting with gifted students, and able to demonstrate advanced knowledge of the subject matter. Evaluate the success of the program through the students' work product and not by tests of mastery of lower-level skills. This may require developing new assessment instruments because most current tests evaluate acquisition of knowledge rather than the application of knowledge in creative ways.

Some Instructional Approaches and Strategies

In an effort to address the needs of students who are gifted in language arts, teachers have devised various instructional approaches and strategies to generate exciting experiences in all aspects of language including vocabulary development, grammar, reading, and writing. Here is just a sampling of those ideas, that, of course, could be appropriate for all students. Many of these activities are explained in greater detail in the **Applications** section at the end of this chapter.

Analyzing Expository Text (Grades K–2): Identifying the topic and main idea of expository text is a common activity for all primary-grade children. Additional tasks can be included for children who show a talent for language processing. For example, kindergarten children can be asked to restate the facts they heard in the text and to answer who, what, where, when, why, and how questions about the text. They could also be asked to identify organizational features of the expository text, such as the title, table of contents, and heading.

After identifying the main idea and supporting details in expository text, first-grade students could be asked to locate facts in response to questions about expository text. They could also be asked the who, what, where, when, why, how questions about expository text, and to infer the author's purpose and intended audience for writing the expository text. Another activity would be to locate specific information by using organizational features such as the title, table of contents, headings, captions, bold print, and italics.

Additional activities for second-grade students could be to locate facts in response to questions about the expository text, and to distinguish fact from opinion. They could also locate specific information by using the text's organizational features as well as locate appropriate print and electronic reference sources, such as an encyclopedia, atlas, almanac, dictionary, thesaurus, periodical, CD-ROM, and Web site, for a specific purpose.

Focus on the Classics (Grades 5 and Higher): To develop verbal talent, students need go beyond the regular basal texts and be exposed to classical literature. Great books are called great because they can have different meaning for different readers. The classics stretch imaginations, challenge ideas, and open a new world of possibilities for expressing the human condition in language. Gifted students often see themselves in classic stories, whose characters can become their virtual mentors.

The classics also provide an exposure to the rich vocabulary that may be lacking from the literature anthologies used in today's classrooms. In addition to their value as sources of mentors and vocabulary, the classics expose students to a wealth of divergent and often conflicting ideas. They shock students into thought, forcing them to confront new concepts.

Author's Chair (Grades 3 and Higher): This is an opportunity for writers to share their final compositions with an audience in order to receive positive feedback that will assist them in future writing efforts. A particular chair in the classroom is designated for this activity. In addition to the value of the feedback, this strategy also develops listening skills for students in the audience.

Student Journal Writing (Grades 3 and Higher): Journal writing provides a natural way to integrate language through reading, writing, and discussion. Gifted students generally enjoy expressing their ideas verbally, but keeping a continuous written journal requires them to write, rephrase, and reflect on their thoughts. Different types of journals can be used for different purposes. *Dialogue journals* are conversations in print, designed to promote fluent oral and written communication. In *literary journals*, students enter their responses to works of literature that they have read. A third type is the *subject journal*, in which students record information related to specific topics (e.g., ecology, dinosaurs, and minerals).

Literature Circles (Grades 3 and Higher): In literature circles, small groups of students discuss a literary work in depth, guided by their responses to what they have read. The circles help students engage in reflection and critical thinking, building on their understanding and ability to construct meaning with other readers.

Writer's Workshop (Grades 7 and Higher): Writer's workshops were first used to develop the work of adult writers who were pursuing writing as a profession. However, the format can be adapted to younger individuals. Essentially, writer's workshop is a thoughtful and more sophisticated form of Author's Chair that is best suited for older middle and high school students who are gifted in language arts. As in Author's Chair, students who have read a writer's paper give feedback that identifies positive features, such as the literary forms and patterns that the author used, and offer constructive criticism as well. The comments are intended to help the author improve the paper, but the author is not obligated to follow all the suggestions. Because it is time consuming, this strategy should be used sparingly and only with students who are comfortable with feedback that includes constructive criticism.

Out-of-School Activities (High School): Opportunities often exist in the local community and region for these students to extend and enrich their experiences with language arts.

APPLICATIONS

IDENTIFYING STUDENTS WITH LANGUAGE TALENT

Students with high ability in language do tend to display common characteristics, especially by the time they reach middle school where language fluency rapidly develops. Use the scale below to help decide if a particular student is gifted in language arts. If you rate the student with scores of 4 or 5 on more than half of the characteristics, then further assessment is warranted.

The student...	A little Some A lot
1. Writes or talks in imaginative and coherent ways.	1 — 2 — 3 — 4 — 5
2. Organizes text in a manner that is exceptional for the student's age.	1 — 2 — 3 — 4 — 5
3. Expresses ideas succinctly and elegantly.	1 — 2 — 3 — 4 — 5
4. Writes with a flair for metaphorical and poetic expression.	1 — 2 — 3 — 4 — 5
5. Takes the lead in helping a group reach its writing goal.	1 — 2 — 3 — 4 — 5
6. Easily grasps the essence of a writing style and adapts it for personal use.	1 — 2 — 3 — 4 — 5
7. Can capture and maintain the attention of an audience by using drama and humor in imaginative ways.	1 — 2 — 3 — 4 — 5
8. Engages creatively and seriously with social and moral issues expressed in literature.	1 — 2 — 3 — 4 — 5
9. Justifies opinions convincingly.	1 — 2 — 3 — 4 — 5
10. Shows special awareness of language features, such as intonation, rhyme, accents in spoken language, and grammatical organization in written texts.	1 — 2 — 3 — 4 — 5
11. Presents reasoned arguments at the hypothetical or abstract level in both spoken and written language.	1 — 2 — 3 — 4 — 5

© 2009 by David A. Sousa. All rights reserved. Reprinted from *How the Gifted Brain Learns,* Second Edition, by David A. Sousa (Thousand Oaks, CA: Corwin). Reproduction authorized only for the local school site or nonprofit organization that has purchased this book.

APPLICATIONS

USING A RUBRIC TO ASSESS STUDENTS' WRITING

A rubric gives a descriptive, holistic characterization of the quality of students' work. It is less concerned with assigning a number to indicate quality than with selecting a verbal description that clearly communicates what the student knows and is able to do. It is also a helpful tool for enhancing gifted learners' understanding of the expectations for specific assignments and the criteria by which they will be assessed. Gifted programs often have the students engage in the development of rubrics and a peer-assessment process to use them. Here is a sample rubric for judging student writing that clearly specifies each category so that the rating can be easily understood (Van Tassel-Baska, 2002).

Rubric for Assessing Student Writing			
Criteria	*A*	*B*	*Other (No grade)*
Organization	Well-organized, easy to follow	Adequately organized, lacks clarity in sections	Is rambling and disconnected
Concept, insight, ideas	Ideas insightful and explain other text and sources well	Ideas are sound and text is adequately explained	Lacks clear presentation of sound ideas
Depth of understanding of selected topic	High level of depth; reflection on readings, class discussion, and experience	Some depth as seen by author; ideas woven into commentary	Shallow, with secondary sources total basis for shaping discussion
Logical argument, persuasion	Highly persuasive, with strong thesis, reasons, and conclusion	Convincing, but weakened by limited examples or reasons	Limited; lack of development of ideas
Use of relevant sources	Highly effective	Effective, but needs better integration	Limited
Form	Mechanical control highly evident	Mechanical control adequate	Mechanical control insufficient

Source: Adapted from Van Tassel-Baska, 2002.

APPLICATIONS

WORKING WITH GIFTED READERS

Young gifted readers are those who start to read early, read better with less drill, read longer, and read a variety of literature. Teachers promote the intellectual development of gifted readers by selecting books and materials that allow the students to do the following (Halsted, 1990; Vosslamber, 2002):

- Work with intellectual peers
- Build skills in productive thinking
- Have more time for processing ideas and concepts
- Share ideas in depth verbally
- Pursue ideas as far as their interests take them
- Encounter and use increasingly difficult vocabulary and concepts
- Draw generalizations and test them
- Anticipate the meaning of text based on visual clues
- Use prior knowledge and experience
- Be aware of cognitive processing of a text for information or concept gathering. Links are made between the present text and what the reader has previously read, and, as a result, concepts are formed or developed.

Promoting Intellectual Development

Teachers can use books to promote intellectual development by requiring students to read whole books in addition to their reading in the basal series. This approach is positive for gifted students because it rewards them for something they already enjoy. To ensure quality control and choice, the teacher should prepare the reading list from which students can choose their required books. Teachers may also suggest that students keep notebooks for recording the title, author, short comments about the book, and the dates the book was read.

Librarians, teachers, and volunteers can lead discussion of the books that students have read. These group discussions should focus on main themes and ideas, encouraging students to pursue higher-level thinking, such as analysis and syntheses, rather than to give just plot summaries and statements of fact.

Books can also be a part of the educational program for individual students, provided that an adult (teacher, parent, librarian, or other mentor) offers guidance appropriate to the student's interests, reading ability, and reading background. Weber and Cavanaugh (2006) recommend that teachers use eBooks with gifted readers. There are currently more than 100,000 books in eBook format, and many are now available for free on the Internet. Today's eBook technologies present features valuable for learners with various abilities, especially gifted and advanced readers. The unique features and capabilities of eBook technologies provide the attraction, options, and accommodations that promote reading.

Nurturing Emotional Development

Gifted children may experience feelings of difference and even inferiority, isolation, and a sense of being misunderstood by others. They must constantly choose between the alternatives of using their abilities and the need to fit into their group. Choices like this make growing up more difficult for them. Consequently, teachers need to nurture the social and emotional development of gifted children, in addition to meeting their intellectual needs. Many novels written for children address these affective concerns. The adults who discuss these books with gifted young students can help them cope with the additional considerations that being gifted add to the process of maturing.

Promoting Emotional Development

Books can be used to help individuals who are facing a particular situation, such as giftedness, become better prepared through reading and discussion. This process, known as developmental bibliotherapy, includes three components: a book, a reader, and a leader who reads the same book and prepares a productive discussion on the issues raised in the book. The goal is to help the reader identify with a character in the book, experience that character's emotions, and apply the experience to the reader's own life. The leader's role is to guide this process and to develop questions that will confirm and expand on these elements. Used appropriately, developmental bibliotherapy can be an effective tool for helping young students cope successfully with their giftedness.

APPLICATIONS

LANGUAGE ARTS STRATEGIES FOR GIFTED ELEMENTARY STUDENTS

Gifted students who have already mastered much of the required oral and written language skills for their grade level need strategies to stimulate imaginative and higher-order thinking. Although the following strategies, suggested by Smutny (2001), are appropriate for all students, they encourage gifted students to work at their own pace and level of complexity.

Exploring Poetic Language: Free Verse

Teachers can use poetry to help gifted students explore the quality of words, the power of metaphoric language, and the subtlety and complexity of meaning. Without the constrictions of a rhyming scheme, free verse allows students to focus on imagery and to experiment with various writing styles.

Creating a group poem. One method for demonstrating the different ways to write free verse is to have the students work as a group to create a free verse poem together. Using a picture or poster as the theme, ask the students to think about the picture's color, any feelings they get, and what the picture's components mean to them. Ask questions that will provoke their imagination: "If you were to think of the animals in this picture as colors, what colors would they be? If they were music, what sounds would you hear?" Write on the chalkboard the words and phrases that the students contribute. Read the words as a poem and talk about the images that are generated.

Creating individual poems. All kinds of media, such as music recordings, games, pictures, posters, puzzles, films, and paintings, can be used as the basis for creating poetry. Help the students select the medium and stimulate original thinking by asking focused questions: "What is the main character in this painting staring at? What mood is he in? What else could be happening around him? What could have happened minutes later?"

Exploring the Elements of Fiction

Divergent thinking. Exploring fiction becomes much more exciting if students think divergently about their stories. Divergent thinking involves pursuing the answers to open-ended questions, such as "How would you change this story, and why? Given all that has happened so far, what are some possible endings to this story? What would you have done in these circumstances, and why?"

Exploring fiction with fractured fairy tales. Altering the plot, setting, or character of a fairy tale in an unexpected way can produce a humorous twist of fiction and stimulate the imagination. For example: What if the big, bad wolf fails to blow down any of the pigs' homes, or the pigs come out and confront the wolf? What if the three bears return home while Goldilocks is still snooping around the place? After presenting a fractured fairy tale, asking some questions can help the students think through what changes have been made and what they mean: "Which events occur in the new tale that do not occur in the original? How do the changes in plot and character behavior affect the overall meaning of the story?"

A Study of Perspective: Biographical and Historical Fiction

Biographies and histories enable gifted students to conceive imaginary versions of actual events from different viewpoints. It gives them an opportunity to critically and creatively debate points in history and politics based on their own revisions of events. By writing biographical and historical fiction, they can explore new and exciting perspectives.

Researching the facts. Use books, short films, and magazines to introduce students to the work of prominent men and women. Get students to research what influenced these individuals in their youth, how they overcame difficulties or obstacles in their lives, and what were the most significant contributions they made to society. As they write down this information, they should also note any questions they have about the person's life. Then ask them to find out the answers to these questions. One of the values of this activity is that it inspires further research and analysis of issues that appear in the story.

Creating a point of view. Ask students to choose a person, animal, or object in this prominent person's life and describe an event from this perspective. Students often discover how individual points of view can create quite a different focus from that of the author who wrote the biography. For historical fiction, students can create a fictional character who, for example, fought in the Civil War. They could devise a fictional biography of this character and write an anecdote of an event that could have happened to this person in this time and place. This approach helps gifted students to see history in a different light, recognizing that within each daily news story, there are many individuals who see an event with slightly different perspectives.

These types of investigations with language arts engage the analytical minds and creative talents of gifted students. The strategies allow these students to expand their experiences with literature through their own creative designing and writing, and to gain a deeper insight into the people and events that have influenced our lives and shaped our world.

APPLICATIONS

USING CLASSICAL LITERATURE TO DEVELOP LANGUAGE ABILITY

Thompson (1999) makes a strong case for using classical literature to lure students away from the basal readers and to encounter new ideas that extend their capabilities in language. Here are some of these suggestions.

- **Identifying with a character.** Encourage students to read classics, such as those found in the Junior Great Books or Great Books programs. The characters in these literary masterpieces provide a powerful source of virtual mentors. Suggest that students talk about which characters they like and explain their reasons. Describe something the character did that they would like to do. What other choices can the character make, and what are their consequences?
- **Enriching vocabulary.** Classic literature offers a rich source of vocabulary not usually found in basal readers. Ask students to select words they found particularly interesting, to define them, and to speculate why the author might have chosen those words. What other words might the author have used? Thompson has compiled a word database, which includes a number of unusual items found in common classics. Here are the first ten books on his list, followed by the number of noteworthy words each contains:

Uncle Tom's Cabin, Harriet Beecher Stowe, 714

Ivanhoe, Sir Walter Scott, 519

Gulliver's Travels, Jonathan Swift, 472

The War of the Worlds, H. G. Wells, 379

Dracula, Bram Stoker, 345

Tom Sawyer, Mark Twain, 293

Robinson Crusoe, Daniel Defoe, 279

Treasure Island, Robert Louis Stevenson, 254

Silas Marner, George Eliot (Mary Ann Evans), 216

To Kill a Mockingbird, Harper Lee, 208

- **Classic ideas.** Classic literature exposes students to the divergent, complex, and conflicting ideas of heroes like Mark Twain, Martin Luther King Jr., Henry David Thoreau, and Thomas Jefferson. These voices express all kinds of humanitarian and uplifting themes: be yourself, be free, be ethical, find happiness, and protect the people.
- **Quality and quantity.** Some of these books will need to be assigned as home reading because few schools can dedicate time for the amount of reading necessary for gifted students. Two classics per semester might be reasonable for middle and high school students. Teachers should also ensure that they assign books rich in vocabulary.
- **The power of ancient words.** Teachers should encourage students with high ability in language arts to study the structure of words, thereby enriching their own vocabulary and ensuring their success in tackling examinations (e.g., the SAT) that assess vocabulary development. Just studying the Greek

and Latin stems, for example, can help a student gain understanding of over 5,000 new words. Some other advantages of learning these stems are

Power learning - Because the stems appear in many words and combinations, this approach to learning vocabulary is more powerful than learning one word at a time.

Spelling - Thousands of English words are nothing more than several stems in a row. By learning the stems, a student learns spelling for many words at the same time.

Standardized tests - The final few, and most difficult, questions on the SAT analogies test contain vocabulary words that are almost always stem-based. Students who have studied these stems, therefore, are likely to do better.

Sense of history - As students study the stems of words, they realize that language was not just invented in our time, but also reflects a historic development of many voices over eons.

Advanced vocabulary - Many stem-based words are big words used by science and technology. The names of biological species and diseases are just two examples of how new words are continually created from Latin and Greek roots.

- **The power of stems.** Greek and Latin stems form the basis for many words in English. Middle school students gifted in language arts may find the pursuit of these stems an enjoyable project. However, it is more important to learn the stem and its definition than the word example. Here are a few common stems for starters.

  ante-, *antecedent, anterior, anteroom*

  anti-, *antibody, antitoxin, antithesis*

  circum-, *circumnavigate, circumspect, circumvent*

  con-, *contract, confine, conjunction*

  equi-, *equivocate, equilateral, equinox*

  intra-, *intramural, intravenous, intracoastal*

  mal-, *malapropism, malodorous, malicious*

  non-, *nonprofit, nonchalant, nonfeasance*

  pre-, *presume, precede, premature*

  semi-, *semifinal, semicircle, semiformal*

  super-, *superb, supervise, superfluous*

  sym-, *symbiosis, symbolic, symphony*

  un-, *unfit, undeniable, unconventional*

- **Pursuing grammar.** Grammar is often viewed by students as tedious and a waste of time. But students gifted in language arts may find studying grammar to be a useful method for critical thinking about language. Grammar provides a way for students to think about how they use language, how grammar can clarify or muddle, and how different authors use language in their own styles. This approach offers a deeper appreciation for literature and the enjoyment of crafting good sentences and compositions.

APPLICATIONS

AUTHOR'S CHAIR

This activity gives writers an opportunity to share their writing products with an audience. A special time and chair are designated for this activity that provides the author with valuable feedback from classmates. It is appropriate for Grades 3 and higher.

Purpose

- To provide students an audience for their writings and motivation to write more in the future.
- To promote listening skills for students in the audience.
- To develop the analyzing and critical thinking skills necessary to critique someone else's work. The critical reviews benefit the writings of both the presenter and the members of the audience.

Procedure

- Select a special chair, such as an overstuffed chair or an office executive's chair, as the Author's Chair. The author orally presents the written material.
- Audience members listen carefully, mentally noting what they like and do not like about the writing.
- The teacher may wish to model the types of responses that would be appropriate from the audience. For example: "The language you used to describe the sunrise at the beach was vivid." "I could really feel the sadness in the character's words when she responded to the bad news."
- Audience members then share only what they liked about the writing, and the author responds to these comments. The author or teacher may set a limit on the number of responses from each audience member or the entire group.
- Set a time limit for the activity. For Grades 3 to 5, 15 to 20 minutes is usually sufficient. Longer sessions may be appropriate for the upper grades.

APPLICATIONS

STUDENT JOURNAL WRITING

Student journals are an effective means for integrating the components of language, and they benefit all students. They are particularly effective with gifted language arts students, who usually enjoy all forms of language expression. Journals invite the students' personal reactions to subject area readings and are considered informal writing. For these assignments, the teacher might suspend (within reason) spelling and grammar concerns and look for evidence of comprehension, analysis, and reflection. Student responses can be used to spark or revive class discussions, and can underscore important points in course readings while reinforcing larger themes of the course.

Students learn best when evaluation of their writing is personalized to indicate an understanding of their work. The journal assignment creates an opportunity for student-teacher interaction by opening a dialogue in a format with which students are already comfortable. It also offers teachers an excellent opportunity to respond, sometimes on a weekly basis, to each student's improvement, ingenuity, or lack of application. The low-risk ground rules of journal writing encourage students to focus on learning and personal expression rather than grades. Technology, such as e-mail, can also become part of the journal writing process. Here are some suggestions for using journal writing effectively (Cobine, 1995; Longhurst & Sandage, 2004).

Format

The journal writing portion of a lesson can be structured in many different ways, depending on the grade level, purpose, and type of journal. For example, the teacher can start with an oral reading of a passage from literature and follow it with journal writing about the passage (Note: *Both* teacher and students write their entries). To model a critical response and to set students at ease about sharing their entries, teachers should read their entry first.

In another format, the teacher initiates a 15-minute focused pre-journal writing session about the day's reading. Afterwards, the teacher separates the class into small groups, appoints a leader, and assigns a focus task or question for discussion. The groups share the results of their discussions with each other and individually write a second version that will become part of their journals.

Types of Journals

Journal writing serves several useful purposes that can be combined into one student notebook. For example, a notebook in English class might be modeled after a book, containing a preface, a body of chapters, and a glossary. These divisions suggest three different types of journal entries, designed to achieve separate goals.

Dialogue journals. Dialogue journals foster communications among students and can serve as the preface for the combined notebook. These journals are personal, informal, succinct, and direct. As a preface for the notebook, students could write about their perspective and respond to questions the teacher may have written alongside their entries. Later, the teacher could write comments about the students' responses. In this way, students have a real audience who helps to enhance their reflection and rhetorical awareness.

Literary journals. The literary journal can serve as the body of chapters for the combined notebook. In this type of journal, students maintain a record of their personal responses to passages from literature. Their writings may include predictions about plot, analyses of characters, and insights about themes. Whenever the plot or actions of a character are suggestive of real-life experiences, the students can also include those personal references in their entries.

Subject journals. The subject journal serves as the glossary for the student notebook. For an English-class notebook, there are several possible uses. One section could be reserved for student responses to the author's biography or about historic events mentioned in the literary work. Another section might represent a personalized dictionary of literary and linguistic terms for further study. A third section could be a personalized stylebook of grammatical, rhetorical, and mechanical concerns about their writings. Here, the students track the progress of their language usage throughout the course.

Journal writing promotes communication, clarity of thought, and investigation into language styles. At the same time, it connects the processes of reading, writing, and discourse. The different types of journals and the diverse student participation accommodate multiple learning styles and offer exciting challenges to gifted students.

From the Classroom — Advice on Journal Writing

I have been using journal writing in my classes for several years along with other classroom teachers in my school. From our experience and student surveys, here are some points to note when using journals as a significant part of a class experience:

- Students who do not understand the purpose of journal writing will need to be prepared with appropriate practice and modeling before they can participate in this process.
- Yet when students learn to use this process, they do see the journals as helping them to think more deeply and seriously.
- While some students prefer to write "in-the-moment" journals, novice writers may need to know how much time they have for completing reflective journals.
- Whether to use guided questions to frame reflections or to write in an open-ended journal should be determined by the content and the purpose of the type of journal used.
- Students usually want feedback. Supportive feedback is most reassuring when the journal content is personal. The Socratic questioning method may be used to respond to journals writing about scholarly subjects.
- Students overwhelmingly view the grading of journal writing assignments negatively, and this diminished the value of the process and outcome for students. Unless a content-based rubric is used, grades should be based on completion rates rather than on grammar, mechanics, or personal perspectives.

APPLICATIONS

LITERATURE CIRCLES

In literature circles, small groups of students read and discuss the same book. The discussions are led by their reactions to the characters and events in the book. Collaboration is critical to the success of this activity because it forms the bridge by which students connect their understandings about the literary work with those of others in the real world.

Procedure

- Students choose their own reading material from a list provided by the teacher.
- Small temporary groups are formed, based upon the book choice of the student. Different groups read different books.
- Groups meet on a regular schedule to discuss their reading. The students use written (or sketched) notes to guide their discussions.
- Discussion topics come from the student but are cleared through the teacher.
- The discussions are open, so personal connections and open-ended questions are welcome.
- Students play a rotating assortment of task roles, which might include the following:

  Discussion director: This student develops a list of questions that the group wants to discuss about the book. The questions should focus on big ideas and stay away from small details.
  Literary presenter: This student selects a few special sections that the group would like to hear read aloud. This is to help students remember some powerful, mysterious, puzzling, humorous, or important sections of the text.
  Connector: This student looks for connections between the group's book and the real world. It may involve connecting the reading to students' lives, to happenings at school or in the community, or to similar events at other times and places.
  Illustrator: This student draws a quality picture related to the reading. Other students should comment on the picture before the illustrator explains it.
  Summarizer: This student prepares a summary of the day's reading, which includes key points, main highlights, and the essential theme of the group's literary choice.

- The teacher serves as a facilitator, not as a group member or instructor.
- The group's work is evaluated by student self-evaluation and by teacher observation.
- When the books are finished, the groups share with each other and new groups are formed around new literary choices.

Guidelines

- Literature circles are *not* meant to be teacher- or text-centered activities.
- Groups should not be formed solely by ability. However, a group formed entirely of students who are gifted in the language arts may be appropriate.
- These circles are not the place to do skills work.
- The group's operating rules should encourage student responsibility, independence, and ownership.

From a Teacher's Desk: *An Elementary Example*

Literature circles meet the needs of gifted students and can be offered to all students. Although class-wide literature circles can start out as chaotic until the routine becomes natural, they are a worthwhile expenditure of time. Allow the students to practice the different roles they will take turns playing during the literature circle meetings. Thereafter, students should carry out meetings at least twice a week, setting and achieving realistic expectations and goals that they help to create. Generally, the purposes and benefits of literature circles are that students:

- View themselves as readers
- Have opportunities to read high-quality books that they might not have chosen on their own
- Are inspired to write
- Develop reading preferences
- Have many opportunities to develop critical and creative thinking
- Learn responsibility for completing assignments
- Learn to self-assess their learning and work habits

Journals can also come into play with literature circles. Students can complete their specific roles (e.g., discussion director, illustrator, etc.) task in their journal. They can also vary the way they take notes or complete their responses. For example, they can use graphic organizers to summarize ideas or to group keywords. They can use the half-page-fold technique to make predictions to return to later for response and reflection. The experience of choice and freedom to guide self-learning is usually a reward in itself for many students but extrinsic rewards, including feedback and praise, are motivating for others.

From a Teacher's Desk: *A Secondary Example*

Classroom Blogs

In Mrs. Richard's 11th-grade English class, students have been examining the role of the playwright. As a result of the unit, Mrs. Richard would like students to understand that (1) each playwright has a voice, and (2) voice is shaped by life experiences and reflects the writer. Mrs. Richard has quite a few gifted students who are ready to move beyond the goals of this unit and so she wants to construct options that will allow those students to be challenged. Beside her general discussion of the role of the playwright, each student has the choice of one of four playwrights to learn about in depth. Students may choose William Shakespeare, Henrik Ibsen, Arthur Miller, or Tennessee Williams. During this unit, the students will have the opportunity to create a piece of writing that reflects their chosen writer's voice and style. In order for her to assess how well the students are progressing on their independent learning in class, Mrs. Richard has each student set up a blog that will be used to reflect on the playwright's work.

Mrs. Richard describes the blog to the class as an online way of journaling. Students will go on the Web site http://www.blogspot.com, register their name, and build their first blog entry. After the teacher has each student's blog address, she will ask students to post their reflections by an established due date. Because she has set each blog site to be accessed only by her, students are assured that their work is protected, and that they are free to openly reflect their feelings about their author's style and voice. She finds that this outlet gives students the ability to communicate with her about their own writing in a private forum. Through classroom blogs, Mrs. Richard feels that she is better informed about student understanding and can quickly adjust to provide the challenge each student is ready to tackle.

Authentic Products in Language Arts

Authentic products help students understand, use, generalize, and transfer essential knowledge, understandings, and skills in a field to discipline-based practices and problems. Students who excel in language arts can benefit from authentic products that allow them to function with increasing skill and competency as a scholar, researcher, problem solver, or practitioner in a field.

At Truman High School, Mrs. Wately discovered that by offering her Advanced Placement English students a choice of authentic products, she tapped into student interests. Students in Mrs. Wately's class had a choice for their upcoming writing assignment. Mrs. Wately told her students that for their upcoming project, they would need to choose a real audience that might benefit from their writing assignment. Some students proposed a letter writing campaign aimed at making changes in the upcoming Prom night, while others sought alternate topics.

One student, Brianne, had been thinking about this project over the weekend. She told Mrs. Wately that she was concerned about the types of magazines that were published for teens. She felt that the teen magazines "promoted stereotypes that made girls feel bad about themselves." She wanted to create a magazine that promoted real people and real life. Mrs. Wately watched with interest as Brianne not only created her magazine, but enlisted the help of other students in the class for her upcoming magazine debut. She ended up publishing her new magazine titled *UnLimited*. In her first issue, she described to her readers the premise of her magazine:

"If there's anything I want you to pick up from my mag, it's that it is real. The stories in here aren't fake and they don't try to be something else. I'll use the trendy words and fonts and feature trendy products, but that's only because it's who I am—and I want *UnLimited* to have personality."

Mrs. Wately's experience with offering authentic product choices to her students resulted in engaging and meaningful writing in her classroom. Offering discipline-based practices and problems in language arts ultimately promotes skill in the field of writing and challenges students as they move along the continuum from novice to expert.

APPLICATIONS

CONDUCTING A WRITER'S WORKSHOP

A writer's workshop is a sophisticated format that is particularly effective in reviewing, evaluating, and improving an author's literary descriptions and style. It was first used with adult writers who were interested in pursuing writing as a career. The basic structure, however, can be modified to accommodate younger writers.

Because it is a labor- and time-intensive strategy, it should be used sparingly and only with more mature middle and high school students who are gifted in language arts, who have a strong self-image, and who can devote the required time and effort. During the workshop, a panel of peers examines the strengths and weaknesses of an author's paper, accentuating positive aspects and suggesting improvements in style and content.

Format

- A group of panel members (usually other student authors) reads the author's paper carefully before the workshop.
- In one format, the author is present but does *not* participate during most of the discussion. The author takes notes in order to respond later to the panelists' comments. Another variation allows the written paper to be discussed by a group that includes the author, a moderator, and several reviewers who are familiar with the author's work. The author selects and reads a paragraph and expresses feelings about the selection. One or two reviewers then briefly summarize their viewpoint of the author's paper, but they should avoid debating inconsistencies between their interpretations of the work's content.
- The panel then discusses and praises what they liked about the paper in terms of content and style.
- Following the discussion on positive aspects, the panel presents ways to improve the content and style of the paper, offering constructive suggestions on how to make the work better. The protocol is to first state the problem and then follow with a suggestion on how to solve the problem.
- During the discussion of both the positive aspects and the areas needing improvement, the author does not participate. Nor do the reviewers address the author directly. The reviewers should refer to the author in the third person and should not look at the author when making comments.
- After this discussion, the author may ask questions of the reviewers to clarify and better understand their comments.
- The audience thanks the author for writing the paper.

Guidelines

- The teacher's main duty during this process is to act as moderator and ensure that the students behave courteously toward each other and toward the author. People feel uneasy when being evaluated, even under the best of circumstances. The teacher needs to insist on an atmosphere that is constructive and conducive to insightful discussions, rather than allowing students to show off their intellect by attacking others.
- Panel reviewers are usually authors themselves, whose papers will also go through this process. In some situations, teachers may wish to include nonauthors in the class as reviewers. Nonauthors may have good comments to contribute but may not be good writers.

APPLICATIONS

OUT-OF-SCHOOL ENRICHMENT ACTIVITIES FOR STUDENTS GIFTED IN LANGUAGE ARTS

Some schools may not offer secondary students who are gifted in the language arts the activities they need to fulfill their potential. Out-of-school activities can frequently offer these students additional opportunities for enrichment in language and for extending their talents. Here are some possibilities for consideration.

- **Local theater and drama groups.** Opportunities to participate in local theater and drama groups that include live performances can be a very enriching experience for these students. The participation can be as passive as just watching rehearsals or involve being an actual member of the production.
- **Reading groups.** Exceptional readers may wish to participate in reading groups organized by older students or an interested parent. The Internet is a useful source of information about these groups and can also provide information on Web sites that show what students are reading in other schools and in other countries.
- **Creative writing and poetry societies.** Some communities have societies dedicated to creative writing or poetry, giving students the opportunity to write for pleasure (and for an audience) outside school.
- **Visiting the media.** Visits to the offices of radio and television stations, newspapers, and publishing companies can provide exciting insights into the world of journalism. Gifted students might even be able to contribute copy of their own.
- **Lectures and seminars.** Gifted students may be able to enroll in lectures and seminars on topics of special interest at local universities, galleries, and museums, as a way of extending the breadth and depth of their subject knowledge.

CHAPTER 6
Mathematical Talent

NUMBER SENSE IS AN INNATE CAPABILITY

Quick, how much is 37 times 489? What is the square root of 7,569? If you are like most people, including some professors of mathematics, you will need a few minutes along with pencil and paper to answer these questions. But there are people who can solve these problems in a few seconds without a calculator or a pencil. How do they do it? Is it an inherited gift? Does this mean that those who cannot solve these problems in their head cannot possess mathematical talent?

Mathematics is often viewed with such awe that those who understand and manipulate numbers with ease are usually considered gifted. Yet, studies show that most infants demonstrate number sense very early in their development and begin to do addition and subtraction much earlier than previously thought. The notion that number sense is hard-wired into the brain makes sense in terms of our development as a species. Counting, such as determining how many animals in a pack represented a danger, and arithmetic operations, such as deciding how much to plant to feed the clan, were major contributors to our survival and, over time, became part of our genetic code.

Research studies continue to find that, even in the first few months of life, babies notice the constancy of objects and detect differences in their numerical quantities (Berger, Tzur, & Posner, 2006). Eight-month-old infants can reliably distinguish individual objects from collections and can discriminate among different objects within their visual field (Chiang & Wynn, 2000). Of course, these babies do not have a sophisticated concept of counting, but they do have a conception of quantity, what scientists call *numerosity* (Sousa, 2008; Wakeley, Rivera, & Langer, 2000).

> It appears that number sense is innate. Even infants can detect differences in numerical quantities.

MATHEMATICAL THINKING AND THE BRAIN

How does the brain process arithmetic and mathematical operations? Is the processing dependent on language or visual-spatial representations? What conditions affect an individual's mathematical competence? These and similar questions have been the focus of scientific investigations for decades. In the past, answers to these types of questions came from observing the behavior of mathematicians and from their own musings about what occurred in their minds while thinking about mathematics. Some mathematicians, including Albert Einstein, insisted that words and language had little or no role in their thought processes; others stressed that language played a vital role in their interpretation of symbol systems. Still others claimed that mathematical insights were opaque operations that did not emerge from conscious, explicit thought. Now brain imaging and stimulation techniques are studying cerebral activity during various types of mathematical operations and have produced some fascinating revelations.

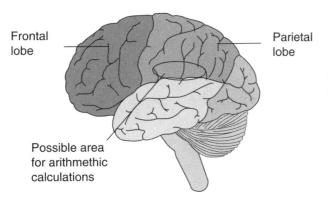

Frontal lobe

Parietal lobe

Possible area for arithmethic calculations

Figure 6.1 One area that appears responsible for arithmetic operations is located in the left parietal lobe, indicated by the circle. This area in Albert Einstein's brain was about 15 percent larger than normal.

Arithmetic Processing and Retrieval

Imaging studies have focused on determining where simple arithmetic functions, such as addition and multiplication, are processed in the brain. One early study found that patients with damage to the left parietal lobe had difficulty with arithmetic operations (Hittmair-Delazer, Semenza, & Denes, 1994). The left parietal lobe is also the part of Albert Einstein's brain that was about 15 percent larger than normal (see Figure 6.1). Because of the size of his related cortical structures, the researchers who examined Einstein's brain estimated that this extensive development of the parietal lobe probably occurred early in Einstein's lifetime, when he was already showing prowess at number manipulation and spatial abilities (Witelson, Kigar, & Harvey, 1999). The unanswered question, of course, is whether the larger parietal lobe is the cause or result of Einstein's intense work with mathematical operations.

Not surprisingly, scans also reveal that the more complicated the mathematical operation, the more brain regions called into action. Numerical calculations requiring substantial retrieval of arithmetic facts, such as the multiplication tables, activated the prefrontal cortex as well as the left parietal area (Ravizza, Anderson, & Carter, 2008). This finding supports the notion that how well and how quickly one can retrieve stored number rules has an impact on that individual's mathematical skills. Are efficient memory and rapid numerical processing, then, keys to mathematical talent? We will have to explore other research findings before we can answer that question.

Number Processing, Language, and Visual-Spatial Dependence

An area of considerable research interest has been the degree to which mathematical operations are dependent on other cerebral functions. If the ability to manipulate numbers is innate, then it would seem that mathematical processing would be associated with other innate human talents, such as language and visual-spatial representations.

Apparently, different brain regions are called into action when we change the way we process numbers. FMRI studies have found that multiplication, subtraction, and number comparison activate different regions of the brain's left and right parietal lobes (Chocon, Cohen, van der Moortele, & Dehaene, 1999; Ravizza et al., 2008). The researchers hypothesized that although both parietal areas are involved in manipulating quantity information, only the left parietal region provides the connection between quantity information and the linguistic code stored in Broca's and Wernicke's areas.

Another fMRI study obtained similar results when examining which brain areas were activated for calculations as compared to those areas activated to perform mathematical reasoning. Once again, the results showed that the regions in left prefrontal cortex and parietal lobe were more active for calculation than for reasoning, whereas regions in right prefrontal cortex and parietal lobe were more active for reasoning than for calculation. Different sorts of mathematical thinking recruit separate neural networks, and logical reasoning goes beyond the linguistic regions of the brain (Kroger, Nystrom, Cohen, & Johnson-Laird, 2008).

Results from these studies support the hypothesis that different brain regions are used for different mathematical operations and thinking. During number comparison, the right parietal region was the most activated region because comparison involves accessing the Arabic number system and does not require any linguistic translation (Figure 6.2). During multiplication, the left parietal lobe was more strongly activated because the brain monitors the results of the process through verbal computations (i.e., verbalized the results internally). Finally, during subtraction, both the left and right parietal lobes were activated because subtraction requires both the internal numbering system and the verbal naming of the resulting quantity.

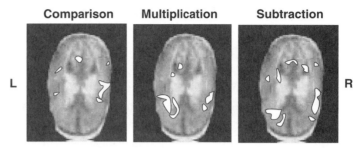

Figure 6.2 These representations of fMRI scans show that the right parietal lobe is most activated during number comparison but the left parietal lobe is most activated during multiplication. However, during subtraction, both lobes are highly activated.

Source: Chochon et al., 1999.

Additional support came from a study of bilingual adults using fMRI techniques to examine brain activity while the subjects performed exact and approximate arithmetic calculations (Dehaene, Spelke, Pinel, Stanescu, & Tsivkin, 1999). For example, in the tasks requiring *exact* addition, subjects were asked to give the sum of two numerically close numbers shown on a card (e.g., 5 + 4 = ?), and to identify the answer on the following card (7 or 9?). Using the same problem, the exercise was repeated and subjects were asked to find an *approximate* calculation (3 or 8?).

The results of the study were quite surprising. First, with repetition, the performance of the subjects improved considerably (i.e., response times dropped about 45 percent), regardless of the language used to present the problem. However, in exact calculations, the bilingual subjects responded significantly faster when the problem was presented in the same language in which they were given the original instructions for the study, but more slowly if the problem was presented in the other language. This was true regardless of the subjects' native language. Apparently, the instructions were stored in a language-specific format that accelerated the exact arithmetic calculations when the language of the problem and instructions were the same, but hindered the exact calculations when the languages were different. In contrast, no differences were noticed because of language changes in problems involving approximate calculations, indicating that those operations were independent of language.

In the second phase of the study, a different group of bilingual adults was asked to perform more complex exact and approximate arithmetic calculations. The fMRI results showed that different areas of the brain were used for exact calculations than were used for approximate calculations. Exact arithmetic calculations activated mainly the left frontal lobe and the left angular gyrus. Both of these areas have been associated with language tasks, indicating that this network is probably using language-dependent coding to carry out verbal processes needed to perform exact arithmetic calculations. In contrast, approximation tasks activated the left and right parietal lobes and portions of the right occipital lobe. These areas are outside the language processing regions and are usually associated with visual-spatial operations, such as mental rotation and guided hand movements (Figure 6.3).

> Exact and approximate arithmetic calculations are processed in different parts of the brain.

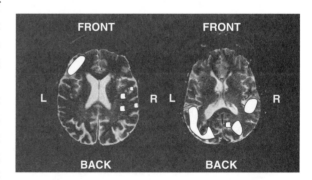

Figure 6.3 The illustration on the left is a representation of an fMRI image showing that the left frontal lobe was the area of main activation during exact calculations. The representation on the right shows that approximate calculations activated the left and right parietal lobes and portions of the occipital lobe.

Source: Dehaene et al., 1999.

Implications for Studying Mathematics: These and other similar studies confirm that there is no one area of the brain for mathematical computation. Different cerebral regions are activated to perform different calculations, some of which require input from the language areas located in the left hemisphere. This would suggest that people who have strong neural connections between the quantity and language centers are likely to be more proficient in mathematics than individuals whose connections are weaker.

Even for simple arithmetic computations, multiple mental representations are used to perform different tasks. To some degree, they also help explain the diverse views that mathematicians have about their own thinking processes. Exact computations seem to involve language-specific operations and rely on left-hemisphere circuits in the frontal lobe to complete their work. Thus, success in learning symbolic arithmetic and calculus may depend heavily on an individual's ability to process verbal language, which may affect the recognition and processing of mathematical language. In other words, good verbal language skills mean good exact computation skills.

Approximate arithmetic, on the other hand, shows no dependence on language and seems to rely more on visual-spatial representations in the left and right parietal lobes. This may be the area where complex spatial portrayals are created and enriched. It is possible that this language-independent representation of quantity is associated with our evolutionary history, whereby approximating the number of animals in a herd or pack was sufficient for our survival. This tendency toward approximation allowed neural networks the freedom to focus on holistic relationships and patterns rather than to get bogged down in handling discrete numbers.

> Exact computation seems related to verbal language skills, while approximate computation is related to visual-spatial skills.

Conceptual and Procedural Knowledge

Understanding mathematics, like most learning endeavors, requires acquiring the grand scheme of a topic, usually referred to as *conceptual knowledge*, as well as the steps and procedures needed to achieve a solution to a problem, known as *procedural knowledge*. Psychologists have long debated how these two components interact with each other during the acquisition of new learning, especially in the early years. A series of studies working with 3- to 6-year-olds found that children have strong addition and subtraction concepts before they can translate the physical effects of these operations into number words. However, using number words does not detract from their calculation procedures. Researchers also discovered that conceptual knowledge and procedural knowledge developed at different rates as children moved from kindergarten to Grade 2 (LeFevre et al., 2006). Even at this early age, conceptual and procedural development are interacting with each other (Canobi & Bethune, 2008).

A study of students in Grades 4 and 5 examined the relationship between the students' conceptual understanding of mathematical equivalence and their procedures for solving problems involving equivalence (e.g., 4 + 5 + 7 = 4 + ?). The students were pretested on their conceptual and procedural knowledge of equivalence. They were split into two groups and taught either the concept of equivalence or the steps needed to solve problems of equivalence. Posttests were given to determine how easily they could transfer their understanding to solve problems (Rittle-Johnson, & Alibali, 1999). Those taught with conceptual knowledge had a good conceptual understanding of equivalence and could also devise the correct procedures for solving equivalence problems. In contrast, the students taught only the procedural knowledge had some conceptual understanding but only limited transfer of the procedure to a new problem.

A similar study of students in advanced mathematics classes had similar results. Students taught in classes emphasizing conceptual knowledge scored higher on standardized mathematics tests than matched students taught in traditional courses focusing on procedural knowledge. Furthermore, students in the conceptual knowledge-based classes had a higher rate of retention of their mathematical knowledge when tested one year later (Kwon, Allen, & Rasmussen, 2005). All of these studies reveal a causal relationship between conceptual and procedural knowledge, and that conceptual knowledge has a greater influence on the acquisition of procedural knowledge than the reverse (Figure 6.4).

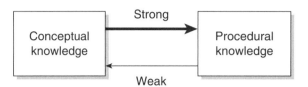

Figure 6.4 Conceptual knowledge has a stronger influence on procedural knowledge than the reverse.

Experienced teachers will not be surprised by the results of these preceding studies. Most of us have experienced learning situations in which we were more or less following a series of steps without really understanding why we were doing it. Beginning cooks can carefully follow a written recipe and even produce a decent product, but they have no clue about how the ingredients came together to make the dish. Moreover, they would not know how to make modifications if they lacked one of the ingredients.

Implications for the Study of Mathematics: In most lessons, teachers should ensure that they find ways to present mathematics conceptually first and check for the students' conceptual understanding before moving on to any procedural steps involved in solving problems associated with the concept.

IDENTIFYING THE MATHEMATICALLY GIFTED

Mathematically promising students are not always easy to spot. They may feel self-conscious about their abilities and may prefer to remain in the background rather than have attention brought to them. As a result, their competence may not be identified at all, or they may be encouraged to skip classes or grades in the hope that their specific needs eventually will be met.

Some Attributes of Mathematical Giftedness

Students with high mathematical ability

- Learn and understand mathematical ideas very quickly.
- Display multiple strategies for solving problems. They prefer to approach the problem from different perspectives and at varying levels of difficulty. The more layers the problem has, the more involved these students become in seeking solutions.
- Engage other students in their activities. They tend to talk to themselves or others as they walk through various approaches to the problem. They make convincing arguments about their views and try to recruit others to their position.
- Sustain their concentration and show great tenacity in pursuing solutions.
- Switch approaches easily and avoid nonproductive approaches.
- Operate easily with symbols and spatial concepts.
- Quickly recognize similarities, differences, and patterns.
- Look at problems more analytically than holistically.
- Work systematically and accurately.
- Demonstrate mathematical abilities in other subject areas by using charts, tables, and graphs to make their points and illustrate their data.

Of course, not all the students who possess these attributes are willing to work hard at mathematics. We see potential, but students may put little effort into using their mathematical capabilities.

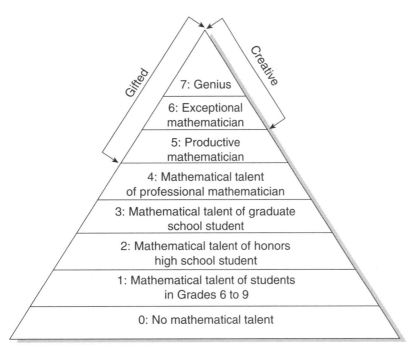

Figure 6.5 This model of Usiskin's hierarchy classifies mathematical talent into eight levels. Mathematicians in Levels 5 through 7 are gifted, but only those in Levels 6 and 7 are creative.

Source: Adapted from Usiskin, 2000.

Mathematical Giftedness and Mathematical Creativity: Some truly gifted students not only possess these attributes but are also creative. Using an eight-tiered hierarchy, Usiskin (2000) maintains that not all mathematically gifted individuals are mathematically creative. His hierarchy ranges from Level 0 to Level 7 and classifies mathematical talent (see Figure 6.5). Level 0 (No Talent) represents adults who know very little mathematics. Level 1 represents adults who have rudimentary number sense to function in their culture, and their mathematical knowledge is comparable to those of students in Grades 6 through 9. A very large proportion of the general population would fall into the first two levels.

The remaining population is thinly spread throughout Levels 2 through 7 on the basis of mathematical talent. Level 2 are the honors high school students who are capable of majoring in mathematics, as well as those who eventually become mathematics teachers in secondary schools. Level 3 are the "terrific" students who score in the 750–800 range on the SATs or a 4 or 5 in the Calculus Advanced Placement exams. These students have the potential to do beginning graduate level work in mathematics. At Level 4 we have the "exceptional" students who excel in mathematics competitions and who receive admission into mathematics and science summer camps and academies because of their talent. These students can construct mathematical proofs and are able to converse intelligently with mathematicians about mathematics.

Level 5 represents the productive adult mathematician, namely, those students who have successfully completed a Ph.D. in mathematics or related mathematical sciences and who are capable of publishing in their field. Level 6 is the rarefied territory of the exceptional mathematicians who move their field forward and who will be found in any history of the fields in which they work. Finally, Level 7 is the exclusive territory of the all-time greats and exemplary geniuses like Leonard Euler, Karl Friedrich Gauss, Henri Poincaré, and others.

Note that in this hierarchy of mathematical talent, gifted mathematicians are at Levels 5 through 7, whereas the creative mathematicians are found at Levels 6 and 7. Therefore, in this model, mathematical creativity implies mathematical giftedness, but the reverse is not necessarily true. Elementary and secondary school students who are gifted and/or creative in mathematics are found at Levels 3 and 4. According to Usiskin, these students have the potential of moving up into the professional realm (Level 5) with appropriate affective and instructional strategies as they progress beyond the K–12 setting into the university environment.

Admittedly, the research literature does not clearly delineate the major differences between *mathematical giftedness* and *mathematical creativity*. Sriraman (2005) suggests that a synthesis of the definitions found in the literature could be summarized as follows:

- Mathematical giftedness means being able to quickly understand *known* mathematical concepts and perform complex mathematical operations at a level well beyond what is typical for the individual's age and schooling.
- Mathematical creativity includes the characteristics of giftedness, but also means the ability to produce *original* work that significantly extends the body of knowledge, or poses new questions for other mathematicians, so that an old problem can be regarded from a new angle requiring imagination.

Sriraman maintains that although schools are doing a better job at identifying the mathematically gifted student, they need to work harder at finding those who are mathematically creative. He suggests that gifted/creative students at the K–12 level with a non-Western ethnic background are rarely encouraged to express or use mathematical techniques they may be familiar with from their own cultures. Instead, they are encouraged to adopt a Western attitude. To some teachers, giftedness is often associated with conformity, whereas creativity is viewed as a fringe commodity, tolerated and nurtured by some teachers, but typically not encouraged.

The earlier that school personnel identify mathematically gifted and creative students, the better. Whether mathematical ability is innate or acquired, however, the early years are an important time for developing the cerebral areas and establishing the neural networks that perform arithmetic computation as well as create and manipulate mathematical abstractions. See the **Applications** section at the end of this chapter for a rating scale that can help identify students who are mathematically gifted.

Some Myths About Mathematically Talented Students: Some myths have emerged about elementary students who are talented in mathematics, most likely because of the difficulty in identifying them. These myths have been collected by Ann Lupkowski Shoplik (2006) at the Carnegie Mellon Institute for Talented Elementary and Secondary Students (C-MITES). Take a look at this list of myths and think about whether any of them exist in your educational environment.

- Mathematically talented students cannot be identified until high school.
- Only students identified for a gifted program are mathematically talented.
- Mathematically talented students are outstanding at computation.
- Results from standardized, grade-level tests are sufficient for identifying mathematically talented students.
- Students who are mathematically talented demonstrate mastery of a topic by earning 100% on tests, including pretests.
- The best option for mathematically able elementary school students is enrichment.
- Students who are mathematically talented shouldn't study algebra until eighth or ninth grade.
- The best way to challenge mathematically talented students is to have them skip a grade and study the regular textbook in the regular classroom.
- Students whose pace of instruction is accelerated cannot cover each section of the text and will have gaps in their mathematics background.
- If mathematically able students study mathematics at an accelerated pace, they will run out of math curriculum before they reach high school.
- Gifted students respond equally well to the same curriculum.

Is it possible that some of these myths could be alive and well in some schools and, as a result, are impeding the development of appropriate measures to identify and accelerate mathematically gifted students?

TEACHING THE MATHEMATICALLY GIFTED

Classroom Challenges

Differentiating Instruction: One reason that mathematically gifted students are not identified may be that the method of teaching mathematics in the classroom does not evoke the type of thinking processes associated with high mathematical ability. Instruction that focuses mainly on memorizing rules, formulas, and procedural steps will provide few opportunities for gifted students to demonstrate their higher-level competencies. In this environment, they are more likely to be bored, withdrawn, or even act out to show their displeasure with activities that offer little or no challenge. Teachers are more likely to spot gifted students when the instruction is differentiated so that the mathematically talented can pursue interesting and thought-provoking problems.

Creating a learning environment that encourages and nurtures the talents of mathematically gifted students, especially in a mixed-ability classroom, requires sustained effort and is no easy task. These students grasp information quickly and seek higher meaning and challenge in what they are learning. Because the mathematics curriculum in most schools today is designed for that school's average learner, the needs of students who are exceptionally talented in mathematics often go unmet. Thus, the teacher has to search for unique opportunities for gifted students, such as designing open-ended problems, setting up cooperative learning groups of high-ability students, and helping students become involved in the talent searches sponsored by nearly a dozen US universities. See the **Applications** section at the end of this chapter for suggestions on strategies for mixed-ability classrooms and the talent searches available for mathematically gifted students.

How Challenging Are the Activities?: Sometimes the activities that teachers view as challenging may not be seen as such by mathematically gifted students. A study of more than 2,000 elementary and 1,500 middle school students asked the teachers and students to self-report on whether they thought the class assignments were challenging (Gentry, Rizza, & Owen, 2002). The gifted students in regular classrooms found their classrooms more than "sometimes," but less than "often" challenging. At the middle school level, there was no correlation between what teachers report they do and what both gifted and other students in regular classrooms perceived as challenging. The study also included gifted students in magnet schools, many of whom perceived a higher level of challenge when compared to the gifted students in regular classrooms. These findings suggest (1) that middle school educators should pay close attention to the level of challenge they provide to all students, and (2) gifted students tend to be more highly challenged in magnet school classrooms than in regular classrooms.

Gender Differences in Mathematics: Do They Really Exist?

In January of 2005, Lawrence Summers, then-president of Harvard University, was speaking at a conference focusing on the representation of women and people of color in science and engineering. During his speech, he created an international furor when he suggested that women may not have the same innate abilities in mathematics and science as men. He soon issued a carefully-worded apology, but he defended his remarks as having some basis in research. Nonetheless, the tumult got only worse, and one month later, Summers submitted his letter of resignation.

Summers may have been referring in his speech to the growing body of research that highlights the differences in male and female brains. To start, the relative sizes of many of the structures inside female brains are different from those of males. Parts of the frontal lobe, which you will recall controls decision-making and problem-solving functions, are proportionally larger in females, as is the limbic area, which regulates emotions. Other studies have found that the hippocampus, involved in short-term memory and spatial navigation, is proportionally larger in females than in males. In males, the proportionally larger areas include the parietal cortex, which processes signals from the sensory organs and is involved in space perception, and the amygdala, which controls emotions and social and sexual behavior (Cahill et al., 2001). Researchers have also found that males and females use different regions of the brain when recalling emotionally charged images they had been shown earlier. Furthermore, the males recalled the gist of the situation whereas the females concentrated on the details. This suggests males and females process information from emotional events in very different ways, using different cerebral mechanisms (Cahill, 2003).

Since the 1970s, gender differences in mathematics performance has been a controversial topic among educators and researchers. Statistical evidence that boys are smarter at mathematics than girls came from the Study of Mathematically Precocious Youth conducted in the early 1980s.

> Gender differences in mathematics seem to be greater for high-ability students than for the general student population.

Gifted seventh-graders were administered the mathematics section of the Scholastic Aptitude Test (SAT-M). Four times as many boys scored above 600 as girls, and 13 times as many boys scored above 700 (Benbow & Stanley, 1983). Male college-bound students also displayed a mathematics advantage by consistently scoring higher on both the SAT-M and the mathematics section of the American College Test (ACT).

Ensuing studies found other differences between male and female performance on specific types of mathematical skills. For example, males seemed to have an advantage over females in mathematical operations involving visual-spatial ability, while females did better in mathematical computation. One possible explanation for these findings is that more male than female brains seem to have a visual-spatial preference (see Chapter 2) and would therefore perform better in solving these types of problems. In contrast, more females have analytic preferences and would tend to do better with computation problems.

Numerous other studies in the 1980s through the mid-1990s yielded conflicting results, especially with regard to the age at which the gender differences emerge. Some studies reported differences in the early elementary years, others by age 12, and still others argued that gender differences did not appear until high school. The discrepancies among these studies can be explained in part by the limited sample sizes and by the use of a select population, such as gifted or college-bound students. A major study by Leahey and Guo (2001) sought to overcome the deficiencies of previous studies by using large samples and data from the National Longitudinal Study of Youth (NLSY) and the National Educational Longitudinal Study (NELS). This approach not only reduced the bias due to small and select samples, but also allowed the researchers to examine mathematical performance from kindergarten to Grade 12, rather than at one or two developmental stages. They were also able to separate out performance differences by mathematical skill and by selected student populations. Table 6.1 summarizes some of their findings.

Subsequent studies continue to show small differences between male and female mathematical processing, yet without substantially changing Leahey and Guo's findings.

> Some gender differences in mathematics ability may be overcome through motivation.

One study's findings reaffirmed that male students had a small advantage over female students in doing mental arithmetic operations, although there were no gender differences in digit span, the ability to repeat a string of numbers read to them by the researcher (Lynn & Irwing, 2008). Another study showed once more that male adolescents did somewhat better with mental rotation tasks than female adolescents, and that this difference increased slightly with age (Geiser, Lehmann, & Eid, 2008). It appears, however, that this small difference in mental rotation tasks may be overcome through motivation. A similar study found that females improved their performance and reached male's scores in the mental rotation tasks when they were led to believe they were better than males (MoP, in press). These results should come as no surprise because numerous studies have shown that how well we *believe* we can do a task affects how well we *actually* do it. This phenomenon appears to be particularly true when females face mathematical processing, more so than males (Chatard, Guimond, & Selimbegovic, 2007; Kiefer & Sekaquaptewa, 2007).

Table 6.1 Gender Differences in Mathematics	
Major Findings (Elementary Students and NLSY data) **No. of Students: 4,126** **No. of Scores: 12,159**	**General Mathematics Skill:** Almost no gender differences in mean scores among the general population. Boys' scores did have more variance than girls' scores, but it was not statistically significant. **High-Scoring Students:** Boys and girls had similar overall averages. Ages 4–7, high-ability girls did better than high-ability boys. Ages 8–10, high-ability boys did better than high-ability girls. Ages 11–13, no significant differences. **Reasoning Skill:** Few differences in younger children; a slight advantage to female students among 11- to 13-year-olds.
Major Findings (Secondary Students and NELS data) **No. of Students: 9,787** **No. of Scores: 26,253**	**General Mathematics Skill:** In 8th grade, males scored an average of 0.5 points higher than females. This difference increased to 1.32 by 12th grade. The difference was not significant at the 5 percent level. **High-Scoring Students:** High-ability boys did better than high-ability girls. **Reasoning Skill:** In 8th grade, no gender differences. In high school, male scores were slightly higher than female, but not statistically significant. **Geometry Skill:** In 8th grade, males held a very slight advantage, which increased to a statistically significant advantage in 12th grade.

Source: Leahy & Guo, 2001.

In summary, the studies by Leahy and Guo and subsequent researchers found that there were a few and slight gender differences that did not appear until the end of high school. These differences also were greater for high-ability students than for the general population. Males seemed to have an advantage in geometry and females, in computation in the early grades. Differences in brain development and learning style preferences may account for these findings. But is it possible that there are societal and cultural factors at work as well? For example, more boys elect to take more mathematics and science courses, which could further develop their visual-spatial abilities and thereby improve their performance on certain tests, such as geometry. These skills are not really emphasized until high school, which could explain the emergence of the gender differences at that time.

Three important points need to be made at this time: First, there are gender differences in mathematics that are slight, develop late, and are subject specific. Second, the findings do *not* support the notion that males generally have a powerful innate superiority in mathematics over females. It may just be that the slight advantage they do have, especially in visual-spatial operations, are more obvious in the later high school years. And females may be able to overcome this male advantage by feeling more positive about their mathematic ability. Third, the fact that much of higher mathematics involves visual-spatial and abstract reasoning may explain why a large portion of top mathematicians are male. But even in this regard, the gap is closing.

APPLICATIONS

IDENTIFYING THE MATHEMATICALLY GIFTED

Students who are gifted in mathematics display certain attributes. Specific classroom activities (see the next application) can often reveal these attributes. Use the scale below to help decide if a particular student is gifted in mathematics. If you rate the student with scores of 4 or 5 on more than half of the characteristics, then further assessment is warranted.

The student....	A little Some A lot
1. Learns and understands mathematical ideas very quickly.	1 — 2 — 3 — 4 — 5
2. Displays multiple strategies for solving problems.	1 — 2 — 3 — 4 — 5
3. Engages others in problem solving.	1 — 2 — 3 — 4 — 5
4. Sustains concentration and shows great tenacity in pursuing problems.	1 — 2 — 3 — 4 — 5
5. Switches approaches easily and avoids nonproductive approaches.	1 — 2 — 3 — 4 — 5
6. Operates easily with symbols and spatial concepts.	1 — 2 — 3 — 4 — 5
7. Quickly recognizes similarities, differences, and patterns.	1 — 2 — 3 — 4 — 5
8. Looks at problems more analytically than holistically.	1 — 2 — 3 — 4 — 5
9. Works systematically and accurately.	1 — 2 — 3 — 4 — 5
10. Demonstrates mathematical abilities in other subject areas.	1 — 2 — 3 — 4 — 5
11. Prefers to present information through charts, tables, and graphs.	1 — 2 — 3 — 4 — 5

© 2009 by David A. Sousa. All rights reserved. Reprinted from *How the Gifted Brain Learns,* Second Edition, by David A. Sousa (Thousand Oaks, CA: Corwin). Reproduction authorized only for the local school site or nonprofit organization that has purchased this book.

APPLICATIONS

CLASSROOM ACTIVITIES TO HELP IDENTIFY MATHEMATICALLY GIFTED STUDENTS

When teaching mathematics at any grade level, offering classroom activities at varying levels of difficulty and complexity can help teachers identify mathematically gifted students. Here are a few suggestions for accomplishing this task (Hoeflinger, 1998).

- Offer open-ended problems that have an array of discrete levels and can be solved using multiple strategies. (A simple test to identify a problem of this type: If you are unsure how to proceed in order to solve the problem, then it most likely requires a multistep approach.)

- Provide thought-provoking and nonroutine problems about once a week. Look for the ways the students organize knowledge, argue their position, make conjectures, and clarify their thoughts. Are they looking for patterns and can they recognize and explain them? What type of reasoning and logic are they using? How quickly and accurately can they solve the problem? Make anecdotal notes on how students respond to specific problems, the types of strategies they use, and their progress.

- As problems are solved, raise the level of complexity for ensuing problems until the students are involved in a spirited debate about potential approaches to solutions. Be certain, however, that the students know and understand the necessary mathematics vocabulary in the event that they need to seek information from other sources.

- Mathematically gifted students often show their talents in other curriculum areas. They tend to view the world in mathematical ways and to use mathematical symbols and language in their other work.

  - In writing, they often demonstrate a clarity of logic, precision, and sequencing, sometimes using tables and charts to organize information.
  - Social Studies offers another area where they can apply their unique abilities to create models and design tables and graphs to illustrate data (e.g., population growth in an area using birth and death rates, etc.). Can they use this information to make and support predictions about future growth?
  - Science experiments also provide many opportunities for these students to show their abilities, especially in collecting, organizing, and manipulating quantitative experimental data. Can they use the data to make predictions when other experimental variables are changed?
  - Avoid giving textbooks to truly gifted students. Suggest that they seek out other sources of information, such as professional journals and Internet research sites, and allow them to move at their own pace. Like other students, they also need nurturing and encouragement to move ahead faster.
  - Cluster the gifted mathematics students in small cooperative groups and give them a complex problem to solve while you carry on instruction with the rest of the class. Ensure that group members have time to discuss their problem-solving strategies and to make connections to curriculum objectives.
  - Look to other sources for mathematical problems, games, and ideas for these students to pursue. Those sources can include texts from higher grade levels, other teacher colleagues, journals published by the National Council of Teachers of Mathematics (NCTM), curriculum materials from the state Department of Education, local public and university libraries, and the Internet.

APPLICATIONS

TEACHING MATHEMATICALLY GIFTED STUDENTS IN MIXED-ABILITY CLASSROOMS

After identifying students who are mathematically gifted, working with them in a mixed-ability classroom can present problems unless the teacher finds ways to differentiate instruction. Mathematically gifted students still have educational needs, but they will be better than other students at handling and organizing data, formulating problems, and expressing and transferring ideas.

Issues

Shoplik (2006) suggests that these are some issues that the teacher might encounter when considering how to teach mathematically talented students in the regular classroom.

- **Students With Varying Abilities.** Because students' abilities vary, programs offered to them should be varied. Matching the curriculum to the abilities of students is done by adjusting the pace and the depth at which the material is presented. Skipping a grade in mathematics might be the most appropriate option for one student, while doing enrichment activities and independent study projects might be the most appropriate for another.
- **Students Might Be Gifted in Mathematics, but Not in Other Subjects.** Many students are gifted in mathematics, but do not have equal strengths in other academic areas. In some cases, these students may not be in their school's gifted program, especially if that program is tailored to students gifted in verbal areas. However, it is important not to deny mathematically talented students enhanced learning opportunities just because they are not labeled "gifted." Gifted programs in many schools are verbally oriented with little time during the academic year devoted to the study of mathematics. The mathematics that is studied might be covered in a random fashion as, for example, challenge problems and enrichment sheets that are unrelated to each other. Gifted programs can meet mathematically talented students' needs only if these students can move ahead in the mathematics curriculum at an appropriate pace and depth as opposed to engaging in random enrichment activities.
- **Acceleration Versus Enrichment Is a False Dichotomy.** Effective acceleration contains some enrichment, while effective enrichment is accelerative. Proper pacing and the opportunity to study the mathematics in depth are both needed for the curriculum to be matched to students' abilities. Students accelerated in mathematics have already demonstrated mastery of most of the topics taught at their current grade level. The task is to determine where the gaps are and to fill them in before the student moves ahead. This can be accomplished by using the five-step model previously described.
- **Mathematical Concepts and Computation.** Some students can be extremely talented in mathematics, but still make mistakes in computations. Studies have shown that mathematically gifted students perform significantly better on conceptual tests than on computational tests. These students show a good intuitive grasp of mathematics, but they lack the same level of skill in computations. Mistakes in computations can occur because the students have developed bad habits such as not writing down their thought processes while solving problems. Another possibility is that their computational skills have not caught up to their advanced conceptual understanding of mathematics because they have not learned the appropriate terminology or algorithms. These students should be

challenged by learning new concepts while improving their computational skills. They should not be held back because of a relative weakness in computations.

Here are some suggestions for differentiating instruction for the mathematically gifted (Johnson, 2000; Shoplik, 2004, 2006).

Assessment

- Give pre-assessments to determine which students already know the material. In the elementary grades, gifted learners still need to know the facts necessary to complete their learning objectives. Work with those students who do not know the basics, and allow the gifted students to complete more complex learning tasks.
- Develop assessments that allow for differences in creativity, understanding, and accomplishment. Give students chances to express themselves orally and in writing to show what they have learned.
- Determine whether a student should move up a grade in mathematics. This is a good option for students who are particularly talented in mathematics. Whole-grade acceleration can also be considered if the child is talented in all subject areas. Advantages include being exposed to more challenging material. The potential disadvantage to this acceleration is that the pace of the new class might still be too slow for quick learners.

Curriculum Materials

- Select textbooks that offer enriched opportunities. Too many mathematics textbooks repeat topics every year prior to algebra. Most texts are written for average students and are not appropriate for the gifted.
- Compact the curriculum. Compacting the regular curriculum opens up more time for mathematically gifted students to study enrichment topics. It also helps match the pace of learning to the abilities of the student. Three basic questions asked during the compacting process are (1) What does the student know? (2) What does the student need to learn? and (3) What differentiated activities will be offered to meet the student's needs? Teachers can address the first two questions using standardized or teacher-made tests. Teachers and students can work together to determine appropriate enrichment topics in the relevant subject area.
- Use multiple resources, such as college textbooks and research reports, because no one textbook can meet the needs of these learners.
- Use technology as a tool, an inspiration, or as an independent learning environment that allows gifted students the opportunity to reach the depth and breadth they need to maintain their interest. Computer programming is a special skill. Using spreadsheets, databases, and graphic and scientific calculators can lead to powerful data analysis.
- The Internet is a vast source of material, contests, student and teacher resources, and information about mathematical ideas usually not found in textbooks.

Instructional Techniques

- Flexibility in pacing is important. Some students may be mastering basic skills while others are working on advanced topics.

- Use inquiry-based, discovery learning approaches that emphasize open-ended problems with multiple paths to multiple solutions. Have students design their own methods for solving complex problems or answering complicated questions. You will be surprised at what gifted students can discover.

- Explore enrichment topics in the regular classroom. One option is to provide learning centers that focus on mathematics topics. For example, most students in the class might be expected to complete Centers A, B, and C, while Centers D and E are available to students who have the time, interest, and motivation to work on additional topics. Ideally, students completing Centers D and E could substitute that work for Center A, B, or C. Examples of enrichment topics in elementary mathematics include probability and statistics, estimation, mental arithmetic, spatial visualization, algebra, geometry, and discrete mathematics.

- Ask lots of higher-level questions that encourage students to discuss and justify their approaches to problem solving.

- Differentiate assignments so that gifted students do not get just more problems of the same type. Offer choices, such as a regular assignment, a more challenging one, or one that matches the students' interests.

- Offer AP level courses in statistics, calculus, and computer science. Students should also be encouraged to take classes at local colleges if they have exhausted all the high school possibilities.

- Provide units and problems that go beyond the normal curriculum and relate to the real world. Use concrete experiences that incorporate manipulatives or hands-on activities.

- Allow students to work on independent study projects as a supplement to the regular mathematics curriculum. However, this should not be a substitute for curriculum compacting and proper pacing. Students can use their time to investigate a topic related to mathematics on their own with the teacher's guidance, or perhaps that of a school community mentor.

- Let gifted students work on the same material as other students, only in greater depth. This approach avoids the problem of students being given more of the same work. Instead, students have an in-depth experience at each level of instruction. Instead of developing a separate program for the gifted, the teacher matches in-depth activities with each level of the existing mathematics curriculum.

- Ensure that students realize that you expect their learning products to be of high quality.

- Offer opportunities to participate in contests, such as the Mathematical Olympiad and eCybermission. Give students feedback on their performance, and use some of the contest's problems for classroom discussion.

- Allow students to participate in mentor-paced programs that replace the regular mathematics curriculum. This option is ideal for those students who are exceptionally talented and need much more challenge and acceleration than the regular curriculum offers. These students are typically capable of working at least two grade levels above their age-group. Students work with a mentor in a program designed for the individual student. To implement this approach, Shoplik (2006) recommends the following five-step process:

  Step 1: Determine Aptitude. Start by selecting the level of a standardized test that is at least two grade levels above the student's current grade. For example: above-level ITBS, the Stanford Achievement Test, or the Metropolitan Achievement Test.

  Step 2: Diagnostic Pre-Test. Measure the talented students' achievements and determine where to begin instruction. For example: Use the Stanford Diagnostic Math test. Also consider end-of-year tests from textbook publishers.

Step 3: Re-administer and Evaluate Missed Items. The purpose is to gain a more complete understanding of topics the student does and does not know. There should be no time limits and the student should show all work.

Step 4: Prescriptive Instruction. Thoroughly analyze the testing results. Consider using a mentor to work with the student on concepts the student doesn't understand. The goal is mastery of the concept. Mentors can be high school mathematics teachers, engineers, college professors, undergraduate mathematics majors, and certified teachers.

Step 5: Post-Testing. Administer a parallel form of the pretest to determine if the student has mastered the content.

Grouping

- Provide some activities that can be done individually or in groups, based on student choice. Grouping is productive because gifted students working alone are learning no more than they would at home. Be sure to give them guidelines on their interactions with other group members and appropriate feedback afterward. One possible strategy is for students to work on assignments in small groups with other advanced students. This option can occur when an entire classroom is composed of students of similar abilities, or when a classroom of students is divided into groups based on ability. The arrangement requires careful planning by the teacher. It can be an effective way to meet students' needs, because the pace of the mathematics curriculum is matched to the pace of a small group of learners rather than to the whole class. Thus, talented students are given challenging activities in mathematics, and they are not forced to wait for everybody else to catch up.

Using differentiated instruction and other strategies in regular mathematics classrooms not only benefits gifted students but also has the potential for enriching the learning experience for all students, because some may also want to try the more challenging tasks. With these approaches, all students will have the chance to work at their own level of challenge.

APPLICATIONS

CHOOSING CONTENT FOR ELEMENTARY SCHOOL MATHEMATICS

Mathematics textbooks and programs for elementary school abound. So how do educators decide which program has the best approach in light of what we know about how the human brain learns mathematics? Although the research is still in its early stages, it seems clear that the young mind is more likely to be successful in displaying mathematical talent if educators are aware of three characteristics:

Multi-Step Learning

Too often, elementary mathematics is presented in textbooks (and therefore taught) as a collection of separate one-step skill operations or routines. Genuine mathematical problems are typically multistep, however, requiring the learner to identify intermediate steps in order to move from what is known to what is sought. These steps should be discovered by students as the teacher guides them along. Some drill and practice are necessary, but too much of these will encourage the memorization of single-step routines, carried out procedurally with little understanding. Thus, a mathematical topic for gifted students should give rise to a rich source of problems that require the integration of several basic steps for analysis and for solving problems.

Making Connections

Gifted students should experience mathematics as a collection of relationships among distinct themes, and not as a body of unrelated methods and rules. The teacher's role here is to help students look for connections among seemingly unrelated ideas. Recognizing that new methods and problems are often more familiar than they seem at first is a basic insight that gifted students need to experience regularly.

Logic and Proof

One important component of understanding the connections between different parts of elementary mathematics is the notion that these connections have a logical basis, and thus must be established by exact calculation. These calculations, or proofs, establish whether a mathematical relationship really is true. Cultivate in gifted students an understanding of the need for proof and help them recognize that, in mathematics, it is exact calculation (or proof) that determines correctness. By gaining this understanding, students realize that the solutions to mathematical problems can be determined objectively and are not subject to the arbitrary whim of any person.

From a Teacher's Desk: *Elementary Examples*

What is often overlooked yet easily integrated in mathematics curriculum are multidisciplinary connections. This is simply merging mathematics into another content area, or adding a layer of meaning by illustrating a real-world application of a mathematical concept. Following are examples of both types of integration.

Merging Mathematics and Language Arts

Begin a lesson with a read aloud from a picture book that relates to the mathematics concept to be learned. Ask students to write out their solutions in paragraphs, perhaps complete with drawings and computations, to word problems using two or more different methods to arrive at the same end result.

Merging Mathematics and Social Studies

After learning how to add/subtract/multiple/divide money, ask students to study how money was used historically by the Native American Indians or during the Gold Rush, etc. They can role-play or write a scenario of how goods and money were exchanged.

Merging Mathematics and Science

Students can use balanced equations and actual balances to understand the concept of equivalency; this can transfer to learning measurement skills and strategies. In a Health class, students can calculate their caloric intake for a day, find their average for a week, etc.

Layering on Mathematics

Ask students to go outside and look for geometric shapes in the real world (e.g., stop sign = octagon, ball = sphere, can = cylinder, etc.).

Ask students to interview adults about when and how often they use mathematics in their everyday lives and routines. For instance, some use it in their occupations, some at the grocery store to figure out what product is the best deal, and some to calculate the tip when eating out at a restaurant. When on a field trip, take the students to places where they must use mathematics.

Give examples of real places and times where greater numbers (e.g., 5 digits or more) are used, including stadiums, carnivals, sporting events, stock market, businesses, population, etc.

APPLICATIONS

SELECTING TEACHING STRATEGIES FOR MATHEMATICS

Teaching strategies in mathematics for gifted students should aim to

- Develop deeper understanding
- Lay stronger foundations
- Foster a willingness to seek out the connections between different aspects of mathematics
- Involve higher-level thinking skills
- Cultivate a desire to understand why particular mathematical methods are correct

The following points also need to be considered:

- Strategies should develop higher-level thinking by challenging students to observe, compare, hypothesize, criticize, classify, interpret, and summarize.
- Teachers should use open-ended problems and make clear what areas the students should pursue, what processes should be involved, and what outcomes are achievable and expected.
- Teachers should not expect gifted students to work in undirected and unsupported ways for extended periods of time.
- Strategies should have clear objectives and be designed to increase the students' ability to analyze and solve problems, to stimulate creativity, and to encourage initiative and self-direction.
- Care should be taken in selecting supplemental strategies so that students see their work as challenging and not as drudgery.
- Be sure to offer opportunities for extended research in areas of student interest.

From a Teacher's Desk: *A Secondary Example*

To me, the key in challenging gifted mathematics students is to offer opportunities for enrichment and to expose them to various approaches to solving problems and viewing concepts.

Here are some examples of what I do:

- I introduce a set of items that represent a concept (e.g., symmetry, prime numbers, equations vs. expressions, variables, etc.) and let the students inductively reason to find the similarities among the set to determine what idea they represent.
- I direct students to use deductive reasoning when presented with a big idea (e.g., "Problem solving is a system that is made up of parts that work together" or "The areas of rectangles, triangles, and parallelograms are all related and can be used to find one other").
- I encourage students to research the origin of mathematical theories and/or biographies of mathematicians (e.g., Pythagoras, Euclid, Sophie Germain, etc.).
- I challenge individual students or a small group of talented mathematicians to find many, varied ways to arrive at the same solution to word problems (e.g., using repeated addition vs. multiplication or making a pictorial depiction vs. using computation only).

From a Teacher's Desk: *A Secondary Example*

Performance Tasks. As research in mathematics has indicated, conceptual knowledge has a strong impact on procedural knowledge. In the mathematics classroom, many assessments test purely procedural knowledge. But in order to assess a student's understanding of the conceptual as well as the procedural, many teachers are turning to performance tasks.

A performance task is any form of testing that asks students to create an answer or a product that demonstrates their knowledge or skills. These tasks require the following:

- Students must be active participants
- Outcomes must be clearly identified
- Students must demonstrate their ability to apply their knowledge and skills to a reality-based situation or scenario
- There must be a clearly presented set of criteria

As teachers continue to look for ways to further challenge mathematically gifted students, performance tasks can help educators to access not only students' procedural knowledge, but conceptual knowledge as well. It is with this information that teachers can make informed decisions about providing challenge in the area of mathematics.

The following is an example of a performance task given in a high school statistics class:

At last, your chance to predict your future in math class! Teachers always say that homework is preparation for the test. Put that allegation itself to the test by investigating the relationship (i.e., correlation) between your own homework scores and your test performance. Then, use the data to make a prediction about your next test score.

After the performance task is given, the teacher gives time for reflection. Students share their findings from the performance task. They respond to the following questions, first individually and then as a class.

- Were you surprised by your results? Why or why not?
- What could you do to improve on the predicted outcome of the next test?

The teacher uses this reflection time to emphasize the purposes of using correlation and regression, especially in research.

Exit and Entry Cards

Mrs. Douglas teaches seventh-grade Algebra to an academically and economically diverse student population. Long ago she realized that if she tried to teach everyone the same way and give everyone the same assignments, she would lose many of her students. She fought hard against the myths that there were some students with socio-economic backgrounds that made them poor students in mathematics and that there were some students who wouldn't need much because they were already "sailing along" in mathematics. She found from personal experience that students who excelled in mathematics deserved to experience rigor, and when given work below their readiness level, they became frustrated. She also knew that there were many students who didn't excel in mathematics, but they deserved to be challenged as well.

To provide challenging and engaging tasks to all students, Mrs. Douglas knew she needed to develop quick ways of assessing each student's understanding along the way. She began early on in her career to use Entry Cards and Exit Cards. An entry card is a problem, question, or task given at the beginning of the class period. Mrs. Douglas sometimes uses these to assess if students remember a formula or concept that was taught in the last class. Sometimes she writes a quick problem on the board and, as students walk into classroom, they quickly write their answer on a slip of paper.

An exit card is a problem, question, or task given at the end of a class period. Mrs. Douglas often finishes the class period with a quick question that students write on an index card or slip of paper and give that to her on the way out. She calls it her "ticket to leave" and the feedback this gives her helps her make decisions that effect the next class.

Entry Cards and Exit Cards have been an invaluable tool for Mrs. Douglas. She has found out what interests her students as well as what mathematical concepts they excel at or struggle with so that she can tailor her teaching to the students' needs. Although entry and exit cards are never graded, students find that these quick assessments help them to express what they are learning and get the assistance they need.

1. What questions do you still have about last night's homework?
2   Which problems challenged you the most/least? Why?

Example of an Entry Card

Draw a graph and label the "x" and "y" axes. Graph a line with the end points (3,5) (7,2). Graph a line with the end points (-3, -5) and (7,2). Provide two ways of writing the equation for a line.

Example of an Exit Card

APPLICATIONS

TALENT SEARCHES AVAILABLE
FOR THE MATHEMATICALLY GIFTED

Talent searches are valuable opportunities for meeting the needs of mathematically gifted elementary and secondary students. Rotigel and Lupkowski-Shoplik (1999) describe the process and benefits of these searches. Thousands of students nationwide take advantage of the programs offered annually by sponsoring universities (see list in **Resources**). Through its selection process, the talent search can not only help teachers identify mathematically gifted students, but can also give guidance for designing educational experiences appropriate to the students' ability levels.

School personnel should realize that talent searches are not restricted to just the most highly gifted, nor just to mathematics. Students who score in the top 5 percent of their age group in just one area (e.g., mathematics) are eligible. Sometimes, these students have not been identified for the school's gifted program because their talent lies in just one area, or because they do not receive high scores in language arts.

The Testing Process

Students who score at or above the 95th percentile on the Composite or Math Total, Vocabulary, Reading, Language Total, or Science subtest on a nationally normed achievement test (e.g., Iowa Test of Basic Skills) are recommended for additional testing. An above-level test is administered next, usually two to five grade-levels above the grade placement of the student. This allows the student to demonstrate mastery of more advanced concepts and results in a greater spread of scores, which can be used by teachers for educational planning. Examples of above-level tests are the Scholastic Assessment Test (SAT) and the American College Testing program's EXPLORE test.

Using the Test Results

The above-level test helps to identify the level of a student's mathematical ability. A student who scores in the 95th percentile on the grade-level test may have demonstrated all he or she knows. Consequently, this student's performance on the above-level test will be low. For another student, the above-level test may show high scores in some or all areas, indicating exceptional achievement and ability.

For example, let's say that two third-graders, Student A and Student B, both scored in the 99th percentile on their grade-level test. However, on the above-level eighth-grade test, Student A scores at the 26th percentile and Student B, at the 96th percentile, compared to other eighth graders. Although the two students' abilities seemed similar on the grade-level test, the above-level results show a very different picture. Both students are in their school's gifted program (as they should be) and both need more challenging activities. Student A needs more enrichment in mathematics, participation in contests, group work with students of similar aptitude in mathematics, and curriculum compacting (perhaps, two years of mathematics in one). Student B needs all the same options as Student A, plus individually-paced instruction as well as course- and grade-skipping. Student B may also be an excellent candidate for a university-sponsored Elementary Student Talent Search.

Benefits of Talent Search Participation

Accuracy of Diagnosis. Because above-level tests have a higher ceiling than grade-level tests, they more accurately measure students' abilities, thereby allowing for the development of specific educational plans for each identified student.

Development of Specific Educational Plans. The scores that the students receive on the above-level assessment lead to the development of specific recommendations that best match the students' demonstrated achievement and abilities. Suggestions can range from enrichment to honors classes to acceleration (see Table 6.2).

Opportunities to Participate in University-Sponsored Talent Searches. Students who enter talent search programs have a broad range of options including summer, weekend, and online programs as well as correspondence courses. These opportunities offer students a chance to study topics that may not be available at their home schools. The summer programs offer the chance for like-minded students to live together for several weeks and to study subjects intensively at a pace consistent with their interests and capabilities.

Learning About Themselves. Students in talent searches gain more insight into their abilities and achievement, putting them in a better position to make important choices, such as which college to attend or which career to pursue.

Recognition of Their Abilities. Some talent search programs recognize students' outstanding abilities through scholarships, awards, and honors. Several colleges and universities that sponsor talent searches, for example, also offer scholarships for students to participate in college courses while still attending high school.

Continuing Information. Talent search programs continue to provide participants with newsletters and other printed information about research findings, scholarships, and other educational opportunities. Studies show that, when compared to gifted nonparticipants, talent search participants pursue more rigorous courses of study, accelerate their education to a greater extent, and participate in more extracurricular activities (Olszewski-Kubilius, 1998).

Table 6.2 shows some guidelines for developing the educational plan for students who achieve different scores on the above-level tests (Rotigel & Lupkowski-Shoplik, 1999).

Table 6.2　Educational Planning Guidelines for Students Who Have Taken Above-Level Tests

Tests and Scores	EXPLORE-Mathematics Scale score 1–13 (taken in 4th grade) OR SAT-Mathematics Score of 200–500 (taken in 7th grade)	EXPLORE-Mathematics Scale score 14–20 (taken in 4th grade) OR SAT-Mathematics Score of 510–630 (taken in 7th grade)	EXPLORE-Mathematics Scale score 21–25 (taken in 4th grade) OR SAT-Mathematics Score of 640–800 (taken in 7th grade)
Components of the Plan	Academic counseling and development of an educational plan In-school enrichment; participation in competitions and contests Supplemental course work; Summer programs for enrichment Algebra I in 7th grade; AP calculus in 11th grade; College-level mathematics courses in 12th grade	Academic counseling and development of an educational plan Curriculum compacting (taking 2 years of mathematics in one year) Summer program of fast-paced classes in mathematics Algebra I in 6th grade; AP calculus in 10th grade; College-level mathematics courses in 11th and 12th grades	All of the options in the previous column, plus: An individualized program of study based on diagnostic testing in mathematics Consider grade skipping, early admission to high school, and taking college classes early Mentorships for advanced study in mathematics

Source: Rotigel & Lupinski-Shoplik, 1999.

CHAPTER 7
Artistic Talent

THE ARTS FOR ALL STUDENTS

Teachers are often among the first adults to discover students who demonstrate artistic talent. This discovery does not only occur in music, dance, art, or theater classes. It can also occur in regular classrooms when subject-area teachers use an art form as a strategy to help students achieve the lesson objective. During these types of activities, teachers may notice individual students who show exceptional capabilities when participating in the art form. Of course, this situation is not likely to occur at all if general education teachers do not use art-form-based activities in their lessons on a regular basis. And that raises an intriguing question: To what degree are educators using the arts in regular classrooms?

Are We Incorporating the Arts in the Regular Classroom?

For decades, the presence of the arts in the U.S. curriculum has varied widely. It often increases when progressive reform movements emerge, such as "educating the whole child." But then their presence decreases when a "back-to-basics" movement becomes the fashion, or simply when school budgets get tight. In recent years, national reform efforts based on educational research (Gardner, 1993; Renzulli, 1994) have encouraged infusing the arts into all areas of the curriculum. (For the purposes of this chapter, the arts refer here to four forms: music, dance, theater, and visual arts.) One of the national initiatives in the arts in the early 1990s resulted in the 1994 publication, *National Standards for Arts Education: What Every Young American Should Know and Be Able to Do in the Arts*. It was the work of the Consortium of National Arts Education Associations, which included representatives from the American Alliance for Theatre and Education, the National Art Education Association, the Music Educators National Conference, and the National Dance Association. The published standards are discipline-specific to dance, music, theater, and the visual arts. From six to nine standards are given in each field, and each standard is articulated across sets of grades: K–4, 5–8, and 9–12. To see the entire list of 90 standards, go to the Web site: http://artsedge.kennedy-center.org/teach/standards.cfm. Given the growing body of research on how the arts contribute to brain development, few educators today would deny that incorporating the arts into all levels of K–12 education is desirable. But translating that desire into actual classroom reality is not as easy as it may seem.

Teacher Training in the Arts: One of the barriers to achieving this goal is teacher training. Only a few teachers outside the arts have had training in how to incorporate the arts into their classroom repertoire on a regular basis. As a result, staff development programs have increasingly included the arts as part of in-service training for general education teachers. How do teachers feel about this? One study of more than 400 K–12 teachers provided some insights (Oreck, 2004). A majority of the teachers in the study reported having had only one year or less of formal arts instruction in their lifetime. Nonetheless, they valued the arts in education, believed in its importance in the curriculum, and recognized its benefits for students. They also expressed the desire for more artistic and creative experiences in their own lives. However, despite these values and attitudes and despite the fact that the arts are offered by their school districts as part of professional development, these teachers rarely used the arts in the classroom. Here are the reasons they cited for this:

- Insufficient time coupled with pressures to cover the prescribed curriculum and to prepare students for standardized tests
- Lack of confidence in their facilitation skills in the arts
- Limited supply of space and materials
- Little or no collaboration and support from arts specialists, teaching artists, or experienced colleagues
- Conflicting perceptions about the autonomy and the support they have from supervisors to use the arts in the classroom

A surprising finding was that prior arts instruction was not a significant predictor of whether a teacher used artistic forms in the classroom. A more reliable predictor was whether teachers felt they had the confidence and autonomy to use the arts in their teaching. Furthermore, some teachers may have recognized the importance of the arts for students but they needed evidence that their own successful inclusion of arts would have a positive impact on student achievement.

The lack of training reflects the low priority given to the arts in pre-service and in-service teacher education. Instructional time in the school day is always a central issue. Using the arts takes time and requires teachers to change pace, expectations, and strategies. Learning through the arts is contrary to the single-right-answer approach of a test-driven curriculum. Ultimately, the ability and motivation of teachers to use the arts as a tool in their practice is related to their education, including their preparation in pre-service courses, and to in-service experiences in the arts and in other subjects.

Let's take a look at some of the research on the art forms of music, dance, theater, and visual art. To date, the majority the research in art forms has been in music. Consequently, that is the major focus of this chapter.

MUSICAL TALENT

Most people view musical talent as a gift. But there is considerable scientific evidence that all of us have some musical capability, and that our recognition of music begins shortly after birth (if not before). A study in Japan used two-day-old infants of congenitally deaf and homebound parents to ensure that the infants had not been exposed to music before birth (Masataka, 1999). The infants heard two types of songs: those that were recorded when sung to infants and those sung for adults. By measuring response times, the researchers found that the infants had a distinct preference for the songs directed toward infants. Because these infants had no pre-natal or post-natal exposure to music, these findings may indicate that infants are born with an innate preference for music—the type they are likely to hear from their parents. Another study showed that eight-month-old infants made a distinction between two pieces of classical music and could remember the distinction two weeks later (Ilari & Polka, 2006).

Researchers conducted experiments with 72 adults who had no musical training or education (non-musicians) and used electroencephalography (EEG) to measure their responses to various musical chords

| Nearly every brain is a musical brain. |

(Koelsch, Gunter, & Friederici, 2000). The subjects listened to chord sequences that infrequently contained chords that did not fit their sound expectations. Brain activity increased when they heard the improper chord and decreased when the expected chord was played. When asked, the subjects could not explain their responses. Apparently, these subjects with no musical training still had an innate and subconscious expectation of which chords did or did not fit a musical sequence.

The study also showed that as the musical keys changed, the subjects could still identify which chord fit which key, and their brain activity increased when a chord did not fit the key. This occurred even though the subjects knew nothing about musical keys or the fit of chords to those keys. The researchers concluded that the subjects' brains were interpreting complex musical relationships, setting up musical expectations, and detecting violations of those expectations with no conscious realization or effort on the part of their owners. Subsequent studies have had similar findings (Green et al., 2008; Katahira, Abla, Masuda, & Okanoya, 2008).These results strengthen the notion that the human brain has innate musical ability. Music may become even more important to us as we age. Researchers have found that the debilitating effects of cognitive dementia and Alzheimer's disease often diminish when one learns to play a musical instrument (Grant & Brody, 2004).

Frankly, we really did not need science to tell us that nearly every brain is a musical brain. Just think of how easily our brain takes a sequence of mixed tones presented at different tempos, groups the sounds, and perceives coherent music. We can detect a wrong note in a musical string, pick out melody and harmony, and respond to tempo and timbre. We can anticipate which note should complete a musical phrase. We can unwittingly memorize tunes and lyrics with no conscious effort and have that tune play incessantly in our head—popularly called an "ear worm." Moreover, we do all this without conscious thought.

Brain imaging studies have not discovered a "musical center." Rather, it seems that multiple interconnected neural networks are engaged when the brain is processing music. These networks, in addition to the encoding of pitch along musical scales, seem to be special cortical processes that strongly suggest the human brain is hard-wired for music. Some people are born with an inherited disorder whereby they fail to recognize common tunes from their culture, do not hear when notes are out of tune, and sometimes report that music sounds like a din or banging (Stewart, 2008). This disorder is known as *congenital amusia* (commonly called tone-deafness), and is estimated to affect about four percent of the population. Further studies of this condition may provide researchers more insights into how the brain processes musical information.

Why Are Humans Musical?

Music *is* everywhere and everyone is musical. Anthropologists have never discovered a culture that did not have music. Although the styles of singing and the type of musical instruments very widely, some form of music exists in all cultures, from Eskimo villages to the tropical rainforests. Of course, the notion that music is innate to all humans raises an interesting question: Why? Some psychologists think music is a useless frill that developed when our neural circuits became more sophisticated. But others feel that the importance of music goes much deeper, given the role it has played in the development of our diverse cultures over thousand of years. The oldest musical instrument found to date is a crude bone flute, discovered in southern Germany with human remains that are about 36,000 years old.

Charles Darwin speculated in 1871 that music evolved as part of courtship. Just as birds sing to attract mates, Darwin suggested that early humans used music to attract and retain sexual partners. Subsequent psychologists support Darwin's ideas but propose that the power of music began at the cradle. Because young humans take so long to develop, anything that bonded mother and infant, such as music, would have immediate survival benefit and genetic staying power. In nearly all cultures today, adults carry on sing-song conversations with babies, often with both ending up in duets and rhythmic movements. Music is also used to bond groups of families into tribes. Listening to the same music, or singing and dancing together, can unite

> Music helped primitive humans find mates, communicate, and care for their young as well as bond with others in the tribe.

teams, villages, and cultures into a productive cluster or a dangerous mob. Music can also be a catharsis, allowing rage or grief to be channeled to public release, as in the case of those singing the national anthem in the days following the collapse of the World Trade Center towers (Milius, 2001).

Although no one knows for sure why humans are musical animals, several theories abound. But, based on historical and evolutionary records as well as the increasingly convincing evidence from neuroscience, the best explanation seems to be that, just as in other primates, singing helped primitive humans find mates, communicate and care for their young, and bond with others in the tribe. All the other benefits of music are secondary but no less enjoyable.

The idea that all human beings are musical has tremendous implications for the teaching of music. Music can help children learn to read faster and more accurately (Downing et al., 2004; Gromko, 2005; Standley, 2008), and enhance academic achievement and performance on cognitive tests (Babo, 2004; Schellenberg, Nakata, Hunter, & Tamoto, 2007). Music education should be available to all members of the school community and not just for students with obvious musical talent or whose parents deem it important.

What Is Musical Talent?

Listening to music is one thing, but being able to *create* music is something else. Most people can process musical input and detect complex rhythm and phrases, as well as produce passable vocal music. But far fewer people seem to possess the capacity to master a musical instrument. Why is that? If music is innate, shouldn't most of us be able to learn how to play musical instruments almost as quickly as running or singing? Is it possible that the skills necessary to play a musical instrument require different brain structures? In other words, is the brain's ability to create music a distinct talent whose development is directed by genetic predispositions not found in most people? The question of how much influence genes have on talent of any kind is currently being questioned by scientists.

Howe, Davidson, and Sloboda (1998) did an extensive study that has stirred debate over how much of talent is the result of genetic predisposition and how much is a matter of sustained and rigorous practice. According to Howe and his colleagues, popular belief in Western cultures holds that talent has four components:

- People are born with the capacity to attain high levels of achievement in various activities, such as mathematics, music, literatures, and sports.
- These talents will be exhibited to some extent early in life.
- Only a small minority of people are born with these talents.
- Talent comes in different amounts, so that the "talented" are only those who achieve the highest levels of expertise or success.

Nature or Nurture?: This "either you are born with it or not" approach to explaining talent is often supported by circular reasoning: "He plays so well because he is talented. How do we know he is talented? Because he plays so well." Music is especially rich in folklore that supposedly substantiates the genetic source of musical achievement. The examples of child prodigies, such as Mozart and Artur Rubenstein, are often used to support the idea that talents appear early in life. Adding to the notion that these children are born with special capabilities, these people cite that perfect pitch (more accurately, absolute pitch) also is innate in these high achievers. Still others refer to the discovery that some parts of the brain in great achievers are larger than average, suggesting that the talent resulted from prenatal changes in brain development.

Howe et al. (1998) suggest that these arguments are weak evidence to support talent as purely genetic and that there may be alternative explanations (Table 7.1). First, they note that much of what is written about child prodigies is anecdotal, and there are very few musical prodigies compared to the larger number of highly successful professional musicians who did not display early signs of talent. Mozart's father, Leopold, was a musician. Would the young Wolfgang have become such a musical wonder had he not been exposed to music from birth? Second, there is evidence that perfect pitch appears in young children who have been given extensive musical training. Consequently, it is just as likely that perfect pitch may be acquired early in life rather than be innate. Third, because brain growth can be affected by experience, increased brain size could be the *result* of musical experiences and practice, rather than being the cause of musical achievement.

Table 7.1 Is Musical Talent Genetic?	
Pros	**Alternative Possibilities**
Child prodigies are evidence that innate talent appears early.	Child prodigies are rare; many professional musicians were not prodigies.
Perfect pitch is innate and a sign of special capability.	Perfect pitch may be acquired early through extensive musical training.
Larger brain areas cause musical talent.	Musical experience and practice cause larger brain areas.

Source: Howe et al., 1998.

Accordingly, is seems that activities, such as practice, accomplished *after* birth may have a significant effect on musical achievement. To examine the power of practice, John Sloboda and his colleagues interviewed 257 young musicians between the ages of eight and 18 about their performance history from the start of playing a musical instrument (Sloboda, Davidson, Howe, & Moore, 1996). Ninety-four of these students kept a diary for a period of 42 weeks to record the amount of time devoted to practice and other activities. The sample included participants with a broad range of musical achievement, from students who were attending a highly selective music school to individuals who had abandoned their playing after a year or less of formal instruction. Music achievement was measured by their degree of skill in playing their musical instruments through an externally validated performance examination.

Participants were divided into five groups on the basis of their level of musical competence. Group 1 was the target group, comprising students enrolled in a highly selective music school. Group 2 were students who had applied for but had not been accepted to the music school. Students in Group 3 had expressed interest in attending a music school but had not followed through with a formal application. Group 4 consisted of students who were learning a musical instrument at a nonspecialist school. Students who had been unsuccessful at instrumental music were in Group 5, having not played for at least one year prior to the study.

Not surprisingly, the researchers found a strong relationship between musical achievement and the amount of formal practice undertaken (see Figure 7.1). High achievers practiced the most (Groups 1 and 2), moderate achievers practiced a moderate amount of time (Group 3), and low achievers barely practiced at all (Groups 4 and 5). Furthermore, the researchers found that

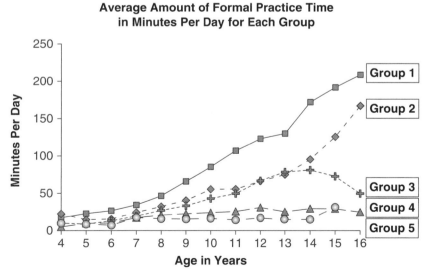

Figure 7.1   The average practice time in minutes per day for the five groups.
Source: Sloboda et al., 1996.

high achievers who practiced less were *no more successful than low achievers*. Another important finding was that differences in practice patterns began very early in age and from the time of starting to learn an instrument. Those who practiced a lot when they were young also practiced a lot when they were older, and vice versa. These results support the premise that formal, intense practice is a major determinant of musical achievement.

Howe and other researchers continue to believe that in order to fully realize potential, an aspiring music performer must acquire the necessary skills and characteristics needed to negotiate the challenges of learning to play a musical instrument competently. Regardless of technical prowess or natural ability, the research literature suggests that individuals in any performance area will only be able to reach the top if they adopt an appropriate focus during training and performance

> Formal, intense practice is a major determinant of musical achievement.

(Abbott & Collins, 2002; Howe & Davidson, 2003). Some researchers in the domain of music now suggest that the ability to succeed is dependent on experience, the influence of others, and the individual's personality. Unfortunately, however, personality profiles in other performance domains, such as sports, have failed to differentiate elite performers from less successful peers, and the weak link between personality and success has often produced ambiguous and unusable findings.

Howe and Davidson (2003) remain skeptical of the belief that innate gifts and talents are vital for the attainment of excellence in music and they have doubts about musical ability being the sole explanation for expertise. Accordingly, they support the research model often referred to as *deliberate practice*. This model suggests that repeated practice influences the development of expertise by improving performance, which in turn leads the participant to choose to engage in more demanding activities. Within this framework, it is assumed that it will take 10 years of deliberate practice to become an elite performer. In this context, the term "deliberate" describes a state where practice is effortful, difficult, and not inherently motivating. To these researchers, it is not only musical ability, but also tenacity, commitment, and other behavioral characteristics that distinguish those individuals who will emerge as talented musicians.

What Has Science Discovered?: As the nature versus nurture debate over musical achievement continues, scientists have been making some interesting observations about music and the human brain. Table 7.2 shows some of their findings. At first glance, getting involved with music, especially at an early age, seems to have significant impact on the growing brain. That may be true. But it is important to point out that probably anything we do at an early age affects brain organization and development. For example, a comparison of the brains of mathematicians to non-mathematicians, of professional dancers to non-dancers, would likely also show structural, and perhaps functional, differences.

Table 7.2 Some Findings From Science on Musical Ability	
Study	**Findings**
Elbert et al., 1995, using PET	Compared to non-players, string players had greater cerebral activity and a larger area of the right motor cortex that controls the fingers of the left hand. The effects were greater for those who began playing at an early age.
Pascual-Leone et al., 1995, using MEG	The area of the motor cortex controlling the fingers increased in size in response to piano exercises.
Schlaug, Jancke, Huang, & Steinmetz, 1995, using PET	(1) Musicians had greater activity in left temporal lobes than non-musicians. (2) Musicians with perfect (absolute) pitch had greater activity in left temporal lobe than musicians without perfect pitch.

Study	Findings
Pantev et al., 1998, using PET	The auditory cortex was 25 percent larger in experienced musicians than in non-musicians, and the effect was greater for those who started studying music at an early age.
Gregersen, 1998	In-depth reviews of genetic data showed evidence of a genetic predisposition to perfect (absolute) pitch, which could be expressed as a result of childhood exposure to music. Some children with perfect pitch also demonstrated exceptional mathematical ability.
Glassman, 1999	Harmonic relationships in music may account for the dynamics and limitations of working memory.
Ohnishi et al., 2001, using fMRI	(1) Musicians processed music in brain areas that were different from the brain areas of non-musicians. Musicians showed more activation in the left temporal lobe but non-musicians had more brain activity in the right temporal lobe. (2) The degree of activation for musicians was correlated with the age at which the individual started musical training; the younger the starting age, the greater the activation. (3) Trained musicians with perfect pitch had greater activation than those without this ability. These findings suggest that early music training influences the brain to organize networks in the left hemisphere to process the analytical data needed to create music.
Itoh, Fujii, Suzuki, & Nakada, 2001, using fMRI	These colleagues reaffirmed the role of the left hemisphere when playing an instrument. The left parietal lobe was more highly activated than the right when musically trained subjects played the piano, regardless of whether they used their left or right hand separately, or used both hands.
Schlaug & Christian, 2001; using MRI	Musicians trained at an early age showed larger gray matter volumes in the left and right sensory and motor cortex regions and the left parietal lobe.
Gaser & Schlaug, 2003	Musicians have larger gray matter volumes in motor, auditory, and visual-spatial brain regions compared to non-musicians. The amounts were correlated with the musician's status (professional vs. amateur) and intensity of practice.
Baumann et al., 2007, using fMRI	Compared to non-musicians, activity in the auditory and motor areas in the brain of pianists was significantly greater and related to degree of intensive practice.
Ruthsatz et al., 2008, testing audiation and measuring practice time	Practice and innate characteristics, such as general intelligence and music audiation (the process of mentally hearing and comprehending music, even when no physical sound is present) together, accounted for more of the variation in music performance than practice alone.

So, Where Are We?: Researchers have to speculate on possible explanations for their findings. At this time, these explanations do not resolve the nature versus nurture debate as it relates to musical performance. However, the research evidence to date suggests that although some genetic predisposition for musical processing is needed (nature), talented performance in music requires considerable and determined practice (nurture). This conclusion is consistent with findings in other research studies examining the nature-and-nurture relationship. In many cases, the nurture component has far greater influence than nature on how a particular behavior is expressed.

Even musically talented students have mixed views on the heritability of their own musical achievement. Tremblay and Gagné (2001) asked 80 musically talented students to use a 100-point Likert-type scale to rate the extent to which they believed seven components of musical ability could be inherited. The heritability scale ranged from *Not at all* to *Completely*. The seven components were as follows: auditory (ability to recognize and discriminate sounds), creativity (ability to improvise or compose melody), interpretation (ability to play a musical piece with feeling), auditory memory (ability to memorize a melody quickly), rhythm (ability to reproduce beats, duration of sounds, pauses, and tempo of a melody), coordination (ability to move hands on the instrument and

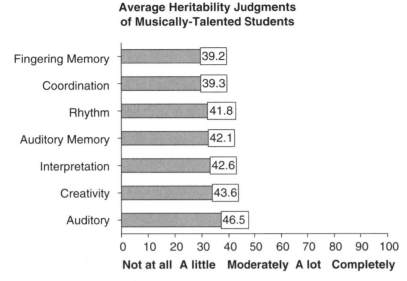

Average Heritability Judgments of Musically-Talented Students

Figure 7.2   The average scores of musically-talented students on their beliefs that these musical abilities are inherited.

Source: Tremblay & Gagné, 2001.

to synchronize both hands), and fingering memory (ability to memorize fingering). Most students' scores fell in the moderate portion of the scale, ranging from 39.2 to 46.5 (see Figure 7.2). Apparently, the music students believed that musical ability is inherited to a moderate degree and that practice and experience did not account totally for their musical achievement.

Ironically, the judgments of these talented musicians may be closer than the scientific studies to explaining what really accounts for musical achievement. On the one hand, the belief that talent is entirely innate has been overworked and, unfortunately, has led people to avoid the challenge of playing a musical instrument altogether. Too often, students invoke the absence of innate talent as the excuse for their failure and readiness to abandon their efforts. "It's not my fault. No one in my family is any good at (fill in the blank, here)," is not an uncommon excuse heard in today's classrooms. However, many accomplished musicians who displayed no early musical talent have become successful through their efforts at regular and determined practice. Granted, they may not be concert virtuosos, but their music can still provide enjoyment for themselves and others.

On the other hand, science cannot discount the possibility of a genetic predisposition to music. This genetic influence, for example, could be in the form of a larger auditory cortex capable of greater sensitivity to, and discrimination of, patterns of sounds. Another possibility is the development of a strong voice box and enhanced breathing musculature to produce powerful and melodic vocal music. Whatever the genetic contribution, such individuals, especially in a strong musical environment, will likely reach exceptionally high levels of musical achievement.

Although our understanding of how music affects the human brain is still far from complete, some of the following points can still be made:

- In most people, the brain has an innate ability to process music from birth.
- When listening to music, the processing may affect and enhance other cerebral functions, such as mathematical operations, kinesthetic performance, and memory recall.
- In most people, musical achievement may result more from efforts at regular and sustained practice than from genetic influences.
- A few people may be born with genetic predispositions that, in the right environment, will allow them to become extraordinary musical performers.
- The musical brain is highly resilient and persists even in people with profound mental and emotional disabilities.

READING AND MEMORIZING MUSIC

Reading Music

Highly successful musicians need to read musical notes and lyrics rapidly in order to produce fluent vocal and instrumental sound. Yet, some of these musically talented individuals have only average abilities in the reading of text. How can this be? Should not the ability to read music with incredible speed also apply to reading text or vice versa? Apparently, this is not the case. A series of brain imaging studies on how the brain processes music in normal and brain-

> The brain uses different storage systems for musical and nonmusical text.

damaged musicians revealed that the ability to read or write music is a functionally distinct process from reading or writing text (Cappelletti, Waley-Cohen, Butterworth, & Kopelman, 2000; Stewart & Walsh, 2001). When the musicians read music, the notes and letters were integrated in the brain along with the acoustic input of what had just been played or sung. A network of brain regions, which Cappelletti and his colleagues called the *abstract musical system*, converted the input into melody and rhythm to produce the playing, singing, or writing of the next musical notes (see Figure 7.3). During this process, the PET studies showed that the lower occipital and the rear

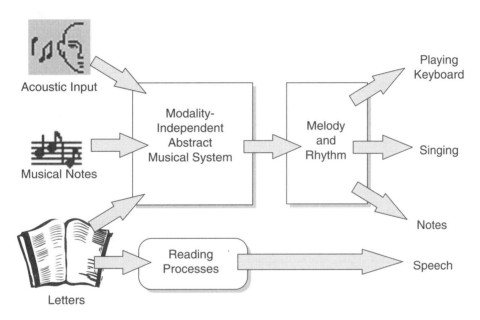

Figure 7.3 The processing of musical notes and letters (lyrics) is functionally distinct from reading text and requires different cognitive operations.

Source: Stewart & Walsh, 2001.

part of the parietal lobes were the most activated areas (Figure 7.4). Damage to these regions resulted in the loss of the ability to read music, but not text. Apparently, different cerebral areas process text that is not related to music, but used instead for the production of speech. These findings may also suggest that there are different memory systems for storing music and nonmusical text. If so, it would explain why some patients with Alzheimer's disease, who have lost their ability to speak, are still able to sing songs and their lyrics with few or no errors. The results of the latest studies seem to be leading away from the earlier theory that music was essentially a right hemisphere function. It seems that music processing is spread throughout the brain and that selectively changing the focus of attention dramatically alters the patterns and intensity of cerebral activation.

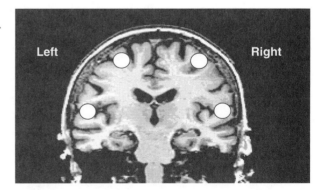

Figure 7.4 The four circles in this representation of a PET scan show the areas of the brain that were most activated while a musician was reading music. Damage to the areas represented by the white circles results in the loss of ability to read music, but not text.

Source: Cappelletti et al., 2000.

Other investigations have revealed just how complex reading music actually is. In a study of nearly 100 high school wind instrument players, researchers found that music sight-reading ability can be predicted by a combination of four cognitive abilities (Gromko, 2004):

- Reading comprehension
- Rhythmic audiation (the process of hearing and comprehending music, even when no physical sound is present)
- Spatial orientation
- Visual field articulation (ability to focus on a specific item embedded in a pattern)

The presence of reading comprehension comes as no surprise and supports researchers who have suggested that reading music may be like reading words because both symbol systems are governed by rules (see Figure 7.3). Rhythmic audiation's presence extends previous research in music education that found rhythmic sight-reading to be the single best predictor of music sight-reading ability. Apparently, precise aural feedback is necessary when processing the rhythmic information contained in music notation.

Spatial orientation ability supports the research suggesting that the pertinent information contained in musical notations is derived not by analyzing the notes but by analyzing the spatial location of the notes. Gromko (2004) believes this finding suggests that reading music is a spatial process that may be like the reading of two-dimensional architectural drawings that are comprehended as three-dimensional objects. In other words, when skilled musicians read musical notation, they may actually be mentally representing the sound as an image with both spatial and temporal dimensions.

Finally, visual field articulation was negatively correlated with music sight-reading ability. Students who scored high on visual field articulation focused on each individual component of the pattern. These students scored lower on music sight-reading, which requires a focus on musical patterns rather than individual notes, and on the spatial location of the notes rather than a discrete analysis of the notes.

Memorizing Music

Professional vocal and instrumental musicians often need to memorize large amounts of music if they want to perform publically. Although musical performance involves recall mainly from long-term memory, working memory is employed whenever the performers begin to improvise on the stored music. Yet, working memory is thought to have a functional limit of about seven chunks in most adults (Sousa, 2006)—a capacity that would seem far too small to explain the rapid and varied modifications that some musicians display during a performance. To do this, they must have some means of binding more items within the chunks, thereby increasing the total item count in working memory. (Although working memory has a functional capacity of only so many chunks that it can process at one time, there appears to be no functional limit to the *number of items* that can be combined into a chunk.)

Some researchers now speculate that harmonic frequencies of brain waves may be the binding medium. This hypothesis holds that (1) items bond into a chunk because some specific property synchronizes and unifies them, and (2) harmonic frequencies within an octave band of brain waves are the synchronizing mechanisms (Glassman, 1999). This theory also suggests that because trained musicians are more attuned and responsive to harmonics, their brains are much better at increasing chunk size than the brains of non-musicians, thereby raising the item count in working memory and significantly improving the efficiency of the transfer of chunks between working and long-term memories.

> Musicians' brains may be much better at chunking information than the brains of non-musicians.

Memory to Performance: As musicians practice and memorize a piece of music, how does the memory information get translated into performance on, say, a piano keyboard? Studies have shown that just listening to a piece of music involuntarily triggers the corresponding finger movements in pianists and violinists, and activates the brain's motor cortex. Conversely, when pianists and violinists silently tap out musical phrases, it causes activation in the auditory regions of their brain (Haueisen & Knösche, 2001; Scheler et al., 2001).

In a follow-up study, researchers used EEG technology to measure changes in the brains of beginning pianists as they were learning and practicing a new piece of music (Bangert & Altenmüller, 2003). The measurements were taken at intervals over a five-week period. Researchers found that, during this period, an area in the rear of the brain's right hemisphere became increasingly activated. All these studies lead researchers to suggest that music training triggers immediate changes in the brain's cortex and that areas in the rear of the right hemisphere provide an audio-motor interface for the mental representation of the musical instrument.

Of course, the inevitable question arises: Is the emergence of this audio-motor interface primarily the result of genetic predispositions or just dedicated practice? Once again, the answer seems to be, both. Just as these studies demonstrate the importance of practice to the development of auditory-motor coordination, other studies weigh in with evidence that some brains are more adept at responding and integrating musical information than others, most likely due to genetic influences (Thaut, Demartin, & Sanes, 2008).

Music As Another Way of Knowing

Findings from cognitive neuroscience and related disciplines are identifying neural networks in the brain that support multiple ways of knowing. These human knowledge networks provide a means for expressing, understanding, sharing, and gaining insights into one's inner and outer worlds. Considered alongside other knowledge systems, such as language and mathematics, what unique contributions can music make? Music allows us to know, discover, understand, experience, share, or express such aspects of the human condition as feelings, aesthetic experiences, thoughts, structure, time and space, self-knowledge, self-identity, group identity, and healing and wholeness (Hodges, 2005).

> Music allows us to know, discover, express, and share aspects of the human condition that we cannot experience through any other means.

Neuroscience research into music supports the notion that music is disassociated from linguistic and other types of cognitive processing. Thus, processing music offers a unique way of acquiring nonverbal information. By studying how the brain processes music, scientists can learn things about the brain that they cannot get from other cognitive processes. Moreover, music allows us to know, discover, express, and share aspects of the human condition that we cannot experience through any other means. For that reason alone, we should be grateful for the music that talented performers create to help us all get a deeper understanding of what it means to be human. If the purpose of an education is to systematically develop the mind and capabilities of every child, then it is clear that music has a unique and necessary role to play.

DEVELOPING MUSICALLY TALENTED STUDENTS

The Identification Process

Identifying musically talented students requires a set of effective criteria and procedures deemed valid by professionals who work with these types of students. Haroutounian (2000) surveyed over 140 teachers, musicians, and arts specialists who work with musically talented students. The following are the most common criteria for identifying musical talent:

Musical Awareness and Discrimination

- Perceptual awareness of sound: internally senses sound and listens discriminately
- Rhythmic sense: fluidly responds to rhythm and maintains a steady pulse
- Sense of pitch: discriminates pitches; remembers and repeats melodies

Creative Interpretation

- Experiments with and manipulates sound
- Performs and reacts to music with personal expression and involvement
- Is aware of the aesthetic qualities of sound

Commitment

- Perseveres in musical activities
- Works with focused concentration and internal motivation
- Refines ideas, constructively critiques musical work of others and self

The identification process should also reach beyond the school to include recommendations from peers, private teachers, music directors, and other community members familiar with the student's musical abilities. An audition would also be appropriate.

The Nature of Practice

The extensive practice required of most musically talented students requires continuing encouragement by parents and teachers. Parents are there at the beginning and establish the routine and habits of practice from the onset. These routines set the work ethic, which can make the difference between the student reaching high or only moderate levels of mastery.

The teacher's role is critical to progressive musical development. As a tutor, the teacher provides a one-on-one environment where there are no limits to the student's progress. Being part of a performance group, such as a band, orchestra, or chorus, can greatly motivate student musicians to try more challenging musical pieces. To do so necessitates a form of practice that requires the student to work at optimal intensity. This is called deliberate practice, and teachers often provide the direction and encouragement that will help students recognize its value. As we discussed earlier in this chapter, the amount of practice time per week needed to produce high levels of mastery depends on the intensity of practice done in the student's early years. Musically talented teenagers who have learned the strategies of deliberate practice can achieve maximum results in less time.

Music teaching in the elementary grades is designed to reach all students. However, in the secondary schools, music classes are elective courses attracting students who have some degree of interest in vocal and instrumental music. They may represent a wide range of musical abilities, from passing interest to extraordinary talent. Given this mix, the music teacher may opt for a performance-based approach, hoping that it will appeal to a majority of the students. Furthermore, public performance helps to highlight the music curriculum and perhaps to garner community support during times when budgets are tight. This single-minded approach, however, is usually not sufficient to meet the needs of students who have already discovered their musical ability, nor will it entice those who have yet to realize their potential in music.

Looking for New Approaches to Teaching Music

Some music educators are examining the research findings in cognitive science and suggesting newer approaches to teaching music in secondary schools. Specifically, attention is focused on three factors that are influencing classroom instruction (Haroutounian, 2000; Webster, 2000):

(1) Shifting from a teacher-centered, didactic format to a student-centered, constructivist approach. The performance-oriented approach requires that the teacher constantly play the role of director, preparing for the next competition, festival, or concert. As a result, performance takes precedence over sharing the process of making musical decisions with students. Constructivism is an instructional format that emphasizes the importance of keeping the learner as an active participant rather than a passive receiver. Guided by the teacher, the students are engaged in creative activities that allow them to show mastery of music through their actions.

(2) Expanding the use of technology and the Internet. Computer software and the Internet provide many new resources for students to deal with music creatively rather than just practicing a musical piece to the teacher's specifications. With project-centered learning, teachers can encourage students to use computers and synthesizers to experiment creatively with sound. See the **Resources** section for suggestions.

(3) Using creative thinking skills and metaperception. One of the major goals of music education is to engage students' imaginations. This is more likely to occur in classrooms where teachers regularly involve students in divergent experiences that require creative thinking. Teachers will help students see music as an art form when they encourage them to create music thoughtfully through composition, performance, improvisation, and active listening. As students absorb abstract musical concepts, they learn to make creative decisions to solve musical problems. In essence, they are combining fine-tuned discrimination of the senses with high cognitive functioning to solve artistic problems. This process, sometimes called *metaperception,* is the artistic equivalent of metacognition. It includes sensing sound internally, remembering this sound, and manipulating the sound to communicate an emotional interpretation to others.

Academic Achievement Versus Musical Study

As musically talented students in secondary schools reach higher levels of performance, they begin to think about the possibility of a career in music. They crave practice time, expand their playing ability to additional instruments, and get involved in more musical performances. Parents, meanwhile, who had been so supportive when the student was younger, may not now welcome the notion of music as their child's career choice. Ironically, the student is then torn between coping with the demands of additional practice and performance time, while simultaneously trying to satisfy parental desires for more intense academic studies to keep career options open. Although it is true that many musically talented students are also gifted academically, this combined pressure can sometimes be too much. As a result, some musically talented students end their music lessons to relieve the pressure.

Working with parents, music teachers may be able to help their talented students deal with this difficult situation by looking at flexible scheduling that allows the student to pursue music lessons at other times. Programs such as MusicLink help schools develop individualized curriculums for talented students.

Implications for Teaching Music in Secondary Schools

Musically talented secondary school students have reached the intermediate to advanced level of talent development. Curriculum programs should be independently developed to meet the needs of these students (Haroutounian, 2000).

Intermediate Level: Lessons should develop the technical skills needed for advancing repertoire and exploring musical structure and style. Students seek opportunities to perform outside the school and wish to do so with technical skill and accuracy. Intermediate level students:

♫ Acquire more refined practice techniques

♫ Enjoy opportunities for performing both in and outside of school

♫ Develop technical proficiency

♫ Desire accuracy and precision in performance

♫ Experience a cognitive shift in musical thinking from active to interpretive understanding

♫ Expand performing opportunities to include occasional judged competitions

♫ Prefer instruction on musical understanding and technical development

♫ Delicately balance input from teachers, parents, and other students on competition, practice, and performance

Advanced Level: Lessons should be designed to hone already-developed technical skills and to enhance personal interpretations appropriate to the style, dynamic qualities, and aesthetic nature of the music. These students are usually already engaged in competition-level performances. Advanced level students:

♫ Analyze musical history, theory, and structure

♫ Understand stylistic differences along with various interpretations that reflect these styles

♫ Develop creative interpretation and artistic reasoning

♫ Fine-tune practice techniques and make maximum use of time for musical problem solving

♫ Use technical skills to create subtle qualities of tonal color

♫ Develop confidence through performances in professional-type settings

♫ Demonstrate subtlety and sensitivity in the critique of music performed by themselves and others

Differentiated Music Curriculum

Different levels of musical talent development in secondary schools can be addressed through differentiated curriculum. For a variety of reasons, the musical talents of some students do not emerge until they reach high school. Many vocal musicians, for example, do not begin taking singing lessons until adolescence, usually at the urging of a school choral director. Potential composers emerge when they start using computers to manipulate music in creative ways. Wind or brass instrument players often do not get serious about their musical studies until high school. And then there are the self-taught musicians, who are more likely to be discovered displaying their skills outside the school setting. Because these students are at varying levels of development, the music curriculum must be sufficiently flexible to meet their different needs. Haroutounian (2000) separates these students into five categories and suggests different curriculum options for each.

Advanced students who are conservatory-bound. Maximum practice time should be allotted to exceptionally talented students who are serious about pursuing a musical career. If they plan to attend a conservatory, the entrance audition is likely to be the major determinant for admissions. Consequently, the demands of intense practice may result in less time devoted to other academic studies. Guidance counselors can be helpful in developing curricular options for these exceptional talents. Although some of these students attend Saturday classes and lessons at conservatories, those who remain in a normal high school setting need independent study options to allow sufficient flexibility for practice.

Advanced students not yet committed to a career. Advanced musically talented students who have not yet committed to a performance career should have curricular options that extend beyond performance. These options could include creative work in composition, improvisation, and even collaborative projects with other art forms. The goal is to move these students out of a performance-based focus from time to time, getting them involved in creative ventures rarely offered in the traditional high school music curriculum.

Self-taught students. The talents of self-trained students lie outside the traditional secondary school music program. They have learned to develop their skills in a haphazard way, rather than through formal training. Offering instruction in the traditional studio setting may not be successful. The differentiated curriculum for self-taught students should investigate topics such as creative composition exploration, which can also include instruction in basic musical notation.

The critical listener. Critical listeners translate musical ideas into words. Their written or verbal critiques demonstrate astute musical awareness and creative verbal talents. Differentiated curriculum for critical listeners should offer comparative listening and critique of professional recordings, mentoring with a professional music critic, and opportunities for writing music reviews for the school paper.

The musical history student. Outstanding history students with musical training may be fascinated with the musical significance of historical eras, musical styles emerging from cultural influences, or other musicological connections. The curricular framework for these students should aim to link music and history in independent study or projects located within the regular gifted education program.

See the **Applications** section at the end of this chapter for suggestions on how to address the needs of these students.

Conclusion About Music

All students can develop their knowledge, understanding, and skills in music. Some may need more help than others, but that is true in any subject. Students who are generally gifted will need challenging musical contexts that will enable them to extend and apply their more general abilities. Music provides a context in

> Music can help teachers recognize giftedness in students who are not yet strong in language, especially those students whose first language is not English.

which generally gifted students can deal with a range of complex factors and bring them together when making and responding to music. Generally gifted students already have the ability to think quickly and assimilate information, so these talents will also be evident when engaging in music. Furthermore, because music is abstract, it provides a means of identifying and developing skills that are not dependent on language skills. Thus, music can help teachers recognize giftedness in students who are not yet strong in language, especially those students whose first language is not English. Students who display strong musical interest and are vocally or instrumentally accomplished will need special attention so that the school environment continues to develop their talents.

Musically talented students should have every opportunity to complete their talent development through high school, regardless of their future career decisions. They should be allowed to engage in challenging curricular experiences in their specialized field of interest. Schools can offer differentiated curriculum through student-developed interdisciplinary and independent study options, accelerated learning in performance classes, and courses in musical theory, composition, and music history. Teachers working with these students can serve as liaisons between the school and community to ensure student access to community resources related to music.

DANCE TALENT

When we hear music, we often rock, sway, or tap our feet to the beat, perhaps totally unaware that we are even moving. This instinctive response likely evolved together with music as a way of generating rhythm. Dance is a fundamental form of human expression found in all cultures. It requires specialized mental skills. One part of the brain serves as a synchronizer to enable us to pace our actions to music. Another part helps direct our body's orientation and movements through space. Dance demands a type of time and space coordination not found in any other social context.

Public schools in general often relegate dance to the realms of play, physical exercise, recreation, and theatrical performance. Unlike music, it is only recently that the discipline of dance has developed its own notation system, and that universities have recognized it as a rigorous intellectual as well as physical activity.

> First-grade students who participated in a 20-session Basic Reading Through Dance Program improved significantly more than control students on all the reading skills that were tested.

Indifference toward dance and the few resources that schools have devoted to developing dance programs have kept dance education on the sidelines or completely out of the K–12 curriculum. This, despite the fact that dance has long had a significant role in the education, religion, ethnic identity, and social and political organization of many cultures. We have never discovered a culture that does not have dance!

Nonetheless, apart from the limited government-funded arts-in-the-schools programs of the 1990s, our current education system gives strong support for verbal communication but not much for nonverbal communication. Yet research on cognition and nonverbal communication is providing new insights into ways of knowing and communicating through dance education. For example, one study found that dance can improve basic reading skills in beginning readers. The study of more than 600 first-grade students in Chicago showed that students who participated for 20 sessions in the Basic Reading Through Dance program improved significantly more than control students on all the reading skills that were assessed (McMahon, Rose, & Parks, 2003).

Dance As an Academic Discipline

The discipline of dance is a lot more than moving around and making body motions to music. Hanna (2008) explains that dance can be conceptualized as a human behavior composed of purposeful, intentionally rhythmical, and culturally influenced sequences of nonverbal body movements and stillness, expressed in time and space, and with effort. Dance has inherent and aesthetic value. It is often accompanied by music, with its range of sounds and rhythm, and sometimes by costume and props. A dancer's purpose may be to provide an emotional experience, such as telling a story or expressing a troublesome theme. Dance is multisensory, and so it heightens one's awareness of the meaning of different kinds of emotional expression. In this sense, dance is a vehicle for purposeful nonverbal communication.

Because communication without meaning is of little value, research on different forms of dance has revealed complex ways of conveying meaning in dance that students can use, depending on their intellectual development and teacher instruction. Dancers may use one or more of the following six symbolic devices to encode meaning (Hanna, 2008).

- *Concretization* describes the dance movement that produces the outward aspect of something, such as a warrior dance displaying battle tactics for advancing or retreating.
- *Icon* represents most of the characteristics of something, and is responded to as if it actually were what it represents. For example, a Haitian dancer manifests through a specific dance the presence of Ghede, the god of love and death, and is then treated by fellow Haitians with genuine awe and gender-appropriate behavior—just as if the dancer were actually the god himself.
- *Stylization* encompasses arbitrary and conventional gestures or movements, such as a ballet dancer pointing to his heart as a sign of love for his lady.
- *Metonym* is a motional conceptualization of one thing representing another of which it is a part, such as a romantic duet representing an affair.
- *Metaphor* is the most common way of encoding meaning in dance. It is the expression of one thought, experience, or phenomenon in place of another that it resembles.
- *Actualization* is a portrayal of one or several of a dancer's usual roles, such as a woman who performs in a dance for mothers, to convey her maternal role.

Brain Areas Involved in Dance: Although there are numerous brain imaging studies of movement of specific body parts, those relating to dance movement and expression are limited, largely because of the physical constraints imposed on the subject by the scanner. Nonetheless, the few findings are fascinating, especially in how they involve the brain's language areas. As explained in Chapter 5, Broca's and Wernicke's areas (see Figure 5.1), located in the left hemisphere, have long been associated with verbal language expression and comprehension, sequential information processing, abstract symbolic and analytic functions, and more recently, complex patterns of movement. The process of making a dance engages some of the same components in the brain for conceptualization, creativity, and memory as do verbal poetry or prose, but not the same procedural knowledge (Cross, de C. Hamilton, & Grafton, 2006).

One study of 10 experienced adult dancers looked at the neural basis of dance using MRI and PET scans (Brown, Martinez, & Parsons, 2006). The dancers performed (1) repeated tango steps on an inclined surface to the regular beat of tango music and (2) step movements to irregular rhythms. The researchers found an interacting network of brain areas active during the performance of specific movements in the tango. A region near Broca's area was involved during motor sequencing, which may be the result of activation in the

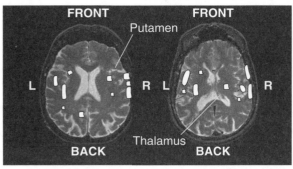

FRONT   **FRONT**

Putamen

L   R   L   R

Thalamus

BACK   **BACK**

Metered Rhythm   Irregular Rhythm

Figure 7.5   These representative PET scans show the brain areas that were activated during dancing with metered and irregular rhythms. Many of the areas are similar. However, the putamen was activated during dancing to metered rhythmn (left image) but the thalamus was activated during dancing to irregular rhythmn (right image).

Source: Adapted from Brown et al., 2006.

abstract musical system explained earlier in this chapter (see Figure 7.3).

Not surprisingly, the dance movements activated the right hemisphere, which seems to involve elementary perceptual tasks, nonverbal processing of spatial information, music, and emotional reactivity. Furthermore, the left image in Figure 7.5 shows that an area involved in motor control and intentional movement, called the *putamen,* was activated when the subjects danced to regular, metered rhythms. But when they stepped to the irregular rhythms, the right image shows activation in the *thalamus,* a structure that monitors most sensory input before sending it to other parts of the brain for processing. Though limited, these studies highlight the complex nature of dance and the extensive network of brain regions that are recruited to perform it successfully.

Just as the brain controls dance movements, so does practicing dance affect the brain. Repeated dance movements cause positive plastic changes in the brain for young and old alike. Physical activity produces neurobiological changes that encourage brain cells to associate with one another, reflecting the brain's fundamental ability to adapt to new challenges. Physical exercise that requires complex motor movement, such as dance, exercises those areas of the brain involved in the full range of cognitive functions, causing the brain to fire signals along the same network of cells, which solidifies their connections (Ratey, 2008). Thus, extended or deep learning in dance affects how well the brain processes other tasks. In a neurological study of which activities lowered the risk of seniors developing Alzheimer's disease, researchers found that seniors who did crossword puzzles cut the risk by 38 percent, those who played musical instruments lowered it to 69 percent, and those who played board games by 74 percent. But dancing lowered the risk by an astonishing 76 percent (Verghese et al., 2003). This unexpected result may be because dancing requires the complex cognitive tasks of remembering dance steps, executing them sequentially in response to music, and coordinating with a partner or group in time and space.

Dance in the K–12 Curriculum

As educators contemplate starting dance programs in K–12 schools, here are some of the questions that need to be addressed:

- Should dance be part of the art education or physical education curriculum?
- What curriculum framework will offer the highest quality dance program?
- Who should teach dance?
- What should be taught?
- Who should have access to dance education?

Cone and Cone (2007) suggest that dance programs remain sidelined in many schools because arts education and physical education are forced to compete for scarce resources such as space, staffing, money, and public support. Consequently, dance is rarely present in the arts curriculum and frequently excluded from physical education programs. Dance educators should insist that dance be taught as an aesthetic art form by qualified dance educators who focus on learning dance technique, creating choreography, and developing performances. In contrast, physical educators see dance as a way of moving that offers creative, social, and cultural experiences for all students. Dance in the performing arts and dance in physical education share some similar concepts and skills, although their outcomes are very different.

> Dance requires complex motor movement that exercises those areas of the brain involved in the full range of cognitive functions, causing the brain to fire signals along the same network of cells, which solidifies their connections.

Maintaining dance as a component of the physical education curriculum is likely to give many students the opportunity to participate in dance. However, schools should also offer dance as a component of the arts curriculum, or as an "Artist in Residence" program to address the needs of students for whom dance is an area of major interest. Dance taught within the arts provides students with the ability to gain technical skills in different dance forms. It enables them to compose and perform dances, to develop the critical thinking skills needed to respond to their own dances and the dances of others, and to understand how dance influences and is influenced by history, culture, and society. In this context, students have an opportunity to learn all aspects of dance as a performing art, learn about dance careers, and become advocates for dance as a way of learning and experiencing the world around them. When dance is taught as a rigorous year-long program, students develop and master technical skills, deepen their aesthetic understanding and appreciation, and learn to collaborate with others to create and perform dances (Cone & Cone, 2007).

See the **Applications** section at the end of this chapter for suggestions on how to incorporate dance programs in the K–12 curriculum.

THEATRICAL TALENT

Shakespeare reminds us that "All the world's a stage, and all the men and women merely players." Playacting is a form of deception, and the fact that all humans do it indicates that deception is very likely a trait that has enhanced our species' chances for survival. Curiously, the word *person* comes from the Latin word *persona*, meaning a mask or character in a play. We all put on masks at one time or another and for many different reasons. Whether it is to gain peer acceptance, attract a mate, or sooth a friend's sorrow, we slip on masks to say and do things that fit the role we are playing at that moment.

Our playacting may involve intentional deception or merely the demeanor and behavior needed to accomplish a particular task. For example, Devine (2006) notes that in addition to playing the role of an employee, a teacher may also play the roles of spouse, parent, and student. The role of teacher requires one to act, react, interact, take action, and keep one's act together. Some people are much better at assuming different roles than others. One's ability to play a role convincingly to observers (an audience) was so highly admired by the ancient Egyptian, Greek, Middle Eastern, and Asian societies that it became a ritual unto itself—and the theater was born.

Theater Programs in Schools

Elementary School Activities: Theater art in elementary schools is usually centered around classroom skits along with the occasional grade-level or school play. Many children participate in these exercises because they enjoy performing for their admiring parents. Although these performances help build socialization skills and self-esteem, they usually are not the type of presentation where students who have genuine theatrical talent will be noticed. That is more likely to happen in secondary schools where theater classes are a formal part of the curriculum.

Using theater in elementary classrooms can bear fruit in other areas. Worthy and Prater (2002) describe the effective use of readers' theater to increase reading fluency and motivation. They found that the readers' theater performance becomes an effective vehicle for reading at an appropriate rate while attending to meaning, rather than reading fast without understanding the contextual meaning of the words. By reading and interpreting texts regularly and evaluating others' performances, the students develop important reading skills. Other studies have yielded similar results with reluctant and struggling readers in middle school (Brinda, 2007).

Secondary School Programs: Secondary school theater programs vary from barely existing to flourishing, from a single class with an annual play or musical to comprehensive curriculums and production seasons led by several certified theater teachers. In many secondary schools, parents often voice their support for the arts, including theater. But when school budgets are tight, those same voices are not there to insist that theater get its fair share of the resource pie. Part of that may be due to the changing American culture where, some say, theater has less relevance in today's technology-centered world. Fewer resources are devoted to theater education because of the fear that lack of technology training may put America's children at a disadvantage in the global market. Yet people around the world still spend billions of dollars a year on movies and theatrical performances. Where will these actors come from? If the purpose of high school is to prepare students for life, and if life includes theater, should not high schools have programs that allow theatrically talented students to emerge and achieve?

What does an outstanding educational theater program look like? Woodson (2004) believes that theater programs focused on developing the theatrical talent of young people should do the following:

- **Treat young people as active agents rather than passive observers.** The program should allow students to practice the artistic identities of playwright, producer, performer, director, and designer. Treating teens as active agents allows them the safety to take risks and to feel vulnerable. Vulnerability is important to theater's artistic process and product. Programs should concretely focus on helping students write, produce, and direct their own plays, screen plays, and alternative performances. It should also assist students to study reflexively and seriously their own work, words, and lives. Students need opportunities to explore the process of becoming artists.

  Beyond class opportunities to write and produce plays, however, programs could be set up that give the entire means of production over to the students. Allow them to elect a seasonal artistic director and give them a production budget. At the least, allow students a voice in choosing a season, making teachers responsible for providing students the opportunities to make informed decisions. Students are more than capable of learning the realities of producing theater in a tight economic climate, as well as balancing the conflicting needs of box office, student actor pool, and educational community. Theater should not be something we do to students or even for students, but *with* them. Educational theater produces and is produced by high school culture, and we must allow our students the ability to reflect and to construct their own versions and understandings of that environment.

> Theater arts programs should use popular culture forms to explore major social issues and problems.

- **Be unafraid to explore big questions, social issues, and problems.** A theater for and about young people also would be a critical theater practice focused on defining and capturing special moments in the present. As an art form, theater is centered in the complex web of human affairs.
- **Create advocates for the arts while exploring what it means to be an artist in the twenty-first century.** A theater program for the twenty-first century would be focused on giving our students the ability to notice those social interactions, to see the underlying motivations, the differences in power, gender, class, and that are just below the surface of all human interaction.

- **Celebrate and use popular culture forms.** In many ways, theater can function as a type of gatekeeper for cultural knowledge as, for example, producing works by the great playwright. Classic plays provide a ready laboratory for students to see that culture is a product of the values of the time (values produced in many different ways and forms by science, art, religion, and daily living). By interpreting cultural symbols, religious myths, and the like, students do not just become sophisticated thinkers, but depart from conditions that limit their ways of interacting with the environment. It teaches them to think like artists. Popular culture defines who and what we are. Respecting the value of young people's literacy in that culture allows us to create and use common vocabularies.

- **Create and promote caring kinship bonds deeply connected into both the school and surrounding communities.** A theater practice based on a narrative of respect for the lived experiences of being young provides for the formation of supportive communities. Theater ultimately and fundamentally remains a dialogue. The theater can also be a home for the building of positive peer relationships at the school, district, and even national level. Many programs already do this, reaching into the community for resources, stories, and audiences. This does not mean only student stories, however, for students should not collaborate only with one another. Rather, it opens up the possibility of a circle of sharing and learning from one another. Ultimately, a theater program for the twenty-first century recognizes that educational theater is a journey, not a destination, for both our students and ourselves.

If, as mentioned earlier, theater seems to have less relevance for students in today's technology-centered culture, then why not reignite interest in theater through technology? With this in mind, Jensen (2008) suggests we should ask ourselves how learning in the theater classroom specifically aids students in effectively succeeding in technology-driven domains. Educators will be most successful in their conversations with students, parents, and policymakers if they are willing and prepared to use technology and incorporate new literacies related to that technology as part of the theater classroom framework. To accomplish this, teachers should embrace theater's essential quality—making meaning.

> If theater seems less relevant in today's technology-centered culture, then why not reignite interest in theater through technology?

Theater skills are a significant mode of production and reception through which students can articulate who they are in the world. For example, we should look for ways to combine traditional theater principles with popular media tools to enhance students' ability to talk with their peers, experiment with new texts and literacies, and explore the theater creation process through popular tools and technologies. Theater educators should explore ways to incorporate other technologies into their classrooms. For instance, teachers could capitalize on students' interest in online affinity groups or generate e-portfolio projects for their theater classrooms that document theater learning processes and promote interactive discussions and reflections on theater projects. These technologies even allow for the audio or video capture and dissemination of student-created products that could be viewed by larger, remote audiences (Jensen, 2008).

VISUAL ART TALENT

Imagery and Visual Processing

Imaging is the ability to generate and manipulate mental images in our brain and is a component of fundamental cognitive processes. In particular, imaging is of special relevance to artistic skills. Although it seems logical that people who are talented in visual arts, such as drawing and painting, would possess good imaging skills, neuroscience now produces the scientific evidence. Studies show that successful visual artists have above-average mental imaging skills and high imaging capacity (the number of mental images they can hold in their mind at the same time). One study of 72 fine arts students found that their imaging capacity was closely related to spatial skill, spatial manipulation skill, and visual memory (Pérez-Fabello & Campos, 2007).

The process by which the brain creates and manipulates mental images is complex. Scans of the brain generating visual imagery have usually come from studies of visual artists who suffered brain damage that affected their talent. These studies provide an unexpected window to the neurology of art, and they have produced some intriguing results. Recent reports of changes in art performance among patients with dementia in the brain's frontal and temporal lobes confirm that visual art is predominantly in the right hemisphere and suggest the existence of a neuroanatomical network for artistic creativity (see Figure 7.6). The right parietal region is critical for the visuospatial prerequisites of art, and the right temporal lobe integrates and interprets these perceptions. The right temporal lobe appears necessary for extracting and exaggerating the essential features of an artistic composition. In contrast, the left parietal region and the left temporal lobe have inhibitory effects on artistic expression through attention to visuospatial detail and semantic labeling. Frontal lobe executive functions are also required for artistic expression, particularly toward the rear of the frontal lobe's right side where the network for novelty-seeking behavior is believed located (Mendez, 2004).

What happens to visual artists with neuropsychological deficits, such as the inability to see any color or to interpret objects in the visual field, epilepsy, migraine, dementia, and autism? It seems that artists are not spared visual or motor deficits despite their special graphic abilities. Rather their talents allow them to express visual deficits with particular eloquence. The history of visual art has many stories of physically and mentally ill artists who continued to paint or sculpt. Thus, neuropsychological problems may be associated with positive outcomes. Such outcomes induced by epilepsy or migraines can serve to inspire artists. In fact, artists with neuropsychological deficits do not necessarily produce art of lesser quality. Rather, their art may change in content or in style, sometimes in surprising and aesthetically pleasing ways. The neuropsychology of visual art also touches on a few central questions about the nature of artistic expression itself. For example, what forms can artistic representations take? How are visual features used descriptively and

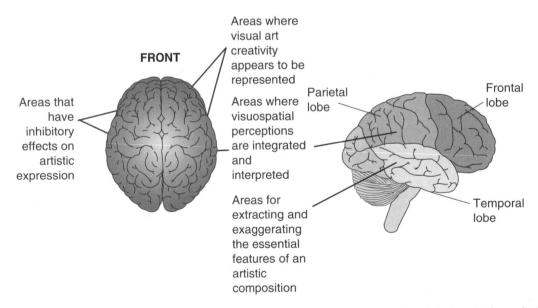

Figure 7.6 The areas of the brain involved in visual art processing. Areas in the right hemisphere facilitate the generating and interpreting of visual art, while areas in the left hemisphere appear to inhibit artistic expression. The unique interaction of all these areas will influence what the individual produces for visual art.

Source: Adapted from Mendez, 2004.

expressively? What roles do knowing and seeing play in depicting the subject of a visual art form? These questions still remain unanswered as research probes further into how visual processing, imagery, and cognitive thought interact to produce art (Chatterjee, 2004).

Using Technology With Visual Arts Teaching

Walling (2001) notes that computer technology in visual art education can be used to create and manipulate images as well as to investigate the visual arts. The first involves art making, while the second involves art history, art criticism, and aesthetics. Students who make art are finding many uses for the computer: (1) to create plans for sculptures (or ceramics or anything three-dimensional); (2) to produce finished "virtual" objects; and (2) to render preliminary, intermediate, or finished two-dimensional works. For example, a student can create a sketch, electronically scan the sketch onto a disk, and then use a computer program such as Adobe Photoshop to manipulate the image. The manipulated image may be recovered for additional work by hand, or it can be refined solely by using the computer application. Finally, the computer output could be an electronic art "product" or a more traditional work that is frameable. This computer-assisted manner of working has already revolutionized the field of commercial art and, consequently, altered the curriculum for students who plan to enter that field. But computer technology is also making changes in the fine arts, as students explore alternatives to traditional methods of art making.

Teachers of aesthetics, art history, and art criticism have two forms of computer technology at their disposal: CD-ROMs and the Internet. CD-ROM versions of printed text and images, from encyclopedias to art collections, offer students and teachers a wealth of information at reasonable prices. These CD-ROMs often include sound and video clips, such as film footage of historic events and excerpts from famous speeches. Not available in standard print resources, these multi-modal pieces enliven and expand the resources, so that students do not merely read the information but experience it. Although CD-ROMs cannot replace the many books that provide useful, in-depth information about art, they frequently offer highly accessible basic information and, as such, are excellent starting points for study. Most students also find CD-ROM resources motivating, because they are interactive and because the computer technology itself is engaging.

The Internet is a valuable resource because a growing number of museums, galleries, archives, and libraries maintain Web sites, which are continually updated and expanded. These Web sites contain images of artworks, reference collections, online texts, and other information that can vastly expand the instructional reach of most teachers. Many also include lesson plans and sample lessons to make the teacher's work easier. The Internet can also take students on virtual field trips. A number of institutional Web sites offer online field trips, or virtual tours, of their facilities, from the massive Louvre Museum (the tour can be taken in several languages for crossover language study) to more intimate collections, such as the Andy Warhol Museum, which is housed in a seven-story converted warehouse in Pittsburgh and can be found on the Web at http://www.warhol.org.

APPLICATIONS

IDENTIFYING YOUNG STUDENTS WITH MUSICAL TALENT

Identifying musical capabilities in young students is not easy because most children enjoy making music, especially when listening to it. But there are some general characteristics that are likely to identify those individuals who have a greater than average interest in music. When trying to determine if a specific student has musical talent, rate the individual on the degree to which they possess the characteristics listed below. This instrument works best with elementary school children. The list is by no means exhaustive. But if the child rates high on most of the items, talk with the parents and other professionals for their input.

The student...	**A little**	**Some**	**A lot**
1. Is captivated by sound and engages fully with music.	1 — 2 — 3 — 4 — 5		
2. Selects an instrument with care and is unwilling to relinquish it.	1 — 2 — 3 — 4 — 5		
3. Memorizes music quickly without any apparent effort.	1 — 2 — 3 — 4 — 5		
4. Can repeat, usually after just one hearing, complex melodic phrases given by the teacher.	1 — 2 — 3 — 4 — 5		
5. Can sing and/or play music with a natural awareness of musical phrasing.	1 — 2 — 3 — 4 — 5		
6. Often responds physically to music.	1 — 2 — 3 — 4 — 5		
7. Demonstrates the ability to communicate through music.	1 — 2 — 3 — 4 — 5		
8. Shows a sustained inner drive to make music.	1 — 2 — 3 — 4 — 5		

© 2009 by David A. Sousa. All rights reserved. Reprinted from *How the Gifted Brain Learns*, Second Edition, by David A. Sousa (Thousand Oaks, CA: Corwin). Reproduction authorized only for the local school site or nonprofit organization that has purchased this book.

APPLICATIONS

SUGGESTIONS FOR ENCOURAGING MUSICALLY TALENTED STUDENTS

Research studies indicate that the earlier individuals begin to use their musical talents, the more likely they are to continue their practice through their adolescence and young adulthood. Although musical talent generally appears in the younger years, there may be secondary school students whose talents have not yet been recognized. One of the goals of working with students who have already developed skills playing an instrument is to develop broader musical skills, as well as inspiring a deeper knowledge and understanding of music. This can occur in nearly all elementary classrooms whenever teachers feel comfortable addressing the skills of musically talented children.

The teacher helps build these skills and talent by

- Setting up challenging musical tasks and expecting a high-quality response. Students tend to meet the expectations that are set for them, provided the expectations are realistic and consistent with the students' goals in music.
- Allowing students to take the lead in a class activity, such as starting a song or conducting the class.
- Including quick recall activities whereby students echo increasingly complex patterns given by the teacher. This choral response approach should be used sparingly, but it does encourage participation by those young students who may be shy.
- Encouraging special instruction in voice or on an instrument. This may occur within the school, through a recognized community mentor, or using a paid tutor.
- Providing open-ended tasks or new contexts in which students can apply previously learned skills. Musically talented students usually seek out ways to apply their musical interests to classroom projects.
- Allowing opportunities in the classroom for students to use skills, such as instrumental skills, that they have learned outside the classroom.
- Enabling students to use improvisation in their work, within certain limits identified by the teacher. Improvisation is an important component of creativity in music.
- Asking students, when appropriate, to analyze and evaluate music in relation to how it is constructed and produced. Further discussions can include identifying how music can be affected by different influences and the various ways that music can affect us.
- Encouraging students to participate in school choirs, bands, and orchestras. Although some students are reluctant to perform for an audience, appropriate coaching can often help students overcome their misgivings about public performance.
- Providing opportunities for students to perform outside of school at public events throughout the community. These engagements have the added benefit of showing the public how their schools encourage and educate musically talented students.
- Ensuring that students experience live professional musical presentations at regular intervals, followed by an analysis and constructive critique of the performances.

From a Teacher's Desk: *An Elementary Example*

In elementary classrooms, music can easily be integrated as a regular part of the schedule. The spectrum of levels of integration ranges from playing music for listening to creating music as a group.

In primary classrooms, we use songs to start the day. Lyrics can be learned in parts or segmented for small groups to master parts and then rotate. Words can be supplemented with movements to increase comprehension and encode meaning faster. In the upper grades, we ask musically talented individuals to lead a song and eventually, the entire class sings along without the teacher.

Traditionally, national or state songs in the curriculum provide a link to social studies. As time goes by, music changes with each generation so that music from just 10 years ago is already unknown. Exposure to various past genres of music is novel and exciting for all learners, especially gifted students who make deep connections to the rhythm and poetry inherent in the beats and patterns. A study of poetry and music can be connected to language arts content, particularly scouring lyrics for the parts of speech used and how they create a coherent structure.

APPLICATIONS

TEACHING MUSICALLY TALENTED STUDENTS IN SECONDARY SCHOOLS

Music educators are suggesting that discoveries in cognitive science should have an impact on the teaching of music in today's schools. Webster (2000) suggests that the following three factors need to be considered by music teachers in designing their lessons for musically talented students in secondary schools.

♫ **Constructivism.** This instructional approach focuses lesson design on activities that engage students in creative experiences so that they can construct their own understanding of the learning with the teacher's guidance. For example, instead of teaching music reading, listening, and movement through a teacher-centered approach with fact- and skill-oriented content, use small, interactive groups where students can discuss and create ways of including composition and improvisation. Other strategies might include asking students to write reports about the music they are playing, discussing the music content ("Why did the composer use this key?"), or even using student conductors on the podium.

♫ **Technology and the Internet.** Computers, software, synthesizers, and the Internet are just some of the new ways that students can manipulate musical sounds. Music sequencing notation and digital audio software allow students to compose music in ways that were not possible just a few years ago. For example, numerous software programs available on the Internet permit students to write musical notation and to experiment with tempo, dynamics, and choice of timbre. As the students become more familiar with revision and other musical ideas, some program allows them to manipulate motives and phrases.

♫ **Creative Thinking Skills.** When teachers resort to problem-centered learning, students are able to pursue tasks that have more than one correct answer. Working alone or in groups, students are allowed to create their own examples of musical structures rather than be limited just to the teacher's example. This balance of convergent and divergent activities can be especially effective in performance venues by encouraging students to give their opinions about interpretations, by asking probing questions about the musical works they are performing, and by requiring them to practice music that creates solutions to various problems of performance. Internet resources can extend these activities further. With this approach, students of all ability levels get a deeper understanding of the learning because they are directly involved in solving problems. Moreover, these types of projects allow students to make judgments about musical content and context, use their creative thinking skills, constructively criticize others' works, and develop with other students a collective understanding of the music being studied. Although all students benefit, divergent activities such as these are particularly meaningful for the more musically talented students.

See the **Resources** section for Internet sites that relate to music education and support students with musical talent.

APPLICATIONS

DANCE AS PART OF THE K–12 CURRICULUM

Although all students can benefit from experiencing dance education, students who are particularly talented in dance need specialized teaching and practice. Hanna (2008) suggests that a curriculum that looks at different aspects of dance as an art form can be a strong framework for developing dance talent. Here are some of those aspects:

A Performing Art

As an imaginative, skillful, and communicative art, dance can be included in a sequential performing arts curriculum. This type of curriculum is typically offered in dance academies and arts magnet schools that accept students on the basis of audition for pre-professional training. Such a curriculum might include the following.

- Studying classical ballet, focusing on a codified technique and skill taught through teacher direction and visual models, repetitive drill, and teacher assessment of the student's mastery of skills and expression
- Exploring the approaches of the early choreographers who distinguished themselves by developing distinct styles and techniques, such as Martha Graham, José Limón, Merce Cunningham, and Katherine Dunham
- Other forms of dance also may be studied, emphasizing dancer responsiveness to changes in music and setting

A Liberal Art

Associated Fields of Study. Dance has context, which makes it a liberal art, part of the humanities and social and behavioral sciences. The study of dance can be related to the following:

- **History, Anthropology, and Sociology:** When individuals explore the culturally specific nature of dance, as well as the commonality of all of dance
- **Psychology and Philosophy:** When individuals learn to critically perceive, respond to, and judge the elements of dance and their connections, and to realize the qualities of dance that contribute to the aesthetic response
- **Business:** When dance is placed in the spheres of economics, arts administration, and law
- **Anatomy, Biomechanics, Kinesiology, Health, Physiology, Computer Science, and Physics:** When dance is studied as a series of body movements in time and space

Basic Concepts and Activities. This curriculum also focuses on the following:

- The process of students creating dances—the path a student takes to find and solve problems in choreography and its realization—rather than the product and performance
- The concepts behind dance: self-expression and evaluation, curiosity, exploration, skepticism, and reflection on dance-making
- Movement, including various modern dance and folk dance techniques

- How visual models, oral commentary, and student kinesthetic imagination aid learning
- The use of metaphor in dance to provide insights to explore such things as power relationships in society
- Students learn how the human body moves through space, in time, and with effort. Students learn that space has direction, level, amplitude, focus, grouping, and shape. Rhythm has tempo, duration, accent, and meter. Effort, or dynamics, is force or energy, tension, relaxation, and flow. Shape is the changing relationship of the mover to another person, object, or space. Locomotion includes a walk, run, leap, hop, jump, skip, slide, and gallop. Gesture, movement that does not carry weight, may be rotation, flexion, extension, and vibration. A phrase is a group of movement sequences that coheres and makes a distinctive statement. A motif is a movement portion of a dance that can be presented in different ways, such as fast or slow or with more or less force.
- Students learn how the body itself works when constrained by cognition, anatomy, physiology, and physics. They explore kinesiology and nutrition. In addition to gaining an understanding of mind–body processes that can be expressed in words, procedures, diagrams, and computer animation, students acquire knowledge about their body.

Learning Sequence: The progression of learning could be as follows:

- Begin with mastering a specific dance vocabulary and locomotor and gestural movements, and then putting these together by following a grammar to make phrases, and then combinations of phrases that become a dance.
- Students go on to dissect the process of choreography, describing its physical characteristics and interpreting meaning of the kinetic images. They note the emotional responses of the dancer, choreographer, and viewer.
- A sequential curriculum that becomes increasingly complex also involves knowing the music, history, and culture of different dances, writing about these dances, and, if producing a show, understanding the mathematics to work within budgets and the English to write program notes. Here it is useful to recall the similarities of the nonverbal communication of dance to verbal communication and its critical role in teaching and learning.
- Students may also learn Laban Motif Writing, a form of symbolic kinetic literacy derived from the more complex Labanotation of dance. Motif writing is a memory aid to dance-making and yet another intellectual challenge.

The substance of K–12 dance, especially for students who are talented in dance, encompasses a range of concepts and skills that students think about and experientially and symbolically integrate. In addition to gaining declarative and procedural dance knowledge, the students acquire various skills as they exercise their multiple intelligences that are applicable in realms outside of dance.

An Applied Art

Looking at dance as an applied art refers to its integration with other academic subjects. Some arts educators believe that dance education is valuable in and of itself and argue that dance integration with other subjects makes it open to exploitation and dilution (Davis, 2008). However, this integration does not devalue dance as a distinct domain but acknowledges its power and scope. Integrating dance with other subjects often entices students to pursue in-depth study of dance at an arts magnet school or an outside dance studio. Moreover, dance as solely an aesthetic "art" phenomenon is a narrow Western concept. Throughout history and across the world, dance is far more, whether it is a means to educate, praise the gods, or celebrate a wedding or rich harvest.

Dance often facilitates the learning of other subjects by engaging students, giving concrete movement and immediacy to abstract concepts, and by promoting creativity. Dance education can hook and sustain students' attention and focus by learning on their feet. Creatively expressing themselves, students take ownership of their dance creations and enter a world in which they are in control, no matter what else is going on in their lives. They can take risks and bring others into a realm they cannot verbalize. Once students are anchored in dance, other educational options present themselves. Although some students may be inspired to become professional artists, few actually realize dance career aspirations. More become motivated to go into dance-related careers, such as becoming a dance program fundraiser, promoter, writer, administrator, photographer, or therapist, or they may acquire an appreciation of the arts while preparing for a career outside dance.

From a Teacher's Desk: *An Elementary Example*

As a way of developing the concepts behind dance, I ask students to explore emotions and learn vocabulary at the same time. I challenge students to define, through movement, what an emotion looks and feels like. Here are examples that are appropriate for various grade levels, ages, and developmental stages:

- happiness
- anger
- surprise
- excitement
- confidence
- boredom
- fear
- pride
- passion
- depression
- love

The ambiguous nature of dance interpretation requires the learner to be open to multiple perspectives about showcasing a movement, idea, or word. There is no room for convergent, closed-ended thinking. Students can take pride in expressing themselves as independent personas.

APPLICATIONS

ACTIVITIES FOR DEVELOPING THEATRICAL TALENT

Woodson (2004) suggests that effective theater programs in secondary schools should include active student participation, explore social issues, uses popular culture forms, and emphasizes the building of deep relationships within the school and community. Here are some activities that she has seen and asks theater teachers to consider.

- A play like Ibsen's *An Enemy of the People* provides a forum for the discussion of civic responsibility and social contract. Teachers could add talk-back sessions for each performance, maybe even bringing in local officials. The topic could be integrated into other classes, such as letter writing and library research in English, local environmental problems in government, and wetland biomes in science.
- A production of Shakespeare's *A Midsummer Night's Dream* could focus on the different worlds, such as cliques and classes, of the student population. To make the production about these students, the forest scenes could be set in an urban blight area and costume choices could focus on reproducing the cliques within the school.
- A twenty-first century theater program should not shy away from asking or addressing large questions in our classrooms or in our productions. The standard should be: Does this activity, play, or curriculum illuminate the lives and social experiences of our student populations? How do we let our students know that theater is there for them and about them? For example, is Shakespeare's *Taming of the Shrew* really, or still, a comedy? A production of this play aimed at exploding gender constructions and power relationships could stage (and restage) key scenes from the play to explore the silencing of Kate's voice. Perhaps using other texts to provide a counterpoint, such as Mary Pipher's *Ophelia* series, Kate could be played by more than one person (or even puppets). One teacher had Kate played by actors of both genders in order to explore male and female identity in key scenes.
- Integrating other media arts into theatrical performance can provide experiences in media literacy, rather than allowing young people to believe in media as a realm of the miraculous. One theater teacher, for example, asks students to bring in their favorite music videos (with guidelines for appropriateness) to practice the role of critic. The class views the videos through Goethe's three dramaturgical questions: What was the production team trying to do? How did they go about doing it? And was it worth doing? This activity helps students to think critically about performance events, gets them to watch and share their favorite music, enables them to begin analyzing media through how that media is constructed. It also moves students beyond passive reception by basing the activity in the realm of popular culture.
- One teacher created a multimedia performance using PowerPoint, collage artworks, and popular culture forms to explore the question, "What makes me, me?" Her students wrote personal ads, created and performed poetic monologues (setting some to music), and even wrote commercials selling themselves. Another program used the format of public service announcements to combine peer counseling and theater. There, the theater teacher partners with a school counselor and a residential police officer to create small scenes about issues relevant to the school community.

From a Teacher's Desk: *A Secondary Example*

Using RAFTs to Enhance Theatrical Talent

As mentioned in this chapter, only a few teachers outside of the arts have had the training to foster artistic talent within their classroom on a regular basis. One strategy that has been helping teachers connect their students' artistic learning preferences and interests to classroom content has been the RAFT. RAFT is an acronym for Role, Audience, Format, and Topic. It encourages students to assume a role, consider their audience, examine a topic from their chosen perspective, and communicate in a particular format.

RAFTs can be used to differentiate a student's readiness, interest, or learning profile and some teachers have discovered that it can also provide a way to foster a student's artistic talent outside of the traditional art, music, or drama classroom. The following are examples of what our high school teachers have created to encourage artistically talented students in their classrooms:

Subject: High School English

Topic: Shakespeare's play *Romeo and Juliet*

ROLE	AUDIENCE	FORMAT	TOPIC
Love	Romeo and Juliet	Mixed media collage of words and images	What I am and what I cost
Romeo	Self	Personal journal entry	Was Juliet really worth it?
Dr. Phil	TV Audience	Debate	Romeo & Juliet: True love or teenage rebellion?
Juliet	Teenagers everywhere	Musical score or song	What I did for love!

Subject: High School Civics

Topic: Electoral College

ROLE	AUDIENCE	FORMAT	TOPIC
Yourself	Friend in Civics class	Telephone conversation	How I feel about the presidential election process
U.S. Senator	The voting people	A speech	Why the electoral process is fair
Concerned citizen	Public	YouTube movie posting	The future election process
Voter in the 2000 election who voted for Al Gore	United States Congress	Graffiti art	The voting process let me down

APPLICATIONS

DEVELOPING OBSERVATION SKILLS IN VISUAL ART

Successful visual artists have highly developed observation skills. Teachers working with students who are talented in the visual arts can develop instructional units that developing the students' perceptual abilities through their direct experience with works of art. Careau (2008) has developed such a unit for older adolescents that focuses on observing physical reality and thinking about what is observed. His approach uses questions that cover a wide range of issues, such as material, process, place, scale, and time, and which ultimately lead to the discussion of various cultural aspects of invented physical reality. The goal is for the students to understand what they are observing, and the questioning serves to unlock information, ultimately allowing students to grasp the essential nature of the pieces they are experiencing.

Though the questions deal primarily with the physical aspects of invented visual reality, issues of cultural significance, of history, context, and theory, inevitably arise in discussion. Thus culture, the individual, and the physical are seen in dynamic interrelationship. Here are some beginning questions:

- **Do you recognize it?** We can imagine all artwork falling into a continuum of recognition. On one end of the continuum is the familiar and the other extreme is the new. When looking at a painting of a horse, for instance, the viewer subconsciously knows it is a horse. Even with an abstract of a horse where only a hint of "horse" is present, the viewer will most likely still see a horse. Our minds recognize shapes and contexts automatically, often with very little visual information provided. But when confronted with something new, something that is not yet named, we must come to an understanding of its nature without the aid of recognition. Strangeness often bothers us exactly for this reason: we do not recognize what we see.

  In this question, the "it" could be a shape (such as a horse) or perhaps a style or strategy used by a particular artist or tradition. For example, seeing an even repetition of forms might remind us of minimalism or bizarre imagery and strange juxtapositions as in surrealism. Some artists, through the uniqueness of their innovation, have become closely tied to some shape, gesture, strategy, or material. They are the originators and own that aspect of visual culture. The capacity for recognition is one tool for gaining an understanding of what we see.

- **How big is it?** We all understand and respond to size, our bodies serving as innate instruments of measure. Since birth, we have navigated our way through an ever broadening environment of objects and spaces and have measured them in relationship to our bodies, experiencing the world of "larger than" and "smaller than." With that knowledge, we have come to understand that size is power. "Larger" demands respect and may evoke confidence, awe, or intimidation, while "smaller" allows control and perhaps greater intimacy. With time and education, we learn the systems of measurement— of inches, feet, and kilometers—and come to see the world in a non-intuitive fashion. We learn to describe aspects of the physical world in a more formal fashion, so that we are able to describe an object sitting on the table, for example, as four inches high and quite easy to pick up and use.

- **Where is it?** A dialogue exists between object and place. Consider a hardwood forest in summer. Trees, bushes, and flowers fill our view, surrounding us in all directions. Above the canopy of trees is the sky. Through the air fly birds and insects. The atmosphere is warm and humid, the odors multiple and changing as we move through the forest. Sounds of all sorts fill the air. Let us now put a cube of stainless steel, five feet wide, flat on the forest floor, among the tall trees. Listen to its voice, its identity—hard, solid, almost changeless, its surface reflecting sunlight and capturing the colors of the sky and forest. Its shape proclaims geometry. Here, in the forest, the contrasts between object and place are marked, and we instinctively understand differences of identity. If we were to place the cube within a white-walled room, such as a gallery space, the differences would be dramatically lessened. In fact, the cube might seem to fit right in.   Awareness of place suggests a related concept, the idea of normal place. We come to know and expect objects within certain contexts. Books, for instance, belong on shelves and on desks and tables, but toothbrushes, in a bathroom. Throughout history, the normal place for artworks has been fluid, changing over time. Sculptural objects, once placed on pedestals, now stand or lie or hang free. Conventions change, indicating cultural shifts in thinking, so that objects once placed inside a building, on a pedestal, might today be found outside, in a forest perhaps. We do not see these objects as being in an abnormal place. Rather, the normal has grown or shifted to include that which would previously have been considered abnormal.

- **What is it made of? How is it put together?** All objects are made of a material or combination of materials formed or put together by some method. Locked within these materials and methods is a history, a history of transformation, of change over time. Each material speaks the language of its physical characteristics, of its texture, durability, and color. The processes by which objects are formed are often hidden from immediate recognition. The wood of the table hides the secrets of the table's creation to all but the most informed. We forget, or do not see, the tools and techniques of felling, transporting, milling, drying, and assemblage. Once wood has been assembled into a recognizable object, a table, it is oftentimes easier for us to see and understand the scratch on the surface, the dent on the leg, or the ring left by the glass, obvious reminders of past events. The future also speaks to the attentive. That which was once considered worthy of special care and attention might, at some future time, be considered of little value and discarded.

Many other questions guide the investigation, such as:

- **How many are there?**
- **How is it organized?**
- **Is it stable?**
- **Does it move?**
- **Is anything implied?**
- **Is it unified or separated?**
- **Are differences stated boldly or subtly?**
- **What do one's senses, besides sight, register?**

The assignment is intended to challenge students to be not only observant but thoughtful as well. By starting with a familiar object, students feel more confident in their abilities to describe what they are observing. Since artworks are often seen as heavily laden with a mysterious significance, the choice of an ordinary object at first, rather than an art object, might lessen the burden of significance, allowing students to feel more comfortable and secure as they proceed in their study. At appropriate intervals, the teacher can increase the challenge by introducing visual art of increasing degrees of abstractness.

To make the unit more personal, the teacher can ask students who are talented in the visual arts the following questions as well:

- **Has any of the art you have seen during this unit of study influenced the kind of visual art you would like to produce? If so, in what way?**
- **Think of a piece of visual art that you have produced, or plan to produce. How would you answer all of the questions above as they relate to your own work?**

From a Teacher's Desk: *A Secondary Example*

Digital Storytelling

Mr. Hamm teaches High School American History and every year he is presented with the same setbacks as he gets ready to talk about America's role in World War II. He has quite a few high school students who struggle with the readings associated with this time period as well as students who seem bored with his presentations. He loves to talk about World War II and he carefully crafts his presentation to highlight key events as well as interesting facts. During the last faculty meeting, the media teacher approached him and told him that there were four or five students in his history class who really excel in technology and are doing some amazing work with digital storytelling. The media teacher explained that digital storytelling is the practice of using computer-based tools to tell stories. She told him that much like documentary filmmaker Ken Burns has done with his Civil War series, digital storytelling can help people make a story with pictures. She led him to a site where he could learn all about digital storytelling, The Center for Digital Storytelling at http://www.storycenter.org. Mr. Hamm was excited to learn about this new technology and saw it as a way to engage students in his classroom.

On the first day of the World War II unit, Mr. Hamm introduced the class project of digital storytelling. The two main goals of the project were to

- Provide students the opportunity, training, and equipment to do personal interviews to capture World War II veterans' experience organized around an inquiry-based, digital storytelling learning experience
- Provide students with creative authentic connections, which foster a deeper understanding and knowledge of the purpose of World War II

Not only were students in his class engaged in the project, he found that class discussions were lively as students shared their personal interviews in a way that brought life to the lessons. When the unit was over, students posted their digital stories for other class members to view. In addition to being an engaging activity, it provided those students with visual art talent the opportunity to use their talent in designing and organizing their project.

CHAPTER 8

Putting It All Together

In the preceding chapters, we have discussed the nature of the gifted brain and suggested strategies that can help gifted students succeed in school. We have looked at general giftedness as well as at some of the specific types of giftedness in the areas of language, mathematics, and the arts. The problem of underachieving and twice-exceptional students was also examined, including specific strategies to meet their atypical needs.

As educators reflect on how to best meet the needs of gifted students, they must do so at a time when changes are occurring in the structure and organization of schools and classrooms. Inclusion policies are returning more students with special needs to the regular education program, and budget cuts are trimming pull-out programs targeted for identified gifted and talented students. Consequently, teachers are now faced with trying to address curriculum standards and high-stakes testing while dealing with a range of student abilities that is broader than ever. Although resources are available both in and outside the school for gifted students, the regular classroom teacher is most likely to be their primary educator. With that reality in mind, this chapter suggests how teachers can identify gifted students, establish an effective learning environment to meet their needs, and incorporate relevant teaching strategies within the context of the inclusive classroom.

> In today's schools, the regular classroom teacher is likely to be the primary educator of gifted students.

IDENTIFYING GIFTED STUDENTS

Because some students do not begin to show their gifts until after entering school, teachers may be the first to recognize potential areas of giftedness. As teachers observe their students, they begin to assess intellectual potential along with other factors, such as emotional and social needs.

Preliminary Assessment for Giftedness

The first indications that a student may be gifted will most likely come from observations of high performance in one or more of the following areas:

- **General intellectual ability.** Students who have high intelligence test scores, usually two standard deviations above the mean, on individual and group measures.
- **Specific academic aptitude.** Students who show outstanding performance in a specific area (e.g., language arts, science, or mathematics) and who score above the 95th percentile in achievement tests.

225

- **Leadership ability.** Students who can direct individuals or groups to a common decision or action. They can negotiate and adapt in difficult situations.
- **Creative and productive thinking.** Students who can produce new ideas by bringing together dissimilar or independent elements, and who have the aptitude for developing new meanings that have social value.
- **Psychomotor ability.** Students who have outstanding motor abilities such as practical, mechanical, spatial, and physical skills.
- **Visual and performing arts.** Students who demonstrate talent in visual art, dance, music, drama, or related studies.

Follow-Up Assessments: If there is evidence of high intellectual or performance ability, the teacher must determine whether the student is truly gifted. Before submitting the student to a barrage of tests, the teacher should assess the student's capabilities on a number of characteristics that the research literature associates with giftedness. Numerous rating scales exist to help teachers determine whether the behaviors exhibited by students represent giftedness. The *Characteristics of Giftedness Scale* (Silverman, 1993) and the *Gifted Rating Scales for Grades 6–8 and 9–12* (DoDEA, 2006) in the **Applications** section at the end of this chapter identify characteristics that are common among gifted students. Using these scales can help teachers make a more valid preliminary judgment about a specific student's abilities.

Students who are gifted in the performing arts usually display many of the characteristics of giftedness in addition to their advanced skills in the main area of competence. Thus, the scale can be used to identify students who are talented in different domains. Although these characteristics can distinguish between gifted and average students, they have not been shown to distinguish different levels of giftedness. Some students who score high on the characteristics scale do not get high scores on tests of achievement. These students may have other problems, such as hearing and vision deficits that impair their classroom participation and depress scores on standardized tests. In this event, it helps to look at the subtest scores to determine areas of strength and weakness. Gifted children often score high on subtests that measure abstract reasoning.

Identifying Minority Students

Minority students continue to be underrepresented in gifted programs, although the gap is closing. One reason for this persistent situation is not that they are less talented than the other classmates, but that their different experiences, values, and beliefs have prevented them from demonstrating their abilities through the assessment instruments that are commonly used for selection into gifted education programs. These students often do better on nontraditional assessments. More recent standardized tests are designed to reduce cultural bias. They include Mercer's System of Multicultural Pluralistic Assessment, Renzulli and Hartman's Scale for Rating Behavioral Characteristics of Superior Students, Bruch's Abbreviated Binet for the Disadvantaged, and the Naglieri Nonverbal Ability Test.

Ability and Achievement: Are We Adequately Assessing Both?: Some researchers now suggest that school-based gifted and talented programs look not only at the students' ranks on achievement and ability tests when compared to all age or grade peers, but also at their rank relative to those with similar backgrounds. Furthermore, even though achievement should be given priority over reasoning abilities, it is generally wiser for school-based programs to test all students in both areas, rather than screen on one test alone. If one test is used to screen applicants, then a much lower cutoff score should be used than is typically adopted. Lohman (2005) believes that an identification program that contains the following components is likely to successfully find minority as well as non-minority gifted students.

- **Except for very young children, academic giftedness should be defined primarily by evidence of academic accomplishment.** Measuring what students currently know and can do is much easier than measuring potential for future accomplishment. Good measures of achievement are critical. Start with an on-grade achievement test and, if necessary, supplement it with above-grade testing to estimate where instruction should begin. Look for other measures of accomplishment, especially production tasks that have well-validated rating criteria. For English language learners (ELLs), attend particularly to mathematics achievement. High levels of current accomplishment should be a prerequisite for acceleration and advanced placement.

- **Measure verbal, quantitative, and figural reasoning abilities in all students.** The majority of students (minority and non-minority) show uneven profiles across these three domains and that the predictors of current and future achievement are the same in White, Black, Hispanic, and Asian American groups. Testing only those students who show high levels of achievement misses most of the students whose reasoning abilities are relatively stronger than their achievement. Because of regression of the mean, it also guarantees that most students will obtain lower scores on the ability test than they did on the achievement test.

- **For young children and others who have had limited opportunities to learn, give greater emphasis to measures of reasoning abilities than measures of current accomplishment.** When accomplishments are few—either because students are young or because they have had few opportunities to learn—then evidence of the ability to profit from instruction is critical. As children mature and have opportunities to develop more significant levels of expertise, then measures of accomplishment should be given greater weight. In all cases, however, evidence of high levels of accomplishment trumps predictions of lesser accomplishments.

- **Consider nonverbal/figural reasoning abilities as a helpful adjunct for both minority and non-minority selections, but only as a measure of last resort.** Scores on the nonverbal tests must always be considered in conjunction with evidence on verbal and quantitative abilities and achievements. Defining academic giftedness by scores on a nonverbal reasoning test simply because the test can be administered to native speakers of English and ELL students serves neither group well. They are measures of last resort in identifying academically gifted children.

- **Use identification tests that provide useful information for all students, not just the handful selected for inclusion in the gifted and talented program.** Teachers should see the test as potentially providing useful information about all of their students and how they can be assisted. A test that supposedly measures innate capabilities (or is easily misinterpreted as doing so) is rightly resented by those who are not anxious to see scores for low-scoring students entered on their records or used in ways that might limit their educational opportunities.

- **Clearly distinguish between the academic needs of students who show high levels of current accomplishment and those who show promise for developing academic excellence.** Academic programs that combine students with high levels of current achievement with those who exhibit *potential* for high achievement often serve neither group well. When accelerating students, the primary criteria must be high levels of accomplishment in a particular domain. Measures of developed reasoning abilities and other aptitudes (such as persistence) are best viewed as indicators of potential for future achievement. Students who show high potential but only moderate levels of current achievement need different types of enrichment programs than those who currently show superior achievement.

- **Use common aptitude measures but uncommon cutoff scores (e.g., rank within group) when identifying minority students most likely to profit from intensive instruction.** Since the predictors of future accomplishment are the same for minority and White students, the same aptitudes need to be taken into account when identifying minority students who show the greatest potential for developing academic excellence. However, even with the best measures of aptitude, predictions will often be wrong. Because judgments about potential are inherently even more uncertain than judgments about accomplishment, a uniform cutoff score is difficult to defend when students come from different backgrounds. Both psychological and ethical issues must be addressed when making such decisions.

- **Do not confuse means and correlations.** A biased selection procedure is one that, in any group, does not select the students most likely to profit from the treatment being offered. Nonverbal reasoning tests reduce, but do not eliminate, differences in mean scores between groups, and they are not the best way to identify those students who either currently exhibit or are most likely to achieve academic excellence. When used alone, they increase bias while appearing to reduce it. A more effective and fairer procedure for identifying academic potential is to look at both within-group and overall distributions of scores on tests that measure the most important aptitudes for successful learning. In particular, look at the domains such as prior achievement and the ability to reason in the symbol systems used to communicate new knowledge in that domain.

Other Methods of Identification: In addition to testing, other methods for selecting students could include the following:

Observation. Information from parents, educators, and classmates can draw attention to the talents of others. Parents can notice their child's degree of interest in intellectual tasks. Teacher observations allow for the evaluation of a child's development over time. How students use their time, how they solve problems, and what interests them can all be indicators of giftedness. Also, just asking students who is the most helpful among them can turn a teacher's attention to an otherwise unnoticed child.

Self-Identification. Students can sometimes reveal through interest inventories the talents they display in nonschool settings, such as participation in community theater or music groups. They may also describe the type of role they play in the family at home.

Portfolios. Materials in student portfolios often show the learning, progress, and applications of knowledge that these students have made. Also, unlike standardized tests, portfolios permit the assessment of students' creativity. An assessment rubric that has been mutually developed by student and teacher can help to make the evaluation of portfolios easier and more objective.

Educators should ensure that procedures are in place to identify the special talents of students from diverse backgrounds. Moreover, the gifted education programs should reflect and respect their culture and learning styles. Doing so will help these students obtain the enriching educational experiences and materials they need to fully reach their potential.

DEVELOPING THE LEARNING ENVIRONMENT

Some teachers deal with a widely heterogeneous class by establishing greater control, reducing flexibility of assignments, and presenting more teacher-centered lessons. Although this approach may work for some students, gifted students need to develop their knowledge and practice their skills in a flexible and secure learning environment that

- Encourages students to use a variety of resources, ideas, tasks, and methods as they pursue learning goals. By having these options, the gifted students can continue to pursue learning objectives on their own while the teacher attends to other students who may need more help in the inclusive classroom.
- Is student-centered and that values and accepts the variety of student interests and learning styles. The more heterogeneous the class, the greater the variety of learning styles among students.
- Encourages students to be open to ideas and initiatives offered by others.

- Allows students to work in a variety of interactive settings, such as individually, in pairs, in small groups, or with students in other classes, as appropriate. Also, using gifted students as mentors for other students can enhance the spirit of learning as a cooperative venture.
- Supports student independence and autonomy within reasonable limits that are mutually set by the students and teacher, where appropriate.
- Is not constrained by subject boundaries or other conventional curricular limitations. Gifted students often have strong interests in specific areas. Look for ways to connect the curriculum to their interests.
- Encourages students to reflect on the processes they use to learn and on the factors that help them to make progress.

STRATEGIES FOR THE GIFTED IN THE INCLUSIVE CLASSROOM

Numerous books and Internet sites offer suggestions on practices that address the needs of gifted students. Implementing some of these practices, however, becomes particularly challenging in heterogeneous classrooms where teachers are dealing with a range of abilities. Nonetheless, the current reality is that many gifted students still spend most of their school day in the mixed-ability classroom, especially in elementary schools. Rogers (2007) has reviewed the research on many of these practices. She and her colleagues believe that, even in the inclusive classroom, the following five principles should guide instruction if gifted learners at all grade levels are to meet their potential:

- **Gifted and talented learners need daily challenge in their specific areas of talent.** The extensive novice-expert or mentoring research has made it abundantly clear that consistent practice at progressively more difficult levels in skill, coupled with the gifted learner's natural ability to link new knowledge to prior knowledge and skill, accounts for what ultimately is perceived as expert performance. Furthermore, studies of talented teenagers also note the rise in psychological distress, stress, and boredom when these individuals cannot advance—either individually or in socialized situations—in their area of talent. This may require some form of regrouping for such instruction, whether that be for a whole class of high talent students, a like-performing cluster group, or a like-ability cooperative group, for which the students are provided with cooperative challenges to be completed with their peers. If this grouping is not possible, then a structured program of independent learning supervised by a gifted resource teacher, media specialist, or talent area mentor either within or outside of the schools must be developed.

    Every identified gifted child must be given consistent, progressively more difficult curriculum that has been articulated across grade and building levels and has been consciously delivered. Across 40 studies that gifted students at various grades were provided with a challenging, articulated curriculum in a variety of curriculum areas, the results have indicated significantly higher test performance (Tieso, 2002; Tomlinson et al., 2002) and improved self-efficacy and motivation (Swiatek & Lupkowski-Shoplik, 2003). The implications of this are that some form of structured regrouping by ability level or structured independent learning will be needed to ensure this consistency of challenge.

- **Opportunities should be provided on a regular basis for gifted learners to be unique and to work independently in their areas of passion and talent.** A synthesis of the research on gifted learning shows that, compared to typical students, gifted learners are significantly more likely to prefer independent study, independent project, and self-instructional materials. Of course, being gifted does not guarantee that one can be effective in an independent learning activity. Independent study does have an impact on motivation to learn, and it is possible that with appropriate structuring through the use of a curriculum model, well-trained teachers, and collaboration between the teacher and the media center, that the independent skills learned through individual study will be transferable to other academic areas, ultimately affecting overall academic achievement. Curriculum compacting (see Chapter 2) at all grade levels is a very useful practice, even in heterogeneous classrooms. The academic effects of compacting are powerful, especially in mathematics and science, when the replacement activities have been accelerated and advanced in complexity.

- **Provide various forms of subject-based and grade-based acceleration to gifted learners as their educational needs require.** At the elementary level, representative studies reporting the academic effects of early entrance to kindergarten or first grade show a consistent picture of high achievement, good social adjustment, and stability of self-esteem measures. A review of 21 studies of early entrants found that they kept pace with their classmates academically and in many cases surpassed them. Gagné and Gagnier's (2004) comparative study of early typical entrants in Quebec schools found no differences in academic maturity, academic achievement, conduct, or social integration, suggesting that social and emotional adjustment are not impacted when a child enters early. Studies of subject acceleration, especially pertaining to science or mathematics, show dramatic achievement gains for gifted elementary students.

  Although gifted secondary level students may be mainly in mixed-ability classes, subject-based options may be available. Some subject-based accelerative options include

- Subject acceleration: Exposing the talented learner to content in the talent area that is one or more years in advance of the learner's actual grade placement
- University-based programs: Residential, Saturday, summer, or commuter courses for middle and high school gifted learners held on college campuses
- Individualized distance or online learning: Courses offered via television or Internet that offer advanced content set at an individualized pace and complexity
- Cross-graded classes: Students cross grade lines within a school in a content area taught at the same time in all grade levels, to work at the level of curriculum they are currently in the process of mastering
- Advanced Placement or International Baccalaureate courses: Provision of college-level content in specific content areas to high school learners, with college credit provided on successful performance on an external national or international examination
- Dual enrollment: Allowing students course work at the next higher building level in their area of talent
- College-in-the-schools: Offering college courses on the high school campus for both high school and college credit
- Mentorships: Connecting the talented learner with a content expert who structures the learning experiences over a specific period of time

Despite the many myths rampant about forms of grade-based acceleration, the evidence suggests that the social impacts are very positive for options such as grade skipping and slightly positive for the other forms of acceleration. Emotional impacts are small and positive throughout.

- **Provide opportunities for gifted learners to socialize and to learn with like-ability peers.** The research on the grouping of gifted learners shows the greatest positive academic effects occur in full-time ability grouping (providing all academic learning for gifted learners within a self-contained setting such as a special school or full-time gifted program), and in performance grouping for specific instruction (sorting and placing students in a classroom with others who are performing at the same level of difficulty in the curriculum). If these options may not be available at the elementary level, other possibilities include within-class grouping (individual teachers sorting children in their own classroom according to their current performance in the curriculum), cluster grouping (placing the top 5 to 8 students at a grade level in an otherwise heterogeneous class so that they become a critical mass for whom the teacher can find time to—and does—differentiate), and pull-out groups (gifted students removed for a consistent set time to a resource room for extended curriculum differentiation). Within-class grouping is superior to no grouping. However, the materials or curriculum tasks must be differentiated for these within-class groups according to their readiness for the learning outcomes planned. Differentiation of materials has been strongly emphasized in the studies on regrouping for specific instruction.

- **For specific curriculum areas, instructional delivery must be differentiated in pace, amount of review and practice, and organization of content presentation.** At the elementary level, faster paced lessons are an alternative to the issues of boredom and perceived stress for gifted children as discussed earlier. There will be less down time in which these students will lose focus, become distracted, act out, or perhaps misinterpret the concepts presented because of their lack of attention to the presentation. If bright children are to retain what they have learned, it must be presented at their actual learning rate, not considerably slower than that rate. Studies show that secondary students in otherwise heterogeneous classes who participated in fast-paced mathematics classes (usually given at a university) successfully completed 2 years of advanced mathematics in 1 year's time, with just 2 to 3 hours of teacher contact time per week during the year. Similar findings have been reported for Saturday and summer courses offered on university campuses in areas such as foreign language, science, history, and mathematics. The implications are that there should be a qualitatively different presentation of K–12 content, especially in mathematics, science, and foreign language, for students who are extraordinary in these areas. This will require separate instruction, either individually or in a like-performing group, rather than delivery through the more traditional whole class concept presentation followed by individual practice and application.

  As to the amount of practice and review, studies indicate that secondary students who had the accelerated pace of instruction needed to do considerably less homework practice before moving on to the next level of difficulty or conceptual level. Yet their performance on national tests substantially showed their ability to accurately retain and apply what they had learned in these classes when compared to their older peers. Gifted students also seem to have a preference as to how content is presented. Some researchers believe that many gifted students acquire information as a whole and store it in long-term memory as a whole, whereas typical learners tend to acquire and store information in small, disparate chunks, from which their teachers will need to help them make connections to ultimately see the whole of a concept. Also, gifted learners are more likely to switch to an alternative strategy when faced with a problem they cannot resolve, rather than to resort to trial and error. They tend to identify or at least search for a "rule" to make their guesses rather than just hit or miss.

  For a teacher to radically quicken the pace for gifted learners, eliminate most practice and review, and teach in a whole-to-part fashion than from the base of facts and parts of a whole idea is almost an impossibility. Some form of at least temporary regrouping or clustering of the highest ability or highest performing learners in the classroom is necessary along with a commitment to spending a proportionate amount of classroom time differentiating instruction.

Strategies on specific curriculum topics and instructional strategies will be found in the **Applications** sections of previous chapters.

WHERE DO WE GO FROM HERE?

Researchers and practitioners in gifted education are concerned that gifted students are still not being adequately identified or challenged in our schools. Parents complain that their children are usually bored and unengaged in school. These students are often underachievers and tend to be highly critical of their teachers, who they feel know less than they do. In many instances, teachers fail to recognize a student as gifted and may think the student is unmotivated or learning disabled. If the student is recognized as gifted, the teacher may have few opportunities to offer curriculum at the appropriate level, and the student may have to learn independently. Surely, we can do better than this.

One study looked at the educational opportunities offered to more than 4,500 students in Grades 3 to 6 from public, private, and parochial schools (Swiatek & Lupkowski-Shoplik, 2003). These students had been identified as gifted by scoring at the 95th percentile or higher on tests administered by the Carnegie Mellon Institute for Talented Elementary Students. Through a survey, researchers found that 37 percent of these students said they were not currently enrolled in a gifted program at their school. This is a surprising finding, given that research studies show that elementary students in any type of gifted program format attain higher levels of achievement than their high-achieving peers who were not in such programs (Delcourt, Cornell, & Goldberg, 2007). Further, 75 percent of students said they had not skipped any grades or subjects. Of those students who were receiving services for the gifted, the pull-out program was the most common, serving 40 percent of the group. Elementary school educators may find the survey in the **Applications** section at the end of this chapter useful in assessing how the gifted students in their schools are being served.

> A study of more than 4,500 gifted elementary students found that 37 percent were not enrolled in a gifted program at their school.

Why Are We Not Doing More for Gifted Students?

Despite the best of intentions, our schools are not doing enough to meet the needs of our gifted students. This is at a time when the serious problems facing our society, such as global warming and energy consumption, will need the most creative people to solve them. Nonetheless, there are still several major factors that, in my opinion, contribute to the lack of progress in serving our gifted students, namely: budget constraints, egalitarianism, and anti-intellectualism.

> The obstacles to doing more for our gifted students are
>
> - Budget constraints
> - Egalitarianism
> - Anti-intellectualism

Budget Constraints: Although some school districts are making valiant efforts to maintain high quality programs for gifted and talented students, the reality is that budget constraints are forcing cutbacks on programs already in place or preventing new programs from getting off the ground. The requirements of the No Child Left Behind legislation have further strained district budgets because the associated federal funding has been considerably less than promised. As the number of students diagnosed with learning disabilities grows, more funds must be shifted to that area, often reducing the amount available for other programs. This "rob Peter to pay Paul" approach is lamentable, but it is still the way most school districts allocate budgetary resources when expenses are rising faster than revenues.

The Egalitarian Compromise: Underlying much of the concerns over how to provide for gifted education has been the ongoing tension between conceptions of excellence and egalitarianism in Western society from the beginning of public education. Reconciling these apparently competing educational ideals has long been a troubling challenge to educators, and gifted education acts as a flashpoint for this debate. As far back as the 1940s, noted educator and then-President of Harvard University, James B. Conant, expressed this as a tension between "discovering and giving opportunity to the gifted student" and "raising the level of the average student" (Conant, 1946). Others have worried that the special learning needs of the gifted could be ignored if equality were overemphasized.

In many cases, primary and secondary schools, at least in the United States, place too much emphasis on equality of outcome at the expense of individual intellectual achievement. Shifting funds from gifted programs to special education needs is sometimes justified by our need to maintain an egalitarian society. This need may seem more pressing as an increasing number of diverse cultures and languages settle in our land. However, we too often see little reason for helping the gifted—presuming that they already have an advantage—and turn our attention primarily to students at the other end of the ability spectrum. But the truth is that many potentially gifted students come from families who do not have the financial means to provide all the resources necessary to fulfill their child's potential. These parents must rely on the public schools to perform that important task. The notion that "those bright kids don't need more money" is not only wrong, but it undermines the mission of public schools: to help all children fully develop into learned citizens.

Anti-intellectualism: Some form of anti-intellectualism has always run through the fabric of American culture, its presence rising and falling as events unfold. Today, the 24-hour news cycle offers some commentators who pride themselves on having anti-intellectual atmospheres on their shows. The word "intellectual" itself has been used as an insult by some commentators. Consequently, the debate between the left and right in America often centers on the relationship between the intellectual class and the public as a whole. Anti-intellectualism in schools resides is a youth subculture associated with those students who are more interested in social life or athletics than in their academic studies. Such subcultures exist among students of all groups. Commercial youth culture also generates a dizzying variety of fads, especially in the area of technology. Keeping up with the trends is difficult, and their content is frequently criticized for being simple-minded and pandering to unsophisticated appetites. Furthermore, pursuing popularity may be a full-time job that leaves little time for intellectual interests.

It is difficult to determine the impact that anti-intellectualism has on educational policy. But it does seem that students with different gifts and talents get a different slice of the educational dollar. Talented athletes and musicians usually have their sports and music activities fully funded and often have plenty of additional opportunities outside of school. On the other hand, students who are intellectually gifted or talented in dance and theater may get placed in a pull-out enrichment program that meets once or twice a week. This is a weak program compared to the opportunities available to the athletically or musically gifted.

Some Considerations for Helping Gifted Students

Intellectual giftedness, of course, runs on a spectrum from mildly to moderately to profoundly gifted. The mildly gifted stay in regular classes because they often fail to meet the minimum scores necessary for selection into the gifted programs. The moderately gifted (usually IQ scores of around 130) can become candidates for gifted programs if other conditions, such as teacher recommendations, are met. This group represents the vast majority of the gifted students who participate in gifted education programs. Students who are profoundly gifted (generally with IQ scores of 160 and higher) are not challenged by current public education gifted programs and probably will not find appropriate educational experiences until they reach college.

Are Part-Time Pull-Out Programs Worth It?: If the reality is that there will be limited funding for gifted education programs in the foreseeable future, then we need to look carefully at how we are spending the money that is available. Although pull-out programs are popular at the elementary level, they allow only a few hours a

> Part-time pull-out programs for gifted students are of modest benefit.

week of instruction for moderately gifted students. Typically, these classes offer little continuity, rarely allow students to study something in depth, and usually offer just one kind of curriculum to all gifted children, no matter where their gifts lie. To measure achievement outcomes, the gifted children's achievement in the pull-out program has been compared with mainstream classroom gifted children's achievement on the same specific test of achievement. Research on these programs has shown them to be of modest benefit. This may be in part because teachers of pull-out programs are more extensively trained than are homogeneous classroom teachers, have more access to differentiated materials, and come to the program excited by their work rather than burdened by daily responsibilities for differentiation. But in actuality, these classes are not much different from good classes for ordinary children. Students of any ability level would probably benefit from the kinds of open-ended, project-based learning that goes on in the best enrichment classes. Nonetheless, the research evidence shows that students in pull-out programs are more positive about school, have more positive perceptions of giftedness, and are more positive about their program of study at school than are gifted students not participating in pull-out programs (Rogers, 2007). Apparently, even limited like-ability grouping is better than no grouping.

Are Full-Time Gifted Classes Better?: A few school districts have established full-time gifted classes that include moderate grade skipping. Because the entrance requirement for these classes is typically a score of 130 or higher on an IQ test, these programs serve moderately gifted students. Research studies show that students in these classes do achieve significantly more than equally gifted children who remain in a mixed-ability classroom, and better than in part-time pull-out programs. As for grade skipping, studies of moderate skipping show that this kind of acceleration has substantial beneficial effects for students and is not harmful socially or emotionally (Rogers, 2007).

The School-Within-a-School Approach. Full-time gifted programs within schools, however, pose a quandary. One of the challenges of designing programs for gifted students is to resolve the apparent conflict between meeting their special learning needs while promoting social equity. As we have previously discussed, exceptionally able learners have special needs that cannot be met without differentiating the pace, depth, and complexity of the curriculum and instruction that is typically offered at the student's age and grade level. At the same time, gifted students must coexist with others, and it is best for everyone if the coexistence is experienced as mutually beneficial rather than as antagonistic and elitist. A school-within-a-school approach is one way to offer gifted programming as well as opportunities for exceptionally capable learners to interact with the general school population in ways that can be mutually enriching.

School-within-a-school programs are generally housed in larger high schools. Studies indicate that for these programs to be successful in both meeting the needs of gifted students while maintaining a positive relationship with the entire school, the following five recommendations should be considered (Matthews & Kitchen, 2007):

- **Transparency and communication.** Open channels of communication are essential to helping others understand the nature of, and reasons for, special enrichment programs. The school needs to make information available about the special programs, including admissions criteria and academic standards. Because students in the regular program may have misconceptions about aspects of the special programs in their school, educators should make efforts to proactively provide all relevant information. As new students enter the school each year, and as the entire student population changes during the course of four years, awareness needs to be raised and maintained every year.
- **Flexible access to gifted programs.** Exclusivity is a frequent concern, especially if there is a strong sense that the gifted program forms a segregated group within the school. More flexibility in access and more frequent entry points may be the best way to alleviate this concern. When enrichment

programs offer reasonably flexible access, it is important that this information about flexibility be disseminated widely and that other students be encouraged to see that they have some choice about participation. Again, transparency and communication are key.

- **Equitable access to equipment, facilities, and field trips.** Some students in the regular program may show resentment of gifted program students' perceived access to more or better equipment, facilities, and field trips. Because teachers in the regular program may be less involved in creating similar opportunities, some perceptions of privilege are almost inevitable and not unfounded. Schools that have special high-ability programs need to work proactively to ensure that all students have access to the kinds of resources and field trips that are provided to the gifted program students. Also, teachers and principals need to communicate effectively with the school community about the nature of access to equipment, facilities, and field trips and look for ways to get teachers and parents of students in the regular program as actively engaged as are those in the gifted program.

- **Educators' awareness of misconceptions and stereotypes.** The teachers' perceptions are likely to be more positive than those of their students regarding the interaction between the gifted program and regular students. Although the teachers' perceptions may in fact be more accurate, it is important to address the nature of students' perceptions. It is also important that educators be aware of potential tensions between students in gifted programs and their peers in regular programs. Informed by this awareness, stereotypes and misconceptions can be addressed and cross-group interaction promoted.

- **Recognition of diverse pathways to excellence and achievement.** At large high schools there are many special programs in addition to the gifted program that receive attention for their exceptional participants and achievements, both within and outside the school. Actively celebrating diverse kinds of excellence and achievement goes a long way toward lessening resentment of any one program or group of students, including the gifted program and its participants. Schools can increase the acceptance and understanding of gifted academic programs by providing all students in the school with many possible pathways to excellence, recognition, and notable achievement.

What Are We Doing for the Profoundly Gifted?

In Chapters 1 and 2 we explained a few of the structural and functional differences that brain research has so far discovered in gifted brains compared to average brains. But no brain research to date has determined how the brains of those who are at the far end of the gifted scale, often called profoundly gifted, are unusual in structure or function. From time to time, children with extraordinary gifts cross the threshold of the public school. What can we do for them?

> Schools need to do more to address the needs of profoundly gifted students.

Programs for gifted students, as currently formatted in most public schools, do not address the needs of the profoundly gifted. First, these students need to be evaluated in terms of their specific talents rather than by a composite IQ score, which often reveals nothing about a student's unique abilities. Second, school districts should develop fast-paced and intensive courses for these students, either during the school year or in the summer. Many of the talent search programs sponsored by universities suggest model programs to address the needs of these extremely gifted students (see the **Resources** section). Allocating resources and devising courses for the profoundly gifted need not mean sacrificing the needs of the moderately gifted. For, if we elevate our expectations, the moderately gifted also would be appropriately challenged.

Teacher Training

Teacher training institutions must recognize that gifted education is the responsibility of all teachers, not just the few who specialize in that particular area. At least some training in gifted education should be provided to undergraduates and graduate students who plan to become professional educators. School administrators, too, must endeavor to ensure that policies on meeting the needs of gifted students are developed and translated into practice within each classroom. Only through our concerted efforts will we be certain that our schools are doing their best to meet the needs of our brightest students.

Preparation Standards for Teachers of the Gifted: A set of standards for the field of gifted education was developed in 1985 by the Council for Exceptional Children, The Association for the Gifted division (CEC-TAG). The purpose of the standards was to guide preK–12 and higher education teachers to instructional strategies that would improve teaching and enhance learning for students. In the early 2000s, the standards were revised and updated, and in 2006, the National Council for Accreditation of Teacher Education (NCATE) approved new *Teacher Preparation Standards in Gifted Education* that were developed by National Association for Gifted Children (NAGC) and the CEC. The new standards, which are the foundation for the knowledge and skills in which teacher candidates demonstrate competency, as determined by the field of gifted education, are to be used by college and university teacher preparation programs in gifted education and are to be a model for district-based professional development programming. See the NAGC Web site, www.nagc.org, for the complete list of standards, knowledge, and skills. Here is a brief summary of the 10 standards (NAGC, 2006).

- **Standard 1: Foundations.** Educators of the gifted
  - Understand that gifted education is an evolving and changing discipline based on philosophies, evidence-based principles and theories, relevant laws and policies, diverse and historical points of view, and human issues. These perspectives continue to influence the field of gifted education and the education and treatment of individuals with gifts and talents both in school and society.
  - Recognize how foundational influences affect professional practice, including assessment, instructional planning, delivery, and program evaluation.
  - Understand how issues of human diversity affect families, cultures, and schools, and how these complex human issues can interact in the delivery of gifted and talented education services.

- **Standard 2: Development and characteristics of learners.** Educators of the gifted
  - Know and demonstrate respect for their students as unique human beings.
  - Understand variations in characteristics and development between and among individuals with and without exceptional learning needs and capacities.
  - Express how different characteristics interact with the domains of human development and use this knowledge to describe the varying abilities and behaviors of individuals with gifts and talents.
  - Understand how families and communities contribute to the development of individuals with gifts and talents.

- **Standard 3: Individual learning differences.** Educators of the gifted
  - Understand the effects that gifts and talents can have on an individual's learning in school and throughout life.
  - Are active and resourceful in seeking to understand how language, culture, and family background interact with an individual's predispositions to impact academic and social behavior, attitudes, values, and interests. The understanding of these learning differences and their interactions provides the foundation upon which educators of the gifted plan instruction to provide meaningful and challenging learning.

- **Standard 4: Instructional strategies.** Educators of the gifted
  - Possess a repertoire of evidence-based curriculum and instructional strategies to differentiate for individuals with gifts and talents.

○ Select, adapt, and use these strategies to promote challenging learning opportunities in general and special curricula and to modify learning environments to enhance self-awareness and self-efficacy for individuals with gifts and talents.

○ Enhance the learning of critical and creative thinking, problem solving, and performance skills in specific domains.

○ Emphasize the development, practice, and transfer of advanced knowledge and skills across environments throughout the lifespan, leading to creative, productive careers in society for individuals with gifts and talents.

- **Standard 5: Learning environments and social interactions.** Educators of the gifted

  ○ Actively create learning environments for individuals with gifts and talents that foster cultural understanding, safety and emotional well being, positive social interactions, and active engagement.

  ○ Foster environments in which diversity is valued and individuals are taught to live harmoniously and productively in a culturally diverse world.

  ○ Shape environments to encourage independence, motivation, and self-advocacy of individuals with gifts and talents.

- **Standard 6: Language and communication.** Educators of the gifted

  ○ Understand the role of language and communication in talent development and the ways in which exceptional conditions can hinder or facilitate such development.

  ○ Use relevant strategies to teach oral and written communication skills to individuals with gifts and talents.

  ○ Are familiar with assistive technologies to support and enhance communication of individuals with exceptional needs.

  ○ Match their communication methods to an individual's language proficiency and cultural and linguistic differences.

  ○ Use communication strategies and resources to facilitate understanding of subject matter for individuals with gifts and talents who are English language learners.

- **Standard 7: Instructional planning.** Educators of the gifted

  ○ Develop long-range plans anchored in both general and special curricula.

  ○ Systematically translate shorter-range goals and objectives that take into consideration an individual's abilities and needs, the learning environment, and cultural and linguistic factors. Understanding of these factors, as well as the implications of being gifted and talented, guides the educator's selection, adaptation, and creation of materials, and use of differentiated instructional strategies. Learning plans are modified based on ongoing assessment of the individual's progress.

  ○ Facilitate these actions in a collaborative context that includes individuals with gifts and talents, families, professional colleagues, and personnel from other agencies as appropriate.

  ○ Are comfortable using technologies to support instructional planning and individualized instruction.

- **Standard 8: Assessment.** Educators of the gifted

  ○ Use the results of such assessments to adjust instruction and to enhance ongoing learning progress.

  ○ Understand the process of identification, legal policies, and ethical principles of measurement and assessment related to referral, eligibility, program planning, instruction, and placement for individuals with gifts and talents, including those from culturally and linguistically diverse backgrounds.

  ○ Understand measurement theory and practices for addressing the interpretation of assessment results.

  ○ Understand the appropriate use and limitations of various types of assessments.

  ○ Employ alternative assessments such as performance-based assessment, portfolios, and computer simulations, to ensure the use of nonbiased and equitable identification and learning progress models.

- **Standard 9: Professional and ethical practice.** Educators of the gifted
  - ○ Are guided by the profession's ethical and professional practice standards. They practice in multiple roles and complex situations across wide age and developmental ranges. Their practice requires ongoing attention to professional and ethical considerations.
  - ○ Engage in professional activities that promote growth in individuals with gifts and talents and update themselves on evidence-based best practices.
  - ○ View themselves as lifelong learners and regularly reflect on and adjust their practice.
  - ○ Are aware of how attitudes, behaviors, and ways of communicating can influence their practice.
  - ○ Understand that culture and language interact with gifts and talents and are sensitive to the many aspects of the diversity of individuals with gifts and talents and their families.

- **Standard 10: Collaboration.** Educators of the gifted
  - ○ Effectively collaborate with families, other educators, and related service providers. This collaboration enhances comprehensive articulated program options across educational levels and engagement of individuals with gifts and talents in meaningful learning activities and interactions.
  - ○ Embrace their special role as advocate for individuals with gifts and talents. They promote and advocate for the learning and well-being of individuals with gifts and talents across settings and diverse learning experiences.

CONCLUSION

Neuroscientists are continually probing the human brain to discover the mechanisms and networks that allow it to carry out its many functions. They are exploring concepts as diverse as intuition, psychic phenomena, mind-body connections, and how the brain manages the information that creates consciousness. Surely the revelations that are to come will offer a deeper understanding of how the brain learns so that we can be more successful in helping *all* our children reach their fullest potential. Yet despite our good intentions, gifted students are still not getting the resources they need. In our effort to be egalitarian, our curriculum is regressing toward the mean. One curriculum does *not* fit all. We must take great care to ensure that while we leave no child behind, we do not prevent a child from moving ahead.

> We must take great care to ensure that while we leave no child behind, we do not prevent a child from moving ahead.

APPLICATIONS

THE CHARACTERISTICS OF GIFTEDNESS SCALE

The following scale may help the teacher and parent make a more valid preliminary judgment about a specific student's abilities. Research studies conducted in recent years have identified characteristics of gifted individuals and Silverman (1993) compiled that research into the giftedness scale found on the following pages. More recent experimental and clinical studies continue to support these characteristics.

Guidelines:

- On this scale, the teacher or parent should rate each characteristic by checking the column that best describes how often that characteristic is evident. The scale is just a guide and is by no means a definitive indicator of giftedness. However, if the teacher or parent scores the student at the "True" or "Very True" end of the scale on more than half of the characteristics, further assessment is warranted.

- Students gifted in the performing arts usually display many of the characteristics of giftedness on this scale in addition to their advanced skills in the main area of competence. Thus, the scale can be used to identify students who are talented in different domains.

- Although these characteristics can distinguish between gifted and typical students, they have not been shown to distinguish different levels of giftedness.

- Students who score high on the characteristics scale but who do not get high scores on tests of achievement may have other problems, such as hearing and vision deficits that impair their classroom participation and depress scores on standardized tests. In this case, look at the subtest scores to determine areas of strength and weakness.

CHARACTERISTICS OF GIFTEDNESS SCALE

Name of Child_____Date_____ Parent/Teacher_____

Compared to other children this child's age, to what extent do these descriptors fit this child?

Characteristic	Not True	Uncertain	True	Very True
1. Reasons well (good thinker)	_____	_____	_____	_____
2. Learns rapidly	_____	_____	_____	_____
3. Has extensive vocabulary	_____	_____	_____	_____
4. Has an excellent memory	_____	_____	_____	_____
5. Has a long attention span*	_____	_____	_____	_____
6. Sensitive (feelings easily hurt)	_____	_____	_____	_____
7. Shows compassion	_____	_____	_____	_____
8. Seeks perfection	_____	_____	_____	_____
9. Intense	_____	_____	_____	_____
10. Morally sensitive	_____	_____	_____	_____
11. Has strong curiosity	_____	_____	_____	_____
12. Perseverant when interested*	_____	_____	_____	_____
13. Has high degree of energy	_____	_____	_____	_____
14. Prefers older companions/adults	_____	_____	_____	_____
15. Has a wide range of interests	_____	_____	_____	_____
16. Has a great sense of humor	_____	_____	_____	_____
17. Early or avid reader**	_____	_____	_____	_____
18. Concerned with justice, fairness	_____	_____	_____	_____
19. Judgment mature for age at times	_____	_____	_____	_____
20. Is a keen observer	_____	_____	_____	_____
21. Has a vivid imagination	_____	_____	_____	_____
22. Is highly creative	_____	_____	_____	_____
23. Tends to question authority	_____	_____	_____	_____
24. Shows ability with numbers	_____	_____	_____	_____
25. Good at jigsaw puzzles	_____	_____	_____	_____

*(Long attention span or perseveres if interested; Does the child stay with tasks for long periods of time?)

**(If the child is too young to read, is intensely interested in books)

Please give examples:

1. Reasons well _____

2. Learns rapidly_____

3. Has extensive vocabulary_____

4. Has an excellent memory_____

5. Has a long attention span_____

6. Sensitive (feelings easily hurt)_____

7. Shows compassion_____

8. Seeks perfection_____

9. Intense_____

10. Morally sensitive_____

11. Has strong curiosity_____

12. Perseverant when interested_____

13. Has high degree of energy_____

14. Prefers older companions or adults_____

15. Has a wide range of interests_____

16. Has a great sense of humor_____

17. Early or avid reader_____

18. Concerned with justice, fairness_____

19. Judgment mature for age at times_____

20. Is a keen observer_____

21. Has a vivid imagination_____

22 Is highly creative_____

23. Tends to question authority_____

24. Shows ability with numbers_____

25. Good at jigsaw puzzles_____

Source: Copyright 1993 by Linda K. Silverman. Used with permission.

APPLICATIONS

MIDDLE SCHOOL GIFTED RATING SCALE (6–8)

The first step in helping gifted middle school students is to identify them. At times students who are truly gifted are overlooked because their interests and learning patterns do not necessarily match classroom activities. Some gifted students may even exhibit negative behaviors. They may challenge authority and school routines. They may show little tolerance for others or extreme sensitivity to others. Gifted students may be compliant or forceful, but the more important thing is what they are revealing about their capabilities for deep, rich, and complex thought. If not identified, their need for challenges may be compromised and their social and emotional vulnerabilities may be heightened. High achieving students are frequently perceived as gifted. Although many gifted students exhibit strong academic performance, this is not always the case. Likewise, many bright, high achieving students who are successful because of hard work and strong support do not require differentiation.

The Middle School Rating Scale is an instrument designed to help identify students who may be exhibiting behaviors indicative of giftedness. The fifteen characteristics on the rating scale are traits that have been documented in a number of research studies as characteristics of giftedness. Think about students in your class and the degree to which they exhibit behaviors that match characteristics of giftedness. Please take time to consider each of your students as you complete the rating scale. By focusing on a profile of each child's strengths, you will be more empowered to work with everyone's potential.

MIDDLE SCHOOL GIFTED RATING SCALE (GRADES 6–8)

- On a class list, check the names of all students in your class who come to mind when you think of giftedness. Do not hesitate to list a student.
- For each student you select, rate each characteristic on the 1–4 scale. Use the rating scale descriptors provided to select a rating.

1 = Typical for grade/age.		3 = Quite advanced for grade/age.					
2 = Above average for grade/age.		4 = Remarkable for grade/age. One in fifty.					
	STUDENT NAME(S)						
1.	Thinks abstractly, generalizes						
2.	Enjoys intellectual activity						
3.	Can persuade others						
4.	Shows power of concentration						
5.	Has storehouse of knowledge						
6.	Is intense, goal-directed						
7.	Experiments, explores						
8.	Exhibits sensitivity						
9.	Has many and/or intense interests						
10.	Adapts to new situations						
11.	Exhibits expertise in one or more areas						
12.	Displays subtle humor						
13.	Is expressive with words, numbers, symbols						
14.	Sees and solves problems						
15.	Invents, creates						
	TOTAL						

Source: DoDEA, 2006.

APPLICATIONS

HIGH SCHOOL GIFTED RATING SCALE (GRADES 9–12)

Identification of students for gifted program services often becomes a function of self-referral at this level. Students request advanced courses and other opportunities that match their potential and performance. However, some gifted students have never been identified and may benefit from recognition by a knowing educator. Students who exhibit gifted characteristics should be identified and counseled into appropriate courses, mentoring, and other experiences that match their needs.

Although most high school students are identified for gifted program services because of past participation or academic records, some may be located through a current analysis of behaviors within and outside the classroom. Some students have been overlooked because their strengths and learning patterns show up in extracurricular activities or in behaviors that may seem less than appropriate in the classroom. They may question teachers and challenge their opinions. They may exhibit extreme political or social positions. Some may be overly-focused on success and perfectionism. Gifted adolescents may be compliant or forceful, but the more important thing to consider is what they are revealing about their capabilities for deep, rich, and complex thought. If not identified, their need for challenges and their social and emotional vulnerabilities may be compromised. This is particularly true for youngsters with very strong potential who are not finding correlating success in academic work.

High achieving students are frequently perceived as gifted. Although many gifted students exhibit strong academic performance, this is not always the case. Likewise, many bright, high achieving students who are successful because of hard work and strong support systems do not require differentiation. Gifted program services are not a reward for good work and good behavior. Rather, the gifted program provides support and challenges for highly capable students whose needs are beyond the standard curriculum.

The High School Rating Scale is an instrument designed to help identify students in your classes who may be exhibiting behaviors that indicate giftedness. The fifteen characteristics on the rating scale are traits that have been documented in a number of research studies as characteristics of giftedness. Think about your students and the degree to which they exhibit behaviors that match characteristics of giftedness. Please take time to consider each of your students as you complete the rating scale. By focusing on a profile of each child's strengths, you will be more empowered to work with everyone's potential.

HIGH SCHOOL GIFTED RATING SCALE (GRADES 9–12)

- On a class list, check the names of all students in your class who come to mind when you think of giftedness. Do not hesitate to list a student.
- For each student you select, rate each characteristic on the 1–4 scale. Use the rating scale descriptors provided to select a rating.

1 = Typical for grade/age. 2 = Above average for grade/age.				3 = Quite advanced for grade/age. 4 = Remarkable for grade/age. One in fifty.			
	STUDENT NAME(S)						
1.	Demonstrates insight						
2.	Thrives on intellectual activity						
3.	Is persuasive; can influence others						
4.	Sustains concentration						
5.	Is widely informed						
6.	Enjoys interactions with adults						
7.	Experiments, explores, pursues ideas						
8.	Is concerned with justice, fairness						
9.	Has multiple and/or extended interests						
10.	Is self-motivated, goal-oriented, persistent						
11.	Exhibits expertise in one or more areas						
12.	Displays mature sense of humor						
13.	Uses subtleties of words, numbers, symbols						
14.	Is resourceful, flexible						
15.	Is original, unconventional, imaginative						
	TOTAL						

Source: DoDEA, 2006.

APPLICATIONS

LOCAL SURVEY ON HOW ELEMENTARY GIFTED STUDENTS ARE BEING SERVED

The following survey has been adapted from Swiatek and Lupkowski-Shoplik (2003), and is designed to help educators who work with gifted elementary students review how these students' needs are being met. Of particular concern is whether opportunities are being offered to elementary students who are talented in mathematics.

After completing the survey, respondents may wish to examine the results and decide whether the current program is truly addressing the needs of the gifted or whether adjustments need to be made.

Part I. Which of these activities have the gifted elementary student done over the past year, and what percent participated in each? (Circle "Yes" or "No" and enter the percentage)

a. Participated in an academic competition. Yes/No %____

b. Attended a summer academic program. Yes/No %____

c. Participated in a weekend academic program. Yes/No %____

d. Participated in an after-school academic program. Yes/No %____

e. Taken a computer-based academic course. Yes/No %____

f. Taken a correspondence course through the mail. Yes/No %____

Part II. In what kinds of gifted classes or programs do gifted students participate? (Circle "Yes" or "No")

a. They get special assignments within the regular classroom. Yes/No

b. They leave the regular classroom one or more times a week to go to a gifted class. Yes/No

c. They meet individually with a teacher or mentor regularly. Yes/No

d. They are grouped for instruction with other gifted students in the regular classroom. Yes/No

e. They are in a special class with other gifted students for one or more of their subjects. Yes/No

Part III. Check all of the following that apply to gifted students. (Circle "Yes" or "No")

a. Students have skipped one or more years/grades of school. Yes/No

b. Students go to a higher grade for instruction in a subject. Yes/No

c. They are doing work at a higher grade level in a subject in their regular classroom. Yes/No

d. They have not skipped any grades or subjects. Yes/No

Part IV. How do they study mathematics? (Circle "Yes" or "No")

a. They are in the regular classroom, learning the same
    mathematics as all of the other students.   Yes/No

b. They work with a small group of other mathematically talented
    students studying advanced topics in the regular classroom.   Yes/No

c. They can move up a grade for mathematics.   Yes/No

d. They study mathematics in a special math class for gifted
    mathematics students.   Yes/No

e. They work individually with a teacher or other adult to study
    advanced mathematics.   Yes/No

f. They participate in a distance learning program.   Yes/No

After reviewing your responses, write here what you may need to do._____

_____

_____

Glossary

Acceleration. Presenting information at a fast pace that corresponds more closely to the pace at which gifted students learn.

Adaptive decision making. The process of solving a problem that has multiple solutions depending on the context and priorities of the moment, as in, "What gift should I buy for my nephew's birthday?"

Alphabetic principle. The notion that written words are composed of letters of the alphabet that intentionally and systematically represent segments of spoken words.

Amygdala. The almond-shaped structure in the brain's limbic system that encodes emotional messages to long-term memory.

Angular gyrus. A brain structure that decodes visual information about words so they can be matched to their meanings.

Asperger syndrome. A developmental disorder also known as high functioning autism because people with the disorder generally display higher mental performance.

Attention-deficit hyperactivity disorder (ADHD). A syndrome that interferes with an individual's capacity to regulate activity level, inhibit behavior, and attend to tasks in developmentally appropriate ways.

Autism. A spectrum disorder that affects an individual's ability to communicate, form relationships with others, and relate appropriately to the environment.

Bloom's Taxonomy of the Cognitive Domain. A model developed by Benjamin Bloom in the 1950s for classifying the complexity of human thought into six levels. It was revised in 2001.

Brain stem. One of the major parts of the brain, it receives sensory input and monitors vital functions such as heartbeat, body temperature, and digestion.

Broca's area. A region in the left frontal lobe of the brain believed responsible for generating the vocabulary and syntax of an individual's native language.

Cerebellum. One of the major parts of the brain, it coordinates muscle movement.

Cerebrum. The largest of the major parts of the brain, it controls sensory interpretation, thinking, and memory.

Chunking. The ability of the brain to perceive a coherent group of items as a single item or chunk.

Compacting. Eliminating drill and repetitious material from the curriculum so that gifted students can move on to more challenging material.

Conceptual knowledge. The ability to acquire the grand scheme of a topic.

Constructivism. This theory of learning states that active learners use past experiences and chunking to construct sense and meaning from new learning, thereby building larger conceptual schemes.

Corpus callosum. The bridge of nerve fibers that connects the left and right cerebral hemispheres and allows communication between them.

Cortex. The thin but tough layer of cells covering the cerebrum that contains all the neurons used for cognitive and motor processing.

Dendrite. The branched extension from the cell body of a neuron that receives impulses from nearby neurons through synaptic contacts.

Differentiated curriculum. An approach where the teacher adjusts the curriculum content, the instructional process, and the student product in response to student readiness, interests, and learning profile.

Electroencephalograph (EEG). An instrument that charts fluctuations in the brain's electrical activity via electrodes attached to the scalp.

Frontal lobe. The front part of the brain that monitors higher-order thinking, directs problem solving, and regulates the excesses of the emotional (limbic) system.

Functional magnetic resonance imaging (fMRI). An instrument that measures blood flow to the brain to record areas of high and low neuronal activity.

Genotype-environment correlation (GEC). The extent to which genes can be modified by the environment.

Gray matter. The thin but tough covering of the brain's cerebrum also known as the cerebral cortex.

Hemisphericity. The notion that the two cerebral hemispheres are specialized and process information differently.

Hippocampus. A brain structure that compares new learning to past learning and encodes information from working memory to long-term storage.

Hyperlexia. A term describing children who have precocious reading skills but who also have significant problems with learning and language.

Imagery. The mental visualization of objects, events, and arrays.

Immediate memory. A temporary memory where information is processed briefly (in seconds) and subconsciously, then either blocked or passed on to working memory.

Inclusion. Grouping students into a regular classroom without regard to ability.

Limbic system. The structures at the base of the cerebrum that control emotions.

Long-term memory. The areas of the cerebrum where memories are stored permanently.

Magnetic resonance imaging (MRI). An instrument that uses radio waves to disturb the alignment of the body's atoms in a magnetic field to produce computer-processed, high-contrast images of internal structures.

Motor cortex. The narrow band across the top of the brain from ear to ear that controls voluntary movement.

Neuron. The basic cell making up the brain and nervous system, consisting of a globular cell body, a long fiber called an axon that transmits impulses, and many shorter fibers called dendrites that receive them.

Neurotransmitter. Chemicals circulating in the brain that transmit impulses from one neuron to another.

Number sense. The innate ability to detect differences in numerical quantities without counting.

Overexcitabilities. Innate characteristics that reveal a heightened ability to respond to stimuli due to an increased sensitivity of the neurons.

Phonemes. The smallest units of sound in a language that combine to make syllables.

Positron emission tomography (PET) scanner. An instrument that traces the metabolism of radioactively tagged sugar in brain tissue producing a color image of cell activity.

Prefrontal cortex. The foremost part of the brain's frontal lobes, responsible for coordinating all cognitive and executive functions.

Procedural knowledge. The steps and processes needed to solve a problem.

Prodigy. A child of high intelligence who is able to perform a specific skill at an adult level of competence, and is aware of thinking strategies.

Rehearsal. The reprocessing of information in working memory.

Retention. The preservation of a learning in long-term memory in such a way that it can be identified and recalled quickly and accurately.

Savant. An individual with an exception ability to perform a specific skill, usually artistic, musical, or mathematical, but who often displays flat emotions and is unaware of thinking strategies.

Self-concept. Our perception of who we are and how we fit into the world.

Thalamus. A part of the limbic system that receives all incoming sensory information, except smell, and shunts it to other areas of the cortex for additional processing.

Twice-Exceptional. A term used to describe gifted individuals who also have a learning disability.

Underachievement. A significant difference between an individual's ability and performance.

Veridical decision making. The process of solving a problem that has only one correct answer, as in, "What is my dentist's telephone number?"

Wernicke's area. A section in the left temporal lobe of the brain believed responsible for generating sense and meaning in an individual's native language.

White matter. The support tissue lying beneath the cerebrum's gray matter (cortex) containing neuron branches that allow communication with distant parts of the brain.

Working memory. The temporary memory of limited capacity wherein information is processed consciously.

References

Abbott, A., & Collins, D. (2002). A theoretical and empirical analysis of a "state of the art" talent identification model. *High Ability Studies, 13,* 157–78.

Achor, T., & Tarr, A. (1996, Spring). *Underachieving gifted students.* Arlington, VA: ERIC Clearinghouse on Disabilities and Gifted Children.

Aguirre, N. (2003). ESL students in gifted education. In J. A. Castellano (Ed.), *Special populations in gifted education. Working with diverse gifted learners* (pp. 17–27). Boston: Allyn and Bacon.

Alexander, J., Carr, M., & Schwanenflugel, P. (1995). Development of metacognition in gifted children. *Developmental Review, 15,* 1–37.

Alsop, G. (2003, Spring). Asynchrony: Intuitively valid and theoretically reliable. *Roeper Review, 25,* 118–127.

American Psychiatric Association (APA). (2000). *Diagnostic and statistical manual of mental disorders (DSM-IV-TR,* 4th ed., text revision). Washington, DC: Author.

Anderson, L. W. (Ed.), Krathwohl, D. R. (Ed.), Airasian, P. W., Cruikshank, K. A., Mayer, R. E., Pintrich, P. R., Raths, J., & Wittrock, M. C. (2001). *A taxonomy for learning, teaching, and assessing: A revision of Bloom's Taxonomy of Educational Objectives* (Complete edition). New York: Longman.

Assouline, S. G., Colangelo, N., Ihrig, D., & Forstadt, L. (2006). Attributional choices for academic success and failure by intellectually gifted students. *Gifted Child Quarterly, 50,* 283–294.

Babo, G. D. (2004). The relationship between instrumental music participation and standardized assessment achievement of middle school students. *Research Studies in Music Education, 22,* 14–27.

Baddeley, A. (2003). Working memory and language: An overview. *Journal of Communication Disorders, 36,* 189–208.

Bangert, M., & Altenmüller, E. O. (2003, October). Mapping perception to action in piano practice: A longitudinal DC-EEG study. *BMC Neuroscience, 4.*

Barnhill, C. (2001, May). What's new in AS research: A synthesis of research conducted by the Asperger syndrome project. *Intervention in School and Clinic, 36,* 300–305.

Baron-Cohen, S., & Hammer, J. (1997). Parents of children with Asperger's syndrome: What is the cognitive phenotype? *Journal of Cognitive Neuroscience, 9,* 548–554.

Bauer, S. (2008). Asperger syndrome. *Online Asperger Syndrome Information and Support.* Available at http://www.udel.edu/bkirby/asperger.

Baum, S. M., & Owen, S. V. (2004). *To be gifted and learning disabled: Strategies for helping bright students with LD, ADHD, and more.* Mansfield Center, CT: Creative Learning Press.

Baumann, S., Koeneke, S., Schmidt, C. F., Meyer, M., Lutz, K., & Jancke, L. (2007, August). A network for audio–motor coordination in skilled pianists and non-musicians. *Brain Research, 1161,* 65–78.

Beatty, J. (2001). *The human brain: Essentials of behavioral neuroscience.* Thousand Oaks, CA: Sage Publications.

Benbow, C. P., & Stanley, J. C. (1983). Sex differences in mathematical reasoning ability: More facts. *Science, 222,* 1029–31.

Berger, A., Tzur, G., & Posner, M. I. (2006, August). Infant brains detect arithmetic errors. *Proceedings of the National Academy of Sciences USA, 103,* 12649–12653.

Bernal, E. M. (2002). Three ways to achieve a more equitable representation of culturally and linguistically different students in GT programs. *Roeper Review, 24,* 82–88.

Berns, G. S., Cohen, J. D., & Mintun, M. A. (1997). Brain regions responsive to novelty in the absence of awareness. *Science, 276,* 1272–1275.

Bischoff-Grethe, A., Proper, S. M., Mao, H., Daniels, K. A., & Berns, G. S. (2000). Conscious and unconscious processing of nonverbal predictability in Wernicke's area. *Journal of Neuroscience, 20,* 1975–1981.

Blackwell, L. S., Trzeniewski, K. H., & Dweck, C. S. (2007, January/February). Implicit theories of intelligence predict achievement across an adolescent transition: A longitudinal study and an intervention. *Child Development, 78,* 246–263.

Bloom, B. S. (1956). *Taxonomy of educational objectives (cognitive domain).* New York: Longman.

Bock, M. (2001, May). SODA strategy: Enhancing the social interaction skills of youngsters with Asperger's syndrome. *Intervention in School and Clinic, 36,* 272–278.

Bortfeld, H., Wruck, E., & Boas, D. A. (2007, January). Assessing infants' cortical response to speech using near-infrared spectroscopy. *Neuroimage, 34,* 407–415.

Bouchard, C., & Shepard, R. J. (1994). Physical activity, fitness, and health: The model and key concepts. In C. Bouchard, R. J. Shepard, & T. Stephens (Eds.), *Physical activity, fitness, and health* (pp. 77–88). Champaign, IL: Human Kinetics.

Briggs, C. J., Reis, S. M., & Sullivan, E. E. (2008, Spring). A national view of promising programs and practices for culturally, linguistically, and ethnically diverse gifted and talented students. *Gifted Child Quarterly, 52,* 131–145.

Brinda, W. (2007, June). Three acts to engagement and enjoyment: Theatre brings literature back to life for reluctant and struggling readers. *Literacy Learning: The Middle Years, 15,* 29–36.

Brown, S., Martinez, M. J., & Parsons, L. M. (2006, August). The neural basis of human dance. *Cerebral Cortex, 16,* 1157–1167.

Brown, S. W., Renzulli, J. S., Gubbins, E. J., Siegle, D., Zhang, W., & Chen, C-H. (2005). Assumptions underlying the identification of gifted and talented students. *Gifted Child Quarterly, 49,* 68–79.

Bruguier, A., Preuschoff, K., Quartz, S., & Bossaerts, P. (2008, May). Investigating signal integration with canonical correlation analysis of fMRI brain activation data. *Neuroimage, 41,* 35–44.

Brunyé, T. T., & Taylor, H. A. (2008, April). Working memory in developing and applying mental models from spatial descriptions. *Journal of Memory and Language, 58,* 701–729.

Buescher, T. M., & Higham, S. (1990). *Helping adolescents adjust to giftedness.* Arlington, VA: ERIC Clearinghouse on Disabilities and Gifted Education.

Burruss, J. D. (1999). Problem-based learning. *Science Scope, 22,* 46–49.

Byrd, S. (2007, November). *Advanced Placement and International Baccalaureate: Do they deserve gold star status?* Washington, DC: Thomas P. Fordham Institute.

Cahill, L. (2003, December). Sex- and hemisphere-related influences on the neurobiology of emotionally influenced memory. *Progress in Neuro-Psychopharmacology and Biological Psychiatry, 27,* 1235–1241.

Cahill, L., Haier, R. J., White, N. S., Fallon, J., Kilpatrick, L., Lawrence, C., et al. (2001, January). Sex-related difference in amygdala activity during emotionally influenced memory storage. *Neurobiology of Learning and Memory, 75,* 1–9.

Callahan, C. M. (2005, Spring). Identifying gifted students from underrepresented populations. *Theory Into Practice, 44,* 98–104.

Canobi, K. H., & Bethune, N. E. (2008, September). Number words in young children's conceptual and procedural knowledge of addition, subtraction and inversion. *Cognition, 108,* 675–686.

Cappelletti, M., Waley-Cohen, H., Butterworth, B., & Kopelman, M. (2000). A selective loss of the ability to read and write music. *Neurocase, 6*, 332–341.

Careau, S. G. (2008, Fall). A pedagogy for understanding the visual arts. *Community College Enterprise, 14*, 7–21.

Carroll, J. B. (1993). *Human cognitive abilities: A survey of factoranalytic studies.* New York: Cambridge University Press.

Cash, A. B. (1999, September). A profile of gifted individuals with autism: The twice-exceptional learner. *Roeper Review, 22*, 22–27.

Centers for Disease Control and Prevention (CDC). (2007, February). *Prevalence of autism spectrum disorders—Autism and Developmental Disabilities Monitoring Network, 14 sites, United States, 2002.* Atlanta, GA: Author.

Chatard, A., Guimond, S., & Selimbegovic, L. (2007, November). "How good are you in math?" The effect of gender stereotypes on students' recollection of their school marks. *Journal of Experimental Social Psychology, 43*, 1017–1024.

Chatterjee, A. (2004). The neuropsychology of visual artistic production. *Neuropsychologia, 42*, 1568–1583.

Chávez-Eakle, R. A., Graff-Guerrero, A., Garcia-Reyna, J-C., Vaugier, V., & Cruz-Fuentes, C. (2007). Cerebral blood flow associated with creative performance: A comparative study. *NeuroImage, 38*, 519–528.

Chiang, W. C., & Wynn, K. (2000) Infants' tracking of objects and collections. *Cognition, 77*, 169–195.

Cho, S., & Ahn, D. (2003, Summer). Strategy acquisition and maintenance of gifted and nongifted young children. *Exceptional Children, 69*, 497–505.

Chochon, F., Cohen, L., van der Moortele, P. F., & Dehaene, S. (1999). Differential contributions of the left and right inferior parietal lobules to number processing. *Journal of Cognitive Neuroscience, 11*, 617–630.

Chong, H., Riis, J. L., McGinnis, S. M., Williams, D. M., Holcomb, P. J., & Daffner, K. R. (2008, January). To ignore or explore: Top-down modulation of novelty processing. *Journal of Cognitive Neuroscience, 20*, 120–134.

Clark, G., & Zimmerman, E. (1998). Nurturing the arts in programs for gifted and talented students. *Phi Delta Kappan, 79*, 747–751.

Cline, S., & Hegeman, K. (2001, Summer). Gifted children with disabilities. *Gifted Child Today, 24*, 16–24.

Cobine, G. (1995). *Effective use of student journal writing.* Bloomington, IN: Indiana University, ERIC Clearing House on Reading, English, and Communication.

Colangelo, N., & Zaffran, R. T. (1979). *New voices in counseling the gifted.* Dubuque, IA: Kendall Hunt.

Coleman, M. R. (2003). The identification of students who are gifted. *Eric Digest.* (ERIC Document Reproduction Service No. ED480431).

Conant, J. B. (1946). *General education in a free society.* Cambridge, MA: Harvard University Press.

Cone, T. P., & Cone, S. L. (2007, January). Dance education: Dual or dueling identities. *The Journal of Physical Education, Recreation & Dance, 78*, 6–7, 13.

Cortina, J. M., & Nouri, H. (1999). *Effect size for ANOVA designs.* Thousand Oaks, CA: Sage Publications.

Coutinho, S. (2008, March). Self-efficacy, metacognition, and performance. *North American Journal of Psychology, 10*, 165.

Cowan, N. (2001). The magical number 4 in short-term memory: A reconsideration of mental storage capacity. *Behavioral and Brain Sciences, 24*, 87–114.

Cowan, N., Fristoe, N. M., Elliott, E. M., Brunner, R. P., & Saults, J. S. (2006, December). Scope of attention, control of attention, and intelligence in children and adults. *Memory and Cognition, 34*, 1754–1768.

Cross, E. S., de C. Hamilton, A. F., & Grafton, S. T. (2006). Building a motor simulation de novo: Observation of dance by dancers. *Neuroimage, 31*, 1257–1267.

Cross, T. L., Cassady, J. C., Dixon, F. A., & Adams, C. M. (2008). The psychology of gifted adolescents as measured by the MMPI-A. *Gifted Child Quarterly, 52*, 326–339.

Cunningham, C. M., Callahan, C. M., Plucker, J. A., Roberson, S. C., & Rapkin, A. (1998). Identifying Hispanic students of outstanding talent: Psychometric integrity of a peer nomination form. *Exceptional Children, 64,* 197–209.

Cycowicz, Y. M., & Friedman, D. (2007, January). Visual novel stimuli in an ERP novelty oddball paradigm: Effects of familiarity on repetition and recognition memory. *Psychophysiology, 44,* 11–29.

Dabrowski, K. (1964). *Positive disintegration.* Boston: Little Brown.

Dapretto, M., & Bookheimer, S. Y. (1999). Form and content: Dissociating syntax and semantics in sentence comprehension. *Neuron, 2,* 427.

Davis, G. A., & Rimm, S. B. (2003). *Education of the gifted and talented.* Englewood Cliffs, NJ: Prentice-Hall.

Davis, J. H. (2008). *Why our schools need the arts.* New York: Teachers College Press.

Dehaene, S., Spelke, E., Pinel, P., Stanescu, R., & Tsivkin, S. (1999, May). Sources of mathematical thinking: Behavioral and brain-imaging evidence. *Science, 284,* 970–974.

Dehaene-Lambertz, G. (2000). Cerebral specialization for speech and non-speech stimuli in infants. *Journal of Cognitive Neuroscience, 12,* 449–460.

Delcourt, M. A. B., Cornell, D. G., & Goldberg, M. D. (2007). Cognitive and affective learning outcomes of gifted elementary school students. *Gifted Child Quarterly, 51,* 359–381.

Delisle, J. R., & Berger, S. L. (1990). *Underachieving gifted students.* Arlington, VA: ERIC Clearinghouse on Disabilities and Gifted Education.

Department of Defense Education Activity (DoDEA) (2006). *Gifted Rating Scales for Grades 6–8 and 9–12.* Washington, DC: Author.

Depienne, C., Héron, D., Betancur, C., Benyahia, B., Trouillard, O., Bouteiller, D., et al. (2007, July). Autism, language delay and mental retardation in a patient with 7q11 duplication. *Journal of Medical Genetics, 44,* 452–458.

DeThorne, L. S., Petrill, S. A., Hart, S. A., Channell, R. W., Campbell, R. J., Deater-Deckard, K., et al. (2008, April). Genetic effects on children's conversational language use. *Journal of Speech, Language, and Hearing Research, 51,* 423–435.

Devine, D. (2006, Winter). Teaching with many acts: Curriculum as theatre. *Journal of Curriculum Theorizing, 22,* 25–38.

Dix, J., & Schafer, S. (1996). From paradox to performance: Practical strategies for identifying and teaching GT/LD students. *Gifted Child Today, 19,* 22–25, 28–31.

Donovan, M. S., & Cross, C. T. (Eds.). (2002). *Minority students in special and gifted education.* Washington, DC: National Academy Press.

Downing, J. A., Carlson, J. K., Hoffman, J., Gray, D., & Thompson, A. (2004, March). A musical interlude: Using music and relaxation to improve reading performance. *Intervention in School and Clinic, 39,* 246–250.

Engle, R. W., Laughlin, J. E., Tuholski, S. W., & Conway, R. A. (1999, September). Working memory, short-term memory, and general fluid intelligence: A latent-variable approach. *Journal of Experimental Psychology, 128,* 309–331.

Falk, R. F., Lind, S., Miller, N. B., Piechowski, M. M., & Silverman, L. K. (1999). *The overexcitabilities questionnaire-two (OEQ-II).* Denver, CO: The Institute for the Study of Advanced Development.

Fingelkurts, A. A., & Fingelkurts, A. A. (2003). Gifted brain and twinning: Integrative review of the recent literature. *Advances in Psychology Research, 20,* 1–32.

Fink, A., Grabner, R. H., Benedek, M., Reishofer, G., Hauswirth, V., Fally, M., et al. (2009, March). The creative brain: Investigation of brain activity during creative problem solving by means of EEG and fMRI. *Human Brain Mapping, 30,* 734–748.

Ford, D. Y., Grantham, T. C., & Whiting, G. W. (2008). Another look at the achievement gap: Learning from the experiences of gifted Black students. *Urban Education, 43,* 216–239.

Ford, D.Y., Harris, J. J., III, Tyson, C. A., & Trotman, F. M. (2002). Beyond deficit thinking: Providing access for gifted African American students. *Roeper Review, 24,* 52–58.

Foust, R. C., & Booker, K. (2007, Fall). The social cognition of gifted adolescents. *Roeper Review, 29,* 45–47.

Gagné F. (1985). Giftedness and talent: Reexamining a reexamination of the definitions. *Gifted Child Quarterly, 29,* 103–112.

Gagné, F. (2003). Transforming gifts into talents: The DMGT as a developmental theory. In N. Colangelo & G. A. Davis (Eds.), *Handbook of gifted education* (3rd ed., pp. 60–74). Boston: Allyn and Bacon.

Gagné, F., & Gagnier, N. (2004). The socio-affective and academic impact of early entrance to school. *Roeper Review, 26,* 128–138.

Gagné, F., & Schader, R. M. (2006, Winter). Chance and talent development. *Roeper Review, 28,* 88–90.

Galuske, R. A. W., Schlote, W., Bratzke, H., & Singer, W. (2000). Interhemispheric asymmetries of the modular structure in human temporal cortex. *Science, 289,* 1946–1949.

Gardner, H. (1983). *Frames of mind: The theory of multiple intelligences.* New York: Basic Books.

Gardner, H. (1993). *Frames of mind: The theory of multiple intelligences* (Rev. ed.). New York: Basic Books.

Garlick, D. (2002, January). Understanding the nature of the general factor of intelligence: The role of individual differences in neural plasticity as an explanatory mechanism. *Psychological Review, 109,* 116–136.

Gaser, C., & Schlaug, G. (2003, October). Brain structures differ between musicians and non-musicians. *Neuroscience, 23,* 9240–9245.

Gazzaniga, M. S., Ivry, R. B., & Mangun, G. R. (2002). *Cognitive neuroscience: The biology of the mind* (2nd ed.). New York: Norton.

Geiser, C., Lehmann, W., & Eid, M. (2008, November–December). A note on sex differences in mental rotation in different age groups. *Intelligence, 36,* 556–563.

Gentry, M., Rizza, M. G., & Owen, S. V. (2002, Spring). Examining perceptions of challenge and choice in classrooms: The relationship between teachers and their students and comparisons between gifted students and other students. *Gifted Child Quarterly, 46,* 145–155.

Gilger, J. W., Ho, H., Whipple, A. D., & Spitz, R. (2001). Genotype-environment correlations for language-related abilities: Implications for typical and atypical learners. *Journal of Learning Disabilities, 34,* 492–502.

Glassman, R. B. (1999). Hypothesized neural dynamics of working memory: Several chunks might be marked simultaneously by harmonic frequencies within an octave band of brain waves. *Brain Research Bulletin, 50,* 77–93.

Gohm, C. L., Humphreys, L. G., & Yao, G. (1998, Fall). Underachievement among spatially gifted students. *American Educational Research Journal, 35,* 515–531.

Goldberg, E. (2001). *The executive brain: Frontal lobes and the civilized mind.* New York: Oxford University Press.

Grabner, R. H., Neubauer, A. C., & Stern, E. (2006, April). Superior performance and neural efficiency: The impact of intelligence and expertise. *Brain Research Bulletin, 69,* 422–439.

Grant, M. D., & Brody, J. A. (2004, Oct). Musical experience and dementia. Hypothesis. *Aging Clinical and Experimental Research, 16,* 403–405.

Green, A.C., Baerentsen, K.B., Strdkilde-Jrrgensen, H., Wallentin, M., Roepstorff, A., & Vuust, P. (2008, May). Music in minor activates limbic structures: A relationship with dissonance? *Neuroreport, 19,* 711–715.

Grigorenko, E. L., Klin, A., Pauls, D. L., Senft, R., Hooper, C., & Volkmar, F. (2002, February). Descriptive study of hyperlexia in a clinically referred sample of children with developmental delays. *Journal of Autism and Developmental Disorders, 32,* 3–12.

Grigorenko, E. L., & Sternberg, R. J. (1997, Spring). Styles of thinking, abilities, and academic performance. *Exceptional Children, 63,* 295–312.

Grobman, J. (2006, Summer). Underachievement in exceptionally gifted adolescents and young adults: A psychiatrist's view. *The Journal of Secondary Gifted Education, 17,* 199–210.

Gromko, J. E. (2004, Spring). Predictors of music sight-reading ability in high school wind players. *Journal of Research in Music Education, 52,* 6–15.

Gromko, J. E. (2005, Fall). The effect of music instruction on phonemic awareness in beginning readers. *Journal of Research in Music Education, 53,* 199–209.

Habib, R., McIntosh, A. R., Wheeler, M. A., & Tulving, E. (2003). Memory encoding and hippocampally-based novelty/familiarity discrimination networks. *Neuropsychologia, 41,* 271–279.

Haier, R. J., Jung, R. E., Yeo, R. A., Head, K., & Alkire, M. T. (2004). Structural brain variation and general intelligence. *NeuroImage, 23,* 425–433.

Hale, J. E. (2001). *Learning while Black: Creating educational excellence for African American children.* Baltimore: Johns Hopkins University Press.

Halsted, J. W. (1990). *Guiding the gifted reader.* Arlington, VA: ERIC Clearinghouse on Disabilities and Gifted Education.

Hanna, J. L. (2008, November). A nonverbal language for imagining and learning: Dance education in K–12 curriculum. *Educational Researcher, 37,* 491–506.

Harden, K. P., Turkheimer, E., & Loehlin, J. C. (2007, March). Genotype by environment interaction in adolescents' cognitive aptitude, *Behavior Genetics, 37.*

Haroutounian, J. (2000). The delights and dilemmas of the musically talented teenager. *Journal of Secondary Gifted Education, 12,* 3–14.

Harris, B., Rapp, K. E., Martínez, R. S., & Plucker, J. A. (2007, Fall). Identifying English language learners for gifted and talented programs: Current practices and recommendations for improvement. *Roeper Review, 29,* 26–29.

Hartnett, D. N., Nelson, J. M., & Rinn, A. N. (2004, Winter). Gifted or ADHD? The possibilities of misdiagnosis. *Roeper Review, 26,* 73–76.

Haueisen, J., & Knösche, T. R. (2001). Involuntary motor activity in pianists evoked by music perception. *Journal of Cognitive Neuroscience, 13,* 786–792.

Heim, S., Eickhoff, S. B., & Amunts, K. (2008, April). Specialisation in Broca's region for semantic, phonological, and syntactic fluency? *Neuroimage, 40,* 1362–1368.

Heller, K. A. (2004). Identification of gifted and talented students. *Psychology Science, 46,* 302–323.

Henderlong, J., & Lepper, M. R. (2002, September). The effects of praise on children's intrinsic motivation: A review and synthesis. *Psychological Bulletin, 128,* 774–795.

Henderson, L. M. (2001, Summer). Asperger's syndrome in gifted individuals. *Gifted Child Today, 24,* 28–35.

Henshon, S. F. (2006, Summer). The evolution of creativity, giftedness, and multiple intelligences: An interview with Ellen Winner and Howard Gardner. *Roeper Review, 28,* 191–194.

Henson, R., Shallice, T., & Dolan, R. (2000). Neuroimaging evidence for dissociable forms of repetition priming. *Science, 287,* 1269–1272.

Hertberg-Davis, H., & Callahan, C. M. (2008, Summer). A narrow escape: Gifted students' perceptions of Advanced Placement and International Baccalaureate programs. *Gifted Child Quarterly, 52,* 199–216.

Hertz-Picciotto, I., & Delwiche, L. (2009, January). The rise in autism and the role of age at diagnosis. *Epidemiology, 20,* 84–90.

Hittmair-Delazer, M., Semenza, C., & Denes, G. (1994). Concepts and facts in calculation. *Brain, 117,* 715–728.

Hmelo-Silver, C. E. (2004, September). Problem-based learning: What and how do students learn? *Educational Psychology Review, 16,* 235–266.

Hodges, D. A. (2005). Why study music? *International Journal of Music Education, 23,* 111–115.

Hoeflinger, M. (1998, May-June). Mathematics and science in gifted education: Developing mathematically promising students. *Roeper Review, 20,* 224–227.

Howe, M. J. A., & Davidson, J. W. (2003). The early progress of able young musicians. In R. J. Sternberg & E. L. Grigorenko (Eds.), *The psychology of abilities, competencies and expertise* (pp. 186–212). Cambridge, UK: Cambridge University Press.

Howe, M. J. A., Davidson, J., & Sloboda, J. (1998). Innate talents: Reality or myth? *The Behavioral and Brain Sciences, 21*, 399–407.

Humphries, C., Binder, J. R., Medler, D. A., & Liebenthal, E. (2006, April). Syntactic and semantic modulation of neural activity during auditory sentence comprehension. *Cognitive Neuroscience, 18*, 665–679.

Ilari, B., & Polka, L. (2006). Music cognition in early infancy: Infants' preferences and long-term memory for Ravel. *International Journal of Music Education, 24*, 7–20.

Jarrold, C., & Towse, J. N. (2006, April). Individual differences in working memory. *Neuroscience, 139*, 39–50.

Jausovec, N. (2000, September). Differences in cognitive processes between gifted, intelligent, creative, and average individuals while solving complex problems: An EEG study. *Intelligence, 28*, 213–240.

Jausovec, N., & Jausovec, K. (2004, February). Differences in induced brain activity during the performance of learning and working-memory tasks related to intelligence. *Brain and Cognition, 54.* 65–74.

Jausovec, N., & Jausovec, K. (2005, December). Sex differences in brain activity related to general and emotional intelligence. *Brain and Cognition, 59*, 277–286.

Jensen, A. P. (2008, May-June). Multimodal literacy and theater education. *Arts Education Policy Review, 109*, 19–26.

Jin, S. H., Kim, S. Y., Park, K. H., & Lee, K. J. (2007, August). Differences in EEG between gifted and average students: Neural complexity and functional cluster analysis. *International Journal of Neuroscience, 117*, 1167–1184.

Johnson, D. T. (2000, April). *Teaching mathematics to gifted students in a mixed-ability classroom.* Arlington, VA: ERIC Clearinghouse on Disabilities and Gifted Education.

Johnson, S. C., Schmitz, T. W., Kawahara-Baccus, T. N., Rowley, H. A., Alexander, A. L., Lee, J., et al. (2005, December). The cerebral response during subjective choice with and without self-reference. *Journal of Cognitive Neuroscience, 17*, 1897–1906.

Jung, R. E., & Haier, R. J. (2007, April). The Parieto-Frontal Integration Theory (P-FIT) of intelligence: Converging neuroimaging evidence. *Behavioral and Brain Sciences, 30*, 135–154.

Kalyuga, S., Ayres, P., Chandler, P., & Sweller, J. (2003). Expertise reversal effect. *Educational Psychologist, 38*, 23–31.

Katahira, K., Abla, D., Masuda, S., & Okanoya, K. (2008, May). Feedback-based error monitoring processes during musical performance: An ERP study. *Neuroscience Research, 61*, 120–128.

Kiefer, A. K., & Sekaquaptewa, D. (2007, September). Implicit stereotypes and women's math performance: How implicit gender-math stereotypes influence women's susceptibility to stereotype threat. *Journal of Experimental Social Psychology, 43*, 825–832.

Kirschner, P. A., Sweller, J., & Clark, R. E. (2006). Why minimal guidance during instruction does not work: An analysis of the failure of constructivist, discovery, problem-based, experiential, and inquiry-based teaching. *Educational Psychologist, 41*, 75–86.

Klahr, D., & Nigam, M. (2004). The equivalence of learning paths in early science instruction: Effects of direct instruction and discovery learning. *Psychological Science, 15*, 661–667.

Koelsch, S., Gunter, T., & Friederici, A. D. (2000). Brain indices of music processing: "Nonmusicians" are musical. *Journal of Cognitive Neuroscience, 12*, 520–541.

Kroger, J. K., Nystrom, L. E., Cohen, J. D., & Johnson-Laird, P. N. (2008, December). Distinct neural substrates for deductive and mathematical processing. *Brain Research, 1243*, 86–103.

Kulik, J. A. (2003). Grouping and tracking. In N. Colangelo & G. Davis (Eds.), *Handbook of gifted education* (3rd ed., pp. 268–281). Boston: Allyn and Bacon.

Kupperman, P., Bligh, S., & Barouski, K. (2002). Hyperlexia. *Center for Speech and Language Disorders* [Online]. Available at http://www.csld.org.

Kwon, O. N., Allen, K., & Rasmussen, C. (2005, May). Students' retention of mathematical knowledge and skills in differential equations. *School Science and Mathematics, 105,* 227–239.

Lally, A., & LaBrant, L. (1951). Experiences with children talented in the arts. In P. Witty (Ed.), *The gifted child.* New York: D. C. Heath, pp. 243–256.

Leahey, E., & Guo, G. (2001). Gender differences in mathematical trajectories. *Social Forces, 80,* 713–732.

Lee, H. J., & Park, H. R. (2007). An integrated literature review on the adaptive behavior of individuals with Asperger syndrome. *Remedial and Special Education, 28,* 132–139.

LeFevre, J., Smith-Chant, B. L., Fast, L., Skwarchuk, S., Sargla, E., Arnup, J. S., et al. (2006, April). What counts as knowing? The development of conceptual and procedural knowledge of counting from kindergarten through Grade 2. *Journal of Experimental Child Psychology, 93,* 285–303.

Lind, S. (2001). Overexcitability and the gifted. *The SENG Newsletter, 1,* 3–6.

Lohman, D. F. (2005, Spring). The role of nonverbal ability tests in identifying academically gifted students: An aptitude perspective. *Gifted Child Quarterly, 49,* 111–138.

Lohman, D. F., Korb, K. A., & Lakin, J. M. (2008, Fall). Identifying academically gifted English-language learners using nonverbal tests: A comparison of the Raven, NNAT, and CogAT. *Gifted Child Quarterly, 52,* 275–296.

Longhurst, J., & Sandage, S. A. (2004, Spring). Appropriate technology and journal writing: Structured dialogues that enhance learning. *College Teaching, 52,* 69–75.

Lovecky, D. V. (2004). *Different minds: Gifted children with AD/HD, Asperger syndrome, and other learning deficits.* New York: Jessica Kingsley Publishers.

Lynn, R., & Irwing, P. (2008, May-June). Sex differences in mental arithmetic, digit span, and *g* defined as working memory capacity. *Intelligence, 36,* 226–235.

Mahoney, A. S. (2008). *In search of the gifted identity: From abstract concept to workable counseling constructs.* Available online at http://www.counselingthegifted.com/pdfs/insearch ofID .pdf.

Mann, R. L. (2005, Winter). Gifted students with spatial strengths and sequential weaknesses: An overlooked and underidentified population. *Roeper Review, 27,* 91–96.

Mann, R. L. (2006, Winter). Effective teaching strategies for gifted/learning-disabled students with spatial strengths. *Journal of Secondary Gifted Education, 17,* 112–121.

Martin, A., Wiggs, C. L., & Weisberg, J. (1997). Modulation of human medial temporal lobe activity by form, meaning, and experience. *Hippocampus, 7,* 587–593.

Masataka, N. (1999). Preference for infant-directed singing in 2-year-old hearing infants of deaf parents. *Developmental Psychology, 35,* 1001–1005.

Matthews, D., & Kitchen, J. (2007, Summer). School-within-a-school gifted programs: Perceptions of students and teachers in public secondary schools. *Gifted Child Quarterly, 51,* 256–271.

Mayer, J. D., Salovey, P., & Caruso, D. R. (2000). Models of emotional intelligence. In R. J. Sternberg (Ed.), *Handbook of intelligence* (2nd ed., pp. 396–420). Cambridge, UK: Cambridge University Press.

Mayer, R. (2004). Should there be a three-strikes rule against pure discovery learning? The case for guided methods of instruction. *American Psychologist, 59,* 14–19.

McAlonan, G. M., Daly, E., Kumari, V., Critchley, H. D., van Amelsvoort, T., Suckling, J., et al. (2002). Brain anatomy and sensorimotor gating in Asperge's syndrome. *Brain, 127,* 1594–1606.

McCoach, D. B., & Siegle, D. (2003). Factors that differentiate underachieving gifted students from high-achieving gifted students. *Gifted Child Quarterly, 47,* 144–154.

McEachern, A. G., & Bornot, J. (2001, October). Gifted students with learning disabilities: Implications and strategies for school counselors. *Professional School Counseling, 3,* 34–41.

McMahon, S. D., Rose, D. S., & Parks, M. (2003). Basic reading through dance program: The impact on first-grade students' basic reading skills. *Evaluation Review, 27,* 104–125.

Mendaglio, S., & Tillier, W. (2006). Dabrowski's Theory of Positive Disintegration and Giftedness: Overexcitability research findings. *Journal for the Education of the Gifted, 30,* 68–87.

Mendez, M. F. (2004). Dementia as a window to the neurology of art. *Medical Hypotheses, 63,* 1–7.

Milius, S. (2001). Face the music: Why are we such a musical species—and does it matter? *Natural History, 110,* 48–58.

Miller, E. M. (2005, Spring). Studying the meaning of giftedness: Inspiration from the field of cognitive psychology. *Roeper Review, 27,* 172–177.

Miyaki, A., Friedman, N. P., Rettinger, D. A., Shaw, P., & Hegarty, M. (2001). How are visuospatial working memory, executive functioning, and spatial abilities related? A latent-variable analysis. *Journal of Experimental Psychology, 130,* 621–640.

Moe, A. (In press). Are males always better than females in mental rotation? Exploring a gender belief explanation. *Learning and Individual Differences.*

Moreno, R. (2004). Decreasing cognitive load in novice students: Effects of explanatory versus corrective feedback in discovery-based multimedia. *Instructional Science, 32,* 99–113.

Moreno, S., & O'Neal, C. (2008). Tips for teaching high functioning people with autism. *Online Asperger Syndrome Information and Support.* Available at http://www.udel.edu/bkirby/asperger.

Mueller, C. M., & Dweck, C. S. (1998). Praise for intelligence can undermine children's motivation and performance. *Journal of Personality and Social Psychology, 75,* 33–52.

National Association for Gifted Children (NAGC) (2006). *NAGC–CEC Teacher knowledge & skill standards for gifted and talented education.* Available online at www.nagc.org.

National Association for Gifted Children (NAGC) (2009). *Common gifted education myths.* Available online at www.nagc.org.

Newman, T. M. (2004). Interventions work, but we need more! In T. M. Newman & R. J. Sternberg (Eds.), *Students with both gifts and learning disabilities* (pp. 235–246). New York: Kluwer.

Niehart, M. (2006, Summer). Dimensions of underachievement, difficult contexts, and perceptions of self: Achievement/affiliation conflicts in gifted adolescents. *Roeper Review, 28,* 196–202.

Ochsner, K. N. (2007). Social cognitive neuroscience: Historic development, core principles, and future promise. In A. W. Kruglanski & E. Tory (Eds.). *Social psychology: Handbook of basic principles* (2nd ed., pp. 39–68). New York: Guilford Press.

Oktem, F., Diren, B., Karaagaoglu, E., & Anlar, B. (2001, April). Functional magnetic resonance imaging in children with Asperger's syndrome. *Journal of Child Neurology, 16,* 253–256.

Olszewski-Kubilius, P. (1998). Talent search: Purposes, rational, and role in gifted education. *Journal of Secondary Gifted Education, 9,* 106–113.

Oreck, B. (2004). The artistic and professional development of teachers: A study of teachers' attitudes toward and use of the arts in teaching. *Journal of Teacher Education, 55,* 55–69.

Pérez-Fabello, M. J., & Campos, A. (2007, November). The influence of imaging capacity on visual art skills. *Thinking Skills and Creativity, Volume 2,* 128–135.

Peters, W. A. M., Grager-Loidl, H., & Supplee, P. (2000). Underachievement in gifted children and adolescents: Theory and practice. In K. A. Heller, F. J. Monks, R. J. Sternberg, & R. F. Subotnik (Eds.), *International handbook of giftedness and talent* (2nd ed., pp. 609–620). Amsterdam: Elsevier/Pergamon.

Phillips, S. (2008, Fall). Are we holding back our students that possess the potential to excel? *Education, 129,* 50–55.

Plomin, R., & DeFries, J. C. (1998, May). The genetics of cognitive abilities and disabilities. *Scientific American, 278,* 62–69.

Ratey, J. (with Hagerman, E.). (2008). *Spark: The revolutionary new science of exercise and the brain.* New York: Little, Brown.

Ravizza, S. M., Anderson, J. R., & Carter, C. S. (2008, October). Errors of mathematical processing: The relationship of accuracy to neural regions associated with retrieval or representation of the problem state. *Brain Research, 1238,* 118–126.

Rayneri, L. J., Gerber, B. L., & Wiley, L. P. (2006). The relationship between classroom environment and the learning style preferences of gifted middle school students and the impact on levels of performance. *Gifted Child Quarterly, 50,* 104–118.

Reis, S. M., Burns, D. E., & Renzulli, J. S. (1992a). *Curriculum compacting: The complete guide to modifying the regular curriculum for high ability students.* Mansfield Center, CT: Creative Learning Press.

Reis, S. M., Burns, D. E., & Renzulli, J. S. (1992b). *A facilitator's guide to help teachers compact curriculum.* Storrs, CT: University of Connecticut, The National Research Center on the Gifted and Talented.

Reis, S. M., & Colbert, R. (2004, December). Counseling needs of academically talented students with learning disabilities. *Professional School Counseling, 8,* 156–167.

Reis, S. M., & McCoach, D. B. (2000). The underachievement of gifted students: What do we know and where do we go? *Gifted Child Quarterly, 44,* 152–170.

Reis, S. M., Westberg, K. L., Kulikowich, J. M., & Purcell, J. H. (1998, Spring). Curriculum compacting and achievement test scores: What does the research say? *Gifted Child Quarterly, 42,* 123–129.

Renzulli, J. (1978). What makes giftedness? Reexamining a definition. *Phi Beta Kappan, 60,* 180–184, 261.

Renzulli, J. (1986). The three-ring conception of giftedness: A developmental model for creative productivity. In Sternberg, R. J., and Davidson, E. (Eds.), *Conceptions of giftedness* (pp. 53–92). New York: Cambridge University Press.

Renzulli, J. (1994). *Schools for talent development.* Mansfield Center, CT: Creative Learning Press.

Renzulli, J. S., & Reis, S. M. (1985). *The schoolwide enrichment model: A comprehensive plan for educational excellence.* Mansfield Center, CT: Creative Learning Press.

Restak, R. M. (2001). *The secret life of the brain.* Washington, DC: John Henry Press.

Richards, M. R. E., & Omdal, S. N. (2007, Spring). Effects of tiered instruction on academic performance in a secondary science course. *Journal of Advanced Academics, 18,* 424–453.

Rimm, S. B. (1997). An underachievement epidemic. *Educational Leadership, 54,* 18–22.

Rimm, S. B. (2008). *How to parent so children will learn: Strategies for raising a happy achieving child.* Scottsdale, AZ: Great Potential Press.

Ring, H., Woodbury-Smith, M., Watson, P., Wheelwright, S., & Baron-Cohen, S. (2008, February). Clinical heterogeneity among people with high functioning autism spectrum conditions: Evidence favouring a continuous severity gradient. *Behavioral and Brain Functions, 4.*

Rittle-Johnson, B., & Alibali, M. W. (1999). Conceptual and procedural knowledge of mathematics: Does one lead to the other? *Journal of Educational Psychology, 91,* 175.

Rivera, D. B., Murdock, J., & Sexton, D. (1995). Serving the gifted/learning disabled. *Gifted Child Today, 18,* 34–37.

Rizza, M. G., & Morrison, W. F. (2003, Winter). Uncovering stereotypes and identifying characteristics of gifted students with emotional/behavioral disabilities. *Roeper Review, 25,* 73–77.

Robinson, A., & Clinkenbeard, P. R. (1998, August). Giftedness: An exceptionality examines. *Annual Review of Psychology, 49,* 117–139.

Rogers, K. B. (2007). Lessons learned about educating the gifted and talented: A synthesis of the research on educational practice. *Gifted Child Quarterly, 51,* 382–396.

Rotigel, J. V., & Lupkowski-Shoplik, A. (1999). Using talent searches to identify and meet the educational needs of mathematically gifted youngsters. *School Science and Mathematics, 99,* 330–337.

Rudasill, K., Foust, R. C., & Callahan, C. M. (2007). The Social Coping Questionnaire: An examination of its structure with an American sample of gifted adolescents. *Journal for the Education of the Gifted, 30,* 353–371.

Russo, C. F. (2004, Summer). A comparative study of creativity and cognitive problem-solving strategies of high-IQ and average students. *Gifted Child Quarterly, 48,* 179–190.

Ruthsatz, J., Detterman, D., Griscom, W. S., & Cirullo, B. A. (2008, July-August). Becoming an expert in the musical domain: It takes more than just practice. *Intelligence, 36,* 330–338.

Scarr, S., & McCartney, K. (1983). How people make their own environments. *Child Development, 54,* 424–435.

Scheler, G., Lotze, M., Braitenberg, V., Erb, M., Braun, C. & Birbaumer, N. (2001). Musician's brain: Balance of sensorimotor economy and frontal creativity [abstract]. *Society of Neuroscience Abstracts, 27,* 76.14.

Schellenberg, E. G., Nakata, T., Hunter, P. G., & Tamoto, S. (2007). Exposure to music and cognitive performance: Tests of children and adults. *Psychology of Music, 35,* 5–19.

Schmithorst, V. J., & Holland, S. K. (2007, March). Sex differences in the development of neuroanatomical functional connectivity underlying intelligence found using Bayesian connectivity analysis. *Neuroimage, 35,* 406–419.

Shadmehr, R., & Holcomb, H. H. (1997). Neural correlates of motor memory consolidation. *Science, 277,* 821–825.

Shao, Y., Curccaro, M. L., Hauser, E. R., Raifords, K. L., Menold, M. M., Wolpert, C. M., et al. (2003, March). Fine mapping of autistic disorder to chromosome 15Q11–q13 by use of phenotypic subtypes. *American Journal of Human Genetics, 72,* 539–548.

Shaw, P., Greenstein, D., Lerch, J., Clasen, L., Lenroot, R., Gogtay, N., Evans, A., Rapoport, J., & Giedd, J. (2006, March). Intellectual ability and cortical development in children and adolescents. *Nature, 440,* 676–679.

Shaywitz, B. A., Shaywitz, S. E., & Gore, J. (1995). Sex differences in the functional organization of the brain for language. *Nature, 373,* 607–609.

Shaywitz, S. E., Holahan, J. M., Fletcher, J. M., Freudenheim, D. A., Makuch, R. W., & Shaywitz, B. A. (2001, Winter). Heterogeneity within the gifted: Higher IQ boys exhibit behaviors resembling boys with learning disabilities. *Gifted Child Quarterly, 45,* 16–23.

Shea, D. L., Lubinski, D., & Benbow, C. P. (2001). Importance of assessing spatial ability in intellectually talented young adolescents: A 20-year longitudinal study. *Journal of Educational Psychology, 93,* 604–614.

Shearer, C. B. (2004). Using a multiple intelligences assessment to promote teacher development and student achievement. *Teachers College Record, 106,* 147–162. .

Shoplik, A. L. (2004). *Gifted students in the regular classroom.* Pittsburgh, PA: Carnegie Mellon Institute for Talented Elementary & Secondary Students.

Shoplik, A. L. (2006). *Developing mathematical talent: They don't have to be bored to tears.* Pittsburgh, PA: Carnegie Mellon Institute for Talented Elementary & Secondary Students.

Silverman, L. K. (1989a). Invisible gifts, invisible handicaps. *Roeper Review, 12,* 37–42.

Silverman, L. K. (1989b). The visual-spatial learner. *Preventing School Failure, 34,* 15–20.

Silverman, L. K. (1993). *The Characteristics of Giftedness Scale.* Available online at www.gifted development.com.

Sloboda, J. A., Davidson, J. W., Howe, M. J. A., & Moore, D. G. (1996). The role of practice in the development of performing musicians. *British Journal of Psychology, 87,* 287–309.

Smutny, J. F. (2000, May). *Teaching young gifted children in the regular classroom.* Arlington, VA: ERIC Clearinghouse on Disabilities and Gifted Children.

Smutny, J. F. (2001, June). *Creative strategies for teaching language arts to gifted students (K–8)*. Arlington, VA: ERIC Clearinghouse on Disabilities and Gifted Children.

Sousa, D. A. (2006). *How the brain learns* (3rd ed.). Thousand Oaks, CA: Corwin.

Sousa, D. A. (2007). *How the special needs brain learns* (2nd ed.). Thousand Oaks, CA: Corwin.

Sousa, D. A. (2008). *How the brain learns mathematics.* Thousand Oaks, CA: Corwin.

Sousa, D. A. (2009). *How the brain influences behavior: Management strategies for every classroom.* Thousand Oaks, CA: Corwin.

Spek, A. A., Scholte, E. M., & van Berckelaer-Onnes, I. A. (2008, April). The use of WAIS-III in adults with HFA and Asperger syndrome. *Journal of Autism and Developmental Disorders, 38,* 782–787.

Speer, N. K., & Curran, T. (2007, October). ERP correlates of familiarity and recollection processes in visual associative recognition. *Brain Research, 1174,* 97–109.

Sriraman, B. (2005, Fall). Are giftedness and creativity synonyms in mathematics? *Journal of Secondary Gifted Education, 17,* 20–36.

Standley, J. M. (2008). Does music instruction help children learn to read? Evidence of a meta-analysis. *Applications of Research in Music Education, 27,* 17–32.

Stanley, G. K., & Baines, L. (2002, Fall). Celebrating mediocrity? How schools shortchange gifted students. *Roeper Review, 25,* 11–13.

Steiner, H. H. (2006). A microgenetic analysis of strategic variability in gifted and average-ability children. *Gifted Child Quarterly, 50,* 62–74.

Sternberg, R. J. (1985). *Beyond IQ: A triarchic theory of human intelligence.* New York: Cambridge University Press.

Sternberg, R. J. (1997). *Successful intelligence.* New York: Plume.

Sternberg, R.J. (1999). The theory of successful intelligence. *Review of General Psychology, 3,* 292–316.

Sternberg, R. J. (2000, December). Identifying and developing creative giftedness. *Roeper Review, 23,* 60–64.

Sternberg, R. J., Ferrari, M., Clinkenbeard, P. R., & Grigorenko, E. L. (1996). Identification, instruction, and assessment of gifted children: A construct validation of a triarchic model. *Gifted Child Quarterly, 40,* 129–137.

Sternberg, R. J., & Grigorenko, E. L. (2004, Autumn). Successful intelligence in the classroom. *Theory Into Practice, 43,* 274–280.

Sternberg, R. J., Grigorenko, E. L., Jarvin, L., Clinkenbeard, P., Ferrari, M., & Torfi, B. (2000, Spring). The effectiveness of triarchic teaching and assessment. *National Research Center on the Gifted and Talented Newsletter,* 3–8.

Sternberg, R. J., & Zhang, L. (1995, September). What do we mean by giftedness? A pentagonal implicit theory. *Gifted Child Quarterly, 39,* 88–94.

Stewart, L. (2008, April). Fractionating the musical mind: Insights into congenital amusia. *Current Opinion in Neurobiology, 18,* 127–130.

Stewart, L., & Walsh, V. (2001). Music of the hemispheres. *Current Biology, 11,* R125–R127.

Swiatek, M. A. (1995). An empirical investigation of the social coping strategies used by gifted adolescents. *Gifted Child Quarterly, 39,* 154–161.

Swiatek, M. A. (2001, February). Social coping among gifted high school students and its relationship to self-concept. *Journal of Youth and Adolescence, 30,* 19–39.

Swiatek, M. A., & Lupkowski-Shoplik, A. (2003, Spring). Elementary and middle school student participation in gifted programs: Are gifted students underserved? *Gifted Child Quarterly, 47,* 118–130.

Szaflarski, J. P., Holland, S. K., Schmithorst, V. J., & Byars, A. W. (2006, March). An fMRI study of language lateralization in children and adults. *Human Brain Mapping, 27,* 202–212.

Thaut, M. H., Demartin, M., & Sanes, J. N. (2008, May). Brain networks for integrative rhythm formation. *PLoS ONE, 3,* e2312.

Thompson, M. (1999). Developing verbal talent. *Center for Talent Development*. Available online at http://www.ctd.northwestern.edu.

Tieso, C. L. (2002). *The effects of grouping and curriculum practices on intermediate students' mathematics achievement scores*. Storrs, CT: National Research Center on the Gifted and Talented.

Tieso, C. L. (2007, Spring). Overexcitabilities: A new way to think about talent? *Roeper Review, 29,* 230–239.

Tomlinson, C. A. (1995). *How to differentiate instruction in mixed-ability classrooms*. Alexandria, VA: Association for Supervision and Curriculum Development.

Tomlinson, C. A. (1999). *The differentiated classroom: Responding to the needs of all learners*. Alexandria, VA: Association for Supervision and Curriculum Development.

Tomlinson, C. A. (2003). *Fulfilling the promise of the differentiated classroom: Strategies and tools for responsive teaching*. Alexandria, VA: Association for Supervision and Curriculum Development.

Tomlinson, C. A., Kaplan, S. N., Renzulli, J. S., Purcell, J., Leppien, J., & Burns, D. (2002). *The parallel curriculum: A design to develop high potential and challenge high-ability learners*. Thousand Oaks, CA: Corwin.

Tremblay, T., & Gagné, F. (2001). Beliefs of students talented in academics, music, and dance concerning the heritability of human abilities in these fields. *Roeper Review,23*, 173–177.

Tsatsanis, K. D. (2005). Neuropsychological characteristics in autism and related conditions. In F. R. Volkmar, P. Rhea, A. Klin, & D. Cohen (Eds.), *Handbook of autism and pervasive developmental disorders* (pp. 772–798). Hoboken, NJ: John Wiley & Sons.

Tuholski, S. W., Engle, R. W., & Baylis, G. C. (2001, April). Individual differences in working memory capacity and enumeration. *Memory and Cognition, 29,* 484–492.

Turkeltaub, P. E., Flowers, D. L., Verbalis, A., Miranda, M., Gareau, L., & Eden, G. F. (2004, January). The neural basis of hyperlexic reading: An fMRI case study. *Neuron, 41,* 11–25.

Turkheimer, E., Haley, A., Waldron, M., D'Onofrio, B., & Gottesman, I. I. (2003, November). Socioeconomic status modifies heritability of IQ in young children. *Psychological Science, 14,* 623–628.

Tyler, L. K., & Marslen-Wilson, W. (2008). Fronto-temporal brain systems supporting spoken language comprehension. *Philosophical Transactions of the Royal Society, 363,* 1037–1054.

Tyler, L. K., Marslen-Wilson, W. D., & Stamatakis, E. A. (2005, June). Differentiating lexical form, meaning, and structure in the neural language system. *Proceedings of the National Academy of Sciences USA, 102,* 8375–8380.

U.S. Department of Commerce (USDC). *Census Bureau, Current Population Survey, 1979 and 1989 November Supplement and 1992, 1995, and 1999 October Supplement, and American Community Survey, 2000–06*. Washington, DC: Author.

U.S. Department of Education (USDE). (2007, May). *Office for Civil Rights elementary and secondary school survey: 2002, and civil rights data collection: 2004*. Washington, DC: Author.

Usiskin, Z. (2000). The development into the mathematically talented. *Journal of Secondary Gifted Education, 11,* 152–162.

Van Tassel-Baska, J. (2002, Winter). Assessment of gifted student learning in the language arts. *Journal of Secondary Gifted Education, 13,* 67–85.

Van Tassel-Baska, J. (2005, Spring). Gifted programs and services: What are the nonnegotiables? *Theory into Practice, 44,* 90–97.

Van Tassel-Baska, J., Johnson, D. T., Hughes, C. E., & Boyce, L. N. (1996). A study of language arts curriculum effectiveness with gifted learners. *Journal of Education for the Gifted, 19,* 461–480.

Verdejo-García, A., Vilar-López, R., Pérez-García, M., Podell, K., & Goldberg, E. (2006, January). Altered adaptive but not veridical decision-making in substance dependent individuals. *Journal of the International Neuropsychological Society, 12,* 90–99.

Verghese, J., Lipton, R. B., Katz, M. J., Hall, C. B., Derby, C. A., Kuslansky, G., et al. (2003, June). Leisure activities and the risk of dementia in the elderly. *New England Journal of Medicine, 348,* 2508–2516.

Vogt, S., Buccino, G., Wohlschläger, A. M., Canessa, N., Shah, N. J., Zilles, K., et al. (2007, October). Prefrontal involvement in imitation learning of hand actions: Effects of practice and expertise. *Neuroimage. 37,* 1371–1383.

Vosslamber, A. (2002). Gifted readers: Who are they, and how can they be served in the classroom? *Gifted Child Today, 25,* 14–20.

Wakeley, A., Rivera, S., & Langer, J. (2000). Can young infants add or subtract? *Child Development, 71,* 1525–1534.

Walling, D. R. (2001, April). Rethinking visual arts education: A convergence of influences. *Phi Delta Kappan, 82,* 626.

Webb, J. T., Amend, E. R., Webb, N. E., Goerss, J., Beljan, P., & Olenchak, F. R. (2005). *Misdiagnosis and dual diagnoses of gifted children and adults: ADHD, bipolar, OCD, Asperger's, depression, and other disorders.* Scottsdale, AZ: Great Potential Press.

Weber, C. L., & Cavanaugh, T. W. (2006, Fall). Using eBooks with gifted and advanced readers. *Gifted Child Today, 29,* 56–63.

Webster, P. (2000). Reforming secondary music teaching in the new century. *Journal of Secondary Gifted Education, 12,* 17–24.

Westberg, K. L., & Daoust, M. E. (2003, Fall). The results of the replication of classroom practices survey replication in two states. *The National Research Center on the Gifted and Talented Newsletter,* 3–8.

White, D. A., & Breen, M. (1998). Edutainment: Gifted education and the perils of misusing multiple intelligences. *Gifted Child Today, 21,* 12–14, 16–17.

Wilke, M., Holland, S. K., & Krägeloh-Mann, I. (2007, April). Global, regional, and local development of gray and white matter volume in normal children. *Experimental Brain Research, 178,* 296–307.

Willard-Holt, C. (1999, May). *Dual exceptionalities.* Arlington, VA: ERIC Clearinghouse on Disabilities and Gifted Education.

Winebrenner, S. (2000, September). Gifted students need an education, too. *Educational Leadership, 58,* 52–55.

Winebrenner, S. (2003, January). Teaching strategies for twice-exceptional students. *School and Clinic, 38,* 131–137.

Winebrenner, S., & Devlin, B. (2001, March). *Cluster grouping of gifted students: How to provide full-time services on a part-time budget: Update 2001.* Arlington, VA: ERIC Clearinghouse on Disabilities and Gifted Children.

Winner, E. (2000). The origins and ends of giftedness. *American Psychologist, 55,* 159–169.

Witelson, S. F., Kigar, D. L., & Harvey, T. (1999, June). The exceptional brain of Albert Einstein. *The Lancet, 353,* 2149–2153.

Woodson, S. E. (2004, March-April). Creating an educational theatre program for the twenty-first century. *Arts Education Policy Review, 105,* 25–30.

Worthy, J., & Prater, K. (2002). "I thought about it all night": Readers' theatre for reading fluency and motivation. *The Reading Teacher, 56,* 294–98.

Yakmaci-Guzel, B., & Akarsu, F. (2006, June). Comparing overexcitabilities of gifted and non-gifted 10th grade students in Turkey. *High Ability Studies, 17,* 43–56.

Zentall, S. S., Moon, S. M., Hall, A. M., & Grskovic, J. A. (2001, Summer). Learning and motivational characteristics of boys with AD/HD and/or giftedness. *Exceptional Children, 67,* 499–519.

Zhang, L. F., & Sternberg, R. J. (2006). *The nature of intellectual styles.* Mahwah, NJ: Erlbaum.

Ziegler, A. (2005). The actiotope model of giftedness. In R. Sternberg & J. Davidson, (Eds.), *Conceptions of giftedness* (pp. 411–434). Cambridge, UK: Cambridge University Press.

Ziegler, A., & Stoeger, H. (2004). Evaluation of an attributional retraining (modeling technique) to reduce gender differences in chemistry instruction. *High Ability Studies, 15,* 63–83.

Zimmer, C. (2008, October). The search for intelligence. *Scientific American, 299,* 68–75.

Resources

Note: All Internet sites were active at time of publication.

ORGANIZATIONS

The Association for the Gifted
Baylor University
Department of Ed Psychology
One Bear Place 97304, Burleson 216
Waco, TX 76798-7304
www.cectag.org
http://www.hyperlexia.org

Center for Excellence in Education
8201 Greensboro Drive, Suite 215
McLean, VA 22102
Tel. (703) 448-9062
http://cee.org

Council for Exceptional Children
1110 North Glebe Road, Suite 300
Arlington, VA 22201-5407
Tel. (888) CEC-SPED (888-232-7733)
www.cec.sped.org

Davidson Institute for Talent Development
9665 Gateway Drive, Suite B
Reno, Nevada 89521
Tel. (775) 852-3483, ext. 435
www.davidsongifted.org

Educational Theatre Association
2343 Auburn Avenue
Cincinnati, OH 45219-2815
Tel. (513) 421-3900
www.edta.org

ERIC Clearinghouse on Disabilities and Gifted Education

1110 North Glebe Road
Arlington, VA 22201-5704
Tel. 1-800-328-0272
www.ericec.org

The Gifted Child Society

190 Rock Road
Glen Rock, NJ 07452-1736
Tel. (201) 444-6530
www.gifted.org

Gifted Development Center

1452 Marion Street
Denver, CO 80218
Tel. (303) 837-8378
www.gifteddevelopment.com

National Association for Gifted Children

1707 L Street NW, Suite 550
Washington, DC 20036
Tel. (202) 785-4268
www.nagc.org

National Research Center on the Gifted and Talented

University of Connecticut
2131 Hillside Road, Unit 3007
Storrs, CT 06269-3007
Tel. (860) 486-4826
www.gifted.uconn.edu/nrcgt.html

Supporting Emotional Needs of the Gifted

P.O. Box 488
Poughquag, NY 12570
Tel. (845) 797-5054
www.sengifted.org
http://www.udel.edu

TALENT SEARCH PROGRAMS

Program	Address and Web Site	Type of Talent Search
Academic Talent Search	California State University 6000 J Street Sacramento, CA 95819-6098 http://edweb.csus.edu/projects/ats	Elementary and middle school students in northern California

Program	Address and Web Site	Type of Talent Search
Belin-Blank Center for Gifted Education and Talent Development	Belin-Blank Center 600 Blank Honors Center University of Iowa Iowa City, IA 52242-0454 www.education.uiowa.edu/belinblank	For 2nd through 12th graders nationwide
Carnegie Mellon Institute for Talented Elementary Students	Carnegie Mellon University (C-MITES) Margaret Morrison St., MMP 30 Pittsburgh, PA 15213 http://www.cmu.edu/cmites	For kindergarten through 9th graders in Pennsylvania
Center for Talent Development	Northwestern University 617 Dartmouth Place Evanston, IL 60208-4175 http://www.ctd.northwestern.edu	For preK to 12th graders in surrounding states
Center for Talented Youth	Johns Hopkins University McAuley Hall 5801 Smith Avenue, Suite 400 Baltimore, MD 21209 www.cty.jhu.edu	For 2nd through 8th graders nationwide
Halbert and Nancy Robinson Center for Young Scholars	University of Washington Box 351630 Seattle, WA 98195 http://depts.washington.edu/cscy	For 5th through 10th graders in the state of Washington
Iowa Talent Search (Office of Precollegiate Programs for Talented and Gifted - OPPTAG)	OPPTAG 357 Carver Hall Iowa State University Ames, IA 50011-2060 www.opptag.iastate.edu	For 3rd through 11th graders in and around Iowa
Rocky Mountain Talent Search	Center for Innovative & Talented Youth University of Denver 1981 South University Boulevard Denver, CO 80208 www.du.edu/city	For 3rd through 9th graders in Colorado, Nevada, Idaho, Montana, New Mexico, Utah, and Wyoming
Talent Identification Program (TIP)	Duke University (TIP) 1121 West Main Street Durham, NC 27701-2028 www.tip.duke.edu	Elementary and middle school students nationwide
Canada: Center for Gifted Education	University of Calgary 170 Education Block 2500 University Drive NW Calgary, Alberta, T2N 1N4, Canada http://www.gifted.ucalgary.ca	For 2nd through 9th graders in Calgary and surrounding area

WEB SITES

This list of Web sites is just a sampling of the various resources that are available for obtaining information about gifted programs. Some sites offer puzzles, problems, and games for challenging gifted children. The list is by no means complete, but it will serve as a useful starting point for exploring the vast number of resources that are available on the Internet. Nearly all of the sites have hyperlinks to other related sites. The Web site addresses were active at the time of publication.

Creative Learning Press

www.creativelearningpress.com
Provides information for teachers and parents about teaching materials and games as well as other resources to enhance creativity.

eCYBERMISSION

www.ecybermission.org
eCYBERMISSION is a Web-based science, math and technology competition for 6th, 7th, 8th, and 9th grade teams. Teams propose a solution to a real problem in their community and compete for regional and national awards.

Future Problem Solving Program International

www.fpsp.org
The Future Problem Solving Program International (FPSPI) engages students in creative problem solving. FSPI stimulates critical and creative thinking skills and encourages students to develop a vision for the future. FPSPI features curricular and co-curricular competitive, as well as non-competitive, activities in creative problem solving.

Genius Denied

www.geniusdenied.com
This site is sponsored by the Davidson Institute for Talent Development and offers articles, book listings, a newsletter, discussion groups, and much more for parents, teachers, students, and other professionals who work with the gifted and talented.

Hoagie's Gifted Education Page

www.hoagiesgifted.org
Includes the latest research on parenting and education (including academic acceleration or enrichment, home schooling, traditional programs, the highly gifted, etc.).

International Baccalaureate Organization

www.ibo.org
All the information one needs to know about this program and its resources.

Library Spot

http://libraryspot.com
A free virtual library resource center for educators and students, librarians and their patrons, families, businesses, and just about anyone exploring the Web for valuable research information. It serves as a gateway to the Web sites of more than 2,500 libraries around the world.

National Arts and Education Network (Kennedy Center Arts Edge)

http://artsedge.kennedy-center.org/teach/

Offers free, standards-based teaching materials for use in and out of the classroom, as well as professional development resources, student materials, and guidelines for arts-based instruction and assessment.

Mensa for Gifted Children

www.us.mensa.org/giftedchildren

Explains how highly gifted children can become members of Mensa and suggests resources to parents.

Music Link Foundation

www.musiclinkfoundation.org

The Music Link Foundation provides partial or full scholarships to students who have musical talent by linking them with nearby volunteer professional music teachers.

National Conference of Governors' Schools

www.ncogs.org

This national organization establishes and supports summer residential governor's school programs.

Online Asperger Syndrome Information and Support (O.A.S.I.S.)

www.udel.edu/bkirby/asperger

This private site run through the University of Delaware offers lots of resources for parents and teachers of students with Asperger syndrome.

SMARTer Kids Foundation

www.smarterkids.org

This is a private organization that provides opportunities for students and teachers to learn new skills and grow in self-confidence through technology, grants, and programs. The Foundation helps equip classrooms with technology products and generates practical research on the impact and effectiveness of technology in the classroom.

Summer Institute for the Gifted

www.cgp-sig.com

A source for high quality educational and social opportunities for academically gifted and talented students through programs designed to meet their abilities and needs.

TeAchnology

www.teach-nology.com/teachers/lesson_plans

This site has thousands of lesson plans at all grade levels that help teachers differentiate instruction in mixed-ability classrooms.

Virtual Library Museums Pages

http://icom.museum/vlmp/

A comprehensive directory of on-line museums and museum-related resources.

World Wide Arts Resources

http://www.wwar.com

Discover more than 170,000 works of contemporary art. Search by medium, subject matter, price, and theme. Research more than 200,000 works by more than 22,000 masters in the in-depth art history section. Browse through new Art Blogs.

Index

UNIVERSITY H.S. LIBRARY

CORWIN
A SAGE Company

The Corwin logo—a raven striding across an open book—represents the union of courage and learning. Corwin is committed to improving education for all learners by publishing books and other professional development resources for those serving the field of PreK–12 education. By providing practical, hands-on materials, Corwin continues to carry out the promise of its motto: **"Helping Educators Do Their Work Better."**